THE CHILD OF THE

Royal Fairy Tales and Essays by the Queens of Romania, Elisabeth (Carmen Sylva, 1843–1916) and Marie (1875–1938)

Selected, edited, and with an introduction and bibliography by
Silvia Irina Zimmermann

Schriftenreihe der
FORSCHUNGSSTELLE CARMEN SYLVA
FÜRSTLICH WIEDISCHES ARCHIV

Herausgegeben von / Series editors

Silvia Irina Zimmermann
Edda Binder-Iijima

Band 9

Die Schriftenreihe versteht sich als Publikationsforum der Forschungsstelle Carmen Sylva des Fürstlich Wiedischen Archivs Neuwied. Ziel ist es, die wissenschaftliche Beschäftigung mit Elisabeth zu Wied, der ersten Königin von Rumänien und Schriftstellerin Carmen Sylva, zu fördern. Die Bände der Forschungsstelle Carmen Sylva, die in loser Reihenfolge erscheinen, sollen neue Brücken in der interdisziplinären und interkulturellen Carmen-Sylva-Forschung schlagen und die Forschungsergebnisse einer interessierten Öffentlichkeit zugänglich machen.

The series serves as a publication platform for the Research Center Carmen Sylva of the Fürstlich Wiedisches Archiv Neuwied. The focus is the scientific research on Elisabeth zu Wied, the first queen of Romania and the writer Carmen Sylva – her life, her literary works, and her intercultural impact on her time. The volumes of the Research Center Carmen Sylva are meant to build new bridges between the interdisciplinary and intercultural research on Carmen Sylva and to make the results available to the interested public.

THE CHILD OF THE SUN

Royal Fairy Tales and Essays by the Queens of Romania,
Elisabeth (Carmen Sylva, 1843–1916) and
Marie (1875–1938)

Selected and edited, with an introduction and bibliography by

Silvia Irina Zimmermann

ibidem
Verlag

Bibliografische Information der Deutschen Nationalbibliothek

Die Deutsche Nationalbibliothek verzeichnet diese Publikation in der Deutschen Nationalbibliografie; detaillierte bibliografische Daten sind im Internet über http://dnb.d-nb.de abrufbar.

Bibliographic information published by the Deutsche Nationalbibliothek

Die Deutsche Nationalbibliothek lists this publication in the Deutsche Nationalbibliografie; detailed bibliographic data are available in the Internet at http://dnb.d-nb.de.

Cover image and design: © Silvia Irina Zimmermann.

∞

Gedruckt auf alterungsbeständigem, säurefreien Papier

Printed on acid-free paper

ISBN-13: 978-3-8382-1393-4

© *ibidem*-Verlag, Stuttgart 2020

Alle Rechte vorbehalten

Printed in the EU

Contents

The Writing Queens of Romania, Elisabeth (Carmen Sylva) and Marie

Queen Consorts and Writers – a Romanian Phenomenon

The history of the monarchy in Romania and of its four kings would be incomplete without the story of the queen consorts, who seem to have been even more fascinating personalities than the kings. The first two queen consorts, Elisabeth (Carmen Sylva) and Marie of Romania, became famous as writers during their lifetime. They both wrote in their mother tongues, Elisabeth in German and Marie in English, and published many of their books, not only in Romania, but also abroad, thus reaching a widespread readership, worldwide publicity, and literary recognition.

Queen Elisabeth of Romania, born on 29 December 1843 in Neuwied, was the eldest child of Prince Hermann of Wied and his wife Marie, born Princess of Nassau. She had received an intense education and was already 26 years old when she married Prince Karl of Hohenzollern-Sigmaringen in November 1869, who had become the elected Prince Carol I of Romania in 1866. After the Russian-Turkish war in 1878, when Prince Carol won Independence for his country, Romania became a kingdom and Carol I and Elisabeth the first royal couple of the land. Unfortunately for the royal couple, their first and only child, Princess Marie, died very young, in 1873, and they did not have any other children. This was especially hard for Elisabeth, who suffered because she could not offer an heir to the Kingdom Romania. In 1878, she started her literary activity with a volume of translations of Romanian contemporary poetry into German. In 1880, she chose the pen name Carmen Sylva for her writings. She published a variety of writings in almost all literary genres, written mostly in German: poems, fairy tales, novels, stage plays, essays, and aphorisms (in French and German). Many of her writings soon appeared in translations into Romanian, French, and English. In 1882/1883 Queen Elisabeth (Carmen Sylva) published the first volume of fairy tales and legends connected with the name of the Pelesh Castle in Sinaia. The castle was built by King Carol I of Romania and inaugurated in 1883, and it was named after the river close-by who also gave the tales their name: *Pelesch-Märchen* (Tales of the Pelesh). The book was published in Romania and Germany, and some of its tales were later published in English translation in the volume *Legends from River & Mountain* (1896).

The reign of King Carol I ended with his death on 10 October 1914, after 48 years, the longest one of a sovereign in Romania. Queen Elisabeth died on 2 March 1916.

Queen Marie of Romania was born in Eastwell Park in Great Britain on 29 October 1875, as the eldest daughter of Prince Alfred, Duke of Edinburgh and (since 1893) Duke of Saxe-Coburg and Gotha, the second son of Queen Victoria of the United Kingdom of Great Britain and Ireland, and Duchess Marie, born Grand Duchess Maria Alexandrovna of Russia, the only daughter of Emperor Alexander II of Russia. She spent a happy childhood in Kent, Malta, and Coburg and married in January 1893, aged 17, the Crown Prince of Romania, Ferdinand, the second son of Prince Leopold of Hohenzollern-Sigmaringen and nephew of King Carol I of Romania. In October 1893, she gave birth to the next heir of the Romanian dynasty, Prince Carol who would later become King Carol II of Romania.

As crown princess, she began to write fiction, being encouraged by Queen Elisabeth of Romania (Carmen Sylva), who translated some of her stories into German and wrote a preface to Marie's fairy tale *The Lily of Life* (1913). After the death of King Carol in 1914, Ferdinand and Marie became the second royal couple of Romania. During the First World War it was mainly Queen Marie who appeared in public as an author of books, essays, and articles which were meant to promote the national cause of Romania at war while it was partly under the occupation of German and Bulgarian troops. After the war, Queen Marie travelled to Paris and remained there during the Peace Conference held in Versailles in July 1919, in order to campaign for the unification of the provinces Transylvania, Bessarabia, and Bukovina with the Old Kingdom of Romania, all territories with a majority of Romanian population. The enlargement of Romania being recognized in Versailles, King Ferdinand and Queen Marie of Romania thus became the royal couple of Greater Romania. The reign of King Ferdinand ended with his death on 20 July 1927, after only 13 years; Queen Marie outlived Ferdinand for 11 years, and she died on 18 July 1938.

Both first royal couples – King Carol I and Queen Elisabeth as well as King Ferdinand and Queen Marie – are buried in the Cathedral of Curtea de Argeş.

Queen Elisabeth and Crown Princess Marie of Romania had both published some of their fairy tales and fantasy novels in English editions in the United Kingdom and the United States around the year 1900. While the crown princess wrote in English, the German writings of Queen Elisabeth were translated into English. Both queens mentioned their royal status on the titles of their books: *Pilgrim Sorrow. A Cycle of Tales by (Carmen Sylva) Queen Elisabeth of Roumania* (New York, 1884), *Golden Thoughts of Carmen Sylva Queen of Roumania* (London and New York, 1900), *A Real Queen's Fairy Tales by Carmen Sylva (Elizabeth, Queen of Roumania)* (Chicago, 1901), *A Real Queen's Fairy Book by Carmen Sylva (Queen of Roumania)* (London, 1901), *The Lily of Life. A Tale by Crown Princess of Roumania with a preface by Carmen Sylva* (London, New York, Toronto, 1913). After the death of King Carol I, Queen Marie continued to publish her fairy tales, novels, and children's books in the USA and the UK calling herself simply „The Queen of Romania": *The Dreamer of Dreams by The Queen of Roumania* (London, New York, Toronto, 1915) and *The Queen of Roumania's Fairy Book* (New York, ca. 1923). Besides their fairy tales, in which the queen writers combine fictional tales with promoting the Romanian landscape and popular traditions, they also published some autobiographical tales and essays about their Kingdom. From the writings of Queen Elisabeth (Carmen Sylva), which also appeared in English translation, the essays and memoirs are worth mentioning: *Bucharest* (1893), *My Reminiscences of War* (1904), *How I Spent My 60th Birthday* (1904), and *From Memory's Shrine* (1911). The best known book from Queen Marie's English editions would be her memoires: *The Story of My Life* (1934-1935). Further interesting autobiographical writings of Queen Marie about Romania are the books: *My Country* (1916) and *The Country That I Love*, (1925). Finally, her children's book *The Magic Doll of Romania. A Wonder Story in Which East and West Do Meet* (1929), written especially for American children, is an interesting combination of fairy tale with autobiographical aspects and publicity for Romania by the time it was a Kingdom under the reign of King Ferdinand and Queen Marie.

Queen Elisabeth (Carmen Sylva): "How I came to take the name of Carmen Sylva as my nom de plume"

Queen Elisabeth explains her pen name in an autobiographical tale for children, published in German in the volume *Märchen einer Königin* (1901) and in English translation in *A Real Queen's Fairy Tales*[1] (1901):

> I have very often been asked how I came to take the name of Carmen Sylva as my nom de plume. […] I passed my childhood in the forest amidst the loveliest beech forest trees standing far higher than the castle, and growing so close up to it that their shadows fell across the threshold. […] Now it can be imagined how much the forest told me, especially on my solitary walks. The storm-wind was a special friend of mine. When it made the oaks and the beeches sway and groan, sawing the branches asunder till they came crashing down, then I would tie my little hood over my brown hair, and with my two big St. Bernard dogs by my side, I would race through the forest, avoiding all the beaten tracks, and listen to its voices; for the forest told me stories all the time.
>
> The forest sang the songs to me, which I wrote down afterward at home, but which I never showed to anyone. It was our secret – the

---

[1] Carmen Sylva: *A Real Queen's Fairy Tales*, translated by Edith Hopkirk, Chicago: Davis and Company, 1901, p. 211-229.

woods and mine. We kept it to ourselves. No one else should know the songs we sang together, we two, for no one else would understand them as we did. But the songs poured from my pen, and if my thoughts do but go back to the woods, again they come, like a far-off greeting from my childhood's days.

How often have I flung my arms round a tree to embrace it, and kissed the rough bark, for if my fellow-creatures thought me too wild and impetuous, the forest never did. The trees never complained that my young arms hugged them too violently, or that I was too noisy when I sang my songs at the top of my voice. For I could never think my songs to myself unsung. I sang them over and over again, hundreds of times, and always to new melodies. […]

I have lovely woods, also, here in Romania, but fir-trees are mixed with the other trees, and there are no lofty, spacious beech avenues, like the aisles of a Gothic cathedral, as in my woods beside the Rhine. And quite a different set of wild animals – bears, lynxes, chamois, eagles, and moor-fowl – inhabit these forests. It is almost another world here, but very beautiful, nevertheless. […]

As a child I always thought I was not so good as the others, and not so well loved, because I was less lovable. And how I prayed that I might become better and worthier of being loved, and that God would also grant me the power in some way or other to set forth his praises, because my heart was always overflowing with thankfulness to see the world so beautiful, and to feel myself so full of youthful strength. And there in secret he planted in my breast the power of poetic song. But at first I did not understand rightly how glorious a gift God had given to me. I did not value it at all – I fancied every one could do just the same, if they only cared to try. And when I grew older and saw that it was really a gift bestowed upon me from on High, then I became still more afraid to speak of it, lest I should be thought vain and boastful. I did not even dare to learn the rules of my art, nor to correct mistakes that I had made; I felt as if that would be scarcely honest and sincere. When I married, I had already written a large volume of poems, and had tried my hand as well at the drama and at prose, writing my first story at eleven years of age and my first play at fourteen. But I knew quite well that it was all very poor stuff. Not till I was five and thirty did I let anything be printed, and that was only because so many people took the pains to copy verses from my scrap-book that I wanted to spare them the trouble and simplify matters. After a time I began to search for a name under which I could hide myself, so that nobody might ever suspect who I really was.

One morning I said to the doctor: "I want a very pretty, poetic name to publish under, and now that I am in Romania, and belong to a Latin people, it must be a Latin name. Yet it must have something in it to recall the land I came from. How do you say 'forest' in Latin?'

"The forest is called *silva* – or, as some write it, *sylva*."

"That is charming! And what do you call a bird?"

„*Avis.*"

"I do not like that. It is not pretty. What's the word for a short poem or song?"

"In Latin that is *carmen*."

I clapped my hands together. "I have my name. In German I am *Waldgesang*, the song of the woods, and in Latin that is *carmen sylvae*. But *sylvae* does not sound like a real name, so we must take a trifling liberty with it and I will be called Carmen Sylva."

Since then I resemble the linden tree more and more. Many songsters come and take shelter under my branches and sing beneath my roof, and the bees are countless who work in my house. For it is no home for idlers; work is going on there from early morn till evening, my bees are always flying in and out. But I myself begin work earlier than any of them, for winter and summer I am up before the sun and at my work.

Woodsong, Carmen Sylva, is my name – the name under which I hid myself for so long, and if today I come forth from that shelter that was like the broad leaves of the silver-linden spread over me, it is because so many friends, and especially dear children, have asked it of me, and because I have white hair now and would so gladly be a grand-mother if only God had granted me that blessing. I must e'en be all children's grandmother, and never refuse them anything they ask. The Woodsong is indeed for all children if they will only listen to it, and it will gladden them all alike, whether they be rich or poor, well cared for or in want, whether they go barefoot or wear boots lined with costly fur. The Woodsong loves all alike that come to her, and pours out her whole soul for their delight. And her white hair is like the silver lining of the linden leaves – it gives a bright sheen to thoughts that were otherwise too grave, and she desires that within her shadow it may always be light.

What is it then to be a queen, if it is not like the silver linden tree to cast a protecting shadow over the world's sweetest songbirds, to offer shelter and refuge to all those whose finely wrought workmanship vies with the spider's skill; to be the providence of the industrious bees lest they perish in the winter? If all this be done, then indeed may life's autumn be as sunny as that golden foliage which seems to have retained the whole summer's warmth and light to radiate it forth again.

But it is harder for poor Carmen Sylva than for any other silver-linden. For God had once given her the loveliest song of all, and then he took it away from her again, because he wanted it in his own heaven. That song was her only child, a little girl whose name was Marie, but who called herself Itty when she was so small that she could not say little, and so the name Itty clung to her. She glided about like a little fairy, as if she had wings, during the whole of her short life, she said the sweetest things, she would throw herself on the earth to kiss the sunbeams. She loved the trees, and the flowers, and the water; she danced along the steepest mountain paths as if there were no danger, no precipice below. And if ever I were sad, she sprang up behind me in the big armchair, and turned my face round to her and looked in my eyes to ask: "Are you not happy, mama?"

But God called her back to heaven because the little angel was missing there, which he had lent for a short time to earth. And it seemed to the poor linden tree as if it stood there desolate, and as if there were no voices to be heard in its branches, and as if the sky had suddenly darkened overhead, and the sun gave no more warmth.

But years afterward, all at once a soft murmur penetrated the sorrowing tree and stirred it to the very core. And then the sky grew bright again, and the birds sang once more, and the dried blossoms filled with honey, for it was the voice of Song and Story, the nearest approach this world can offer for the voice of Itty – consoling and gladdening the heart by endeavoring to give comfort and joy to others.

***

And now, dear children, I bid you farewell for the present. Next year I may have another volume for you. In the meantime I hope you will tell me which of these tales you like best and perhaps I will write sequels to some of them.

Queen Elisabeth of Romania, the poet Carmen Sylva, ca. 1883.

Queen Elisabeth in Romanian costume, ca. 1883-1886.

Princess Elisabeth with her daughter Maria, ca. 1873.

Queen Elisabeth, ca. 1883.

Queen Elisabeth, coronation photography, 1881.

RĘINE ELISABETH DE ROUMAINE

7086

Queen Elisabeth, ca. 1896, old postcard.

King Carol I and Queen Elisabeth, ca. 1909, old postcard.

King Carol I and Queen Elisabeth, ca. 1913.

King Carol I and Queen Elisabeth at Sinaia, ca. 1913, old postcard.

Queen Elisabeth photographed by Crown Princess Marie on the Serpent-Isle, ca. 1910.

Königin Witwe Elisabeth von Rumänien
(Carmen Sylva)

5478

Phot. B. I. G. Berlin

Queen Dowager Elisabeth, ca. 1914-1915, old postcard.

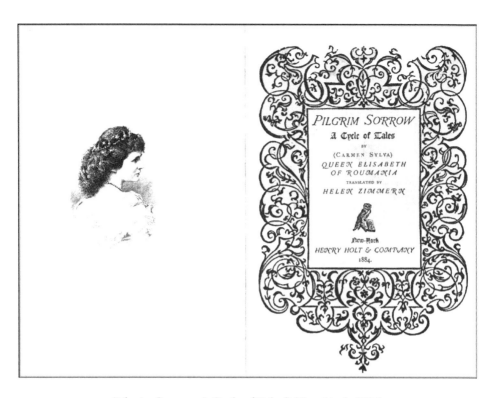

„Pilgrim Sorrow. A Cycle of Tales" (New York, 1884),
American English edition of the book "Leidens Erdengang" (German edition, 1882).
With a portrait of Queen Elisabeth on the frontispiece.

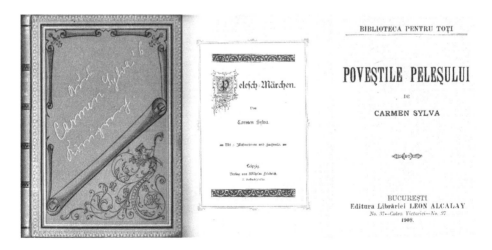

"Pelesch-Märchen" (Tales of the Pelesh) by Carmen Sylva
(cover and title page of the 1st German edition, 1883),
and "Poveştile Peleşului" (title page of a Romanian edition from 1908).

Illustrations of Romanian peasants in "Pelesch-Märchen"
(Tales of the Pelesh, 1st German edition, 1883).

Legends from * * * * *
River & Mountain
By Carmen Sylva (H.M. the
Queen of Roumania) and Alma
Strettell. With Illustrations
by T. H. Robinson

London: George Allen
156 Charing Cross Road
1896

"Legends from River & Mountain" by Carmen Sylva (H.M. the Queen of Romania),
translated into English by Alma Strettel and illustrated by T.H. Robinson
(London, 1896).

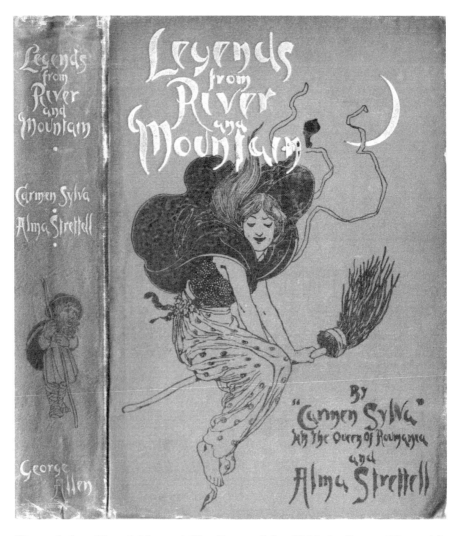

"Legends from River & Mountain" by Carmen Sylva (H.M. the Queen of Romania), translated into English by Alma Strettel (London, 1896), containing tales from the volume "Pelesch-Märchen" (Tales of the Pelesh, German edition: 1883) and legends from the volume: "Durch die Jahrhunderte" (Through the Centuries, German edition: 1885).

„Märchen einer Königin" (A Queen's Fairy Tales, German edition, 1901).

Queen Elisabeth in illustrations for the autobiographic tale "Carmen Sylva"
in "Märchen einer Königin" (A Queen's Fairy Tales, German edition, 1901).

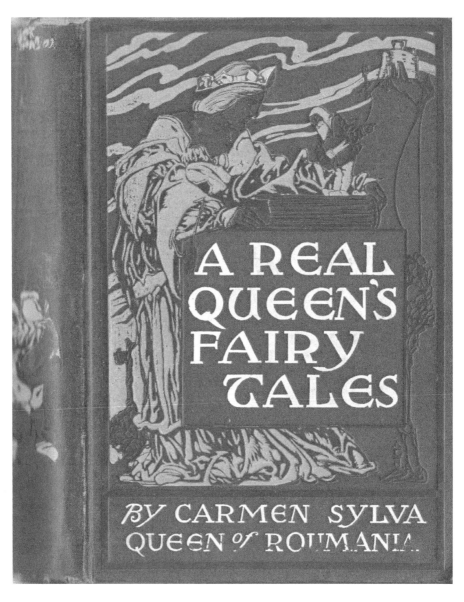

American English edition of the fairy tales by Queen Elisabeth (Carmen Sylva):
"A Real Queen's Fairy Tales" (Chicago, 1901).

The Fairy laid her soft hand on the hot
little head and he was well again.

Carmen Sylva
Elizabeth, Queen of Roumania

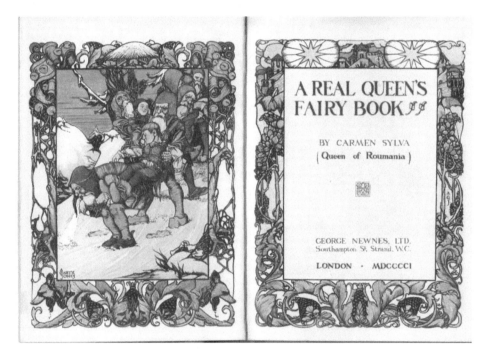

American and British editions of the fairy tales by Queen Elisabeth (Carmen Sylva):
"A Real Queen's Fairy Tales" (Chigaco, 1901),
"A Real Queen's Fairy Book" (London, 1901).

"Meine Ruh'" (My Peace), volume of poems by Carmen Sylva, 1st German edition: 1884.

"In der Lunca" (On the Meadow. Romanian Idyll), a love story of two orphans in the Romanian countryside by Queen Elisabeth (Carmen Sylva), published in Germany in 1904. The volume has a dedication to the musician George Enescu and contains two illustrations of paintings by Nicolae Grigorescu (on the frontispiece is the picture of a young Romanian shepherd, "Ciobănașul", signed and dated: 1900).

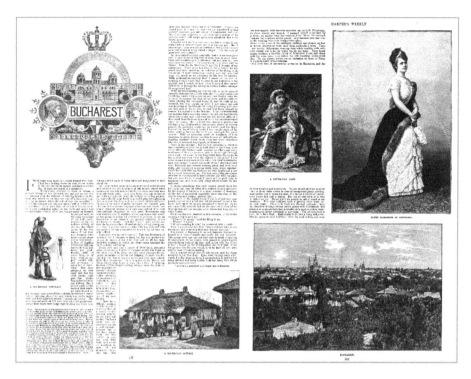

"Bucharest", an essay of Queen Elisabeth of Romania (Carmen Sylva) published in the American political magazine "Harper's Weekly. A Journal of Civilization" (1893).

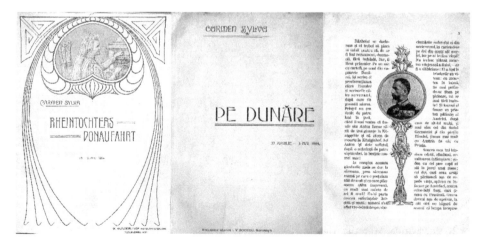

The travel journal of Queen Elisabeth (Carmen Sylva):
"Rheintochters Donaufahrt" (The Daughter of the Rhine Travelling on the Danube, German edition) and "Pe Dunăre" (On the Danube, Romanian edition), both published in 1905.

Queen Marie: "So I began to write fairy-tales"

Queen Marie of Romania relates in her memoirs *The Story of My Life* [2] (1934) the beginnings of her writing activity by the time she was Crown Princess of Romania, while the old Queen Elisabeth of Romania (Carmen Sylva) encouraged her first steps in fictional writing:

> I have not as yet spoken about my writing. It began thus: Even as a child I possessed a vivid imagination and I liked telling stories to my sisters, when at night we all three lay in our small beds, side by side. Later it was to my children that I told my stories, and as I ripened the stories ripened with me and even my growing up children liked to listen. Out of the wealth of the visions that floated before my brain, I built up my tales. They were nearly always fantastic and my imagination was so vivid that I could conjure up marvelous places and wonderful people, sometimes heroic, sometimes grotesque or funny, and their lives were a mixture of pathos and absurdity, but through it all ran a strong strain of idealism, a touch of the romantic.
>
> Beauty played a great part. Beauty in every form attracted me, and so distinctly did I see what I was relating that I made my listeners wander with me through marvelous castles and gardens, through waste lands and up high mountains, upon lone sea-shores, also to terrible places where the four winds met. Then one of my children said to me: "Mamma, you ought to write all this down, it is a pity to allow so many beautiful pictures to fade away; you ought to hold them fast, there are few who can make others follow them into such strange and prodigious worlds ; you are made for writing fairy-tales." Fairy-tales! There was magic in the word. I had always loved fairy-tales, legends and old ballads, the queerer, the more uncanny, the better. I loved the Scotch and Scandinavian Sagas and all the heroic romantic tales of the past.
>
> Fairy-tales, legends... I closed my eyes and saw all the manifold people of my imagination stirring before me, all the colors, all the flowers, all the beauty; there was no end to them, it was a tremendous store of wealth, inexhaustible, endless...
>
> So I began to write fairy-tales. They were not wonderful literature; I knew nothing whatever about writing, about style or composition, or about the "rules of the game," but I did know how to conjure up beauty, also at times, emotion. I also had a vast store of words.

---

[2] Queen Marie of Romania: *The Story of My Life*, New York: Charles Scribner's Sons, 1934, pp. 577-580.

Carmen Sylva, when she discovered that I was writing, instead of laughing at me and being ironical about my modest attempts at literature, encouraged me from the very first in every way. She was getting old, her imagination was running dry and she declared that mine had come just in time to replace hers, which was a generous thing to say. She declared that it was a happy and blessed discovery that I could hold a pen, and no end of kind and enthusiastic things. She spurred me on to write, and each time I had finished a story she immediately wanted to have it so as to translate it into German.

She assured me that, although hers had been rich, I had a larger vocabulary than she ever had, that I saw beauty in a special and particularly intense way, and much else, which made me glad and proud, although I knew that Aunty was too easily enthusiastic and not always a keen discerner as to the value of things.

"Child, child!" she used to exclaim. "How do you know so much? I never dreamt that you knew so much!"

Neither had I ever dreamt that I knew so much; I suppose the subconscious within me had continually absorbed those many things I seemed to pass by without noticing: sights, feelings, emotions, pictures, human passions, human joys, human griefs, also a certain philosophy which comes with living. This was all stored up and stirred in me somewhere and came to life when I put pen to paper, and above all there was beauty, so much beauty everywhere, in every form; it was all mine if I could seize it.

At first I imagined that I could write nothing but fairy-tales, that I must continually describe the fantastic, the superhuman, in unreal worlds of imagination: mold picture upon picture out of nothing but beauty. I was moved by a regular thirst for beauty. And yet with it there was always that queer feeling of never being able to take myself seriously which was mine all through my youth and which now still clung to me when I wrote: "I do not want to pretend to know more than I do, to pretend to be anything else than what I am," were the thoughts that hampered my development. "I do not want to show off or to take anything for myself to which I have no real right, nothing by false means, ever... Rather be considered beneath my own value than above it, no pretending, no shams..."

But one day I discovered that I could describe, depict, a landscape, a village, a sunset, a dusty road; that I could with ease conjure up also visions of everyday places, of everyday people; everything picturesque attracted me. I felt the atmosphere, the pathos, that something which lies beneath what is merely seen by the eye, I felt it all, and whilst I wrote I understood that this had come to me little by little through my growing love for my adopted country. I realized how deeply I had absorbed the beauties, the characteristics, the quaintness peculiar to Romania, and I knew that I should be able to describe it one day—and that knowledge made me feel strong and rich.

I was still extremely hesitant about what form, what style was going to be mine; the weird had a too great attraction for me, and I was so unlearned, but the visions, pictures, emotions, sensations were all there, lying within me ready to be born.

So I simply went on writing, humbly, without any pretensions, because, having begun I could not lay down my pen. That is all there was about it, an inner urge not to be denied; but strangely enough I felt almost ashamed as though I were somewhat of a fraud... a little girl pretending; still that silly fear of taking myself too seriously.

Album: Queen Marie, Portraits and Books

Crown Prince Ferdinand and Crown Princess Marie, 1893.

Crown Princess Marie with her son, Crown Prince Carol, 1894.

Crown Princess Marie of Romania, ca. 1900, old postcard.

A. S. R. Princesa Maria

Crown Princess Marie in Romanian costume, ca. 1900, old postcard.

Crown Princess Marie at the Cotroceni Palace in Bucharest, 1907, old postcard.

Crown Princess Marie with her two sons, Crown Prince Carol and Prince Nicolae,
ca. 1907, old postcard.

Crown Princess Marie with Princess Maria (Mignon) and Prince Nicolae
in Romanian costume, ca. 1910, old postcard.

Crown Princess Marie with four of her children in Romanian costume,
ca. 1910, old postcard.

Queen Marie with her daughter Princess Ileana, ca. 1920, old postcard.

King Carol I and Crown Princess Maria at Sinaia, ca. 1910, old postcard.

King Ferdinand and Queen Marie, ca. 1914, old postcard.

Queen Marie of Romania, coronation photography, 1922, old postcard.

M. S. Regina Maria

187
EDIT. C.SFETEA.BUCURESTI.

Queen Marie of Romania, ca. 1920, old postcard.

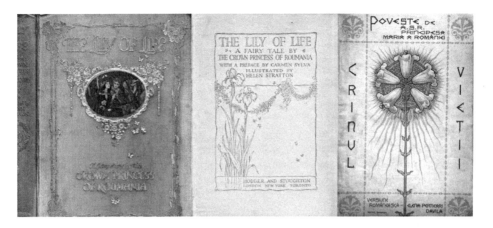

"The Lily of Life" (London, New York, Toronto, 1913), a fantasy novel by
Crown Princess Marie with a preface by Queen Elisabeth (Carmen Sylva),
and "Crinul vieții", the Romanian edition (1913) translated by Elena Perticari-Davila,
with a cover by Ignat Bednarik after a design of Crown Princess Marie.

"The Dreamer of Dreams" (London, New York, Toronto, 1915), a fantasy novel by
Crown Princess Marie with illustrations by Edmund Dulac,
and "Visătorul de vise", the Romanian edition (1914),
translated by Margărita Miller-Verghy.

"Ilderim. A Tale of Light and Shade" (London, 1926) by Queen Marie, with a dedication to her son, Crown Prince Carol. The German edition "Feindliche Brüder" (Hostile Brothers), translated by Queen Elisabeth (Carmen Sylva), was published in 1917.

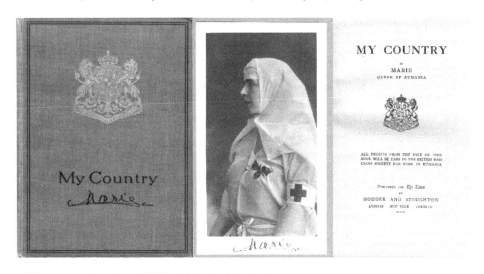

The autobiographical books „My Country" (London, New York, Toronto, 1916) and „The Country that I Love" (London, 1925) by Queen Marie of Romania, containing essays about Romania.

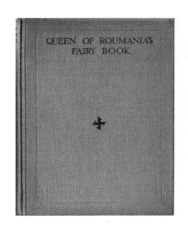

"The Queen of Romania's Fairy Book" by Queen Marie (New York, ca. 1923).

Romanian edition of the fairy book of Queen Marie: "Poveşti" (Fairy Tales, volume 2, 1921), with a dedication of the Queen "to all the children in Greater Romania".

"The Magic Doll of Romania. A Wonder Story in Which East and West Do Meet"
by Queen Marie (New York, 1929), with illustrations by Maud and Miska Petersham.

"The Magic Doll of Romania. A Wonder Story in Which East and West Do Meet"
by Queen Marie (New York, 1929), with illustrations by Maud and Miska Petersham,
the frontispiece showing Queen Marie with her coronation crown and other illustrations
showing the Bran Castle and Queen Marie in Romanian costume.

The Ideal Sovereign in the Vision of the Writing Queens of Romania, Elisabeth (Carmen Sylva) and Marie

Besides their fictional writings, the first two queens of Romania, Elisabeth and Marie, also wrote memories and diaries. Queen Elisabeth signed both her published literary books and her memoirs with her pen name Carmen Sylva, in order to mark a difference between the writer and the queen. Queen Marie, instead, simply used her royal title for her publications with no need to express any difference between the author and her high status. Nevertheless, both the works of the Poet-Queen Carmen Sylva as well as those of Queen Marie contain their reflections about how an ideal sovereign should be and which living royal personality they considered mostly alike to their vision.

Both queens were writing their memories in their native language (Elisabeth in German, Marie in English) and they published their books in their native country (Germany and the United Kingdom), as well as in Romanian translation in the country of their destiny, Romania. Like in the fairy tales, in their autobiographical writings about their kingdom the queens are describing the rich beauties of Romania, its landscape, the rural and monastic architecture, showing their empathy with the Romanian people, and inviting the foreign reader to share their high hopes for their country. While both writing queens describe King Carol I of Romania as a strong personality and a great king, his successor on the Romanian throne, Crown Prince and later King Ferdinand, is either missing (like in Elisabeth's writings), or he is barely mentioned (like in Marie's writings). Thus, for the Poet-Queen Elisabeth (Carmen Sylva) King Carol I is the embodiment of the ideal monarch, while Queen Marie is promoting herself as the caring and visionary sovereign.

King Carol I of Romania, the ruling king and husband, seen by Queen Elisabeth (Carmen Sylva)

In several writings, Queen Elisabeth is focusing on her husband, King Carol I of Romania, and showing him as a devoted monarch who fought to change Romania's status from a vassal state of the Ottoman Empire into an independent state and a new kingdom and who supported Romania's development in economy, culture, arts, society, and technology.

In her essay *Bucharest* (1893)[3], Queen Elisabeth tells the story about the young prince Carol who, when being offered the crown of Romania in

---

[3] A first version of Queen Elisabeth's essay about Bucharest in French was published in: *Les Capitales du Monde*, 1892, nr. 12, Paris, p. 297-320; the English translation appeared in: *Haper's*

1866, saw the future of the country in a vision of achievement und fulfill-ment:

"When the crown of the country, of the very existence of which he was ignorant, was offered to a young Hohenzollern prince, he opened the atlas, took a pencil, and seeing that a line drawn from London to Bombay passed through the principality which called him to be its head, he accepted the crown with these words: 'This is a country of the future!'"[4]

The same story is repeated in the later published book *Rheintochters Do-naufahrt* (1905) – the German title meaning: "The Daughter of the Rhine Travelling on the Danube", the Romanian title being: *Pe Dunăre*, i.e. "On the Danube". In *Rheintochters Donaufahrt / Pe Dunăre* (1905) Queen Elisabeth describes the journey of the Royal Family on the Danube in May 1904.[5] The German title seems to emphasize the importance of the author herself, pointing out that it is Elisabeth, the former princess from the Rhine, sharing her memories about her new country. Nevertheless, her book is more about her husband King Carol I. Elisabeth is relating her observations about the landscape, the people and events along the Danube, while mixing them up with reflections about the life and visions of her husband, the King, and thus bringing out his achievements during his long reign in Romania. From all the achievements of the king, she specifies, Queen Elisabeth considers the bridge across the Danube to be the most important realization of her king and husband, because this symbolized for Romania a bridge to worldwide trading:

"Now we arrived at Cernavodă. I have been there already when the bridge was officially opened. To me, this was the most touching day of the king's whole reign. When he was offered the Romanian crown, he did not know yet anything about the country and he already had refused other crowns, where he could see no future. But now, he opened a map, took a pen, drew a line between London and Bombay and saw that it was passing through Romania. Then he accepted the crown. When I married thirty-five years ago, I saw the first plans for the bridge across the Danube lying on his desk. But he had to wait for thirty years, until his plan could be accomplished. [...] And when the bridge was ready, the King solemnly hit the last nail. [...] And that was the moment when I realized that the King had just ful-

weekly, Saturday, February 4, 1893, New York, vol. XXXVII, No. 1885, p. 107-111; and the German version in: *Die Hauptstädte der Welt*, Breslau: Schottländer, [1898], p. 403-430.

[4] Queen Elisabeth (Carmen Sylva): Bucharest, in: *Haper's weekly*, New York, 1893, p. 111.

[5] Carmen Sylva: *Rheintochters Donaufahrt*, Regensburg: Wunderling, 1905. Carmen Sylva: *Pe Dunăre*, București: Socec, 1905. Two new editions of the journal are published in: Silvia Irina Zimmermann: *Unterschiedliche Wege, dasselbe Ideal: Das Königsbild im Werk Carmen Sylvas und in Fotografien des Fürstlich Wiedischen Archivs*, Stuttgart: ibidem-Verlag, 2014, p. 113-175. Silvia Irina Zimmermann: *Regele Carol I în opera Reginei Elisabeta*, București: Editura Curtea Veche, 2014, pp. 152-199.

filled his mission. Right there, at the bridge of Cernavodă, was now the next connection between London and Bombay. It was this bridge that counted, and that we had waited for thirty years. […] Hitting the last nail in the bridge across the Danube was the quintessence of [our] whole life."[6]

King Carol I of Romania seen by later Queen Marie

In Queen Marie's book, *The Country That I Love*[7] (1925), there are several passages about the old King Carol I, too. Like the Queen consort Elisabeth in her book *Rheintochters Donaufahrt / Pe Dunăre* (1905), Queen Marie emphasizes a good relationship with "the old King Carol" and imitates the way Elisabeth herself evoked the king's confidence in his wife, when he was sharing his thoughts, plans, and visions with her. More than that, Queen Marie somehow puts Queen Elisabeth down, when saying that the king did not ask for his wife's advice and did not value her opinion as to consult her when he planned and decorated the Pelesh-Castle in Sinaia and the Royal Palace in Bucharest. According to the lately published correspondence of the royal couple Carol I and Elisabeth, the first queen of Romania was a confidant of King Carol I and the letters of the king to his wife show that he very much valued Queen Elisabeth's opinion and that they shared with one another not only family issues but also information about social and political matters.[8]

Nevertheless, Queen Marie of Romania leads the reader of her memoires to see herself as the only one who was a true confidant of the old king in the Royal Family and that he somehow considered Marie a conversation-partner at eye-level. Like Queen Elisabeth[9], the later Queen Marie also calls the old King Carol her teacher and friend:

"How often has he related to me tales of these wanderings, when he visited the most distant corners of his land. His eyes would sparkle, his descriptions become vivid, a smile would brighten the usual gravity of his face; so dear to him was the remembrance of those days of travel and discovery in the country he had come to love. […] Loving this country as I do, I grateful-

---

[6] Carmen Sylva: *Rheintochters Donaufahrt* (1905), p. 51-52 and p. 70. Quote translated from the German by S. I. Zimmermann.

[7] Queen Marie of Romania: *The Country That I Love* (1925), p.45-70.

[8] See more in: Silvia Irina Zimmermann (editor): „*In zärtlicher Liebe Deine Elisabeth*" – „*Stets Dein treuer Carl*". *Der Briefwechsel Elisabeths zu Wied (Carmen Sylva) mit ihrem Gemahl Carol I. von Rumänien aus dem Rumänischen Nationalarchiv in Bukarest. 1869-1913*, Stuttgart: ibidem-Verlag, 2018, especially volume I, containing the royal correspondence from the period 1869-1890. Silvia Irina Zimmermann: "Corespondența primei perechi regale a României, Carol I și Elisabeta, păstrată la Arhivele Naționale ale României din București", in: *Revista Bibliotecii Academiei Române*, București, Anul 3, Nr. 1, ianuarie-iunie 2018, p. 3-21.

[9] Zimmermann: *Unterschiedliche Wege…* (2014), see chapter: *Der Lebenspartner* (The Life Partner), p. 59-73, especially p. 67-73.

ly realize how he, who was our forerunner, showed us the way."[10] "Later, as my understanding grew, I learnt to appreciate the value of what often had wearied me at first. I entered more entirely into the wise old man's interests; there was so much knowledge to gain from his experience, and if his judgment was sometimes foreign to my more ardent conception of things, much did I learn from his words, and more still from the example he gave us. [...] Never was man more austere, more simple, more selfless, existing solely for his work. A saint could not have lived a life of greater abnegation. We did not always agree, but each year made of us better friends."[11]

For Queen Marie, the old King Carol was "a great king" with a vision fulfilled and an ideal king for his country – but only up to the point when history changed and he couldn't go any further fighting for his peoples' dream, and when he died just before the First World War broke out:

"He too had a dream, but a dream he realized little by little through many long years."[12] "He had had but one ideal the glory of his country, the good of his people. [...] [Now] He was at rest – his work was over and, at an hour when he and his people could no more follow the same dream, the great King closed his eyes and became silent, leaving unto others the solving of the last question – the one that had been taken out of his hands."[13]

The Hereditary Prince Ferdinand of Romania unmentioned in the works of Queen Elisabeth (Carmen Sylva)

The Hereditary Prince and later King Ferdinand is never mentioned by Queen Elisabeth in her autobiographical writings for the public. Nevertheless, Queen Elisabeth's private correspondence with her princely family in Neuwied and with her husband, King Carol I, reveals that she was disappointed by the lack of charisma and by the indecisiveness of Prince Ferdinand, the nephew of the king and heir to the Romanian throne. In the long run, Queen Elisabeth was content to realize that Crown Princess Marie of Romania was the more active and determined part of the couple, and that she had both the power and the skills to continue the work Elisabeth had begun for Romania and to become a good queen consort and the best match for the future King Ferdinand. Thus, in Queen Elisabeth's book *Rheintochters Donaufahrt / Pe Dunăre* (1905) about the journey of the Royal Family on the Danube in May 1904, when Prince Ferdinand was part of the travelling family group, he appears only in some of the images in the queen's book, but otherwise he is not mentioned at all. Instead, Queen Elis-

---

[10] Queen Marie of Romania: *The Country That I Love* (1925), p. 59-60.

[11] Ibidem, p. 52-53.

[12] Ibidem, p. 46.

[13] Ibidem, p. 54.

abeth writes about the Crown Princess Marie and about the children of the hereditary couple Ferdinand and Marie and focuses on little Prince Carol, the first hereditary prince born in Romania, whom she regards as the high hope of the country and the follower of her husband, King Carol I.[14]

King Ferdinand I of Romania, the ruling king and husband, barely mentioned in the works of Queen Marie

King Ferdinand I of Romania, the ruling king and husband, is barely mentioned by his queen consort Marie, too. In her book, *My Country* (1916) there is no mention of any king. Here the author Queen Marie introduces herself to the English reader with an emphatic affirmation at the very beginning: "The Queen of a small Country!," adding that "she would like the country of her birth [England] to see this other country [Romania] through the eyes of its Queen".[15] When reading this book, one has the feeling that the author Queen Marie is a queen regnant, a queen ruling in her own right, and not just a queen consort. In Queen Marie's book *The Country That I Love* (1925) – a kind of continuation of the book *My Country* (1916) – and in the Romanian edition *Țara Mea* (1917-1919) – containing both *My Country* and *The Country That I Love* in Romanian translation – we can find two chapters about the old King Carol and a few passages about King Ferdinand, too. However, in Queen Marie's second book about Romania, *The Country That I Love*, King Ferdinand is present, but Queen Marie does not mention his name anywhere. Instead, Ferdinand is simply called "the King" or "The King and I".[16] Nevertheless, there are two longer passages, where King Ferdinand becomes more a part of the plot in Queen Marie's book. In the first case, Queen Marie tells about her travelling with the king in the country, while they are both heavy-laden by the thought of the approaching war:
"A heavy feeling of gloom brooded over all things; hearts were uneasy, spirits were troubled, and not least troubled was the heart of the King. Those were days of throbbing anxiety; we knew that the wing of war was already hovering near our country, and, like two anxious parents, we watched the horizon, feeling that the hour of fate was nearing, that naught could now stay the storm that must break over our land. Restless were the King's nights, sleep avoided him, his soul was torn by doubt. Was it the

---

[14] For more details see: Silvia Irina Zimmermann: "Portretul perechii princiare moştenitoare Ferdinand şi Maria din viziunea Reginei Elisabeta a României în scrisori personale şi texte pentru publicul larg", in: *Revista Bibliotecii Academiei Române*, Anul 1, Nr. 2, 2016, p. 11-35.

[15] Queen Marie of Romania: *My Country* (1916), p. 5 and p. 6.

[16] Queen Marie of Romania: *The Country That I Love* (1925): "the King and I", p. 41; "the King", p. 42. The only place where the name of King Ferdinand is appearing in Queen Marie's book is in the obituary for their son Mircea (p. 152).

right moment? If he drew the sword would it be for the good of the country? Would the word he had to say, the word that would cut him off from all the loves of yore, would that word lead his people towards the accomplishment of their Golden Dream?"[17]

Another mentioning of King Ferdinand (again without his name) occurs in Queen Marie's Romanian edition *Țara mea*, when the queen appreciates the appearance of the King and the hereditary Prince Carol, the later King Carol II (also mentioned without his name in Queen Marie's book), in the field hospital where the queen takes care of the wounded soldiers:

"My husband, who had the command upon all the troops, came every day to see how we were getting along. His presence was a huge encouragement and all our sick people welcomed his arrival as a sign that nothing had been left aside from what they would need. My son was with me, too, my elder son; he was my right hand, my workmate, and his young energy could reach the places where my smile could not."[18]

Both Queen Elisabeth and Queen Marie have a similar discomfort with Ferdinand's weaker personality, and seem to compare him with the old King Carol I, expecting from him to have more initiative and to show a more determined attitude towards the people. In consequence, Queen Elisabeth chose not to mention Ferdinand at all in her memoires. Queen Marie, on the one hand, writes about King Ferdinand with respect and sympathy in part II of the Romanian edition of her book. On the other hand, in her diaries, she writes about her being disappointed by the lack of energy and initiative of her husband King Ferdinand and she expresses her wish to take the lead, asking herself: "Oh, why am I not King?"[19]

Regarding the passage in Queen Marie's book *The Country That I Love* about the hereditary Prince Carol ("he was my right hand, my workmate, and his young energy could reach the places where my smile could not"[20]) – this is obviously a euphemism, and Queen Marie here seems to be holding the pieces of the royal family together. In reality, the hereditary Prince Carol had not demonstrated the sense of duty and sacrifice for his country expected from an heir, but more of the contrary. In 1918, Prince Carol had deserted to marry Zizi Lambrino on 31 August 1918. In addition, in 1925, when Queen Marie's book was published in the United Kingdom, Prince Carol would leave his family with a new mistress and renounce his right to the throne on 28 December 1925 in favor of his son by Crown Princess Helen (Elena), Mihai, the later King Mihai I.

---

[17] Queen Marie of Romania: *The Country That I Love* (1925), p. 42.

[18] Regina Maria: *Țara Mea* (1919), p. 97. Quote translated from the Romanian by S. I. Zimmermann.

[19] Lucian Boia (editor): *Regina Maria: Jurnal de Război*, 1916-17, the Queen's note from Sept. 25/ Oct. 8, 1916, p. 164.

[20] Regina Maria: *Țara Mea* (1919), p. 97.

Contrastingly, when talking about herself in her book *The Country That I Love*, Queen Marie emphasizes her strength and courage that caused her to be admired and loved by her people: "Not many princesses and queens are given the chance to be so close to their troops, but because this is a small country, the sovereigns are really taking their part, too. There must be something in my nature that makes me be helpful whenever there is an eager need of help and energy. Then, it's like my forces grow twice as before and my strengths seem never to vanish."[21]

In the context of the First World War, the books of Queen Marie about Romania were not meant to pay tribute to the reigning King Ferdinand (who was a German native), but Queen Marie was addressing herself to the reader from her native country, the United Kingdom, who in the World War was fighting against the German Empire. Thus, it is understandable that Queen Marie's books focused instead on the personality of a queen who not only overshined the defects and drawbacks of both the king and the heir to the throne. More than everything else, her books emphasized that Romania had a determined sovereign fighting for her people's survival during the war and occupation period. For the English reader of Queen Marie's books about Romania it must have been more sympathetic that Queen Marie, an English princess, was bound both to her native country, the United Kingdom, and to her new country Romania, who also was an ally in the war. And for the Romanian reader Queen Marie of Romania embodied the ideal sovereign for Romania more than anybody else, as she not only pictured herself as a monarch determined to fight for her people's dream, but also acted during the war time like a monarch capable of sacrifice for her country, and a devoted monarch, one could rely on.

Regarding the personal understanding of their role as queen consorts, the writing queens of Romania, Elisabeth and Marie, reveal different kinds of images of a queen, though they have the same intent of reaching a large public and both have great power of persuasion.

The Queen Consort Elisabeth (Carmen Sylva): The Personal Image of Her Role and Vision

Queen Elisabeth considers herself a poet-queen and a chronicler writing about the visions and the glory of the first King of Romania, and bringing homage to King Carol I. Queen Elisabeth had dreams and visions, too: She badly wished to have an heir and she had the vision of having a royal court at Bucharest with a high cultural prestige. In the end these would all be

---

[21] Ibidem, p. 102. Quote translated from the Romanian by S. I. Zimmermann.

dreams, which did not fulfil as she expected.[22] Instead, Queen Elisabeth had no heir, and after the death of her only daughter no further children. She went through the bitter experience of a three-year long exile (1891-1894), followed by the loss of her influence at court and the downsizing of her importance and historic memorability – as one can also notice from the portrait made by later Queen Marie, who called the dreams of old Queen Elisabeth ironically: "building castles in the air"[23].

Elisabeth and Marie had a quite difficult relationship at the beginning. In 1893, when Marie became the hereditary princess of Romania, Elisabeth felt like being brushed aside by the young princess, who had taken her place at the Royal Court in Bucharest, while Elisabeth was banned to come back to Romania for another two years of her exile.[24] After her return to Romania, Queen Elisabeth began to realize the talents of the crown princess, and she encouraged her literary activity by translating one of her novels into German and writing a foreword to a long fairy tale of Crown Princess Marie.[25] Nevertheless, long before Marie's appearance at the court in Bucharest, Queen Elisabeth had the vision to be the chronicler of King Carol I of Romania and she wished to write his memoires. She advised the king of the importance that he, who had won the independence of the country and was the first king of Romania, must publish his memories. Obviously, Queen Elisabeth already made a start in writing about his life, as she asked Carol in a letter from 1890 to continue to make some notes, so that they could write it all together later.[26] However, the implication of Queen Elisabeth encouraging a marriage of the Hereditary Prince Ferdinand with her court-lady Elena Văcărescu in 1891 was a fatal mistake of hers, which finally caused Queen Elisabeth to be exiled for more than three years, from 1891 to

---

[22] For more see in: Zimmermann (ed.): *Der Briefwechsel...* (2018), volume II: 1891-1913, p. 65; p. 384.

[23] Queen Marie of Romania: *The Country That I Love* (1925), p. 68.

[24] More about the exile of Queen Elisabeth in: Silvia Irina Zimmermann: "Corespondența primei perechi regale a României..." (*Revista Bibliotecii Academiei Române*, 2018), p. 3-21. Silvia Irina Zimmermann: "Activitatea literară și artizanală a Reginei Elisabeta din perioada exilu-lui (1891-1894) în oglinda corespondenței cu Regele Carol I. Colaborarea reginei cu André Lecomte du Noüy", in: *Revista de Artă și Istoria Artei*, București: Editura Muzeului Municipi-ului București, Nr. 1, 2018, pp. 144-159.

[25] See more in: Hannah Pakula: *The Last Romantic: A Biography of Queen Marie of Roumania.* New York: Simon & Schuster, 1984, p. 66–67, p. 103-104, p. 122-123, p. 143. Gabriel Badea-Păun: *Carmen Sylva. 1843-1916. Uimitoarea regină Elisabeta a României*, București: Humanitas, 2010, p. 204-206, p 210-211. Gabriel Badea-Păun: «Autour d'un récit autobiographique royal», dans: *Reine Marie de Roumanie: Histoire de ma vie. 1875-1918*, Paris: Lacurne, 2014, p. 9-19, especially p. 13-14. Silvia Irina Zimmermann: „*Die Feder in der Hand bin ich eine ganz andre Person.*" *Carmen Sylva (1843-1916). Leben und Werk*, Stuttgart: ibidem-Verlag, 2019, p. 305-312, p. 315-335.

[26] Zimmermann (ed.): *Der Briefwechsel...* (2018), volume I: 1869-1890, p. 342-343.

1894. During the exile-period of Queen Elisabeth, King Carol I began to publish his memoires. In addition, the king chose a former literary co-author of the Queen, Mite Kremnitz, to be the editor of his memoires, which was another blow to Elisabeth, who then blamed Kremnitz for having intrigued against her.[27] Maybe as a compensation for all her losses, Queen Elisabeth published her book about the royal journey on the Danube *Rheintochters Donaufahrt* in 1905, both in Germany and in Romania, thus paying a tribute to King Carol I, and obviously wishing to leave behind a picture of her king and husband in her own words.

The Queen Consort Marie: The Personal Image of Her Role and Vision

The Queen Consort Marie is presenting herself more self-confident than Queen Elisabeth in her writings: Marie is a monarch writing about her peoples' "Golden Dream", the Great Union of Romania. She is a queen fighting with her pen for the glory of her country and paying a tribute to the Romanian soul. Moreover, she pictures herself as an ambassador for her Kingdom, presenting herself and taking an attitude like a reigning queen on her visits abroad when meeting political personalities.[28]

Queen Marie published the book *My Country* first in the United Kingdom, in 1916, during the First World War. By this time, Marie was the Queen of Romania for just 2 years (the old King Carol I had passed away in October 1914), and beginning with August 1916 Romania was at war, on the side of the Allied Powers. Queen Marie's book *My Country* had a note on the front page, too: "All profits from the sale of this book will be paid to the British Red Cross Society for work in Rumania". Queen Marie published the continuation of *My Country* under the title *The Country That I Love. An Exile's Memories* in 1925 in the UK, and this part was about the war-years 1917-1918 spent by the queen in Jassy, when Bucharest and the South of Romania were under German occupation. There also existed a Romanian edition published in 1917 and 1919, a translation by the historian Nicolae Iorga, containing both books of Queen Marie in one volume and entitled *Țara mea.* The Romanian volume had an additional first chapter before part II of the

[27] More about the relation of Queen Elisabeth and Mite Kremnitz in: Zimmermann: *Carmen Sylva. Leben und Werk* (2019), p. 11, p. 164. Zimmermann: *Unterschiedliche Wege…* (2014), see chapter: *Über den Herrscher in republikanischen Zeiten* (On the Sovereign in Republican Times), p. 89-104, especially p. 89-93. Silvia Irina Zimmermann: „Despre regi in vemuri republicane. Portretul regelui în opera reginei Elisabeta a României", in: Claudiu-Lucian Topor, Alexandru Istrate, Daniel Cain (editori): *Diplomați, societate și mondenități. Sfârșit de Belle Époque în lumea românească,* Iași: Editura Universității Alexandru Ioan Cuza, 2015, p. 125-138.

[28] More about the political talent of Queen Marie of Romania and her visits abroad in: Adrian-Silvan Ionescu: *Regina Maria și America*, București: Noi Media Print, 2009. Diana Mandache: *Viva Regina Maria! Un destin fabulous în reîntregirea României*, București: Editura Corint, 2016.

book, about the Romanian soldiers preparing for war and Queen Marie on the field hospitals, a chapter dated 18 August 1916.[29]

As a writer, Queen Marie focuses in her books *My Country* (1916) and *The Country That I Love* (1925) on her feelings towards the country as her peoples' land. The reader does not learn anything about real politics, only a few passages about Romanian history, nothing about its educational system, the beginning industry, or people in the towns and the high society, nor can we read anything about the economy and trading relations of Romania with other countries. In this regard, the books of Queen Marie are very different from Queen Elisabeth's book praising the old King Carol and his achievements in various fields of activity: army, culture, railroad infrastructure, development of the cities, trading, and international politics. Nevertheless, Queen Marie warns the reader right at the beginning about what her book on Romania does not contain:

"I am not going to talk of my country's institutions, of its politics, of names known to the world. Others have done this more cleverly than I ever could. I want only to speak of its soul, of its atmosphere, of its peasants and soldiers, of things that made me love this country, that made my heart beat with its heart."[30]

Thus, Marie describes mostly the landscape of the country, revealing her emotions and the atmosphere of what she can see when she visits the peasants in their villages, the nuns and monks at the monasteries. Nevertheless, Queen Marie offers a brief history of the capital city of Moldavia, Jassy, in *The Country That I Love* (1925) and she describes the castles and palaces in Sinaia and Bucharest, later the Bran castle, the surroundings of Constanţa, and the harbor at the Black Sea. When telling about her own personal dreams, Queen Marie reveals very private and unspectacular joys like the dream to build houses in different beautiful places of her country and to plan new flower gardens. Nonetheless, in regard to her social position as a queen, Marie's vision is the same as her people's "Golden dream" of the union of all Romanians in one country. Obviously, Queen Marie is aiming to personify this dream of the Romanians with her attitude as a confident, caring, courageous, and faithful queen of her people. Above all, the two books of Queen Marie, *My Country* (1916) and *The Country That I Love* (1925) are an homage to the Romanian land, its people and the Romanian soul, because, as she declares: "There is nothing of the Romanian land that I have not loved. […] I have loved it all, loved it deeply ... loved it well!"[31]

For both writing Queens of Romania, Elisabeth and Marie, the ideal sovereign for their country is the caring and visionary monarch. To Queen Elisa-

---

[29] Regina Maria: *Ţara Mea* (1919), p. 89-105.
[30] Queen Marie of Romania: *My Country* (1916), p. 8.
[31] Queen Marie of Romania: *The Country That I Love* (1925), p. 18-19.

beth it is King Carol I of Romania who embodies her ideal of a sovereign, because of all his achievements for the country's independence, welfare, and prosperity during his long reign. Contrastingly, in Queen Marie's books, it is the queen idealizing herself as a monarch, who has the strong character and determined attitude to fulfil her country's dream, the unity of all Romanians. Finally, King Carol I and Queen Marie of Romania appear as monarchs with a vision fulfilled, both gaining greatness through their achievements and attitude.

The Royal Family of Romania, ca. 1906, old postcard.

The Royal Family of Romania, ca. 1906, old postcard.

Bibliography

Queen Elisabeth (Carmen Sylva): Published Works (Selection)

Poems (in German)

1880   *Hammerstein* [epic poem], Leipzig: F. A. Brockhaus.
1880   *Sappho* [epic poem], Leipzig: F. A. Brockhaus.
1881   *Stürme* [Storms, volume of epic poems], Bonn: Strauss.
1882   *Die Hexe* [The Witch, epic poem], inspired by the statue "The Witch" by Carl Cauer, Berlin: Duncker.
1882   *Jehovah* [epic poem], Berlin: Duncker.
1884   *Meine Ruh'* [My Peace, poems], Leipzig: Druckerei W. Druglin; Berlin: Duncker; 3rd extended edition in 5 volumes, Berlin: Duncker, 1901.
1884   *Mein Rhein* [My Rhine, poems], Leipzig: Titze.
1886   *Mein Buch* [My Book, poems] Düsseldorf: Felix Bagel.
1890   *Die Sphynx* [The Sphynx, epic poem from the volume *My Book*], facsimile of the handwriting of Queen Elisabeth, sheet music by August Bungert, French translation by Elena Văcărescu, Berlin: Luckhardt/ New York: Schirmer.
1891   *Heimath* [Homeland, poems], Bonn: Strauss.
1891   *Handwerkerlieder* [Songs of the craftsmen, poems], Bonn: Strauss.
1891   *Meerlieder* [Songs of the Sea, poems], Bonn: Strauss.
1891   *Weihnachtskerzchen von Pallanza* [Little Candles from Pallanza, poems in 4 languages], Pallanza: Vercellini.
1900   *Thau* [Dew, poems], Bonn: Strauss.
1903   *Unter der Blume* [Wine Flavor, poems], Regensburg.

Tales (in German)

1882   *Leidens Erdengang* [Pilgrim Sorrow], Berlin: Duncker.
1883   *Pelesch-Märchen* [Tales of the Pelesh], *Aus Carmen Sylva's Königreich* [From Carmen Sylva's Kingdom], vol. 1, Bonn: Strauss.
1885   *Durch die Jahrhunderte* [Through the Centuries, historical stories and popular legends from Romania from King Decebalus of Dacia to King Carol I of Romania], *Aus Carmen Sylva's Königreich* [From Carmen Sylva's Kingdom], vol. 2, with a dedication to the poet Vasile Alecsandri, Leipzig.
1888   *Pelesch im Dienst. Ein sehr langes Märchen für den Prinzen Heinrich XXXII. von Reuß* [The Duty of the Pelesh. A very long tale for Prince Henry 32nd of Reuss, autobiographical tale], Bonn: Strauss.
1898   *Monsieur Hampelmann. Domnul Pulcinel. Monsieur Polichinelle. The*

Story of Mr. Jumping Jack [a tale in four languages], cover illustration by and facsimiles of the handwriting of Carmen Sylva, illustrations by André Lecomte du Noüy, [Bucureşti: Carol Göbl].

1901   *Märchen einer Königin* [Fairy Tales of a Queen], illustrations by Emma Marie Elias, Fidus and Eduard Kado, Bonn: Strauss.

Tales and novels (in German)

1882   *Ein Gebet* [A Prayer, novel], Berlin: Duncker.
1884   *Handzeichnungen* [Hand Drawings, sketches and tales], Berlin, Duncker.
1887   *Es klopft* [Knocking at the Door, novel], Regensburg: Wunderling.
1890   *Deficit* [novel], Bonn: Strauss.
1904   *In der Lunca. Rumänische Idylle* [On the Meadow. Romanian Idyll, tale], with a dedication to the musician George Enescu, with two illustrations after pictures by Nicolae Grigorescu, Regensburg: Wunderling.
1912   *Aus dem Leben* [Life Stories], Leipzig: Reclam.

Aphorisms (in German)

1890   *Vom Amboß* [About the Anvil], Bonn: Strauss.

Stage plays (in German)

1890   *Frauenmuth* [Women's Courage, volume of stage plays], Bonn: Strauss.
1892   *Meister Manole* [Master Manole], Bonn: Strauss.
1893   *Um ein paar Stiefelchen* [For Some Little Boots], Neuwied: Strüder.

Religious and philosophical essays (in German)

1900   *Seelengespräche* [Conversations of the Soul, religious essays], Bonn: Strauss.
1903   *Geflüsterte Worte* [Whispered Words, essays and poems], 5 volumes, Regensburg: Wunderling, 1903-1912.

Memoirs and autobiographical writings (in German)

1898   *Bukarest* [essay], in: Die Hauptstädte der Welt, Breslau: Schottländer, p. 403-430.
1902   *Es ist vollbracht. Das Leben meines Bruders Otto Nicholas, Prinz zu Wied* [It is consumated. The Life of My Brother Otto Nicolas Prince of Wied, memoirs], Berlin: Duncker.

1905 *Rheintochters Donaufahrt* [The Daughter of the Rhine Travelling on the Danube, travel journal: 10-16 of Mai 1904], Regensburg: Wunderling.

1908 *Mein Penatenwinkel* [My Penates-Shrine, memories from the childhood and adolescence in Neuwied], Frankfurt/ Main: Minjon.

Writings in French

1882 *Les pensées d'une reine* [aphorisms], préface par Louis Ulbach, Paris: Calmann-Lévy; 2nd extended edition [revised by Pierre Loti]: 1888.

1892 *Bucharest* [essay], in: Les Capitales du Monde, nr. 12, Paris, pp. 297-320.

1913? *Aliunde* [aphorisms], Bucureşti: Minerva.

Writings in English

1904 *Sweet Hours* [poems], London: Everett.

Works in collaboration with Mite Kremnitz (double pen name: "Dito und Idem")

1884 *Aus zwei Welten* [epistolary novel], Leipzig: Friedrich.
1886 *Astra* [epistolary novel], Bonn: Strauss.
1886 *Anna Boleyn* [stage play], Bonn: Strauss.
1887 *Feldpost* [epistolary novel], Bonn: Strauss.
1888 *In der Irre* [stories], Bonn: Strauss.
1888 *Rache und andere Novellen* [stories], Bonn: Strauss.

Translations by Carmen Sylva

1881 *Rumänische Dichtungen* [Romanian contemporary poetry translated into German in collaboration with Mite Kremnitz], Leipzig: Friedrich.

1885 Pierre Loti: *Islandfischer* [*Pecheurs d'Islande*, French novel translated into German], Bonn: Strauss.

1889 Hélène Vacaresco [Elena Văcărescu]: *Der Rhapsode der Dimbovitza* [poems in French (inspired by Romanian folk poetry) translated into German], Bonn: Strauss.

1891 Hélène Vacaresco [Elena Văcărescu]: *The Bard of the Dimbovitza* [poems in French (inspired by Romanian folk poetry) translated into English in collaboration with Alma Strettel], London: Harper & Brothers.

1899f Paul de Saint-Victor: *Die beiden Masken* (*Les Deux Masques: tragédie, comédie*) [a history of the dramatic literature, translation from French into German], 3 volumes, Berlin: Duncker, 1899-1900.

1917   Crown Princess Marie of Romania: *Feindliche Brüder* [*Ilderim*, English novel translated into German], Berlin: Oehmigke's.

Translations from the works of Queen Elisabeth (Carmen Sylva)

1882   *Poveştile Peleşului* [Tales of the Pelesh, tales and legends translated into Romanian by Dimitrie A. Sturdza], Bucureşti: Ed. Ministerul Cultelor şi Instrucţiunii Publice.

1884   *Pilgrim Sorrow, A Cycle of Tales*, translated into English by Helen Zimmern, New York: Henry Holt & Company.

1888   *Cuvinte sufleteşti* [religious essays translated into Romanian], Bucureşti: Socec.

1888   *Songs of Toil* [poems, bilingual: German-English], translations into English by John Eliot Bowen, New York: Frederick A. Stokes & Brother.

1889   *Cugetările unei regine* [aphorisms], translated into Romanian by Al. Pencovici, Bucureşti: Imprimeria Statului.

1889   *Peasant Life in Roumania* [essay], translated into English, in: The Forum, June 1889.

1893   *Bucharest* [essay], translated into English, in: Harper's Weekly. A Journal of Civilization, New York, Saturday, February 4, 1893, New York, vol. XXXVII, No. 1885, p. 107-111.

1896   *Legends from River & Mountain* [tales and legends from "Pelesch-Märchen"], translated into English by Alma Strettel, illustrations by T. H. Robinson, London: George Allan.

1896   *Femeia română* [essay translated into Romanian], in: Telegraful român, Sibiu, part I: nr. 98, 31 August/ 12 September 1896, part II: nr. 99, 3/ 15 September 1896, part III: nr. 100 5/ 17 September 1896.

1900   *Golden Thoughts of Carmen Sylva Queen of Roumania* [aphorisms], translated into English by H. Sutherland Edwards, London and New York: John Lane, The Bodely Head.

1901   *A Real Queen's Fairy Tales*, translated into English by Edith Hopkirk, illustrated by Harold Nelson and A. Garth Jones, Chicago.

1901   *A Real Queen's Fairy Book*, illustrated by Harold Nelson and A. Garth Jones, London: Newes.

1904   *How I Spent My Sixtieth Birthday* [memoirs], translated into English by H. E. Delf, Guildford: Astolat Press.

1904   *My Reminiscences of War* [memoirs translated into English], in: The North American Review, October 1904.

1905   *Pe Dunăre* [travel journal translated into Romanian by Al. Tzigara-Samurcaş], Bucureşti: Socec.

1905   *În luncă. O idilă* [tale translated into Romanian], with a dedication to George Enescu and two illustrations after pictures by Nicolae Grigorescu, Bucureşti: Ed. Librăria Socec.

1905 *Les Noëls d'une Reine* [memoirs translated into French], preface by J. Pollio, illustrated by Maurice Toussaint, Henri Toussaint, A. Robia, J. Wagrez, and Émile Robida, Paris: H. Daragon Éditeur.

1906 *Cetatea orbilor* [essay translated into Romanian], in: „Tribuna", Arad, year X, nr. 175, 19 September/ 8 October 1906, p. 1-4.

1906 *Poveştile unei Regine* [tales translated into Romanian], illustrated by Emma Marie Elias, Fidus and Eduard Kado, vol. I, Bucureşti: Alcalay.

1906 *Valuri alinate* [poems], translated into Romanian by George Coşbuc, Bucureşti: Minerva.

1908 *Œuvres choisies* [selected works translated into French], published by G. Bengesco, Paris: Juven.

1910 *De ce ne trebuiesc regii? Umbra lui Ştefan cel Mare* [an essay and a tale], translated into Romanian by Leopold Stern, Bucureşti: Editura Lumen.

1910? *Prinţul Codrului* [The Prince of the Woods, fantasy novel], translated into Romanian by Lia Hârsu, Bucureşti: Editura Librăria Nouă, seria: Biblioteca „Lumina", nr. 7.

1911 *From Memory's Shrine* [memoirs], translated into English by Edith Hopkirk, London: Sampson Low & Marston.

1914? *Poveştile unei Regine* [Fairy Tales of a Queen], translated into Romanian by Lia Hârsu, colecţia „Biblioteca pentru toţi", nr. 856, Bucureşti: Editura Librăriei Leon Alcalay.

Posthumously published works, translations and new editions

1931 *Carmen Sylva povestind copiilor* [fairy tales and legends translated into Romanian], edited by Octav Minar, Bucureşti: Socec.

1933 *Poveştile Peleşului. Pelesch-Märchen* [Tales of the Pelesh, bilingual Romanian-German edition], published on behalf of H.M. King Carol II of Romania, Bucureşti.

1936 *Poezii din Carmen Sylva* [poems], translated into Romanian by Adrian Maniu, Bucureşti: Institutul de Arte grafice „Luceafărul", Fundaţia pentru Literatură şi Artă „Regele Carol II".

1990 *Poveştile Peleşului* [Tales of the Pelesh, translated into Romanian], edited by Doina David and Stela Iancea, Timişoara: Argo.

1991 *Poveştile Peleşului* [Tales of the Pelesh, translated into Romanian], edited by Tudor Nedelcea, Craiova: Casa de editură Nob.

1992 *Insula şerpilor* [fairy tale translated into Romanian], edited by Gabriela Păsărin-Rusu, Craiova: Editura Scrisul Românesc.

1997 *Poveştile Peleşului* [Tales of the Pelesh, translated into Romanian], edited by Silvia Colfescu, Bucureşti: Editura Vremea; 2nd edition:

2016.

1998   *Versuri alese* [selected poems translated into Romanian], edited by Gabriel Badea-Păun, Bucureşti: Editura Eminescu.

1998   *Les pensées d'une reine. Carmen Sylva reine de la Roumanie* [aphorisms in French], preface by Louis Ulbach, edited by Nicolae Ionel, Iaşi: Fides.

2000   *Poveştile Peleşului* [Tales of the Pelesh, translated into Romanian], Bucureşti: Saeculum.

2000   Eminescu, Mihai, *Cele dintâi traduceri în germană. Die frühesten deutschen Übersetzungen* [poems by Mihai Eminescu, the first translations from Romanian into German by Carmen Sylva and Mite Kremnitz], München: Editura Bărbulescu.

2000? *Flüstere weiter, Seele* [selected philosophical essays], edited by Helmut Reimer, Passau: Edition Lionardo.

2001   *Les pensées d'une reine – Cugetările unei regine* [aphorisms, blingual French-Romanian edition], translations into Romanian by Dumitru Scorţanu, Iaşi: Fides.

2002f *Colţul penaţilor mei* [memoirs], translated into Romanian by Dumitru Hîncu, 2 volume, Bucureşti: Vivaldi, 2002-2003.

2003   *Valuri alinate* [poems], translated into Romanian by George Coşbuc, Bucureşti: România Press.

2004   *Stephans des Großen Mutter: rumänische Dichtungen* [Romanian poems translated into German by Carmen Sylva an Mite Kremnitz], Bucureşti: Romania Press.

2011   *Astra* de Dito şi Idem (Carmen Sylva and Mite Kremnitz) [epistolary novel], translated into Romanian and edited by Grete Tartler, Bucureşti: Humanitas.

2012   *Gedanken einer Königin – Les pensées d'une reine* [complete aphorisms in French and German], edited by Silvia Irina Zimmermann, Stuttgart: ibidem-Verlag.

2012   *Gedanken einer Königin* [selected aphorisms], edited by Silvia Irina Zimmermann, Edition Noëma, Stuttgart: ibidem-Verlag.

2012   *Poveştile unei regine* [Fairy Tales of a Queen, translated into Romanian], Bucureşti: Curtea Veche.

2013   *Aus Carmen Sylvas Königreich. Gesammelte Märchen und Geschichten für Kinder und Jugendliche von Carmen Sylva (Königin Elisabeth von Rumänien, geborene Prinzessin zu Wied, 1843–1916)* [complete fairy tales and legends in German by Carmen Sylva] edited by Silvia Irina Zimmermann, 2 volumes (1. *Rumänische Märchen und Geschichten*, 2. *Märchen einer Königin*), Stuttgart: ibidem-Verlag.

2013   *Pelesch-Märchen* [Tales of the Pelesh], edited by Silvia Irina Zimmermann, Edition Noëma, Stuttgart: ibidem-Verlag.

2013   *Sagesse d'une reine* [aphorisms in French], edited by Gabriel Badea-Păun, Versailles: Via romana.

2013   *Fluturi sărutându-se* [aphorisms and poems], edited by Gabriel Badea-Păun, translations into Romanian by: George Coşbuc, Ilie Ighel Deleanu, Doina Jela Despois, Şt. O. Iosif, Elena Poenaru, Bucureşti: Curtea Veche.

2014   *Rheintochters Donaufahrt* [travel journal], in: Silvia Irina Zimmermann: Unterschiedliche Wege, dasselbe Ideal: Das Königsbild im Werk Carmen Sylvas und in Fotografien des Fürstlich Wiedischen Archivs, Stuttgart: ibidem-Verlag.

2014   *Pe Dunăre* [travel journal translated into Romanian by Al. Tzigara-Samurcaş], in: Silvia Irina Zimmermann: Regele Carol I în opera Reginei Elisabeta, Bucureşti: Editura Curtea Veche.

2015   *Prinz Waldvogel* [selected fairy tales], edited by Silvia Irina Zimmermann, Edition Noëma, Stuttgart: ibidem-Verlag.

2015   *Cugetări şi impresii* [selected essays and aphorisms translated into Romanian], edited by I. Oprişan. Bucureşti: Saeculum Vizual.

2016   *Poveştile Peleşului* [Tales of the Pelesh] translated into Romanian, edited by Silvia Irina Zimmermann, Bucureşti: Corint.

2016   *Mein Penatenwinkel* [memoirs], in: Zimmermann, Silvia Irina/ Willscheid, Bernd (ed.): Heimweh ist Jugendweh. Kindheits- und Jugenderinnerungen der Elisabeth zu Wied (Carmen Sylva), Schriftenreihe der Forschungsstelle Carmen Sylva - Fürstlich Wiedisches Archiv, Band 4, Stuttgart: ibidem-Verlag.

2017   *Monsieur Hampelmann – Domnul Pulcinel* [a fairy tale in 5 languages], illustrated by André Lecomte du Nouÿ, with a bilingual introduction (German-Romanian) and edited by Silvia Irina Zimmermann, Schriftenreihe der Forschungsstelle Carmen Sylva, Fürstlich Wiedisches Archiv, Band 5, Stuttgart: ibidem-Verlag.

2017   *Domnul Pulcinel*, fairy tale in 5 languages, edited by Silvia Irina Zimmermann, Bucureşti: Vremea.

2018   *Poveştile Peleşului* [Tales of the Pelesh], edited by Silvia Irina Zimmermann, translations by Romaniţa Constantinescu, Dimitrie A. Sturdza, Elena Radu Rosetti, Silvia Irina Zimmermann, extended edition, Bucureşti: Corint.

2018   *Prosa des Lebens* [Life stories], edited by Martin A. Völker, Berlin: Anthea-Verlag.

2018   *De prin veacuri. Povestiri istorice şi legende populare pentru copii* [Romanian legends and historical tales for children by Queen Elisabeth, translated into Romanian], edited by Silvia Irina Zimmermann, Bucureşti: Humanitas.

Posthumously published correspondence

1916   *Carmen Sylva. Briefe einer einsamen Königin*, edited by Lina Sommer, München: Braun & Schneider.

1920   *Aus Briefen Carmen Sylvas*, edited by Werner Deetjen, Leipzig: Seemann.

1920   *Letters and Poems of Queen Elisabeth (Carmen Sylva),* introduction and notes by Henry Howard Harper, 2 volumes, Boston: The Bibliophile Society.

2015   Hans-Jürgen Krüger: *Briefe Carmen Sylvas im Fürstlich Wiedischen Archiv in Neuwied,* in: Silvia Irina Zimmermann/ Edda Binder-Iijima (coord.): „Ich werde noch vieles anbahnen". Carmen Sylva: die Schriftstellerin und erste Königin von Rumänien im Kontext ihrer Zeit, Stuttgart: ibidem-Verlag, 2015, p. 222-223.

2018   *„In zärtlicher Liebe Deine Elisabeth" – „Stets Dein treuer Carl". Der Briefwechsel Elisabeths zu Wied (Carmen Sylva) mit ihrem Gemahl Carol I. von Rumänien aus dem Rumänischen Nationalarchiv in Bukarest. 1869-1913,* correspondence of Queen Elisabeth with King Carol I, historical-critical edition by Silvia Irina Zimmermann, 2 volumes, part 1: *1869-1890. Anfangsjahre in Rumänien. Unabhängigkeitskrieg. Königreich Rumänien,* part 2: *1891-1913. Exil der Königin. Rückkehr auf den rumänischen Thron,* Stuttgart: ibidem-Verlag.

Queen Marie: Published Works (Selection)

Fantasy stories and novels (in English)

1913　*The Lily of Life*, with a dedication to her daughter Elisabeta, preface by Carmen Sylva, illustrated by Helen Stratton, London, New York, Toronto: Hodder & Stoughton.

1915　*The Dreamer of Dreams*, with a dedication to her daughter Ileana, illustrated by Edmund Dulac, London, New York, Toronto: Hodder & Stoughton.

1916　*The Stealers of Light. A Legend*, with a dedication to King Ferdinand, illustrated by Edmund Dulac, London, New York, Toronto: Hodder & Stoughton.

1923　*Why? A Story of a Great Longing*, with a dedication to Carmen Sylva, Stockholm: Svenska Tryckeriaktiebolaget.

1923　*The Voice on the Mountain. A Story for those who understand*, New York: Alfred A. Knopf.

1926　*Ilderim. A tale of light and shade*, with a dedication to her son, Crown Prince Carol], London: Adelphi Company.

1929　*Crowned Queens. A Tale from out the Past*, London: Heath Cranton.

1935　*Masks. A Novel*, London: Duckworth.

Children's books (in English)

1918　*Peeping Pansy*, illustrated by Mabel Lucie Attwell, London, New York, Toronto: Hodder & Stoughton.

1922　*The Story of Naughty Kildeen*, illustrated by Job, London: Oxford University Press/ New York: Harcourt, Brace and Company.

1923?　*The Queen of Romania's Fairy Book*, illustrated by N. Grossman-Bulyghin, New York: Frederick A. Stokes Company.

1924　*The Lost Princess. A Fairy Tale*, illustrated by Mabel Lucie Attwell, London: S.W. Partridge & Co.

1929　*The Magic Doll of Romania. A Wonder Story in Which East and West Do Meet*, illustrated by Maud and Miska Petersham, New York: Frederick A. Stokes.

Memoirs and autobiographical writings (in English)

1916　*My Country*, London: Hodder & Stoughton.

1918　*From My Soul to Theirs*, in: Will. Gordon: Romania Yesterday and Today, London/ New York: John Lane, p. 149-158.

1918　*A Queen and Her People*, in: Will. Gordon: Romania Yesterday and Today, London/ New York: John Lane, p. 208-218.

1925   *The Country that I Love. An Exile's Memories,* illustrated by Queen
         Elizabeth of Greece, London: Duckworth.

1934f   *The Story of My Life*, vol. I-III, London: Cassell, 1934-1935.

Translations from the writings of Queen Marie

1913   *Crinul vieții* [fantasy novel], translated into Romanian by Elena Per-
         ticari-Davila, cover by Ignat Bednarik, Bucureşti: Socec.

1914   *Visătorul de Vise* [fantasy novel], translated into Romanian by
         Mărgărita Miller-Verghy, Bucureşti: Editura Institutului de Arte
         Grafice „Flacăra".

1915   *Patru anotimpuri din viața unui om* [tale], translated into Romanian
         by Mărgărita Miller-Verghy, illustrated by N. Grant, Bucureşti.

1915   *Ilderim. Poveste in umbră şi lumina* [fantasy novel], translated into
         Romanian by Mărgărita Miller-Verghy, Bucureşti: Institutul de
         Editura şi Arte Grafice „Flacăra".

1917f   *Țara mea* [essays] translated into Romanian by Nicolae Iorga, Iaşi:
         Editura „Neamul Românesc" (part I), 1917; 3rd extended edition
         (parts I and II), Bucureşti/ Sibiu: Tiparul Tipografiei Arhi-
         diecezane, Editura Librăriei Pavel Suru, 1919.

1917   *Feindliche Brüder* [*Ilderim*, fantasy novel], translated into German by
         Queen Dowager Elisabeth of Romanian (Carmen Sylva), Berlin: L.
         Oehmigke's Verlag.

1917   *Mon Pays* [memoirs], translated into French by Jean de Lahovary,
         Paris: Georges Cres & Cie.

1918   *Minola. Povestea unei mici regine triste* [tale], translated into Roma-
         nian by Adria Val, Iaşi: Tipografia serviciului geografic al armatei.

1918   *O poveste de la Sfântul Munte* [essay], translated into Romanian by
         Nicolae Iorga, Iaşi.

1918   *Din mijlocul luptei* [essay], translated into Romanian by Nicolae
         Iorga, Iaşi.

1918   *Povestea unei Domnițe neascultătoare* [tale], translated into Romanian
         by Nicolae Iorga, Iaşi.

1919   *Gânduri şi icoane din vremea războiului* [essay translated into Roma-
         nian], Bucureşti: Editura Librăriei Pavel Suru.

1920   *Dor nestins* [fantasy novel], translated into Romanian by Em.
         Panaitescu, cover by Princess Elizabeth of Romania [later Queen of
         Greece], Bucureşti: Editura Librăriei Pavel Suru.

1921   *Poveşti* [fairy tales], translations into Romanian by Elena Perticari
         and Adria Val, illustrations by N. Grossman-Bulyghin, vol. I,
         Bucureşti: Din publicaţiile „Fundaţiei Culturale – Principele Carol".

1921   *Minola* [story], translation into Greek by Emilios Karavia, Athenais:
         Ekdotikos Oikos „Eleutheroudakes".

1921   *Ilderim. Poveste în lumini şi umbră*, Romanian adaptation as a stage play by Ion Peretz, Bucureşti: Editura Literară a Casei Şcolalelor.

1922 *Kildine. Historie d'une mechante petite princesse* [tale translated into French], Paris: Maison Alfred Mame et Fils.

1923 *Sămânța înțelepciunii* [fairy tale translated into Romanian], Sibiu: Editura „Asociațiunii", Biblioteca poporală a „Asociațiunii", nr. 110.

1923 *Dal mio cuore al loro cuore* [essay], translated into Italian by Pinetta Gerla Antohi and Jean Antohi, Milano: Modernissima.

1923 *Lo Czàr Nicola: ricordi* [memoirs], translated into Italian by Alexandru Marcu and G. F. Cecchini, Foligno: F. Campitelli.

1923? *Poveşti* [fairy tales translated into Romanian], illustrations by N. Grossman-Bulyghin, vol. II, Bucureşti: Editura Cartea românească.

1923? *O legendă de la Muntele Athos* [essay translated into Romanian], illustrations by Ignat Bednarik, Bucureşti: Editura Ig. Hertz.

1925 *Dinainte şi după răsboi* [memoirs translated into Romanian], Bucureşti: Librăria Socec et Compania.

1925 *Ce-a văzut Vasile soldatul. Poveste din timpul războiului* [tale translated into Romanian], illustrations by Ignat Bednarik, Bucureşti: Tipografia Serviciului Geografic al Armatei.

1925? *Poveşti pentru cei mai mici* [fairy tales translated into Romanian], illustrations by M. Teişanu, Bucureşti: Convorbiri Literare.

1927 *Die Stimme der Berge* [novel], translated into German by Amalie Falke-Lilienstein, Leipzig: Renaissance-Verlag.

1928 *Păsări fantastice pe albastrul cerului* [essay translated into Romanian], Bucureşti: Editura atelierelor grafice ale ziarului Universul.

1930 *Casele mele de vis* [essay], translated into Romanian by Emanoil Bucuța, article published in the magazine „Boabe de grâu", year I, nr. 2 (1930), p. 65-77.

1930 *Stella Maris. Cea mai mică biserică din lume* [essay], translated into Romanian by Emanoil Bucuța, article published in the magazine „Boabe de grâu", year I, nr. 9 (1930), p. 515-524.

1931 *Copila cu ochi albaştri* [memoirs], translated into Romanian Bucureşti.

1931? *Glasul de pe munte* [novel], translated into Romanian by Zoe Simpson Ghica, Bucureşti: Editura Națională S. Ciornei.

1932 *Ce-a văzut Vasile soldatul. Poveste din timpul războiului* [tale translated into Romanian], Bucureşti: Institutul de Arte Grafice E. Marvan.

1933? *Regine încoronate. Povestire din trecut* [novel], translated into Romanian by Mărgărita Miller-Verghy, cover by Ignat Bednarik, Bucureşti: Adevărul.

1933 *Königinnen* [novel], translated into German by Amalie Falke-Lilienstein, Wien: Augarten-Verlag Szabo.

1934 *Kildine. Histoire d'une méchante petite princesse* [tale translated into French], Tours: Maison Mame.

1935   *Traum und Leben einer Königin* [memoirs translated into German], Leipzig: Paul List Verlag.

1935f *Mitt livs historia* [memoirs], translated into Swedish by Ingeborg Essén, 2 volumes, Stockholm: Albert Bonniers Förlag, 1935-36.

1936   *Masques* [novel], translated into French by Hélène Claireau, Paris: Éditions de la Nouvelle Revue critique.

1937   *Il mio diario di guerra* [memoirs translated into Italian], 3 volumes, Milano: A. Mondadori.

1937   *La storia della mia vita* [memoirs], translated into Italian by Mario Borsa, Milano: A. Mondadori.

1937f *Historie de ma vie* [memoirs translated into French], Paris: Plon, 1937-1938.

1938   *Vom Wunder der Tränen* [fairy tale translated into German], illustrations by Sulamith Wülfing, Wuppertal-Elberfeld: Sulamith Wülfing Verlag.

1938   *Măşti* [novel], translated into Romanian by Margărita Miller-Verghy, Bucureşti: Editura librariei Socec.

1939? *Povestea vieţii mele*, translated into Romanian by Margărita Miller-Verghy, Bucureşti: Editura Adevărul, o.J.

Posthumously published works, translations and new editions

1944   *Regine încoronate. Povestire din trecut* [novel translated into Romanian], Bucureşti: Adevărul.

1957   *A Christmas Tale* [fairy tale], illustrated by Enrique Espinoza, New York: Aldus Printers.

1969   *A Christmas Tale* [fairy tale], illustrated by Claude S. Seward, private edition Anson C. Miller.

1991   *Insula şerpilor* [fairy tale translated into Romanian], edited by Viorica Mircea, Braşov: Arania.

1991   *Povestea vieţii mele*, [memoirs] translated into Romanian by Margărita [Margareta] Miller-Verghy, Iaşi: Editura Moldova.

1992   *Poveşti* [fairy tales translated into Romanian], Craiova: Biblioteca Ramuri.

1996   *Poveşti* [fairy tales translated into Romanian], Iaşi: Editura Porţile Orientului, 2 vol.

2000? *Regine încoronate* [novel translated into Romanian], Bucureşti: Garamond.

2001   *Miracle of Tears* [fairy tale], illustrated by Sulamith Wülfing, Woodside: Bluestar Communications.

2003   *Kildine. Povestea unei mici principese răutăcioase* [tale] translated into Romanian by H.R.H. Prince Radu of Romania, Bucureşti: Corint.

2004   *Măşti: romanul unei imposibile iubiri* [novel translated into Romanian], Bucureşti: Teşu.

2011	*Poveştile Reginei Maria* [fairy tales translated into Romanian], Bucureşti: Curtea Veche.
2012	*Copila Soarelui. The Sun Child* [fairy tale, bilingual], Bucureşti: Monitorul Oficial.
2013	*Copila cu ochi albaştri. The Child With The Blue Eyes* [memoirs, bilingual], translation into Romanian by Florin Sandu, Bucureşti: Monitorul Oficial.
2014	*De coada cometei. On the Tail of the Comet* [fairy tale, bilingual], translation into Romanian by Florin Sandu, Bucureşti: Monitorul Oficial.
2014	*Povestea unei domniţe neascultătoare* [fairy tale], translated into Romanian by Nicolae Iorga, Bucureşti: Sigma.
2015	*Orfana. The Orphan girl* [fairy tale, bilingual], Bucureşti: Monitorul Oficial.
2015	*Poveşti* [fairy tales translated into Romanian], edited by I. Opriş, Bucureşti: Saeculum.

Posthumously published memoirs, letters and journals

1971	*The Story of My Life,* New York: Arno Press.
1996f	*Însemnări zilnice* [diary], edited by Vasile Arimia, translated into Romanian by Valentina Costache and Sanda Racoviceanu, vol. 1-4, Bucureşti: Albatros, 1996-2005.
1999	*America Seen by a Queen. Queen Marie's Diary of Her 1926 Voyage to the United States of America*, edited and with an introduction by Adrian-Silvan Ionescu, Bucharest: The Romanian Cultural Foundation Publishing House, 1999.
2004	*Later Chapters of My Life. The Lost Memoir of Queen Marie of Romania*, [diary], edited by Diana Mandache, Stroud: Sutton Publishing.
2006f	*Însemnări zilnice* [diary], edited by Vasile Arimia; translated into Romanian by Valentina Costache, Sanda Racoviceanu, vol. 1-9, Bucureşti: Historia, 2006-2012.
2007	*Regina Maria a României. Capitole târzii din viaţa mea. Memorii redescoperite* [diary], edited by Diana Mandache, translated into Romanian by Valentin Mandache, Bucureşti: Editura Alfa.
2009	*Jurnalul Reginei Maria* [diary of the Voyage to America], translated into Romanian and edited by Adrian-Silvan Ionescu, in: Adrian-Silvan Ionescu: *Regina Maria şi America*, Bucureşti: Noi Media Print, pp. 104-350.
2011	*Dearest Missy. The Correspondence between Marie, Grand Duchess of Russia, Duchess of Edinburgh and of Saxe-Coburg and Gotha and her daughter, Marie, Crown Princess of Romania. 1879-1900*, edited by Diana Mandache, Falkoping: Rosvall Royal Books.
2012f	*Însemnări zilnice* [diary], edited by Vasile Arimia, translated into Romanian by Sanda Ileana Racoviceanu, vol. 6-10, Iaşi: Polirom,

2012-2014.

2014f   *Jurnal de război, 1916-1918* [diary], edited by Lucian Boia, translated into Romanian by Anca Bărbulescu, 3 volumes, Bucureşti: Humanitas, 2014-2015.

2014   *Historie de ma vie* [memoirs translated into French], edited by Gabriel Badea-Păun, Paris: Édition Lacurne.

2015   *Queen Mary of Romania. Letters to Her King*, edited by Sorin Cristescu, Bucureşti: Tritonic.

2016   *Queen Marie of Romania. Letters to Her Mother*, edited by Sorin Cristescu, 2 volumes, vol. I: 1901-1906; vol. II: 1907-1920, Bucureşti: Tritonic.

2016   *Corespondenţa Reginei Maria cu mama sa, Ducesa de Coburg (1914-1929)*, translated by Lia Decei, in: Diana Mandache: *Viva Regina Maria! Un destin fabulos în reîntregirea României*, Bucureşti: Corint, pp. 195-319.

2016   *Ţara pe care o iubesc: memorii din exil* [memoirs] translated into Romanian by Maria Berza, illustrated by Queen Elisabeth of Greece, Bucureşti: Humanitas.

2018   *Însemnări din ultima parte a vieţii: (martie 1937-iulie 1938)*, [diary] translated and edited by Sorin Cristescu, Bucureşti: Corint.

2018   *Queen Marie of Romania. Confessions, February 1914 – March 1927* [letters to Loie Fuller and Roxo Weingärtner], edited by Sorin Cristescu, Bucureşti: Tritonic.

Further Bibliography

Badea-Păun, Gabriel: Carmen Sylva. 1843-1916. Uimitoarea regină Elisabeta a României, traducere din franceză de Irina-Margareta Nistor, Bucureşti: Humanitas, 2003; 3rd edition: 2010; 4th edition: 2014.

Badea-Păun, Gabriel: Mecena şi comanditari, artă şi mesaj politic, traducere din franceză de Laura Guţanu, Bucureşti: Noi Media Print, 2010.

Badea-Păun, Gabriel: Carmen Sylva (1843-1916). Königin Elisabeth von Rumänien, eine rheinische Prinzessin auf Rumäniens Thron, ins Deutsche übersetzt und mit einem Nachwort von Silvia Irina Zimmermann, Stuttgart: ibidem-Verlag, 2011.

Badea-Păun, Gabriel: Carmen Sylva, reine Elisabeth de Roumanie, Versailles: Via Romana, 2011.

Badea-Păun, Gabriel: Autour d'un récit autobiographique royal, in: Reine Marie de Roumanie: Histoire de ma vie. 1875-1918, Paris: Lacurne, 2014, p. 9-19.

Badea-Păun, Gabriel: De la Palatul Domnesc de pe Podul Mogoşoaiei la Palatul Regal de pe Calea Victoriei. Arhitectură şi decoruri (1866-1947), Bucureşti: Editura Corint, 2017.

Beldiman, Ruxanda: Castelul Peleş: expresie a fenomenului istorist de influenţă germană, Bucureşti: Simetria, 2011.

Binder-Iijima, Edda/ Löwe, Heinz-Dietrich/ Volkmer Gerhard (coord.): Die Hohenzollern in Rumänien 1866-1947. Eine monarchische Herrschaftsordnung im europäischen Kontext, (Studia Transylvanica; Bd. 41), Köln/ Weimar/ Wien: Böhlau 2010.

Binder-Iijima, Edda: Europäische Integration durch Hofkultur. Die Höfe Bukarest, Sinaia, Sigmaringen und Neuwied und ihre Vermittlungs- und Repräsentationsfunktionen, in: Binder-Iijima etc. (coord.): Die Hohenzollern in Rumänien 1866-1947, 2010, p. 99-121.

Binder-Iijima, Edda: Creating Legitimacy: The Romanian Elite and the Acceptance of Monarchical Rule, in: Anastassiadis, Tassos, Clayer Nathalie (Ed.): Society, Politics and State Formation in Southeastern Europe during the 19th Century, Athens: Alpha Bank, Historical Archives, 2011, p. 177-203.

Burgoyne, Elizabeth: Carmen Sylva. Queen and Woman, Eyre & Spottiswoode, London, 1941.

Carandino-Platamona, Lucreţia: Carmen Sylva, Bucureşti: Editura Ziarului Universul, 1936.

Ciupală, Alin: Bătălia lor. Femeile din România în primul Război Mondial, Bucureşti: Polirom, 2017.

Heitmann, Klaus: Deutsche und rumänische Kultur am Hofe Carols I. und Carmen Sylvas, in: Höfische Kultur in Südosteuropa, hrsg. von Reinhard Lauer und Hans Georg Majer, Göttingen: Vandenhoeck & Ruprecht, 1994,

[Abhandlungen der Akademie der Wissenschaften in Göttingen], S. 305-338.

Ion, Narcis Dorin (coord.): Regina Elisabeta a României. Un secol de eternitate / Queen Elisabeth of Romania. A Century of Eternity, Muzeul Național Peleş, Sinaia, 2016.

Ion, Narcis Dorin (coord.): Maria a României. Portretul unei mari regine, Muzeul Național Peleş, 2. volume, Sinaia, 2018.

Ionescu, Adrian-Silvan: Regina Maria şi America, Bucureşti: Noi Media Print, 2009.

Kallestrup, Shona: "Royalty is no longer quite royal": word and image in the children's tales of Queen Marie of Romania, in: Image & Narrative, vol. 19, Nr.1, Leuven, 2018, pp. 23-45.

[Mandache] Fotescu, Diana (ed.): Americans and Queen Marie of Romania. A Selection of Documents, The Center of Romanian Studies: Iaşi, Oxford, Portland, 1998.

Mandache, Diana: Marie of Romania. Images of a Queen, Falköping: Rosvall Royal Books, 2007.

Mandache, Diana: Balcicul reginei Maria, Bucureşti: Curtea veche, 2014.

Mandache, Diana: Cotroceniul regal, Bucureşti: Curtea veche, 2015.

Mandache, Diana: Castelul Bran. Romantism şi regalitate, Bucureşti: Curtea veche, 2017.

Mandache, Diana: Viva Regina Maria! Un destin fabulous în reîntregirea României. Text, transcrierea manuscriselor din limba engleză şi note Diana Mandache. Traducere la scrisori Lia Decei, Bucureşti: Editura Corint, 2016.

Muellner, Beth Ann: The Walled-up Wife Speaks Out: The Balkan "Legend of the Walled-up Wife" and Carmen Sylva's Meister Manole, in: Marvels & Tales: Journal of Fairy-Tale Studies, Vol. 32, No. 2 (2018), Wayne State University Press, Detroit , p. 245–264.

Nixon, Laura Elizabeth: The "British" Carmen Sylva: recuperating a German-Romanian writer, PhD thesis, University of Nottingham: 2014, Link: http://eprints.nottingham.ac.uk/13946/ [7.7.2019].

Oberländer-Târnoveanu, Ernest (coord.): Maria Regina, Muzeul Național de Istorie a României, Bucureşti, 2013.

Oberländer-Târnoveanu, Ernest/ Ilie, Constantin (coord.): 90 de ani de la încoronarea de la Alba Iulia, Muzeul Național de Istorie a României, Bucureşti, 2012.

Pakula, Hannah: The Last Romantic: A Biography of Queen Marie of Roumania. New York: Simon & Schuster, 1984.

Principele Radu al României: Povestea Castelului Peleş, Bucureşti: Curtea veche, 2017.

Principele Radu al României: Maria. Portretul unei regine, Bucureşti: Curtea veche, 2018.

Principele Radu al României: Elisabeta. Portretul unei regine, Bucureşti: Curtea veche, 2019.

Stoian, Emil: Regina Maria în amintirile Branului / Queen Marie in Bran's Memories, Baia Mare: Marist, 2015.

Willscheid, Bernd (coord.): Carmen Sylva. Elisabeth Königin von Rumänien (1843-1916), Neuwied: Kreismuseum Neuwied, 1999.

Willscheid, Bernd (coord.): Carmen Sylva (1843-1916). Eine Königin aus Neuwied, Roentgen-Museum, Neuwied, 2016.

Woolf, Virginia: Royalty, in: Virginia Woolf: The Moment and Other Essays, New York / London: Harvest, 1975, p. 235-240.

Zimmermann, Silvia Irina: Die dichtende Königin. Elisabeth, Prinzessin zu Wied, Königin von Rumänien, Carmen Sylva (1843-1916). Selbstmythisierung und prodynastische Öffentlichkeitsarbeit durch Literatur, Stuttgart: ibidem-Verlag, 2010.

Zimmermann, Silvia Irina: Der Zauber des fernen Königreichs. Carmen Sylvas „Pelesch-Märchen", Stuttgart, ibidem-Verlag, 2011.

Zimmermann, Silvia Irina: Regina poetă Carmen Sylva. Literatura în serviciul Coroanei, traducere din germană de Monica Livia Grigore, Editura All, Bucureşti, 2013.

Zimmermann, Silvia Irina: Unterschiedliche Wege, dasselbe Ideal: Das Königsbild im Werk Carmen Sylvas und in Fotografien des Fürstlich Wiedischen Archivs, Schriftenreihe der Forschungsstelle Carmen Sylva – Fürstlich Wiedisches Archiv, Bd. 1, Stuttgart: ibidem-Verlag, 2014.

Zimmermann, Silvia Irina: Regele Carol I în opera Reginei Elisabeta. La 100 de ani de la moartea Regelui Carol I al României (1839-1914), Bucureşti: Editura Curtea Veche, 2014.

Zimmermann, Silvia Irina: Despre regi in vemuri republicane. Portretul regelui în opera reginei Elisabeta a României, in: Claudiu-Lucian Topor, Alexandru Istrate, Daniel Cain (editori): Diplomați, societate şi mondenități. Sfârşit de Belle Époque în lumea românească, Iaşi: Editura Universităţii Alexandru Ioan Cuza, 2015, p. 125-138.

Zimmermann, Silvia Irina: Portretul perechii princiare moştenitoare Ferdinand şi Maria din viziunea Reginei Elisabeta a României în scrisori personale şi texte pentru publicul larg, in: Revista Bibliotecii Academiei Române, Anul 1, Nr. 2, 2016, p. 11-35.

Zimmermann, Silvia Irina: „Influenţa lui Alecsandri, Grigorescu şi Enescu asupra operei literare a Reginei Elisabeta a României (Carmen Sylva)", in: Saeculum, anul XVI (XVIII), nr. 1 (43)/ 2017, Universitatea Lucian Blaga Sibiu, p. 176-190.

Zimmermann, Silvia Irina (ed.): „In zärtlicher Liebe Deine Elisabeth" – „Stets Dein treuer Carl". Der Briefwechsel Elisabeths zu Wied (Carmen Sylva) mit ihrem Gemahl Carol I. von Rumänien aus dem Rumänischen Nationalarchiv in Bukarest. 1869-1913. Historisch-kritische Ausgabe. Herausgegeben, kommentiert und eingeleitet von Silvia Irina Zimmermann,

Schriftenreihe der Forschungsstelle Carmen Sylva – Fürstlich Wiedisches Archiv, 2 Bände, Stuttgart: ibidem-Verlag, 2018.

Zimmermann, Silvia Irina: „Activitatea literară şi artizanală a Reginei Elisabeta din perioada exilului (1891-1894) în oglinda corespondenţei cu Regele Carol I. Colaborarea reginei cu André Lecomte du Noüy", in: Revista de Artă şi Istoria Artei, Bucureşti: Editura Muzeului Municipiului Bucureşti, Nr. 1, 2018, p. 144-159.

Zimmermann, Silvia Irina: Corespondenţa primei perechi regale a României, Carol I şi Elisabeta, păstrată la Arhivele Naţionale ale României din Bucureşti, in: Revista Bibliotecii Academiei Române, Bucureşti, Anul 3, Nr. 1, ianuarie-iunie 2018, p. 3-21.

Zimmermann, Silvia Irina: „Die Feder in der Hand bin ich eine ganz andre Person." Carmen Sylva (1843-1916). Leben und Werk, Schriftenreihe der Forschungsstelle Carmen Sylva – Fürstlich Wiedisches Archiv, Band 8, Stuttgart: ibidem-Verlag, 2019.

Internet Resources

Arhivele Naţionale ale României: http://arhivelenationale.ro
Biblioteca Academiei Române: http://www.biblacad.ro/
Biblioteca digitală a Bucureştilor: http://www.digibuc.ro/
Biblioteca Naţională a României: http://digitool.bibnat.ro
Bibliothèque Nationale de France: http://www.bnf.fr
Deutsche Nationalbibliothek: http://www.dnb.de
Enciclopedia României: http://enciclopediaromaniei.ro
Europeana Collections: http://www.europeana.eu
Internet Archive: https://archive.org
Penn Libraries, University of Pennsylvania, Digital collections: A Celebration of Women Writers, edited by Mary Mark Ockerbloom: https://digital.library.upenn.edu/women/
Research Center Carmen Sylva of the Princely Archive of Wied in Neuwied: http://www.carmensylva-fwa.de/
Staatsbibliothek zu Berlin: http://kalliope.staatsbibliothek-berlin.de
Tom Kinter: Web collection of articles, books, quotes, excerpts, art, pohotography about Queen Elisabeth (Carmen Sylva) and Queen Marie of Romania: http://www.tkinter.smig.net
Wikipedia. The Free Encyclopedia: https://www.wikipedia.org/
WorldCat: http://www.worldcat.org
Zentrales Verzeichnis Antiquarischer Bücher: https://www.zvab.com

Photographs and images of the original book-covers, illustration-examples and title pages: private collection of Silvia Irina Zimmermann.

Selected Fairy Tales

Note

The selected tales were published in the following editions during the life-time of the queens of Romania:

Queen Elisabeth of Romania (Carmen Sylva):

Pilgrim Sorrow. A Cycle of Tales, (German edition: *Leidens Erdengang*, 1882) translated by Helen Zimmern, New York: Henry Holt & Company, 1884, *The Child of the Sun*, p. 15-34; *The Treasure Seekers*, p. 241-249.

Legends From River & Mountain, translated by Alma Strettel, London: George Allan, 1896. Tales from the volume *Pelesch-Märchen* ("Tales of the Pelesh", German edition: 1883): *Vârful cu Dor* (The Peek of Yearning), p. 37-54, *The Cave of Ialomitza*, p. 139-148, *Furnica* (The Ant), p. 55-67, *The Witch's Stronghold*, p. 101-120, *The Caraiman*, p. 69-80. Tales from the volume: *Durch die Jahrhunderte* ("Through the Centuries", German edition: 1885): *The Serpent-Isle*, p. 19-36, *Rîul Doamnei* (The River of the Princess), p. 131-138.

A Real Queen's Fairy Tales (German edition: *Märchen einer Königin*, 1901), translated by Edith Hopkirk, Chicago: Davis and Company, 1901, *The Story of a Helpful Queen*, p. 70-77, "*Stand! Who Goes there?*", p. 123-137.

A Real Queen's Fairy Book (German edition: *Märchen einer Königin*, 1901), London: Newes, 1901, *My Kaleidoscope*, p. 263-279.

Queen Marie of Romania:

The Queen of Roumania's Fairy Book, New York: Frederick A. Strokes Company, [1923?]; *The Sun Child*, p. 169-176; *Conu Ilie's Rose Tree*, p. 9-17; *Baba Alba*, p. 39-59; *The Snake Island*, p. 91-110; *Parintele Simeon's Wonder Book. A Very Moral Story*, p. 72-90; *A Christmas Tale*, p. 60-71.

The Magic Doll of Romania. A Wonder Story in Which East and West Do Meet, illustrated by Maud and Miska Petersham, New York: Frederick A. Stokes, 1929, fragments.

Queen Elisabeth of Romania (Carmen Sylva)

The Child of the Sun

Life was a radiant maiden, the daughter of the Sun, endowed with all the charm and grace, all the power and happiness, which only such a mother could give to her child. Her hairs were sun-beams, her eyes gleaming stars. Flowers dropped from her hands, seeds sprang into life from beneath her footsteps; sweet scents and songs of birds floated around her; from her lips uncounted songs welled forth. Sounds like the gurgling of a thousand streams were heard from out her garments, and yet they were only made of flower petals and covered with tender webs, in which numberless dew-drops twinkled. Glow-worms encircled the royal brow like a diadem; birds bore her train over rough paths. When her foot touched thorns, they grew green and blossomed; when she laid her soft hand upon the bare rock, it became covered with moss and fern. The Sun had bestowed on her glorious child power over all things, and as companions and playfellows she had given to her Happiness and Love. In those days, there was much joy and blessedness on earth, and no pen can recount, no pencil paint how glorious it all was. It was just one eternal May day, and the august mother looked down from afar upon her daughter's glad games, and blessed the earth upon which her child was so happy.

But deep down in the earth there lived an evil spirit called Strife. The Kobolds brought him news of all the beauty that was outside, and of the young sovereign who reigned so proudly and lovingly over the whole world, and who played so sweetly with Happiness and Love. First he was angry at the tidings, for he desired to be sole ruler of all things; but after a while a great curiosity took hold of him – and something beside, something hot and wild, he knew not himself what. Only he wanted to get outside at all costs. So he began to move a mighty rock from the center of the earth, and he cast it up on high. Then he kindled a great fire, so that all the rocks and the metals above him melted and poured their glowing, scorching streams over the paradise of earth. And in the midst of these flames Strife rose up, clothed in dazzling armor, with flowing locks and contracted brows. In his hands he held a great block of stone, and he peered around him with his piercing black eyes, seeking what he should destroy first. But of a sudden he let fall the rock, crossed his arms over his breast, and stared down upon the garden of earth, like one in a dream. He stood thus a long, long while, gazing down, silent with wonder, like to a statue. Suddenly he struck his brow with his fist.

"What! I have lived down there, among cold stores, in the darkness, and outside is such beauty! What must the sovereign be like to whom all this belongs?"

The thought brought life once more into this titanic figure. He stepped with giant strides down into the blooming, scented world, treading through it like a storm-wind, stamping down the flowers, breaking down the trees, without knowing it. He must find the mistress of all this fair earth. He even passed across the sea, making it pile up waves tower high, and once more he climbed a lofty mountain, in his hot impatience to gain a survey. Then he saw upon a meadow-side that which he sought so ardently. Resting her foot upon cloudy, silver-feathered flower seeds, her garments gathered up around her, Life was floating by upon her journey from flower to flower, singing as she went. Upon her shoulders twittered a pair of birds; upon her finger she bore a bee, to whom she showed where the best honey lay hid. She had left Love behind her in a wood, busy building a nest, while Happiness was sleeping upon a mossy bed beside a waterfall, after having played antics innumerable. Therefore Life was floating forth alone, singing a morning carol to her mother, the Sun. Of a sudden she beheld something gleam and glitter in front of her, and when she raised her eyes, she saw Strife planted before her, gazing at her fixedly. His bright armor reflected her glistening tresses. Life quailed at the sight of this mighty man with the burning eyes, her foot slipped from its seed-cloud, which sped on without her. She would have fallen had she not grasped a birch branch and slid herself down by it upon a mossy rock.

"Aha!" cried Strife, "have I found you at last, you who dispute my empire, you who wield the scepter here on earth? Who are you, little maiden, who venture upon such liberties?"

These haughty words restored to Life all her pride and loftiness.

"I am the child of the Sun, and the earth is mine; it was given to me by my royal mother, and all bends before my power."

Speaking thus, she threw back her fair head proudly, so that the Sun lighted up all her face.

Strife saw it and was drunk with love.

"If I overcome you so that you are mine, then you and the earth will both belong to me."

"Try," said Life, "I am stronger than you."

"I am to wrestle with you, you tender flower! Well, if I do so I must put aside my armor, or I shall crush you."

And he did so, laying his shield and armor upon the grass. Then he sprang at her to encircle her waist and to lift her into the air. But at that moment roses sprang forth from her girdle, and their thorns pricked him so sharply that he had to let her go. He tried to catch her by the hair, but this scorched him. Then he tore off his golden chain and tried to bind her hands with it. She only bowed her head; then the chain melted in his grasp. Suddenly he felt his wrists clasped by her tender fingers. He tried to shake her off, but she would not let go. He lifted her from the ground; she only floated but would not let him loose, and as often as she grew weary the Sun gave her new strength. Then he strove to draw her under the shade of the trees; but these inclined to one side that the Sun might protect her darling. A whole day did this wrestling last. At last, Strife saw that the Sun inclined towards setting, and though she lingered she had to depart. Then Life lost her strength, but Strife grew doubly strong. He shook her off and rushed upon her. Soon her garments lay torn upon the sward, her hair lost its scorching might, and before dawn broke the chaste maiden knelt trembling and red with shame upon the earth, entreating forbearance and mercy with sobs and tears. At this Strife set up a laugh that made the earth quake, and the rocks re-echoed it like to pealing thunder.

Terrified, Life sank to earth in a swoon. Strife raised her high in air in his mighty arms and bore her away. Her lovely head was bent back, her hair swept the ground, her lips were half opened as though no breath were in them, the wondrous limbs that had resisted him so long hung faint and powerless, and wherever he bore her there the grass faded, the leaves decayed and fell from off the trees, and there blew a storm wind that froze the limbs of Life.

"Wait", said Strife, and he covered her with kisses, "you shall warm at my fires. Only I must hide you from the Sun or I shall lose you again."

And he vanished with her into the mountains.

The whole earth grew barren and desolate, the birds sang no more, the flowers drooped, only on the spot where Life had sunk down fainting there bloomed some crocuses; but even these could not endure. The Sun grew pale with grief, and wept and beckoned with a white sheet that fell upon the earth and dispersed into thousands of tiny fragments, while the mountains upon which Strife's armor had lain became ice for all time.

When Love and Happiness found that they had lost Life they began to roam the world in search of her, asking all things after their beloved companion. They no longer recognized their earth garden in its changed form, and they wept bitterly. They wandered past hill and dale, alongside the rivers that lay frozen and ice-clad, and they called aloud for Life, for they deemed that they must find her. One day they leant wearily against a tall rock, when of a sudden they heard a sound within it as of gurgling waters. Flushed with joy they looked at one another and both exclaimed: "Here she is, here; we hear sounds of Life," and they began to touch the rock and to call and listen round about it, until they found an opening whence a spring gushed forth. Softly they called "Life," and there she stood before them, joyless, downcast, with weary steps, laying her finger upon her lips.

"My lord slumbers, do not wake him," she whispered sadly.

"Dear Life, come out with us; your garden is bare, your mother is pale, and we have roamed so long in search of you. Oh, come forth once more."

And they drew Life forth with them, and as she took the first step outside snowdrops peeped up, and at her next step violets bloomed, and as she laid her weary hand upon a tree, the buds swelled and broke into leaf.

"Behold," cried Love and Happiness, "you still have your old might. Oh, do be joyous! Look up at the Sun that she, too, may laugh."

But when the Sun saw her child so weak and weary, she could not refrain from weeping, though she strove to smile and warm her daughter with her hot rays. Again and again she had to press her cloud-sheet before her eyes, and then her tears dropped down upon the earth. Life still crept along, but wearily.

Then came a swallow: "Hold on, to my wings, dear Life; I will bear you a bit," and thus she once more floated through the blue air, until the swallow was tired. Then the stork came and said: "Kneel on my back and put your arms round my neck; I will carry you further." And he bore her far, far, and wherever he alighted a babe was born, and Love and Happiness followed in their wake, and dwelt beside the child. And the whole earth grew green and bright. The birds sang again, and every sunbeam gave new power to Life, so that once more she could stand on the mountain tops, a blooming, splendid woman, full of grace and majesty, with earnest eyes and serious mouth, her hands filled with the fruits that should make rich the world.

But deep down in the earth, Strife who had awoke long ago, sought for his absent wife. He stormed out into the world, and everywhere he beheld her traces, but herself he could not find. How many of her gifts did he not destroy in his wild haste! Sometimes he would halt puzzled, piercing the distance with his stern looks. Ay, he was near despairing, for she, from whom he could no longer live apart, fled from him ever. Now a tree hid her with his foliage, now a bird in his nest, now a flower beneath its leaves, now the mist in its veil, and if he came too near to her an eagle would bear her on his pinions up to the Sun, until Strife had swept past below, when she returned endowed with new power and glory. But at last, at last, he did catch sight of her as she was pressing a vine wreath upon the locks of Happiness, and sending a gleam from her forehead into the eyes of Love. Then he stepped before her, looked at her and beckoned. He must have done something to her, for of pride and resistance there was no longer a trace. He strode before her without looking round, and she bowed her lovely head and followed him; and when her comrades would have held her back, she only beckoned with her hand, and stepped after him silently, wrapped in robes of mist that swept the falling leaves, and was like to an echo of the gurgling that had once sounded in her robes.

She went into the mountain, bearing with her fruits and grapes, that the Kobolds pressed into wine with which they made to themselves merry days.

And she brought forth two children, a boy and a maid. Both were very pale, and had large dark eyes. The boy had something wild about him, like his father, the maid was tender like her mother; she was named Sorrow, but he was called Death. Sorrow did not remain long in her rocky home. She had inherited from her mother a yearning for earth, and from her father a ceaseless unrest. So she wandered ever backwards and forwards upon the earth, and never returned to her home. The boy followed now his father, now his mother, now his sister, and he made all still and dead upon their paths; the birds grew still and dead, the ears of corn grew empty, the children pale; still and dead all who struggled and suffered.

His mother could only behold him with a shudder; he inspired his father with malicious joy, but only his sister loved him. She ever called him to her, and wept when he would not come. One day he said to Sorrow: "I must kill my mother; ay, if she only looks at me she is dead. But she ever turns aside from me."

Sorrow was terrified at these words, and did all in her power to turn the mother's gaze from the son. But she ever felt his might, and could no longer play with Love and Happiness as formerly. They both, too, feared Life's awful son even more than her grim spouse, for over him they had learnt to exert a certain power; he grew quieter in their presence. But Death remained ever inexorable; his glance now scorching like the Simoon, now numbing like the north; even the Sun lost her strength before this terrible boy, for he laid night upon all eyelids, and froze all things living.

Since that time there is an end of the earth's paradise. That is why Life is no longer a radiant maiden, but a grave woman, full of useful power, of stern demands on that which she has created. She cannot forget how fair all was once, and fain would see it thus again, notwithstanding Strife and Sorrow and Death. She would fain be stronger than all these three, and yet she must succumb and begin again anew, to succumb again, ever and ever.

The Treasure Seekers

The Philosopher and the Poet set out together on a pilgrimage, to seek after the hidden treasure of cognition and to raise it. They had been told that it lay buried there where the rainbow touches the earth, and that it was quite easy to find. The Philosopher dragged instruments with him, and began accurate measurements, and as often as he saw a rainbow he carefully measured the distance, determined the spot with mathematical accuracy, hurried thither and began to dig. The Poet, meanwhile, laid himself in the grass and laughed and toyed with the sunbeams. They played about his happy brow, they told to him bright fairy tales of dreamland, and showed him the life and working of nature. He grew familiar with all plants and creatures, he learnt to know their speech, and he became versed in their secret whisperings and sighs. Ay, all created things came to have faces for him, from the tenderest plant and the most insignificant beast, and before his eyes were unrolled deeds full of woe and joy.

When at last the Philosopher, with solemn look, torn hands, and weary back, rose from his shaft back into daylight, laden with some new stones, he marveled when he saw the Poet's face radiant, as though he had heard wonders.

"How transfigured you are, you lazy one!" he said angrily.

"Who tells you that I am lazy?"

"You always remain here on the surface while I go into the depths."

"Perhaps the surface, too, offers some solutions, and perchance I read these."

"What can the surface offer? One must penetrate into the depths. I have as yet not found the right spot in which the promised treasure lies, but I have made some most important discoveries, though never yet the right ones, those that I apprehend."

"Let us seek further," said the Poet.

Suddenly he held his friend by the arm, and pointed with breathless delight.

"Another rainbow!" cried the Philosopher, and began his measurements.

But the Poet had seen behind the sun-glittering rainbow a wondrous form with black hair and large, sad eyes. She seemed to wait for him; then she turned away slowly. As though demented, the Poet rushed after her; he forgot the aim of his pilgrimage, forgot his friend, who had descended into a new shaft. He only hurried after that wondrous being whose eyes had sunk into his soul. Over hill and dale, from house to house he followed the fair form. He saw the world and its agonies, wherever he looked he beheld woe, for in his own heart dwelt the greatest woe, the gnawing pangs of love. He ever thought he must attain to his enchantress, who stepped in front of him so calmly, through the fallen autumn leaves, across the soft snow, in the bitter north wind – north, south, east, and west, ever unapproachable. Once or twice she looked round after him, and her gaze only increased his yearning.

At last, spring neared on the wings of the wind. At the spot whence the Poet had set out the fair form halted. Now he should reach it. But at that moment a hurricane broke loose that shook the world. Forests were uprooted, and all the sluices of heaven seemed opened. The Poet crossed the foaming mountain stream at the peril of his life, and came up to her who stood calm amid all this uproar, and only gazed at him. He seized her hand.

"You are mistaken in me," she said, sadly. "I wanted to flee from you because I love you, for I bring you no happiness. I am Sorrow, and must leave you a heavy heart and serious thoughts. Farewell! You have found your treasure; now you need me no longer."

So speaking she vanished.

The hurricane had changed into a fine, drizzling rain, through which the spring sunbeams pierced to the Poet. At that moment the Philosopher rose out of the earth richly laden. He let all his burden fall, folded his hands, and cried: "Why, you lucky wight, you stand in the very midst of the rainbow, straight upon the treasure."

"Who? I?" said the Poet, waking from his stupor. Then he threw himself to earth and wept aloud and cried: "Oh that I had never been born! I suffer unspeakable torture."

The Philosopher shrugged his shoulders and began to dig anew.

"There stands one right upon his treasure," he said, "and does not know it; and when I tell him he weeps. Oh, these poets!"

Vârful cu Dor (The Peak of Yearning)

There was once on a time a *hora*[32] at Sinaia, the like of which had never been seen before; for it was upon a great holiday, and the monks in the neighboring cloister had distributed food to everyone, heaping bowls of it, so that all the villagers had eaten their fill. The folk had gathered from far and near, from Izvor and Poiana Ţapului, from Comarnic and Predeal, and from the other side of the mountains. The sun shone down so warm into the valley that the maidens took the kerchiefs from their heads, and the lads pushed their flower-bedecked hats from their brows, so hot had the dancing made them. The mothers stood round about upon the green, suckling their children; their shimmering veils showed afar off, as white and soft as spring blossoms.

What a stamping and shouting there were amid the merry dancers! The maidens seemed to hover in the air, as though their dainty feet, peeping out from the narrow petticoat, never touched the ground. Their shifts were gaily and richly embroidered, and glittered with gold, like the coins that hung on their necklets. The dance moved on, in circles both great and small; ceaselessly it moved, to the ceaseless music of the lute-players, like the pulsation of a vein, or an undulating wave. A little to one side, a handsome shepherd stood leaning upon his staff and watched the *hora* with his dark eyes, dark as blackberries. His form was slender, like a young pinetree; his hair fell in black locks upon his shoulders from under his cap of white lambskin. His shirt was grey, fastened about the hips with a broad leather girdle, and he wore sandals upon his feet. Only for a moment had his eyes glanced uncertainly around; now they had discovered what they sought, and their sparkling gaze was fixed upon a maiden, who did not seem to notice him at all. The maiden was fair – fair as the most beautiful flower; nay, lovelier far than the gentian or the Alpine rose, more delicate than the edelweiss. In each of her eyes shone two points of light, one in the black pupil and the other in the brown circle surrounding it. Her teeth flashed white every time the coral lips parted; her hair was as black as the abyss from whose depths a gleam of water shoots up, and the wreath of flowers upon her head did not fade; it was as though she gave it freshness and life. Such a slender body she had, one might have thought a man could break it with a turn of his hand; and yet the people told tales of her wondrous strength. Yes, Irina was fair, very fair, and Ionel, the young shepherd, gazed upon her ceaselessly. At last, he too drew near the circle and grasped her hand. The maidens looked at one another and laughed, and

---

[32] The *hora* is a Romanian dance, the dancers forming into circles or rounds [note in the first edition].

89

Irina grew crimson. Now of a sudden the lute-players stopped upon a shrill, high note, the lads each turned their partners round under their arms and once about, and then Ionel drew Irina's hand downwards with a firm grasp. There was deep significance in this, but Irina only shrugged her shoulders and laughed.

"Irina," he whispered, "dost thou see the golden leaves on yonder beech? It is time – I must go down with my sheep into the valley, down into the Baragan, perhaps as far as the Dobrudgea, and I shall see thee no more till spring-time. Give me a good word, that my heart may have no cause to tremble when I think of thee looking upon the other lads!"

"What wouldst have me say? Thou dost not love me truly, and I shall soon be forgotten."

"I will die ere I forget thee, Irina."

"These be but words – these I do not believe."

"What must I do, then, that thou mayst believe me?"

Irina's eyes sparkled as she gave him a sidelong glance and answered: "That which thou canst never do."

"I can do anything," said Ionel slowly, as though he scarcely knew that he spoke.

"Nay, thou canst not bide without thy sheep; thou wouldst sooner do without me than them."

"Without my sheep," repeated Ionel, and sighed.

"Dost see," laughed Irina, "the only thing which I require of thee, that thou shouldst stay on yonder mountaintop without thy sheep, that thou canst not do! Words, naught but words!"

"And what if I do it?" said Ionel. He grew pale and clenched his teeth as he spoke.

The youths and maidens had gathered about the pair and were listening. "Do it not!" – "Do it!" cried one and another. Then an old shepherd with silver locks and overhanging brows laid his hand on Ionel's shoulder. "Let the maidens be," he said roughly; "they will but break thy heart and then laugh thee to scorn. Dost thou not know that the shepherd who forsakes his sheep must die?" He shook his clenched fist at Irina: "And thou dost think, because thou art fair, that thou canst dare all, and that nothing shall quell thy mischievous spirit? But the evil thou dost work, to thine own self dost thou work it!"

Irina did but laugh again. "He need not go," said she, "nor do I need him either." And turning, she ran off to drink from the spring that rises beside the cloister.

Ionel would listen to no one, but with pale cheeks and set mouth took his way toward the mountain. He passed Irina by, and only made a gesture of farewell to her with his hand.

"Do it not!" she called after him, and laughed with the other maidens. And the Pelesh stream, as it rushed by, re-echoed the words, "Do it not! Do it not!" But Ionel did not hear it, and went on climbing higher and higher in the noontide sun, over the smooth uplands, beneath the giant pines – whose trunks six men can scarcely span – and through the shady beech-woods, up to the shepherd's hut round which his flock was lying, and whence his dogs ran forth to meet him, barking for joy. He passed his hand caressingly over their rough coats, and then called his Mioritza, or the ewe that led his flock. "Brr, brr, *oitza*[33]," he called, "brr, come hither." She came trotting up with her little lamb, and suffered him to thrust the carnation that he had stolen from Irina into her fleece. Then he begged the other shepherds to take his flock with them, saying that he would follow later, but must first accomplish a vow that he had taken. They all looked at him in wonder. "And if I return no more," he ended, "ye shall say that Yearning hath bidden me to the marriage-feast."

He took his Alp-horn in his hand, and climbed on and on to the very summit of the mountain, whence he could look away across the Danube to the Balkans. There he stood still, and putting his horn to his lips, sent forth a wailing note whose echoes spread far around. But at the call his faithful dog rushed in pursuit, and was soon springing round him, whining for joy. Then, seizing his master's shirt between his teeth, he tried to drag him away toward the valley, so that Ionel scarce knew how to resist, and was obliged at last, with tears in his eyes, to speak roughly to the poor beast and drive him away with stones. And now he had turned away his last friend, and was alone in those desolate mountain wilds. Two eagles circled in the air beneath him; save for this, all was motionless and silent.

He stretched himself upon the turf and sighed so deeply that his breast seemed nigh to bursting. At last he fell asleep, from sheer heart-ache and longing. When he awoke, the clouds were rolling above his head and gathering nearer and nearer; first they moved rapidly, then a sudden calm seemed to fall upon them, and finally they closed about him in a mist so dense that he could not see one step before his face. All at once they appeared to take distinct form, and to be gliding round him in the likeness of wondrously beautiful women, clad in shimmering, snow-white garments, and holding one another by the hand. He rubbed his eyes, for he thought he still dreamed; but presently he heard that they were singing, a song so soft and low that it sounded as from afar off; and now they stretched lily-white arms towards him, while from every side came the cry: "Thou goodly youth, be mine, be mine ! Come with me!"

But he shook his head.

"Do not despise us," cried one, "we will give thee such happiness as shall make thee forget the valley forever!" She parted the mist with her hand, and there appeared before him a mountain meadow, carpeted with flowers as he had never seen one before, and upon the meadow stood a shepherd's

---

[33] Little sheep [note in the first edition].

hut built of roseleaves, and beside it was a spring, whose pearly drops gushed out over the fresh green moss. "Come, we will dwell there together!" called the fair one in silvery tones.

"Nay, come to me!" cried another, and before his very eyes, she built out of the mist a house that shone like a rainbow when the sunbeams fell upon it. Inside it was as downy as though floor and walls alike were of the softest wool; from the roof fell rainbow drops, and no sooner did they touch the earth than grass and flowers sprang up there. "We will dwell here," cried the lovely maiden. "See, I will adorn thee, even as I am adorned," and she cast wreaths and chains of the glittering drops about his head and his neck. But he shook them off again. "One only may deck me," he said, with a darkening brow, "only my bride."

"Then I will be thy bride!" exclaimed a third maiden. "See, here is my dower!" And rolling the mist into balls, she made sheep of it, ever more and more sheep, till the whole mountain – nay, all the mountains and the sky itself were full of them. They were dazzling white, with silver and gold bells about their necks, and everywhere fresh green sprang up beneath their feet. For a moment, the face of the lonely shepherd cleared, but anon he waved the tempting picture aside. "I have but one flock," he said, "my own, and I desire no other."

Then the mist grew thicker and darker again; he was soon surrounded by black clouds once more and from their midst the lightning flashed and the thunder rolled dreadful and near. And in the thunder a voice spoke: "Rash son of Earth, thou that hast dared despise us, to destruction art thou doomed!" Then a fresh peal of thunder seemed to rend the very mountain, and as it rolled on toward the valley, snowflakes began to fall around Ionel, first lightly, then thicker and thicker, till all the mountaintop was covered, and his cloak, his hair and his eyebrows were frosted over. And, 'mid the soft patter of the descending snow, the sweet voices rang out again in rich harmony, the sound of shepherds' pipes and Alpine horns mingled with their song, and a palace built by unseen hands rose before him – a palace of snow so dazzling in its radiance that now and again he had to shield his eyes from it. And lo! When he looked up, the moon and the stars had assembled in the palace, and illuminated it so that the walls shone quite transparent. The moon sat enthroned on high upon a downy couch and watched the stars, that were holding one another by the hand and dancing a *hora*. The blacker the heavens became, the more stars flocked into the palace, and whenever the moon beckoned, another little star left the sky and hurried in. There were quite tiny stars, like children, that rolled about with one another, and laughed and played at the feet of the moon. Others marched in majestically, wearing a long train – a train as long as the whole Bucegi, that swept over all the mountaintops and was borne by a host of little stars, all in shining dresses and decked with wreaths and crowns of wondrous brightness. The gates of the palace opened wider of their own accord as these mighty stars appeared. And one of these commanded the moon to come down from her seat and do obeisance. Then that star beckoned to Ionel and said: "Come, child of man, be thou my consort; with me thou shalt range over the universe, my little stars shall be thy servants, and thou thyself shalt bathe, a shining star, in a flood of radiance!"

Ionel, without knowing it, had drawn close to the gateway, and was listening to these entrancing tones, while the other stars all sang together in soft accompaniment. Then the moon raised her head and looked at him, and she was so like Irina that Ionel clutched at his heart and cried out: "Nay, were the whole world at my feet, I would but offer it to Irina!"

Then there arose a rustling, roaring sound that ended in a fearful crash – the stars swept by towards heaven, in an endless, mighty train, the palace fell, burying Ionel in its ruins, and the moon gazed down pale and sad upon the desolate snowdrifts.

But the dwarfs, who had heard the fearful crash overhead, now climbed painfully forth from the recesses of the mountain to see whether their roof were in danger. And so they discovered the vast heap of precious stones of which the palace had been built, and began in great glee to collect this costly treasure, and to drag it down into the fastnesses of the mountain, where they heaped it up in their mighty vaults.

Thus they came upon poor Ionel, and since there was still some life left in him, and he was so fair to look upon – far more so, certainly, than any of themselves – they dragged him down too, with much trouble, and laid him upon a couch of their softest moss. They drew water from both hot and cold springs, washed and bathed him, and then carried him to the great underground lake that feeds all earthly springs. After they had plunged him once into those waters, he awoke healed of all pain, and looked about him in astonishment.

"Where am I?" he exclaimed at last. And well might he be amazed. For above him vaults of shimmering rock rose to giddy heights and were lost in darkness; and at his feet a lake stretched forth, so far, so far, that it seemed as though it must fill up the whole earth within, and it too was lost in dark distance. All around thousands of gnomes were standing, running, or climbing; they wore long beards, and carried lights, some in their girdles, some upon their heads. Countless hosts of them were busy carrying jewels to the lake, washing them in its water – whereby their radiance was greatly enhanced – and storing and arranging them in chambers or upon heaps. Many of the gnomes came in upon rafts, bringing treasure of hitherto unknown stones with them; others loaded up rafts for a far voyage and pushed off from shore.

There was such a stir and din of lights and voices in the great vault that Ionel was fairly bewildered. Yet all seemed to understand their business quite clearly, save those who surrounded him, and they did not appear to know what they should do with him. But a sudden longing seized him to journey away into the unknown, dark distance, and he hurried towards a raft that was just about to put off. Then there arose from the waves a beautiful woman; she was as like to Irina as though she had been her sister, and she stretched out her arms towards Ionel. With a great cry of "Irina!" he would have flung himself down to her, but that twenty strong arms held him back, and twenty others as strong began to rain blows upon him. He made resistance, for the beautiful woman still beckoned to him from the water; but his captors would not let go their hold, and even began to stone him in their anger.

Then on a sudden, there appeared before him a dwarf who wore a crown upon his head, and who, commanding the others to desist, said: "Thou art mistaken, Ionel; thy bride is not here; she waits for thee in the valley. This is my appointed bride, and for her I have tarried many a long year." At this an angry look, that yet only enhanced her charm, crossed the fair woman's face, and with a threatening gesture, she dived beneath the waves.

The little king sighed, and Ionel sighed, and all the dwarfs, being good, faithful subjects, sighed too; yet they still held their stones in readiness, lest perchance Ionel should be condemned to die. But the king gazed pityingly at the goodly shepherd-lad, and bade his people wash him once more in the waters of the healing spring, since he was bleeding from many wounds. With youth and beauty thus renewed, he was escorted, by the king's orders, to the mountaintop where they had found him, and as the little monarch bade him farewell he added: "Thou art surely to blame, Ionel. Thou hast forgotten thy duty for the sake of a fair woman. Thy faithfulness to her is beautiful and great, but thine unfaithfulness to thy duty is greater; and though I may understand the feeling that overmastered thee, I cannot avert the punishment that awaits thee."

With a heavy heart did Ionel take his stand once more upon the lonely peak, around which the storm was still raging.

Its violence increased with every moment, as though it would fain have cast down the solitary mortal from the height whereon he stood, to dash him into a thousand pieces. Ionel took firm hold of a projection in the rock, and glanced wildly about him, expecting to see new enemies, new dangers and temptations, rise up on every side. He felt as though the storm were crushing him to the earth, as though it were tearing and dragging at his heart, as though he were dying of his agony and grief. He clung yet more closely to the rock, that seemed to reel beneath the pressure.

And amid the raging and the din round about him he caught sounds, now as of many voices, and again as of one voice alone, calling, enticing, threatening; then there was a blare of trumpets, that seemed to cleave his very brain; and suddenly his love for Irina changed into bitter, burning hate, since it was she who with laughing lips had sent him to his death. Yea, he would wait out his time here, unshaken to the end; but in spring he would go down and take leave of her with scorn, forever! No woman should possess his heart; that should be for his flock alone, the flock he had shamefully forsaken.

Then there rang forth from the rock a deep and mighty voice: "Nay, lad! Thou art mine, in my power, irrevocably and forever!" and in a moment the rock changed into a giant woman's form that embraced Ionel with stony arms and kissed him with lips of stone. In horror, he strove to free himself from her, and could not. "Who art thou?" he cried. "Have all the powers of hell conspired together against me? Who art thou – unless thou be Velva?"

But the woman had turned to rock again, and through the storm these words echoed: "I am the Spirit of Yearning, and thou art mine – mine the last lips thou shalt ever kiss."

Then a great silence fell upon the place, and the sun broke forth from behind the clouds. It shone upon a pale man, who stood leaning upon his Alpine horn and gazing into the valley, and far away to the Danube. He neither sighed nor moved, and the beating of his heart did not stir his arms, which were folded upon his breast.

Save for the languid motion of his eyelids no one could have told that he still lived. Anon the surrounding world began to awake to life. Ice and snow melted and ran down in streams to the valley, while young green crept forth upon the spots the snow had covered. But Ionel never moved. The forest shook off its withered leaves and the new buds began to swell. But Ionel never seemed to heed them. Up the mountain slopes came the voices of twittering birds, and the sound of the woodland streams rushing on under the warm rain. But Ionel did not hear. It seemed as though all things living had drawn near to awaken him, yet in vain; he only gazed forth toward the Danube, as though he were turned to stone. Then all at once his face awoke to life, his eyes shone, a faint color came upon his cheek and with open arms and outstretched neck, he stood listening as the sound of barking dogs and tinkling bells drew nearer. Now he could plainly see the white fleeces of his flock, and he put his horn to his lips to sound a welcome. But even as he did so he clutched at his heart, and wailing forth the words "I die!" he sank upon the earth.

In vain did his dogs lick him lovingly on hands and face, in vain did his Mioritza stand bleating beside him and his fellow-shepherds call him by name; he lay still, with a happy smile upon his wan face, and gave answer to none. The Alpine horn, whose voice his breath had so lately stirred, lay broken beside him, and naught around him bore witness to the battles the young warrior had fought. They buried him where he lay, and named the mountain *Vârful cu Dor* – "the Peak of Yearning". Often have I been up there and seen his grave, and the sheep love to browse upon it still.

The Cave of Ialomitza

In crossing the pass between the peaks of Vârful cu Dor and Furnica, on the other side of the Bucegi, you come upon the Ialomitza river. One of the springs, which feed it, rises hard by, in a vast stalactite cave, at the entrance of which stands a small cloister. From time immemorial, it has always been said that there is no ending to this cave, and that a man who once went in there has never been seen again to this day.

The cave was once inhabited by a terrible enchanter, of whom it was told that he carried off all the fairest maidens roundabout – carried them off out of the fields, from their parents' cottages, yes, even from before the marriage-altar. They all followed him, without resistance, but no one ever saw them more. Many a bold youth had sworn to go and free them, and had even marched bravely into the cave and called the enchanter by name: "Bucur! Bucur!" but not one had ever caught a glimpse either of Bucur or of the maidens.

But in the pretty village of Rucar, at the foot of the Bucegi, there dwelt a beautiful maiden, named Ialomitza, who had been rash enough to say that she engaged never to follow the enchanter, no matter in what shape he might appear before her, or with what promises he might try to entice her.

"And though he should even drag me into his cave," she said, "I would still get forth again."

This was a very daring speech, and the old folks shook their heads at it, and shrugged their shoulders, saying: "If he were really to come, she would yet go with him gladly, just like all the others."

A short time passed, during which no one appeared, and nothing happened, to try the young girl's courage. She was a joy for all men to look upon, with her red cheeks, her fresh, cool lips, her waving auburn hair, and her great blue eyes. Her nose was delicately cut, with transparent nostrils, only the tip had just a little impudent, upward turn. Her throat rose snow-white from her richly embroidered shift, and upon her forehead, temples, and neck the pretty reddish locks curled in wild abundance, escaping from the plaits and rebelliously defying all the efforts of the comb. When Ialomitza loosened her plaits she was as though clothed from head to foot in a golden mantle, of which she could not see the half in her little mirror when she was decking herself on a Sunday for the *hora*.

There was one in the village, who was forever running after her, to the well, in the fields, and at the dance. But she did not care to have much to do with poor Coman, and yet he was a fine lad, and rich. He owned broad meadows, with horses, cows, buffaloes, and sheep, and wore a fine, embroidered white leather jerkin, and a long white cloak lined with red, and richly adorned with gold and colored threads. Many a maiden looked round after Coman, but Ialomitza never did. She thought only of the enchanter Bucur, and of how she would strive with him and avenge all the poor maidens who had fallen into his clutches.

One beautiful Sunday afternoon, when the heated dancers were standing still to rest for a moment, there was heard close by the sweetest sound of flute-playing – so sweet that every heart in that gay young throng beat high with delight. All turned curiously to see who the player was, and there stood a handsome young shepherd, leaning against a tree, with his feet crossed, as quietly as though he had been there forever – and yet no one had seen him come, and no one knew him. He played on and on, as if he were alone in the world; only once he raised his eyes and looked at Ialomitza, who had drawn quite near, and was listening to those heavenly melodies with parted lips and quivering nostrils. After a while he looked at her again, and presently a third time. Then Coman whispered to her from behind: "Come away, Ialomitza; yon is an impudent fellow!" An impatient motion of the girl's shoulders and elbows was the only reply. "Ialomitza!" whispered the jealous lover once more, "art thou not ashamed to let thyself be stared at thus?" Again she made no answer, but turned her back upon him. "Ialomitza, I tell thee, yon shepherd is no other than Bucur, the enchanter!" Just at that moment the shepherd, without leaving off his playing, nodded his head, and Ialomitza's heart turned cold and her throat dry. "What dost thou know about it?" she rejoined defiantly, yet her voice trembled a little.

"I know it, I can feel it! I feel it because I love thee – and because I love thee I see, too, that he has taken thy fancy, and that thou wilt fall a prey to him, as all the others have."

"I! Never – I swear it!" cried Ialomitza, and turned deadly pale.

"Here is my flute; do thou play for us a while," the shepherd now called out, handing his flute to Coman.

Without knowing what he did, Coman grasped the flute and began to play, and he played more beautifully than he had ever done in his life; but he presently perceived, to his horror, that he could not leave off. He improvised new *horas*, such as he had never heard before – *brâus*, *kindias*, he played them all, and could see, as he did so, that the stranger was always dancing with Ialomitza. Then he began to play a *doina*[34], and the air was so passing sad that tears stood in all the women's eyes, and Ialomitza implored him to stop. But he played on and on, looking round with terror in his glance, for the flute would not be silent. Evening closed in; the people, in twos and threes, began to turn homewards, and still Coman blew upon the flute, and Ialomitza stood beside him as though spellbound. The strange shepherd had disappeared.

---

[34] *Hora, brâu, kindia, doina*: Romanian folk songs.

"Leave off, Coman," said she, "thou art breaking my heart. Thou knowest I do not love thee; but I have sworn to thee never to belong to that other. Leave off, Coman; be sensible!"

But Coman played on, now merrily, as though he would have laughed, and now in so sad and melting a strain, that the nightingale made answer from the depths of the dewy valley. Nearer and nearer drew the nightingale; Ialomitza could see it in the moonlight, how it came and settled above Coman's head, and sang with the flute. Then it flew off, still uttering its sweet, entrancing note, and Ialomitza followed it the whole night through, without knowing whither she went. Coman too, with his flute, followed the wonderful bird through the dewy valley, along by the edge of the stream.

Morning broke, and Ialomitza smote her hands upon her head in terror: "Where am I? I am far away from home, and this place is strange to me. Coman, where are we? I am affrighted! That bird was Bucur!"

Coman gave no answer, but only played a merry dance. Then a horse came galloping towards them over the meadow, and circled about the maiden, offering her his back to mount, and rubbing his head against her.

"Ah, me!" she cried, "I know the dread one again! If I were but a bird and could flee away!" She had scarcely said this before she was flying away in the shape of a dove, far away into the dewy morning. But thereupon the horse was changed into a hawk, that shot down upon her from a giddy height, and bore her away in his talons toward the mountains.

"Ah, would I were a flower down in the meadow!" thought the terrified maiden; and the next instant she was growing beside the stream, a blue forget-me-not; but then the hawk became a butterfly, and circled about the flower, settling upon it, and swinging with it to and fro.

"Oh, were I rather a trout in the stream!" thought Ialomitza; and in a moment she became a trout, but the butterfly turned into a net, caught her, and lifted her up into the air, till she was like to die.

"I would I were a lizard!" thought the poor maid as she lay dying in the net. And lo! In the twinkling of an eye, she was gliding as quick as thought among the grass and flowers, and fancying she was hidden beneath every stone and leaf. But from under the nearest stone a snake crawled forth, and held her spellbound beneath his dreadful eyes, so that she could not move. They tarried a long while thus, and the little lizard's heart beat to bursting against her sides.

"Would I had become a nun! I should have been safe in the cloister!" she thought; and in a moment the lofty dome of a church rose above her head, she saw tapers burning, and heard the voices of many hundreds of nuns re-echoing in a mighty wave of song. Ialomitza knelt, in the guise of a nun, before the picture of one of the saints; her heart was still throbbing with fear, and she rejoiced to think that she was hidden in this sanctuary. She raised her eyes in thanksgiving to the picture above her – and behold! Bucur's eyes were gazing at her from out its face, and cast such a spell upon her, that she could not quit the spot, even when the church grew empty. Night fell; the eyes began to shine and glitter, and Ialomitza's tears fell ceaselessly down on the stones where she knelt.

"Ah, me!" she cried, "even in this holy place I find no rest from thee! Would I were a cloud!" As she spoke the vaulted roof above her changed to the blue vault of heaven, and she was floating as a cloud through its boundless heights. But her persecutor turned into the wind, and hunted her from south to north, and from east to west, over the whole earth.

"I had better have been a grain of sand," said the little cloud to itself at last. Then it sank to earth, and fell, in the form of a tiny grain of golden sand, into the Râul Doamnei[35]. But Bucur became a peasant, wading with naked feet in the river to seek for gold, and he fished up the little grain of sand out of the depths. It slipped hastily through his fingers, and turned into a doe, that fled away toward the woodland thickets. But before the doe could reach the shelter of the forest, Bucur became an eagle, shot down upon her from above, and once more bore her off in his talons toward his eyrie in the Bucegi Mountain. Hardly had he loosed his grasp of her before she fell, as a dewdrop, into the cup of a gentian blossom. But he became a sunbeam, and glanced down upon her to drink her up. Then at last, in the shape of a wild goat, she dashed, without knowing whither she went, straight towards his cave. Laughing, he pursued her in the guise of a hunter, and murmured: "I have thee now." She ran into the cave, ever deeper and deeper, and on a sudden perceived that all the stones round about were beautiful maidens, from whose eyes tears dropped unceasingly down.

"Oh, flee, flee from hence!" a hundred voices called to her. "Thou unhappy maid! If once he kisses thee, thou wilt turn to stone like us!"

At that moment, an arrow flew through the whole length of the cave, and struck the little goat as she fled. In deadly anguish she cried: "Oh, would I were a stream! Then I could flow away from him." Instantly she felt herself rushing out of the cave as a foaming mountain torrent; the enchanter uttered a terrible curse, turned into rock, and caught in his arms the little stream, that still kept on ever escaping him.

Just then Coman reached the cave, and recognizing his Ialomitza by her voice, as she uttered a heartrending cry of "Coman, Coman!" he gathered up all his remaining strength, and hurled his flute against the rock, in the outlines of which he could discern Bucur's cruel grin. And now the spell was broken. Bucur could no more change his shape again than Ialomitza hers, and so she flows on to this day, away over his stony, immovable arms. But Coman built a little church before the cave, and became a monk, dwelling there in holiness, and gazing upon his fair beloved, unto his life's end.

---

[35] The River of the Princess.

Furnica (The Anthill)

There was once a beautiful maiden, Viorica by name; she had hair like gold, and eyes like the blue sky, and cheeks like carnations, and lips like cherries, and her body was as lithe as the rushes that sway by the riverside. All men rejoiced when they beheld this fair maiden, yet not so much on account of her beauty as because of her wondrous diligence. When she went to the spring with her pitcher on her head, she carried her distaff in her girdle and spun the while. She could weave too, and embroider like a fairy. Her shifts were the finest in the whole village, wrought with black and red stitches, and with wide seams of broidery on the shoulders. She had adorned her petticoat, and even her Sunday hose, with flowers wrought in the same way. In short, it seemed as though the little hands could never rest; in field and meadow, she did as much work as in the house; and all the lads turned their eyes upon the fair Viorica, who should one day be such a notable housewife. But she never turned her eyes toward them; she would hear no talk of marriage; there was plenty of time for that, she said, and she had to care for her old mother. Thereupon the mother would bend her brows, and say that, for her part, she thought a stalwart son-in-law would be but a prop the more. But this troubled the little daughter, who would ask whether she were of no more use at all, that the mother should be so set upon having a man into the house.

"The men do but make a deal more work for us," said she, "for we must spin and stitch and weave for them as well as ourselves, and then we never find time to get the field labor done."

Then the mother would sigh, and think of her dead son, for whom she had made so many fine linen shirts, and washed them so dazzlingly white that all the village maidens gazed their eyes out, looking after him. It had never been too much trouble for her – but then, what will not a mother do, indeed, and never be weary!

The hour came when Viorica had to own that her mother had been right to wish for a son-in-law, even as though something had warned her that she was not much longer for this world. She began to fail, and all her daughter's love was powerless to hold her upon earth. The fair maiden had to close the beloved eyes; and now she was all alone in the little house. For the first time her hands lay idle in her lap. For whom, indeed, should she work now? There was no one left to her.

One day, as she sat upon her threshold and gazed sadly forth, she saw something long and black moving across the ground towards her. And, behold! It was an endless procession of ants. No one could have told whence the creeping host had travelled; it reached so far into the distance. But now it halted, forming into a mighty circle round about Viorica, and one or two of the ants stepped forth and spoke thus: "Well do we know thee, Viorica, and oft have we admired thy industry, which we may liken to our own; and that is a thing we seldom notice among mortal men. We know, too, that thou art now alone in the world, and so we pray thee to go hence with us and be our queen. We will build thee a palace, finer and larger than the largest house thou hast ever seen. Only one thing thou must promise – that thou wilt never return to dwell among men, but stay with us faithfully all thy life long."

"I will stay with you gladly," replied Viorica, "for I have nothing more to hold me here except my mother's grave; but that I must still visit, and bring flowers, wine, and cake to it, and pray there for her soul."

"Thou shalt visit thy mother's grave; only thou must speak with no man on the way, else wilt thou be unfaithful to us, and our revenge shall be terrible."

So Viorica went forth with the ants, a far, far way, until they reached the spot that seemed most fitting for the building of her palace. Then Viorica saw how far the ants surpassed her in skill. How could she have raised up such a building in so short a time? There were galleries, one above another, leading into spacious halls, and farther yet, into the innermost recesses where the pupae, or infant ants, dwelt, that were carried out whenever the sun shone, and brought quickly under shelter again as often as there was a threatening of rain. The chambers were daintily decked with the petals of flowers, fastened on to the walls with pine needles; and Viorica learnt to spin cobwebs, out of which canopies and coverlets were fashioned. Higher and higher grew the building, but the apartment that was prepared for Viorica was more beautiful than any vision of her dreams. Many galleries led to it, so that she could hold communication with all her subjects with the greatest rapidity. The floors of these galleries were laid over with poppy-leaves, so that the feet of the queen should rest on nothing but purple. The doors were of roseleaves, and the hinges were spiders' threads, so that they could open and shut noiselessly. The floor of the room was covered with a thick velvety carpet of edelweiss, into which Viorica's rosy feet sank softly down; for she needed to wear no shoes here, they would have been far too clumsy, and would have trodden the flower-carpets to pieces. The walls were hung with a tapestry cunningly woven of carnations, lilies of the valley, and forget-me-nots, and these flowers were constantly renewed, so that their freshness and perfume were always entrancing. The ceiling had a tent-like covering of lily-leaves stretched across it. The bed had taken the diligent little ants many weeks to prepare; it was all made of pollen, the softest they could find, and a cobweb of Viorica's spinning was spread over it. When she lay there asleep, she was so lovely that the stars would have fallen from heaven, could they have seen her. But the ants had built her room in the most secret recesses of the palace, and guarded their beloved queen jealously and well; even they themselves scarcely dared to look upon her in her sleep.

Life in the anthill could scarce have been made happier or fairer than it was. One and all, they took a pride in doing the most they could, and trying to surpass each other in pleasing their industrious queen. They were as quick as lightning in carrying out her every command; for she never gave too many orders at once, and never unreasonable ones; but her gentle voice sounded ever as though it were but giving some friendly advice or opinion, and her eyes expressed her thanks in a sunny glance. The ants often declared that they had the sunshine dwelling within their house, and exulted over their good fortune. They had made a special terrace for Viorica, where she could enjoy air and sunlight when her room grew too confined; and from thence she could observe the progress of the building, which was already as high as many a mountain. One day she sat in her room embroidering a dress, upon which she had sewn butterflies' wings with the threads from a silkworm that the ants had brought in for her. None but her dainty fingers could have accomplished such a task. All on a sudden there was a tumult round about her mountain; the sound of voices rang forth, and in a moment all her little kingdom was thrown into alarm, and her subjects came breathlessly crowding about their queen and crying: "They are overthrowing our house; evil men are trampling it down. Two, nay, three galleries have fallen in, and the next is threatened. What shall we do?"

"Is that all?" asked Viorica calmly. "I will bid them stay their course, and in a few days the galleries will be built up again."

She hurried through the labyrinth of galleries, and appeared suddenly upon her terrace. Looking down, she beheld a splendid youth, who had just dismounted from his horse, and was engaged with some of his followers in turning up the anthill with sword and lance. But when she appeared they all stopped short, and the noble youth stood shielding his dazzled eyes with his hand as he gazed upon the radiant figure in its shining draperies. Viorica's golden hair fell in waves to her very feet, a delicate color flooded her cheeks, and her eyes shone like stars. She dropped them, indeed, a moment before the young man's glance; but soon she raised them again, and from her rosy mouth her voice came ringing forth: "Who are ye that have laid such rude hands upon my kingdom?"

"Forgive, fairest lady!" cried the youth, "and as surely as I am a knight and a king's son, I will henceforth be thy most zealous defender! How could I guess that a fairy – nay, a goddess – reigned over this kingdom?"

"I thank thee," answered Viorica. "I need no other service save that of my faithful subjects; and all I ask is, that no foot of mortal man shall intrude upon my kingdom."

With these words she disappeared as though the mountain had swallowed her up, and those outside could not see how hosts of ants were kissing her feet and escorting her back in triumph to her chamber, where she took up her work once more as calmly as though nothing had happened. And outside, there, before the mountain, the king's son stood as though in a dream, and for hours could not be prevailed upon to remount his horse. He still kept hoping that the beautiful queen would appear again – even though it were with angry word and glance; he would at least see her once more! But he only saw ants and yet more ants, in an endless stream, busying themselves with all diligence in repairing the mischief that his youthful thoughtlessness had occasioned. He could have crushed them under foot in his anger and impatience, for they seemed not to understand, or perhaps not even to hear, his questions, and ran quite boldly in front of him, in their new-found sense of security. At last he dejectedly mounted his steed, and so, plotting and planning how he might win the loveliest maid his eyes had ever beheld, he rode on through the forest till nightfall, to the great discontent of his followers, who consigned both anthill and maiden to the devil, as they thought of the supper-table and the bumpers of wine that had long been awaiting them.

Viorica had gone to rest later than any of her subjects. It was her wont to visit the nurseries herself, to see to the infants and feel if their little beds were soft enough; so she glided about, lifting one flower-curtain after another, with a fire-fly clinging to her finger-tips, and looked tenderly after the little brood. Now she went back into her room, and dismissed all the fireflies, who had been lighting her about her work for many hours. She only kept one little glow-worm beside her while she undressed. She was used to fall at once into the deepest and quietest sleep, but tonight she tossed restlessly to and fro, twisting her hair about her fingers, sitting up and then lying down again, and all the time feeling so hot – oh, so hot! Never before had she been sensible of a lack of air in her kingdom, but now she would gladly have hurried forth, only that she feared to be heard and to corrupt others by her bad example. Had she not already, though under much pressure from the others, been obliged to pass many a harsh sentence, to banish some ants from her jurisdiction, because they had indulged in forbidden wanderings – nay, even to condemn some to capital punishment, and, with a bleeding heart, to see them ruthlessly stung to death?

The next morning she was up earlier than any of the rest, and gave them a surprise by showing them one of the galleries that she had built up all alone. Doubtless, she herself did not know that whilst doing so she had cast several glances towards the forest, and had even stood listening for a few moments. She was scarcely back in her chamber again before some of the ants hurried to her in terror, crying: "The bad man who came yesterday has returned, and is riding round our hill!"

"Let him be," replied Viorica, the queen, quite calmly; "he will do us no more harm." But the heart of Viorica, the lovely maiden, beat so fast that she could scarce draw breath.

A wondrous unrest had come over her; she roamed about far more than was her wont; she was always thinking that the baby-ants were not enough in the sunshine, and carrying them out herself, only to bring them in again as quickly; and she often gave contradictory orders. The ants could not tell what had befallen her, and took twice the pains to do all their tasks quickly and well. They surprised her with a splendid new vaulted hall, too; but she gazed at it with an abstracted air and praised it but scantily.

The sound of horses' hoofs was now constantly heard, both late and early, round about the mountain; but for many days Viorica never showed herself. A desperate yearning for the companionship of human beings, which she had never yet felt, now seized upon her. She thought of her native village, of the *hora*, of her little house, of her mother, and of her mother's grave, which she had never again visited. After a few days she announced to her subjects that she thought of making a pilgrimage to her mother's grave, and at this the ants inquired, in alarm, whether she were no longer happy with them, since she had begun to think of her home again.

"Nay," replied Viorica, "I would go for a few hours only, and be back among you before nightfall."

She refused all escort, but one or two of the ants followed her, unobserved, afar off. Everything looked greatly changed to her, and she thought she must have been away a long time. She began to reckon how long it could have taken the ants to build the great mountain wherein they dwelt, and said to herself that it must have been years. Her mother's grave was no longer to be found, the spot was so overgrown with grass and weeds, and Viorica wandered about the churchyard weeping, since here too she was naught but a stranger. Evening drew on, and still Viorica was seeking for the grave she could not find. Then close beside her she heard the voice of the King's son. She would have fled, but he held her fast and spoke to her of his mighty love, with such gentle and moving words that she stood still with bowed head, listening to him. It was so sweet to hear a human voice once more, and to hear it speak of love and friendship. Not until the night had grown quite dark did she remember that she was no forlorn orphan, but a queen forgetful of her duties, and that the ants had forbidden her to hold any further converse with mankind. Then she broke away and fled in haste from the King's son; but he pursued her, with caressing words, to the very foot of her mountain. Here she prayed and implored him to leave her, but he would only consent upon her promising to meet him again the following evening.

She glided noiselessly in, feeling her way along the galleries, and looking fearfully behind her, for she fancied she heard the sound of hurriedly tripping feet and whispering voices all around. No doubt, it was but the anxious beating of her heart, for as soon as she stood still all was silence. At last, she reached her chamber and sank in exhaustion upon her couch, but no soothing sleep fell on her eyelids. She felt that she had broken her promise; and who would now hold her in respect, since her word was no longer sacred? She tossed uneasily to and fro; her pride revolted against any secrecy, and yet she knew the ants only too well – their implacable hate, their cruel punishments. Many times she raised herself on her elbow to listen, and always she seemed to hear the hurried tripping of thousands of little feet, as though the whole mountain were alive.

When she felt that morning drew near, she lifted one of the roseleaf curtains to hurry out into the open. But what was her amazement when she found the doorway completely stopped up with pine-needles! She tried another, then a third, until she had been the round of them all. In vain – they were all filled in to the very roof. Then she called aloud. And lo! The ants appeared in hosts, creeping in through countless tiny, invisible openings.

"I must go forth into the air," said Viorica in commanding tones.

"Nay," replied the ants, "we cannot let thee forth, or we shall lose thee."

"Do ye then obey me no more?"

"Yea, in all things, save this one. Crush us under foot in punishment if thou wilt; we are ready to die for the good of our community, and to save the honor of our queen."

Viorica bowed her head, and tears gushed from her eyes. She implored the ants to give her back her freedom, but the stern little creatures held their peace, and all at once she found herself alone in those dark halls.

Oh, how Viorica wept and wailed and tore her beautiful hair! Then she began to try and dig an opening with her tender fingers, but all she scooped out was filled in again as quickly, so that she was fain at last to throw herself upon the ground in despair. The ants brought her the sweetest flowers, and nectar and dewdrops to quench her thirst, but all her prayers for freedom remained unanswered.

In the fear that her wailing might be heard without, the ants built their hill higher and higher, till it was as high as the peak Vârful cu Dor, and they called their mountain *Furnica*, or "the ant". The King's son has long since left off riding round about the mountain, but in the silence of the night one can still hear the sound of Viorica's weeping.

The Witch's Stronghold (Cetatea Babei)

Going up the Prahova valley one cannot see "Cetatea Babei", the Witch's Castle, because it is hidden by the Bucegi Mountain. It is a jagged peak, and looks as though it were covered with ruins. A field of eternal snow lies between it and the Jipi. In far-off times, when wolves guarded the flocks, and eagles and doves made their nests together, a proud castle stood there, and within the castle busy doings went on. From morning till night it rang with pattering, clanging, bustling sounds, and hundreds of hasty footsteps scurried to and fro therein. But at nighttime a light shone forth from the tower, and the humming of a mighty wheel was heard, and above the hum of the wheel a wondrous, soft song seemed to hover, keeping time with it. Then people would glance fearfully up toward the castle and whisper: "She is spinning again!" And she who sat spinning there was the mistress of the castle, a very evil witch, to whom the mountain-dwarfs brought all the gold that they found in the depths of the earth, that she might spin threads of gold for all the brides to wear upon their heads on their wedding day.[36] The gold was unloaded in heaps in her castle, and she weighed it and chose it out. And woe to the dwarf who did not bring the required weight; he was thrust between the stem and bark of a huge tree, and squeezed until he gave up the very uttermost grain of gold. Or he would be caught by the beard only in the tree, and there he might struggle and writhe as he pleased, and cry for mercy – the old witch turned a deaf ear to it all. The name of *Baba Coaja* ("Mother Bark") had been given her, perhaps because of this cruel custom of hers, perhaps because she was as hard as a stale crust of bread, and as wrinkled as the stem of an old oak. She alone understood the spinning of the golden threads, and she went on preparing them for hundreds of years in advance.

Baba Coaja had a wondrously beautiful daughter, named *Alba* ("The White One"), for she was as white as the snow that covered the mountaintops. Her skin was like velvet, and like velvet, too, were her brown eyes, and her hair was like the goldthreads that her mother spun. She was always kept shut up, for Baba Coaja had plenty of work for her to do; and, besides, no one was to be allowed to see her, still less to woo her. She had to wind all the golden thread on reels, and store it up in underground cellars, ready for all those hundreds and hundreds of years to come. This work was very burdensome to the sweet maiden, because her mother would sing and mutter all sorts of evil spells and sayings as she spun, so that a portion of sorrow and heartache was already prepared for each bride, so soon as the

---

[36] The bridal veil of Romanian girls is composed of a shower of loose golden threads [note in the first edition].

golden threads should have rested upon her head. And Alba thought sadly of all the trouble that was being thus determined beforehand. Indeed, she once sat down herself to the great wheel, while her mother was away, and spun a length of thread into which she worked nothing but good wishes. But when Baba Coaja came home she was very wroth, and beat her daughter unmercifully, saying, as she threw the thread upon a heap with the rest: "Thou shalt never wed until thou canst tell thine own spinning apart again!"

In her heart, the old witch was glad to have a pretext for keeping her daughter to herself, for it had been prophesied that Alba would be very unhappy, and would die young. The only being that she loved in the world was her beautiful child. Yet, however much trouble she took to please her with fine clothes and all sorts of pretty trifles, she could not bring a shade of color to her cheek or a smile to her eyes, for the only thing the maiden yearned after was freedom, and that was never hers. How she longed to go wandering for once beneath the trees that clothed the foot of the mountain whereon she dwelt. Up there nothing grew, save a little short grass; and the winter lasted far longer than the summer. When the wind howled round the castle, raging as though he would tear it to pieces, then her heart would grow heavy indeed; she would sit for hours before the hearth, staring into the fire, watching the sparks fly, and thinking of nothing at all. Or again, she would listen to her mother's uncanny singing, while the humming of the wheel and the howling of the storm mingled in one dreary accompaniment. And then she would wonder why she spun so much sorrow for the brides into the goldthreads – why men were not suffered to be happy and gay, out there in the beautiful sunshine, for that always looked bright and merry. But she could never make out the reason why, and would fall asleep at last from sheer thinking. The great reels of gold in the cellars all had one and the same face, yet she would play with them, and pretend they were people, and make up their histories, and try and fancy what would befall the brides that were to wear those golden threads. But as she knew nothing of the world, all her stories were very unlikely ones.

"Mother," she asked one day, resting her chin upon her hand, "are the people in the world just as we are, thou and I – or have they other forms, and other thoughts?"

"What are the people in the world to thee? They are all very bad, and would only do thee harm if they got hold of thee."

"But a while ago a beautiful creature came up our mountain, and there sat one upon him, one who was fairer far to see than any of the little dwarfs; he had black locks, and no beard, and a purple mantle. Was not that a man?"

The old witch was terror-stricken at this speech, and answered: "If he does but ride up here again, I will break his neck for him, and those in the valley shall never see him again!"

„Oh, mother! Do not thus – he was so fair!"

"If thou dost think but once again of him, I tell thee I will lock thee in the cellar, and make thee weigh gold out night and day. As it is, thou art grown so idle in these latter times, and dost naught but sit there and ask useless questions! Hast thou not all thy heart can desire?"

"Nay, mother; I too would fain have a beautiful creature, such as yonder man had, and sit upon it. Up here there are but sheep, and one cannot sit upon them."

"Now thou wouldst have a horse indeed, wouldst thou, foolish child! Dost not see that it were dangerous to life to ride here? The grass is slippery and the abyss deep. One false step, and thou wert lying shattered to pieces down below."

Alba thought over this for a long while, and wondered why it was dangerous for horses to go where sheep could tread in safety; but to this question also she got no reply, for she did not dare to ask it. Only, the dwarfs appeared much uglier to her than before, and the gold became so distasteful to her that she could not bear to look at it. She constantly thought of the beautiful horse, and of the youth who was to have his neck broken if he showed himself there again. Why did her mother want to break his neck? This time, too, she found no answer, however much she puzzled over the matter.

Some time after, the handsome youth rode up to the mountain again; he was tormented by curiosity to discover who lived in that mighty castle, whose walls were hewn out of the living rock. He was a king's son, and his name was Porfirie. He was not used to being unable to do things, and any obstacle was welcome to his impetuous nature. When they spoke to him of marriage, he was wont to reply that he should win his bride from the clutches of a dragon, or pluck her down from a cliff, but never have her tamely wooed for him by a deputy, and end up with a commonplace wedding!

Just at that moment Alba was busy bedecking herself, by way of passing the time, after having worked at reeling off gold all the morning. She had bathed her hands and face, and combed her long hair with her ivory comb, and about her brow she had bound a double row of pearls, in which she had fastened an alpine rose sideways. Her robe was white, with a golden girdle, and over it flowed a green velvet mantle, held on either shoulder with chains of pearls. Around her snow-white throat she laid a string of emeralds, as large as pigeons' eggs, a present from the mountain-dwarfs; and then she looked at herself in the glass, in which, however, she could not see how her golden hair gleamed upon the green velvet mantle. Indeed, she could not have seen aright at all, or the glass was bad, for now she smote her face, crying: "How ugly I am! Oh, how ugly! That is why my mother hides me from all men, and gives me fine dresses, and jewels like a queen's – that it may be forgotten how ugly I am!"

Just then the sound of horses' hoofs echoed among the rocks, and with horror-stricken gaze she beheld the handsome stranger, who was to lose his life if he appeared again before the castle. He must be warned at any cost. She sprang like a wild goat down the mountainside, with fluttering mantle and waving hair, in which the sunbeams seemed to catch as she went. The young king saw her speeding towards him over the rocks, her feet scarcely seeming to touch the stones upon the way, and reined in his horse in wonder-struck admiration. He asked himself what princess, or mountain-fairy, this might be, flying down to him thus. And now she waved both her arms, crying breathlessly: "Back, back! Do not come up hither – it were thy death!"

"And though it should be my death," he exclaimed, "I would die gladly, seeing I have beheld the fairest maid that ever trod this earth!"

Alba stood still before him, a faint blush overspread her cheeks, and looking at him with wide-open eyes, she said: "Am I fair?"

"Yea, verily, wondrous fair! So bewitching art thou, with thy golden hair and thy golden eyes, that I love thee from this hour!"

"And I love thee, too," replied the guileless maiden, unaware of the fact that it is not customary among men to say what one thinks. "But do not say my hair is golden, for gold is so ugly!"

"Ugly!" the king's son laughed. "I have never heard that of it before. Hast thou, then, seen so much gold that it has grown to seem ugly to thee?"

"Ah, yes! I see naught save gold – instead of green trees, gold – instead of flowers, gold – instead of men, gold – heaps of it, like that." And she spread out her arms and turned herself about. "Oh, how much rather would I sit upon yon beautiful creature! I have never seen a horse before – may I touch it?"

"Yes, indeed, and stroke it too, and climb up beside me. Thou shalt ride as long as thou hast a mind to."

Then he bade her rest her foot on his and give him both her hands, and so he drew her up before him on the saddle, clasped his arm about her, and gave his horse the spur. He fancied she would be frightened, but no such thought occurred to the gentle, innocent creature, for she knew naught of danger. As soon as the ground was soft beneath them he loosened the reins, and away they sped, through the woodland shade, and over the flowery meadows. Alba shouted and clapped her hands for glee, crying: "Faster, faster yet!" So they drew near to the city, through which they had to ride before reaching the hill upon which the royal castle stood. Then suddenly fear came upon the maiden.

"Are all these human beings?" she asked, as they rode at a foot's-pace through the streets. "And does not the wind blow down these tiny houses?"

"Nay," laughed Porfirie. "The wind does not blow here as hard as it does up yonder."

110

"See, my people," he cried to the folk as he passed, "here I bring you your queen. She is a fairy-blossom, and I plucked her from yonder cliff!"

"But I am no queen," said Alba in affright.

"I am a king, and since thou art to be my wife, thou wilt become queen also."

"Thy wife? But I was to have no husband, my mother said."

"She only said that because she knew that none was to have thee, save I alone."

"Art thou not at all bad, then?"

"No, I am not bad."

"Then art thou not a human being?"

"Nay, but I am."

"Yet my mother said that all human creatures were bad, and that I must have naught to do with them."

"Who is thy mother, then?"

"That I do not know. She spins gold."

"Spins gold? And for what?"

"For bridal veils – but I will have no gold at my wedding!" added Alba hastily, and she clutched at her head as though she would defend it from that dangerous contact.

"But thou canst not do otherwise," said Porfirie, "or everyone would wonder. Here we are at my home; we are even now riding into the courtyard, and thou must speak pleasantly to my mother."

"Is she old and ugly?"

"Nay, she is fair and proud."

"What does 'proud' mean?" asked Alba.

Porfirie looked into her eyes – they were as clear and unsullied as the sun itself. He pressed the maiden to his heart; then throwing the reins to the attendants who came forward, he sprang from his horse, lifted Alba gently to the ground, and offered his hand to lead her up the broad stone steps. They entered a lofty hall, and there sat a tall, noble lady, surrounded by many maidens, and she was spinning beautiful gold-colored silk. All rose from their work, and gazed in delighted amaze on the beautiful pair standing beneath the portal, that was just then flooded by the glory of the setting sun.

"Here, mother," cried Porfirie, "is thy dear daughter, my sweet bride, whom I found up yonder, quite near the sky; and I am not yet sure whether she be not indeed one of the heavenly inhabitants, that will presently spread wings and flee away from us!"

"Oh, thou beauteous lady!" cried Alba, and fell at the feet of the queen, who raised her up and kissed her with great kindness.

"And thou art spinning too", she went on, "only far, far more beautifully than my mother; for what thou dost spin is as soft and fine as snowflakes, or the petals of flowers."

"What does thy mother spin, then?"

"Oh, always that hard, ugly gold!"

"Gold!" echoed the bystanders; and many laughed, and did not believe the maiden's words.

"Canst thou, too, spin gold?"

"I can, but I may not."

"Why not?"

She was opening her lips to tell what her mother did over her spinning, but all at once she felt strangely ill at ease, and realized how angrily everyone would look at her if the maidens knew that all kinds of sorrow was spun for them into their bridal veils. And here they were all looking so happy and so kind, these bad people, against whom her mother had warned her! They seemed far better, indeed, than that mother herself, of whom the mountain-dwarfs were always so horribly afraid.

She was relieved of her perplexity by hearing one of the maidens whisper: "Her dress is velvet – real white velvet!

"And the jewels – from whom did she get her jewels?" said another, rather louder.

"From my friends," answered Alba. "Would you like them? I have many more such playthings at home." And taking the emeralds from her neck, she gave each of the girls one. She would have done the same with her strings of pearls, had not the queen prevented her.

"Are thy friends so rich, then?" inquired the latter.

"I do not know. What is 'rich'? They bring it all up out of the earth in sacks; and when they do not bring enough, they are punished."

Then the queen's face darkened; she drew her son aside and said: "This maiden is none other than the daughter of the abominable witch, Baba Coaja. Take her back as quickly as possible to the spot where thou didst find her. She will only bring trouble upon our house."

"Ask anything of me but that, mother," replied the young king, turning pale. "I love this sweet and innocent maid with my every thought, with my every breath, with all the blood in my veins, and though she were Baba Coaja her very self, I could not give her up!"

The queen sighed. But she gave orders that an apartment should be made ready next to her own for the maiden; and the wedding was fixed for the following day.

The queen desired to adorn her new daughter for it with her own hands. But she had a bitter struggle with her, because the maiden would on no account suffer any goldthreads to be laid upon her head. She fled from one end of the castle to the other like a hunted doe, she cast herself upon the ground, and hid beneath the coverings of the divans; she begged and prayed with streaming eyes that she might be spared.

"Let the queen put some of the beautiful silken threads of her own spinning upon her hair, only not the horrible gold!"

But as she knelt wailing and praying before her, the queen gave a sign, and two of the attendant maidens bound her hands, while a third fastened on the golden veil. They all expected to see an outbreak of rage and despair; but Alba grew quite quiet. As pale as death, she bowed her head beneath its burden. "Thou art harder than my mother," she said, "for she would not give me a husband, lest I should be unhappy, but thou dost thyself call down sorrow upon me!"

No one understood these words. Alba could not be prevailed upon to explain them, whereby the general mistrust of her was yet further increased. She looked so sad that the people no longer even recognized in her the beaming maiden of yesterday; and all her young husband's words of love could not chase the clouds from her brow.

At court there was presently no talk of anything but the countless treasures of the young queen, and many people urged the king to go up the mountain and examine them for himself. He cared nothing for the treasures; he only thought of how he could bring back the smile to his young wife's face, and fancied that perhaps, if he fetched her the ornaments she was fond of, she would grow merry again. For she smiled pityingly at the little stones other people called jewels, and could not at all understand that such trifles should be costly. But as soon as she learnt that Porfirie intended to ride up to her castle again, she was terror-stricken, and implored and conjured him not to do so. "It will surely be thy death," said she. He, however, would not be convinced, and the more she depicted the dangers that awaited him there, the more did these very dangers attract him; so that one morning he set off secretly, while she still lay in a deep slumber.

With only a few followers, he dashed up towards Baba Coaja's castle. But she spied his coming from afar, and cried out to him as he drew nearer: "A curse upon thee – thou who didst ravish my child, only to bring her to sorrow! See here, then – satisfy the greed that has driven thee back hither, miserable wretch! I never desired to have aught to do with thee – why didst thou seek me out?"

With these words she began to scatter down jewels in endless quantities upon the horsemen; but as they fell, the precious stones were changed into ice and snow, and whirled through the air in such clouds that the unhappy men were unable to shield themselves, and were, moreover, so dazzled that they could no longer see their way. The greater number of them fell over the precipices. But the young king, who, thirsting for vengeance, tried to reach the castle that he might strangle the terrible witch, was so completely caught in the avalanche that ere a moment was past he could no longer move a limb, and before he had time to utter a word he was buried deep beneath the snow. As he disappeared, Baba Coaja said, with a malicious laugh: "Now she will come, to him, not to me – yet it will be to me, not to him, that she comes. I shall have my child again, for she may not remain in the wicked world, and among men, whom I hate."

And indeed it was not long before Alba, weary with her long journey afoot, her white velvet dress dusty and travel-stained, came hastening up the mountain.

"Where, where is he?" she asked, with blanched lips.

"So!" said the old witch, "thou hast run away from me with a strange man, and now comest back, and dost not ask after me, but after him? He is not here."

"Yes, yes, he is! I traced him, up to the edge of yonder snow!"

"He came no further, indeed!" laughed the old witch. "He is smothered beneath thy jewels!"

With a terrible cry, Alba cast herself down upon the patch of snow and began to shovel it away with her hands. But in vain! The covering that lay upon her beloved was too heavy, it was frozen too fast. With one cry – "Oh, mother, mother! What hast thou done to me!" – Alba fell dead beside the ice and snow.

Then Baba Coaja hurled forth so terrible a curse, that the very mountain reeled, and the castle fell with a crash, burying her and her gold beneath its ruins. But on the spot where the beautiful Alba had drawn her last breath, there sprang up a white flower, in a white velvet dress, which has ever since been called "Alba Regina", or *Edelweiss*. This flower only blooms close to the eternal snow, which covered her beloved, and is as white and pure as she was herself. Perhaps the snow will turn to jewels again some day, if an innocent maiden should pass over it. The piece of goldthread that Alba spun is still being sought for, and every bride hopes that it is she who has found it. That is why not one of them ever fears the golden threads that are so dangerous, but still believes that happiness will be her portion.

The Caraiman

The Caraiman towers up, dark and threatening of aspect, with his mighty peak of rock that looks as though a great fragment of it had been partly loosened, and were hanging in mid-air. That part of the rock is shaped like a set of bagpipes – and this is the tale they tell about it.

Long, long ago, when the sky was nearer to the earth than now, and there was more water than land, there dwelt a mighty sorcerer in the Carpathians. He was as tall as the tallest pine-tree, and he carried upon his head a whole tree with green twigs and budding branches. His beard, that was many yards long, was of moss, and so were his eyebrows. His clothing was of bark, his voice was like rolling thunder, and beneath his arm he carried a set of bagpipes, as big as a house. He could do anything he liked with his bagpipes. When he played softly, young green sprang up all round about him, as far as his eye could reach; if he blew harder, he could create living things; but when he blew fearfully loud, then such a storm arose that the mountains shook and the sea shrank back from the rocks, so that more land was left uncovered. Once he was attacked by some powerful enemies, but instead of having to defend himself, he merely put the bagpipes to his lips, and changed his foes into pines and beech-trees. He was never tired of playing, for it delighted his ear when the echo sent back the sound of his music to him, but still more was his eye delighted to see all grow into life around him. Then would thousands of sheep appear, on every height and from every valley, and upon the forehead of each grew a little tree, whereby the Caraiman might know which were his; and from the stones around, too, dogs sprang forth, and every one of them knew his voice. Since he had not noticed much that was good in the inhabitants of other countries, he hesitated a long while before making any human beings. Yet he came to the conclusion that children were good and loving, and he decided to people his land with children only. So he began to play the sweetest tune he had ever yet composed – and behold! Children sprang up on every side, and yet more children, in endless crowds. Now you can fancy how wonderful the Caraiman's kingdom looked. Nothing but play was ever carried on there; and the little creatures toddled and rolled around in that beautiful world and were very happy. They crept under the ewes and sucked the milk from their udders; they plucked herbs and fruit and ate them; they slept on beds of moss and under overhanging rocks, and were as happy as the day was long. Their happiness crept even into their sleep, for then the Caraiman played them the loveliest airs, so that they had always beautiful dreams.

There was never any angry word spoken in the kingdom of the Caraiman, for these children were all so sweet and joyful that they never quarrelled with one another. There was no occasion for envy or jealousy either, since each one's lot was as happy as his neighbor's. And the Caraiman took care that there should be plenty of sheep to feed the children; and with his music he always provided enough of grass and herbs, that the sheep, too, might be well nourished. No child ever hurt itself, either; the dogs took care of that, for they carried them about and sought out the softest, mossiest spots for their playgrounds. If a child fell into the water, the dogs fetched it out; and if one were tired, a dog would take it upon his back and carry it into the cool shade to rest. In short, the children were as happy as though they had been in paradise. They never wished for anything more, since they had never seen anything outside their little world. There were not yet any "smart" or "ugly" clothes then; nor any fine palaces with miserable huts beside them, so that no one could look enviously at his neighbor's belongings. Sickness and death were unknown, too, in the Caraiman's country; for the creatures he made came into the world as perfect as a chick from its shell, and there was no need for any to die, since there was so much room for all. All the land which he had redeemed from the sea had to be populated, and for nothing but sheep and children there was room on it, and to spare, for many a long day. The children knew nothing of reading or writing; it was not necessary they should, since everything came to them of itself, and they had to take no trouble about anything. Neither did they need any further knowledge, since they were exposed to no dangers.

Yet, as they grew older, they learnt to dig out little dwellings for themselves in the ground, and to carpet them with moss, and then of a sudden they began to say: "This is mine." But when once a child had begun to say, "This is mine," all the others wanted to say it too. Some built themselves huts like the first; but others found it much easier to nestle into those that were already made, and then, when the owners cried and complained, the unkind little conquerors laughed. Thereupon those who had been cheated of their belongings struck out with their fists, and so the first battle arose. Some ran and brought complaints to the Caraiman, who in consequence blew a mighty thunder upon his bagpipes, which frightened all the children terribly. So they learnt for the first time to know fear; and afterwards they showed anger against the talebearers. In this way even strife and division entered into the Caraiman's beautiful, peaceful kingdom.

He was deeply grieved when he saw how the tiny folk in his kingdom behaved in just the same way as the grown people in other lands, and he debated how he might cure the evil. Should he blow them all away into the sea, and make a new family? But the new ones would soon be as bad as these, and then he was really too fond of his little people. Next he thought of taking away everything over which they might quarrel; but then all would become dry and barren, for it was but over a handful of earth and moss that the strife had arisen, and, in truth, only because some of the children had been industrious and others lazy. Then he bethought himself of making them presents, and gave to each sheep and dogs and a garden for his particular use. But this only made things far worse. Some planted their gardens, but others let them run wild, and then perceived that the cultivated gardens were the fairest, and that the sheep that had good pasture gave the most milk. Then the trouble became great indeed. The lazy children made a league against the others, attacked them, and took away many of their gardens. Then the industrious ones moved to a fresh spot, which soon grew fair also under their hands; or else they refused to be driven out, and long conflicts arose, in the course of which some of the children were slain. When they saw death for the first time they were greatly frightened and grieved, and swore to keep peace with one another. But all in vain – they could not stay quiet for long; so, as they were now loth to kill one another, they began to take away each other's property by stealth and with cunning. And this was far sadder to see; the Caraiman, indeed, grew so heavy of heart over it that he wept rivers of tears. They flowed down through the valley and into the sea. Yet the wicked children never considered that these were the tears their kind father was weeping over them, and went on bickering and quarrelling. Thereupon the Caraiman wept ever more and more, and his tears turned to torrents and cataracts that devastated the land, and ended by changing it into one large lake, wherein countless living creatures came to their death. Then he ceased weeping, and blew a mighty wind, which left the land dry again; but now all the green growth had vanished, houses and gardens lay buried under heaps of stones, and the sheep, for lack of pasture, no longer gave any milk. Then the children cut their throats open with sharp stones, to see if the milk would not flow out in a fresh place; but instead of milk, blood gushed out, and when they had drunk that they became fierce, and were always craving for more of it. So they slew many other sheep, stealing those of their brethren, and drank blood and ate meat.

Then the Caraiman said: "There must be larger animals made, or there will soon be none left!" and blew again upon his bagpipes. And behold! Wild bulls came into the world, and winged horses with long scaly tails, and elephants, and serpents. The children now began to fight with all these creatures, and thereby grew very tall and strong themselves. Many of the animals allowed themselves to be tamed and made useful; but others pursued the children and killed them, and as they no longer dwelt in such peace and safety, many grievous and dangerous sicknesses appeared among them. Soon they became in all respects like the men of other lands, and the Caraiman grew more and more soured and gloomy, since all that, which he had intended to use for good, had but turned to evil. His creatures, too, neither loved nor trusted him, and instead of perceiving that they themselves had wrought the harm, thought that the Caraiman had sent sorrow upon them out of wanton cruelty and sport. They would no longer listen to the bagpipes, whose sweet strains had of old been wont to delight their ears. The old giant, indeed, did not often care to play on his pipes now. He had grown weary for very sorrow, and would sleep for hours together under the shade of his eyebrows, which had grown down into his beard. But sometimes he would start up out of sleep, put the pipes to his mouth, and blow a very trumpet-blast out into the wicked world. Hence there at last arose such a raging storm that the trees ground, creaking and groaning, against one another, and caused a fire to burst out, so that soon the whole forest was in flames. Then he reached up with the tree that grew upon his head, till he touched the clouds, and shook down rain, to quench the fire. But all this while the human beings below had but one thought – how to put the bagpipes to silence forever and ever. So they set out with lances and spears, and slings and stones, to give battle to the giant; but at the sight of them he burst into such laughter that an earthquake took place, which swallowed them all up, with their dwellings and their cattle. Then another host set out against him with pine-torches, wherewith to set his beard on fire. He did but sneeze, however, and all the torches were extinguished and their bearers fell backwards to the earth. A third host would have bound him while he slept, but he stretched his limbs, and the bonds burst, and all the men about him were crushed to atoms. Then they would have set upon him all the mighty wild beasts he had created. But he swept the air together and made thereof an endless fall of snow, that covered them over and over, and buried them deep, and turned to ice above them; so that after thousands of years, when their like was no more to be seen on earth, those beasts still lay, with fur and flesh unchanged, embedded in the ice. Then they bethought themselves of getting hold of the bagpipes by stealth, and carrying them off while the giant was asleep. But he laid his head upon them, and it was so heavy that men and beasts together could not drag the pipes from under it. So at last they crept up quite softly and bored a tiny hole in the bagpipes. And lo! There arose such a storm that one could not tell earth, or sea or sky apart, and scarcely anything survived of all that the Caraiman had created.

But the giant awoke no more; he is still slumbering, and under his arm are the bagpipes, which sometimes begin to sound, when the storm-wind catches in them, as it hurries down the Prahova valley. If only someone could but mend the bagpipes, then the world would belong to the children once more.

The Serpent-Isle

The great Latin poet Ovid was banished by the emperor of Rome, no one knew why, to a desolate spot near the mouth of the Danube, on the shores of the Black Sea. That land has had many masters, and last of all the Romanians, under King Carol[37], took it from the Turks. Where Ovid once wandered by that lonely shore there is now a grand hotel, where fashionable ladies and officers sit and listen to the music of the band; a large town, too, lies hard by, but in the poet's days only a small collection of miserable huts stood there, which men called the city of Tomi. On one side there was nothing to be seen, as far as the eye could reach, but sand and marshes, where at intervals a solitary tree stretched out its barren boughs over some evil-smelling mere; while on the other the endless sea, black and cheerless, rolled its monotonous waves towards the shore. Snowstorms, unknown to an inhabitant of Rome, swept over the land in winter; and in summer, the sun beat down with scorching heat, setting the brain on fire and parching the tongue. Wells were scarce here, and Ovid learnt to prize a draught of pure water more than he had ever prized the choicest wines in his Roman cellars. The inhabitants of the country were few – dark-skinned men, whose language was strange to him. The only Romans were men whom he would in former days have thought unworthy of his slightest glance or word – thieves, galley slaves, or fraudulent officials. Surely he could never have borne such a life, and must have died of misery, save for one only consolation. Every man must have some such, be it only a dog, a flower, or a spider. Ovid had a snake, a tiny, bewitching snake, that always lay curled about his neck or his arm, and in whose eyes he read the most wondrous tales. To his mind she was very likely the victim of some spell – a banished princess in a serpent's shape – for did he not write the "Metamorphoses"? – and he wove fancies about her by the hour together – of how fair she was in reality, and how unfortunate, his shining little Colubra, as he called her. And as his thoughts wandered thus, and he sat gazing out upon the sea, his eyes would close and he would sink into peaceful sleep.
One day, as he thus slept, he dreamed a strange dream; his little snake had suddenly become possessed of human speech, and was whispering softly

---

[37] King Carol I of Romania ruled from 1866 to 1914. During his reign Romania gained its independence from the Ottoman Empire (when fighting successfully on the Russian side in the Russo-Turkish War, also called the Romanian War of Independence, 1877-1878), and became a kingdom in 1881. Dobrudja (Romanian: Dobrogea) and the Serpent-Isle (or: Snake Island, Romanian: Insula Şerpilor) in the Black Sea became in 1878 a part of Romania as a compensation to the loss of South Bessarabia, which was annexed to the Russian Empire. Today the Snake-Island belongs to the Ukraine.

in his ear: "Come, come with me to the island at the mouth of the Danube – that which they call the Serpent-Isle. There thou shalt witness transformations indeed." He awoke with a start of surprise; but his little snake was lying quite quietly about his neck, as though she had never spoken a word. Again he fell asleep, and again Colubra whispered: "Come to the Serpent-Isle. Come; trust thy little friend." The poet awoke once more and gazed at the little creature that still clung motionless to his throat, and met his eyes with a strange look of comprehension. He slept for the third time, and for the third time Colubra whispered: "Come with me; thou wilt not repent it." But this time he awoke before she had finished speaking, and she gave him so expressive a glance that Ovid thought to himself: "Why should I not go to the Serpent-Isle? It cannot be a more desolate spot than this is; and if the serpents devour me, then there is an end of my pain forever."

So he manned a sailboat with stout rowers, took provisions with him for several days, and set out across the sea. He reached the island, not without trouble, for the Black Sea has its evil moods, far worse than those of the ocean itself. The heartsick poet was in danger of being punished for his desire to be quit of life, for it came near taking him at his word. But the boatmen were less weary of life than he, and fought bravely with the stormy elements, grumbling all the while at the enterprise.

"So much pain and danger for the sake of a desert island full of poisonous reptiles," they would mutter, casting dark glances upon the poet. Several times was he minded to put back, for fear of a mutiny among the crew, but each time a slight movement from the little creature about his throat admonished him to pause. Once or twice he was even aware of an impatient stroke from the slender tail, and the tiny head would be raised aloft, ever gazing in the same direction.

"There is the island," muttered the sailors at last.

"Where?" asked Ovid, for he could see nothing.

"That strip of land there, at the river's mouth, that is the Isle of Serpents."

As he saw the bank of sand covered with stunted bushes, the poet's heart sank, more on account of the men's discontent than because of the uninviting aspect of the place. To his mind the whole country was equally desolate, and whether it were somewhat more or less so was of little moment. But the little snake about his throat began fairly to dance for joy, and the lonely man felt glad of the pleasure he could give to the only creature he loved. As he stepped on shore he felt for her about his neck. What was his amazement at finding nothing there! His little Colubra was gone! Sore at heart, he thought to himself: "So that was why thou wert so fain to reach the island – only to forsake me! Thou art not a human being, yet thy deeds are even as theirs." And, lost in bitter thought, he waded onward through the deep sand, having promised the sailors to go and seek water for them. But the wine to be found on board was far more acceptable to the men, and soon they lay wrapped in a drunken sleep. Ovid went sorrowfully on his way. "Now have I lost my all," he sighed; and since no one saw him, he was not ashamed of the tears that filled his eyes.

Was it the gleam of those tears or the light of the sun that blinded him? Was a midsummer madness upon him? He passed his hand over his brow again and again and closed his eyes; but each time he reopened them his bewilderment increased. For there rose before him a magic garden, with shady trees, undulating lawns, and plashing fountains. A carpet of forget-me-nots and poppies spread out on every side, and the tender petals of the flowers seemed transfused with sunlight. Marble steps led down to the sea, and smooth paths wound in and out among hedges of rose and myrtle. Wondrous birds perched among the planes and chestnut-trees, and poured out a song that no nightingale could rival. Beneath the poet's feet, violets and mignonette gave forth well-nigh too unrestrained a perfume; and sprays of lilac and jessamine caressed his brow. The lonely exile fancied himself transported to one of the fairest gardens of Rome, and his heart beat high with joy, till it seemed ready to burst in his bosom. But what was his delight when he suddenly became aware of a crowd of beautiful maidens, gliding about among the trees and over the smooth turf chasing and embracing one another in the wildest glee, swinging upon the thick, tangled boughs of the hedge-roses, and tripping down the marble stairs to the sea, to bathe, and splash each other with the clear water. He saw, too, Roman matrons clad in long robes and snowy veils, whose faces seemed familiar, and men wearing the toga and mantle, who paced to and fro, as though in eager discussion over the topics of the day, just as of old in the Roman Forum. But before he could draw near them, a lovely maiden hastened up to him with a gesture of familiar greeting and took his hand, saying: "I warrant thou dost not know me in this shape; yet I am thy little Colubra! Come with me and I will show thee all." And she drew him away, through the undulating crowd of people, who were all speaking Latin and Greek, so that he could understand their every word. He seemed to recognize them too, and would fain have accosted many a one by name, for they appeared to him to be courtiers of the emperor, whom he had been wont to see every day. But his little guide clung to his hand with slender, caressing fingers and led him on. He heard around him the names of Greek sculptors or philosophers and Roman statesmen; and though these names might once have been indifferent to him, they now made his heart leap and brought the moisture to his eyes, only because it was so sweet to hear the familiar sounds once more. Several persons approached him with an expression of delighted surprise, but Colubra motioned them all aside with an impatient stamp of her little foot, and if they did not heed, her delicate eyebrows would contract and her dark eyes flash – those eyes which were the only reminder of her serpent nature. Once, however, it is true that she thrust the tip of her rosy tongue between her lips – a little tongue as sharp as though it could prick.

There were very few children to be seen in the magic garden, and those few, the poet noticed, crept sadly about, holding one another by the hand, and gazing with wide-open eyes at this gay, merry world, which seemed quite strange to them. No one spoke to them or took any notice of them, for here each seemed to think of nothing but his own pleasure. Ovid would have given them a kind word, but Colubra drew him past them also, and led him to an arbour hidden among the thick bushes, hard by a bubbling spring. There she fed him with the most luscious fruits, and making a cup out of a broad leaf, she fetched a draught of water for him. Then, swinging herself up on one bough and clasping her white arms round another, she began in triumphant tones: "Now, what dost think of thy little friend?"

"I think thou art lulling me with a faery dream."

"Nay, nay, thou art not dreaming! Thou art on the Serpent-Isle, whither all men are banished who have lied during their lifetime. Once in every thousand years the island grows green, and we can take our own shapes again, and wander in this magic garden. But no living man may look upon us save a poet, and he must be a sorrow-stricken creature; nor must he speak with anyone, for should he utter the smallest lie he would be changed into a serpent for a thousand years. And it will no longer be fair here tomorrow."

"But I can surely speak without lying?"

"Yea, with thy little Colubra, or on the mainland yonder, in Tomi, where thou dost need to ask for naught but bread, water, and wood, and where it avails thee nothing to be gracious or witty, since none would understand thee. But amid this company thou wouldst be tempted to speak as they do, and then I would not stand warranty for thee!"

"But I see statesmen here, high officials, artists and philosophers, matrons who are held in esteem, and even little children."

With a pitying smile she replied: "All these spoke untruths while they lived; and because even in the underworld they and their false tongues are dreaded, they have been sent here on to this island, where they can do no harm, or at least only hiss, and strangle one another. It is saddest of all for the children, because they are such strangers here, and belong to no one, neither are they remembered by any earthly friends. Even this festive day is sad for them, since it makes them feel lonelier than ever. This evening the old boatman, Charon, will sail to the shore of the island, and those who have spoken nothing but the truth during the last thousand years he will suffer to enter his boat, and to journey with him to the underworld. But thou must not await that moment, for then everything will be changed. I, truly, am privileged, for I may stay with thee, and thou art safe on the island, because thou art doing penance enough in thy lifetime."

"But thou – what hast thou done?" asked the poet.

"I?" The maiden blushed, and springing from the bough, answered carelessly: "I suppose I lied like the rest." And she drew him hastily away to join a group of dancing maidens. Yet, with a look round at him, she laid her finger on her lip.

It was high time, for an ancient dame approached Ovid with a friendly grimace and began: "Why, see! Our great poet! Is he too, like us, banished from the earth and the underworld alike? Poor Ovid, art thou thyself metamorphosed? What a trick they have played us clever people, have they not? Were we to blame for being wiser than the rest? And thy sweet companion! I have known and loved her this long, long while."

"Thou liest!" cried Colubra, beside herself.

In the twinkling of an eye the old dame was changed into a huge snake, which darted hissing upon the young girl, coiled round her, and would surely have throttled her, had not Ovid used all his strength to wrestle with the noxious creature, and tearing it off, cast it far away from them. The maiden kissed his hands in a passion of gratitude, and the dancers crowned him with roses and myrtle. Presently a little boy ran up to him and cried in pleading tones: "Take me away with thee! Oh, take me away, and I will be as truthful as the sunbeams and as transparent as the clearest brook. Only take me with thee! I have seen that thou art a hero, and I – I was once a hero too; I was so strong that all my playmates feared to feel my fists!" While he yet spoke a little sharp, forked tongue shot out between his rosy lips, and before the poet's very eyes he was changed into a tiny slow-worm, that wound itself about his feet.

"And canst thou not speak truth for one hour, thou miserable little worm?" cried Colubra angrily. Yet Ovid looked compassionately upon the tiny snake, and did not move for a long time, for fear of hurting it.

But his friend was in haste to draw him from the spot: "Dost thou not see the sun is setting? Methinks I already hear the keel of Charon's boat rushing through the smooth water. Thou must away from here. The reality here is ugly, terribly ugly. Thou shalt only keep the memory of the beautiful dream."

Still Ovid lingered. He plucked blossoms and threw them to the laughing girls; he stood gazing out over the sea that was now bathed in a flood of purple and golden light. But presently, like the very night itself, a ship with dusky sails moved silently towards the shore, spreading darkness around it as it came. The ship was large, but only one boatman stood therein, an old man with snowy beard and sunken eyes. His bony hands held a huge pole, with which he steered the ship, till he brought its keel grating upon the shore. Now he raised his pole aloft, so that the trickling water-drops shone like pure gold in the last rays of sunshine.

"Come," whispered Colubra, growing pale. But Ovid stood as though spellbound. Charon raised his pole again and smote it against the trees with a sound like thunder. Then, behold, all the forms that moved upon the island pressed toward the ship and held out imploring hands. But Charon asked in deep, dread tones: "Who hath spoken the truth these thousand years?"

"I! I!" came the answer from every side: but all who spoke the word were instantly changed into serpents.

"I," cried a wondrously beautiful woman, forcing her way through the mass of writhing reptiles, her white veil shining as it floated in the twilight air. "I have kept silence for a thousand years, that I might rejoin my seven children in the Elysian fields. I will go to my children!" And with this cry she sped over the sand into the ship.

"I," said Colubra quite low.

"Thou?" asked Ovid sadly. "Then must I lose thee?"

Colubra looked at the poet and then at the ship.

"If I could but remain a maiden, I would love thee only, and belong to no other."

"O Colubra, thou liest! Keep silence!"

But he had scarcely spoken the words ere she was changed into the same little snake as of old.

Now the keel grated on the sand once again and Charon pushed off from the shore. And lo! The trees came crashing down, the flowers turned to dust, and the grass withered; while far, far away Charon's white beard and the woman's waving white veil shone out in the moonlight. But upon the sandy shore and among the stunted, thorny bushes only the smooth, gleaming serpent-forms crawled and writhed. Then horror fell upon Ovid, and he hastened towards his own boat. With the cry of "Serpents!" he awakened the sleeping men, who rubbed their eyes, muttering discontentedly: "For this we came hither, then to see serpents!" – "Away now, away!" cried Ovid, who, for the horror that was upon him, had well-nigh forgotten his little friend. But as they were pushing off he remembered her, and called aloud: "Colubra! My faithful little Colubra!" Then a faint, very faint sound of laughter smote his ear, and something wound itself caressingly about his neck, and two eyes gazed steadily up into his in the clear moonlight. The sailors thought their master had taken leave of his wits, for he spoke no more, save to murmur from time to time: "A thousand years! And for me!" while he stroked something which shone round his throat, and which they took to be a jewel. But, laughing softly once more, Colubra hissed into his ear: "Be not over vain, my soft-hearted poet. Not for thee alone did I give way to lying. For I found my lost lover again, yonder among the serpents, and a serpent he must remain. Yea – and I will remain even as my beloved is, until we can belong to one another."

Since that day the Serpent-Isle has been green and lovely once again, and only once, but no one was there to see it. Ah, if one could but be a poet, and alive in the year 2000!

Râul Doamnei (The River of the Princess)

Not far from the pretty little mountain-town of Câmpulung, a clear, cool stream winds along, called Râul Doamnei – "the River of the Princess". This stream washes down gold along its bed, sometimes a bit half the size of one's nail; and it was a custom in times gone by that all the gold found there should belong to the princess, the wife of the ruler of the land. And this is the reason why:

There was once a great famine in the land of Romania, such a famine as had never been known in the memory of man. First the locusts had come into the land, in such swarms that the sun was darkened; and wherever they settled they devastated everything, so that in a few minutes the fairest field of corn would be left bald as a threshing-floor, and the trees, stripped of every leaf, stretched out their naked boughs against the summer sky, beneath whose cloudless blue the heat grew ever greater and greater, so that even at night there was no longer a breath of coolness in the air. As soon as all things around were devoured, the cloud of locusts would arise, only to settle instantly again upon the next green patch. And so it went on unceasingly; and in those days folk were not so clever as they are now, when they cover the great stretches of land where the insects have settled, with petroleum, and set it all on fire. Nor were there then any cannon with which they could shoot into the swarm of flying locusts, as they do now, and so sometimes contrive to scatter them.

After the locusts came the Poles from the North, the Hungarians from the West, and the Turks from the South, and fell upon the land, and by them all the houses were burnt and the cattle stolen away. At last these foes, too, quitted the country, but they left behind them fever and pestilence, both among man and beast. Men went about with blackened lips, and grievous sores on their bodies. The cattle perished together in heaps on the barren fields, where not a single blade of grass was standing. Only the dogs and the ravens were in good case; they tore the flesh from the bones of the dead creatures, and for miles around nothing was to be seen but white bones with red flesh hanging to them, and millions of flies, that shone with gorgeous prismatic colors, settling upon them. The air quivered with heat, and pestilential odors spread far over the land, so that men were stricken as with a plague, and died in a few hours. Complaints were heard no longer, for dull despair had reduced all men to silence; and when the starving people tore one another to pieces, no one even told of it. The bells rang no more; there was no keeping Sundays or holidays, nor was there any work done, for no one had any oxen for the ploughing, or any seeds to sow. Men crept about like ghosts, with their bones staring through the skin, their lips drawn back so that the teeth lay bare, and only a few rags upon their bodies. There was hardly anyone found to bury the dead, and many remained lying, like the cattle, upon the fields.

The beautiful Princess Irina felt her heart breaking for pity. She had given away all her jewels for the poor; she had spent her last coin to buy cattle for the peasants, but they had all been slain by the plague as soon as purchased. She had fed the hungry, till she had scarcely enough left to feed her own four little children. She stood at her window wringing her hands in despair, and prayed thus: "O good God! Hast Thou, then, quite forsaken me? Wilt Thou bring our poor land to destruction? Have we sinned yet more, that we must endure such searchings-out of Thy wrath?"

Then a soft, cool breath stole in, bearing a perfume as from the most beautiful of gardens, and a silvery voice spoke: "Help shall arise for thee out of a river. Only seek."

Then she went to the prince, her husband, and to her children, and bade them farewell, promising soon to return, and saying she now knew where to seek for that which should free them all from their misery. She spoke with such cheerful assurance that it brought trust and hope to every man, for she never told them that she did not even know what she was to seek. Then, through the burning summer heat, she began a weary pilgrimage toward the rivers. Sometimes she would still chance upon a poor, starved little horse, that would carry her a short distance, and then fall down dead, even beneath her light weight. She went up the Olt river, the Jiu, the Buzau, the Siret, all the rivers, both great and small. They flowed but meagerly over their stony beds, and those once mighty waters scarcely whispered as they went, they that of old were wont to rush and roar.

"Merciful God!" prayed the princess, "let but a little cloud appear when I have found the river that is to help us!" But there arose no cloud. She was wandering for a second time up the banks of the Arges, and was just about to turn sadly back, when she caught sight of the mouth of a little stream that she had not noticed before. She turned her steps hesitatingly in that direction, her heart growing heavier and heavier as she saw the stream grow smaller and more insignificant. Wearied by her hard journey over the stones, she stood still a moment and sighed: "I can find nothing, nothing at all, and perchance my children are starving and dying! Perhaps my thought was but a foolish one – a cobweb of the brain, a lying fancy!"

Even as she spoke a shadow seemed to fall upon her. She thought it was only caused by the tears which for the first time were filling her large, wan eyes. She wiped them off. Nay, there was indeed a shadow lying over the treeless waste, and when she raised her eyes, lo! The sun had hidden itself behind a tiny cloud that yet was growing slowly larger. Irina began to tremble for joy, that yet was mingled with dread. Had God heard her, or was it only another mistake? "Dear God," she prayed again, "if this be the river, suffer the cloud to become larger and the rain to fall, for rain alone would be a blessing, and a great help to us in our need." She went on a little – yes, the cloud was growing larger; she hurried forward, she ran, till she grew too weak to go farther; then a few great, heavy drops began to fall. She drank them in, with lips and eyes, with hands and hair. Now a light patter and plashing began round about her, and all at once, a perfect waterspout broke forth. She struggled on in the wet loam of the river-bed as well as she could, till the stream began to swell, and dashed by in a brown, foaming flood, like a broad river. Sometimes she was forced to stand still and seek for her path, but yet she went on and on, for fear the rain should leave off. It rained all day and all night. The princess was so wet that a stream flowed from her garments. But she wrung them out, girt them up higher, and still went on, for one whole day and night longer. Now she had reached the mountains, and often fell to the ground from exhaustion after her long journey. At last she lay down upon the riverbank and fell asleep, while the rain streamed down upon her, and the river rose higher and higher, as though it would have snatched her down and floated her away.

She awoke trembling with cold. There stood the gleaming sun, looking as fresh in the bright morning air as if he had had a bath himself. And behold! The river was no longer brown, but clear and blue as the air, and at the bottom of the water something shone and glittered like the sunbeams themselves. Irina again girt up her garments and waded in – she must see what it was that shone with so wondrous a gleam. And lo! It was pure gold. She fell on her knees, there in the stream, and gave God thanks, aloud and earnestly. Gold! Gold! Now she could help! She went carefully on through the water and gathered up the golden grains and little fragments, filling her mantle with them, till the burden was almost too heavy for her. And now she hurried home with her treasure, and poured it out before her husband. Her children were yet alive, though weak and sorely exhausted; and they scarcely knew her again, she was so emaciated and sunburnt. Yet now messengers went forth into distant lands and bought corn, maize and hay, seeds and cattle; and the river never grew weary of giving till the famine was at an end, and laughing green, and sleek cattle, covered the Romanian meadows once more. And the thankful people called the river *Râul Doamnei*, and no one was to touch any of the gold therein, to possess it, save the princess of the land.

But the princesses who came after this one, no doubt made a less good use of their riches, for the river has become more niggardly, and the gold that the peasants still find in it now and then, is saved up for exhibition in the State Museum.

The Story of a Helpful Queen

Once upon a time, there lived a good queen. She would fain have assuaged all the suffering she saw on earth, but the more good she did, the more distress seemed to increase. Her means were inadequate to help the poor, her words proved unequal to the task of freeing those in sorrow from their grief, and her hands were unable to bring healing to the sick. Then the thought occurred to her that it must be impossible that God should have intended the world to be so full of misery; she felt that mankind was destined to be happy, if only it knew how.

One day she entered a church and prayed to God with an intensity the full strength of which she was unable to realize at the time. She prayed – as many other foolish mortals pray, who do not know what it would mean to them if their prayers were granted – she prayed: "Oh, Lord! Let me he able to bring happiness to those that suffer, even if I must take their burden upon myself." She left the church with an anxious heart, wondering whether God had heard her prayer; for sometimes God does not seem to hear us when we pray. But on the very same day it was made clear to her that her prayer had been heard.

She met a boy being wheeled in his sick chair, who had never been able to walk a step in his life. She had known him for long, and he loved the good queen with all the strength of his soul. As was her habit, she went up to him, took his thin hand in hers, and spoke to him in her melodious voice of his early recovery. The boy's eyes seemed to grow larger as she spoke. She felt as if his glance drew all the strength from within her; she was suddenly overtaken by a sense of fatigue such as she had never known before. And, all at once, the boy rose up straight from his couch and said, as if in a dream: "I think I can walk." Then he got on his feet and stepped out as though he had never been lame in his life.

The queen smiled sadly at the sight of his gladness. She went home and lay many weeks in bed suffering from lameness. Her limbs were as though they had perished. Still, she declined the help of the doctor, and said that in due time God would take her suffering from her. And so it was. Henceforth she suffered from one illness after the other; she became blind, deaf, mute, and fell into high fever; but only to emerge younger and more beautiful – glorified, as it were, by every trial through which she passed. Nobody ever heard her utter a word of complaint. Her miraculous powers for healing the sick became known far and wide, although she never spoke of them, and people thronged around her and besought her to relieve their sufferings, without having an idea of the sacrifice it involved for her. It was only rumored that the queen exposed herself to all kinds of infection, and would take no precautions against them, particularly where children were concerned. Her poverty soon became equal to her other trials.

She was ingenious in procuring work for others, but she herself had long since had nothing left to give. She was forced to begrudge herself the smallest luxury, for she was bereft of every means for procuring it. And although her devoted husband often assisted her from his own, yet she fell at last into the same plight as Saint Elizabeth of old – she had scarcely a gown left to cover her. And still her name was blessed a thousand times. People came to her from far and near. They tried to grasp her hand, to catch a glance from her eyes, the splendid radiance of which soothed all those who looked into them. She spread an atmosphere of peace and happiness around her, and even those gained joyful contentment who had been most ungodly. Nobody could resist the placid influence, which emanated from her person.

But what was harder to bear than all were the dark hours of misconception, when she had been the means of fostering peace and was only requited by the slander of evil tongues in her own home. This almost made her forget that it was all part and parcel of the blessings, which her miraculous gift had vouchsafed her. She wept in silence. But soon the clouds lifted again and she realized that she was ordained to take the spiritual sufferings of others upon herself. From that moment her patience became inexhaustible. And people forgot that they had ill-treated her, and fancied that they had always venerated her, and never misunderstood or maligned her. She smiled sadly as she thought of all this in her solitude. One glance from her had enabled them to forget the past.

It was a remarkable experience to her to have to suffer the pangs of repentance of a guilty conscience, as if she herself had committed some great crime. This was the result of bringing back to the right road one who had fallen away under great temptation. This was, indeed, hard to bear; for she knew herself to be free from guilt or blame, and yet her poor heart beat day and night in mortal anguish. At times she was conscious that this could only be a transitory state of mind of hers, like all the others she had passed through; but her sufferings were great, indeed.

One day she was visited by a poor woman. "Oh, dear, gracious queen," she cried, "my only son is dying! And I know that you possess miraculous herbs which can effect a cure in cases where no mortal can afford help!"

Without hesitation the queen hurried to the bedside of the gasping youth. He opened his eyes, which were already nearly closed, and looked at the queen; and that one glance rekindled the dying flame of life. Breath returned to him; the pallid, cold lips grew red and warm, and the grateful mother sank down before the queen, embracing her feet, and then fondling her son who was saved.

On her return home the queen did not feel so weary as usual, and yet she fully expected to be struck down by a severe illness, if not, indeed, by death. But what was her agony when, the very next day, her only child fell seriously ill and appeared to be hurrying towards certain death.

"O, Lord! O, Lord!" she cried, "do not ask this sacrifice of me, for it is beyond my strength."

But her supplications were in vain. In vain was her experienced nursing. The glance of her eyes had lost its power here. The child did not look up again, and only murmured at times of beautiful angels and flowers, until at last it lay pale and cold in her arms – and she a broken woman, bereft of tears, without strength to utter a moan, utterly consumed with grief. Henceforth her miraculous power seemed to have deserted her.

People said she had lost faith in her mysterious herbs. Dark days, indeed, were in store for the poor queen. She cursed herself and her prayers. She said to herself that it was her fault that the husband she adored was now as unhappy as she was herself. The world seemed to her to be dark indeed. She only saw night around her; no sunrise, no lovely trees, and no heavenly justice; naught of all that which in other days had gladdened her heart. She who had never complained before, so long as she thought she could relieve others from their suffering, now thought heaven to be cruel, and she no longer possessed the strength to rejoice with the mother whose child she had saved from impending death. For the first time for many a day, during which she had been ceaselessly racked by anguish and doubt, she fell asleep.

And it seemed to her that the door opened, and her child came towards her, happy and radiant. He sat down by her bedside and took her hand, and the dull heaviness of pain was lifted from her heart. He breathed with a breath as of violets, and joy possessed her. He spoke to her with the voice of a clear and resonant bell: "Mother, weep not! You have given me a greater happiness than is known on earth – even through the sublimity of love; for you have opened up the heavens to me, and I have been permitted to return there without pain and sorrow – thanks to your self-sacrifice. Mother, weep not! I am ever near you. You were guilty of a pious error when you undertook to banish all suffering from the world, and this error you had to atone for in sorrow and ashes. For the world is exactly as God ordains that it should be – a mine, a furnace, a crucible – a brief passage from one existence unto another, which is higher or meaner, in accordance with the life we have practiced on earth. Be patient, mother – your hour of release is near, and I am always by your side, with all my fervor and strength. You can still console others, because you believe in the world to come – yes, because you know for certain that it awaits us all. There is no such thing as death! There is only a re-birth. And if – oh, mother! – you only knew how beautiful it is, you would await it radiant with joy, and never sigh again! It is necessary that poverty, sickness, injustice, and war should exist; for these are means of purification, of mutual help and mercy. Therefore are all those blessed who help them that suffer with all their strength, with all self-sacrifice staking all they have to give. But they cannot make this world a paradise; that is not permitted to them. For the world is, indeed, a laboratory, which, according to worldly conceits, we call hell or purgatory."

Here the queen awoke, and from that hour peace entered into her soul. She was able to do good, to console and to give pleasure to others, but no longer to cure them! And she no longer asked for power to do these things, for she was quiet and content, and peace reigned around her.

My Kaleidoscope

I write a great deal during the night, and in summer I always leave the door wide open on to my balcony so that the moon and stars may shine in, and I can see the tall fir-trees standing out black against the sky, like giant sentries ranged around the castle – a screen protecting it from the outside world. Down below I hear the river Pelesh rippling, and the fountains in the courts and on the terraces splashing the whole night long, and then the fairies come to see me – the fairy with the glossy white hair and the white spindle, and the Fairy Imagina, and all the fairies from the trees, and out of the flowers, which are all fast asleep, under the weight of dew that bows their little heads down almost to the ground.

I always keep a bright light burning to welcome my visitors. I am fond of having my rooms well lighted. It is an encouragement to cheerful thoughts, and then also it is more likely to attract the fairies. I often wander out on to the balcony and pace up and down, and if the sentinel looks up and sees me he must take me for one of my own fairy visitors, and wonder if he ought to salute or not. For it would never occur to him that people who live in a castle, and have good beds to sleep in, could get up at two or three in the morning to please themselves! He does not know that that is the very best hour for the fairies, for they only tell their stories when everything sleeps, and in the evening there are always some people awake, but towards early morn everyone is asleep – only the moon and stars still keep watch, shining very brilliantly.

One morning the fairy with the white hair entered my room, holding something in her hand.

"I have brought you something," she said, smiling, "into which you have only to look, and you will behold most wonderful scenes from real life. It is a fairy kaleidoscope, such as human beings never have been able to manufacture. They make theirs of little bits of colored glass and amuse themselves with the different arrangements of color they produce, but we put very different things into ours, and from the way they come together and arrange themselves, we are able to see the whole world in our kaleidoscope!"

I thanked the fairy for her charming gift, but I did not thank her enough, for I did not yet know all the pleasure it would give me. When I first looked into it, I perceived only a confused scene resembling an anthill; there were little specks running about, some in one direction – some in another. I took it away from my eyes and looked at the fairy inquiringly. She smiled.

"Can you make nothing of it?" she asked.

"No, I cannot at all understand what the turmoil means."

"Look a little longer, and you will see what it is."

And after a little time I distinguished a town, in which human beings were rushing to and fro in the utmost haste, and soon I recognized that it was London. There was Westminster Abbey, and there were the carriages and riders in the Row, and the Thames with all its shipping, and the poor quarter, with all its nameless misery. Just then, however, I moved and involuntarily I gave the instrument a little turn, and behold I was standing before Vesuvius in eruption. Suddenly such a burning flood of lava came streaming down that I shuddered and turned the kaleidoscope again, glad to escape from the terrible scene. Next I found myself in a land in which the people were all graceful and pleasant; lively, without being hurried in their movements. I knew that I could only be among the Japanese. Now full of curiosity I turned again, and this time I was at the exhibition in Chicago, but that was such a crowd, with so much hurry and bustle, I felt quite dizzy and tired, and put the fairy toy down for a moment to rest myself.

"Now what do you say to my present?" said the fairy. "Are you pleased with it?"

"Yes," I replied, "I like it very much, but you could have given me much more pleasure still with a kaleidoscope that would let me look into human hearts. The traffic in the streets has but little interest for me. I can easily imagine that for myself, but I should like to see what people think and feel, so that I might comfort them when they are unhappy, and find out the kindest words to say to them to give them pleasure."

The fairy laughed. "You shall have that too," she said. "I like your frankness. One shows you the whole world, and you are not yet satisfied."

"What is the whole world in comparison with a single human heart? I have very little curiosity about the affairs of men, and have no wish to make descriptions of travel. But that which men think and feel is what I wish to know and to be able to describe, and since they shut their lips and do not let their eyes speak for them, how can I tell what goes on within them? I want to see their inmost thoughts as if no skull were there, no bolts, no mystery at all."

"Alas!" said the fairy, "you will often see things that will grieve you."

As she spoke the fairy gave another turn, and then I saw something I had never seen in my life before – the thoughts of other people displayed before me in a series of pictures. It was so marvelous I almost shouted in sheer astonishment. It was infinitely richer than the busy movement of the crowded streets. One heart I looked into was that of a child who was envious of her little playfellow, and had all the toys and playthings of the other little one stored up in her heart. But none of these things looked quite so beautiful as in reality, for a black veil was thrown over them which rather spoiled them. There was a doll's house that was, oh! so lovely; with so many rooms, and cellar and pantry, and water-pipes with real water, and lamps alight everywhere, and a kitchen with a real stove, at which a real dinner was being cooked, and such pretty dolls, just like real children, to live in the house. It was all charming if it had not been spoiled by the horrid dark veil. The child knew these things were not its own, and could therefore take no pleasure in them. I looked next into the heart of the child to whom the toys belonged, and saw that her pleasure in her new present was also spoiled by the thought of her little friend's envy. This one was a dear little child who could not bear to see her companion unhappy, and all the time she was tormenting herself with the thought that she ought perhaps to give the other her doll's house. It was a long struggle, but I did not tire of looking into this little heart that had no dark gloomy corners, but was all bright and warm and loving, and at last the generous impulse prevailed, and she said to the other: "Take my pretty doll's house; it shall be yours now, only let me play with it too, whenever I want to."

"No," replied the envious child, "I want to have it all to myself. I do not care to share things."

"Then you will not have it at all." And a dark shadow fell over the heart that had so far been all sunshine, and the poor little girl was quite sad, for she could not understand such selfishness – she had rejoiced so in the thought of the happiness she could give, but now that the other should wish to take her beautiful plaything away from her altogether, that seemed too unjust, for, after all, the doll's house had been given to her.

I was very sorry for the poor child, but the next little heart I peeped into made me sadder still. It was that of a boy who had a sick mother, and the poor little fellow loved her so passionately there was no room in his heart for any other thought. The image of the pale suffering mother filled it entirely, and my own heart ached to see his sadness. Indeed, I very soon became aware of one very decided drawback to my wonderful gift, and that was that I could now read hearts without being able to help them, since very often they were too far off for me to reach; sometimes I did not even know where they were to be found, so that I could not possibly do anything to help or comfort, and this made me quite melancholy, as I had not thought of such a contingency.

So I sat in my room with the magic kaleidoscope in my lap, not caring to put it to my eyes, as it revealed so much misery which I could not take away – so much unhappiness, where I could be of no service, and even close around me I beheld faults which I would rather not have known. Each time I looked, I saw something that distressed me, and at last I made up my mind that I would look no more.

But that same night Fairy Imagina floated into my room upon a moonbeam, and said: "I see that you do not value my sister's gift as you should. You wanted to see into the hearts of men as they lay before you. We have given you the means of satisfying your wish, and already you have laid it aside, and do not use it any longer. Is that right?"

I felt quite ashamed as I explained to the fairy: "I should never tire of using it, if I could only do some good afterwards. Then I should continually consult it."

"But you forget that even we fairies cannot always help those in need! What then can you hope to do who are only a poor mortal?"

"Only as much as may be permitted me. But I do not wish to witness sufferings which I may not relieve!"

"Well," said the fairy, "I will help you this much: I will lend the kaleidoscope the power to send a bright warm ray, full of hope and comfort, in any direction where you see misery, which you earnestly desire to relieve. More than that I cannot grant. Will that content you?"

I thanked the fairy, but had no very great confidence in the effect of the magic ray. I had too frequently seen how often the sun itself fails to content the people, sending too much warmth and brightness to suit some, too little to satisfy others.

When next I tried my new present again, I saw an awful scene. A great flood was sweeping through a village, and I saw multitudes of poor people into whose houses the water was streaming, and threatened every moment to carry away. The poor things climbed on to the roofs and wrung their hands in despair – no boat was to be seen. Then, with the strength of my whole heart and soul, I prayed: "Let the inundation subside!" And, wonderful to relate, in another moment the water had begun to flow on, and soon the little huts and cottages lay high and dry in the sunshine. I was overjoyed and all the more delighted when I saw the thankfulness of the people at their escape, and how they thought heaven had worked a miracle to save them. In my glad surprise I gave the kaleidoscope a little twist without noticing, and the scene had vanished before I knew where it had taken place. Instead I saw a little girl, sitting by the wayside, crying bitterly and trembling with cold, looking eagerly for something, which she evidently could not find in the growing darkness. I put all my power of wishing into the ray I directed on the spot to help her, and it seemed as if the working of the charm depended on the depth of my compassion, for the more earnestly I desired to help the warmer and brighter grew the ray. The child looked about in astonishment for the cause of this sudden and extraordinary brightness, and then resumed her search. Soon by the aid of that bright light she found the penny she had lost, and ran jumping for joy to a cottage close at hand. The bright light from the kaleidoscope fell on her little form, warming and gladdening her, and by it I could also see a cross and careworn-looking woman standing in the doorway to await the child, apparently prepared to scold her. But her angry look changed when she saw the little one hold up the piece of money, and when the child pointed out the beautiful glowing light, and drew her gently into it, she seemed at last quite softened, and smiled and patted the little cheek. So they went into the cottage together, hand in hand.

Now the fairy gift really came up to my expectations. I was so astonished at its power that I began to wonder if even now I had discovered the whole extent of the power possessed by the fairy's present, and I asked her one day if it would be possible for me to take a peep through it into Fairyland itself.

"Certainly," she replied, "whenever you are tired of the world, then you may always refresh your soul with a peep into my Wonderland."

How can I describe what I saw there? What is there in this dull world of ours to compare with the Fairy-world? In a twinkling I beheld glorious gardens where the loveliest flowers blossomed, each of which was the home of a little elf – a lovely little being that rocked itself in the heart of the flower, or floated about in the air, or bathed in streamlets of crystal dew, or swung itself in the spider's webs, or, taking hands with its companions formed a joyous circle. It was wonderful to see the graceful little creatures winding in and out among the flowers, then suddenly bounding from the earth and dispersing in all directions on the breeze, looking like winged seeds driven hither and thither by the wind. Love and peace and goodwill reigned perpetually in these regions. The elves were clothed in transparent raiment of the color of the blossoms in which they lived, so that the rose-elves wore pink, and the elf of the forget-me-not blue, and those that came out of the autumn crocus mauve, and all the dwellers in the grasses green. I could never tire of watching them, all these colors were such a treat for my eyes. All at once I saw how the good fairy summoned the little flower-elves around her, while she gave them instructions. A moment later they were hurrying away in all directions. I watched them through my magic glass, and I saw some fly down to earth and enter the gardens of human beings to tend all the flowers that seemed to be suffering from neglect or from any other cause. And the plants and blossoms that looked most parched and withered revived as the fairy gardeners passed along. Some of the elves flew across the meadows, lifting up the drooping heads of the daisies, the buttercups and harebells, which careless children had trodden down in the grass. The flowers evidently told their little friends the story of their wrongs, for the elves often shed pitying tears, which fell into the flower-cups, refreshing them, and the tender caressing touch of the fairy fingers completed the cure. But some of the poor little flowers were past help, they could not summon up strength to raise themselves again on their stalks, so the elves smoothed them out gently and turned sadly away.

Some of the bigger elves had the task of looking after the trees, and they too had much to complain of, owing to the carelessness of human beings, for too often picnic-parties lighted their fires so near the trunk of some fine old tree that it would catch on fire also, and the fairies had much trouble to stop the blaze. Generally, the poor tree was all black and charred after-wards, and the elves were sad to see the mischief they could not prevent, caused by the thoughtlessness of men. It was almost more than I, too, could bear, so I turned the kaleidoscope quickly, to escape the horrid sight.

The next scene was no longer in Fairyland, but it was nevertheless a most pleasing sight. I beheld a little colony of beautiful houses built for workmen by their employer. All were clean and neat and well kept, and the occupants were so smiling and contented that it was almost like Fairyland. In the midst of the village stood a great hall where grand concerts were held weekly, and where the men could rest at the end of the day's work. There were schools and kindergartens for the children, and the young daughters of the factory owner often came to teach the little ones, or play with them and tell them stories. It was exactly like one big happy family, and the scene greatly encouraged me after the unhappy sights I had witnessed in so many countries, where the men looked overworked and discontented, and their wives sad and pale, with poor sickly children. Of course I could never hear what was said, but I could see so clearly in my kaleidoscope that I could follow every movement and gesture, and could generally understand all that took place.

One night the kaleidoscope showed me a poor woman watching by the bedside of her sick child. It was a miserable little room, without fire or light, and at first I could hardly distinguish the two figures – the poor mother leaning her head in her hand and straining her ears to catch the fitful breathing of the little sufferer, who tossed feverishly on the wretched truckle-bed. Every time a restless movement of the child threw off the thin patched blankets, the woman drew them over the little limbs again in anxious haste. She might well dread the effect of that icy temperature, in which she herself sat shivering, on her child in its state of high fever. At once I bethought me of the fairy's gift.

"Here at least I can be of some use," I thought, and at once put all the warmth of the compassion I felt into the ray I directed on to the bed. The charm worked instantaneously. An expression of happiness and comfort came over the poor little face, while the child stretched its arms towards the light, smiling at the stray sunbeam that danced before its eyes. Soon, to my great joy, the eyes closed and the child sank into a refreshing slumber. The anxious lines on the mother's wan face now relaxed, for she knew that sleep was the best restorer, and that this might be the turning point in her darling's illness. Gradually she also yielded to the pleasant sensation of unaccustomed warmth. Her head sank forward on the bed, and in a few minutes she too was asleep. But I knew that warmth was not the only necessity, that food also would be required for the little invalid and the mother. I glanced round the room. There was not a trace of anything to eat. What could be done? Food must be there for them when they awoke. But was it not beyond the power of my kaleidoscope to procure it? I turned it a little and saw a baker's shop in the street below, with all sorts of cakes and fancy bread in the window. Just inside the glass door stood a dear little girl, prettily dressed, choosing a number of these. Her nurse was beside her with a big basket on her arm, into which they put the hot cakes and rolls that were evidently meant for a children's party. I turned the light from my magic glass full on them as they left the shop, and the little girl, enchanted, began to dance in the wonderful ray. Then I put all the brightest colors of the kaleidoscope into it, and made it dance before her eyes, drawing her on until she reached the door of the house where the poor mother and child were fast asleep. The nurse followed her, trying in vain to stop her, but the child could think of nothing but this beautiful changing light that seemed to be always just in front of her steps, tantalizing her. In this manner I led her inside the house and right up the narrow dingy staircase until she had reached the room where the sick child had just awakened. The poor mother was bending in rapture over her little one, who had been saved by that refreshing sleep. But a new suffering was about to make itself felt, for the child was hungry and inclined to cry for food, and the mother had none to give it. At this moment the magic ray shone in once more through the open door, and like another ray of sunshine the little girl burst into the room. I sent the light full on the bed, on to the sick child and on to the poor pale mother, and their wasted features told their own story. Quickly the little girl called to the nurse, who was already on the stairs, and in a moment the contents of the basket were handed to the two poor hungry ones. I saw also how the nurse ran quickly downstairs and brought up a can of warm new milk, from which the sick child and mother drank eagerly. I saw also how before the little girl went away she had the nurse write something down, and I knew that it was the poor woman's name and address, and that she would be well cared for hereafter.

These were only a few of the marvelous deeds wrought by the aid of the kaleidoscope. In my heart I continually thanked the good fairy, who had given me so many opportunities of making myself useful, and helping those who were in trouble. It was certainly not as much as I could have wished to do, but I could not assist all of those in need, even if I had sat all day and night at my kaleidoscope. As it was, the bright light of the magic instrument weakened my eyes by its constant use, and I should surely have become blind in course of time, had not the fairy observed this and taken her magic gift away from me. This made me unhappy, but the fairy said: "Your eyesight is required for yourself and for those about you; for their sake you must not endanger it. It is unjust towards those who are close at hand if your thoughts and eyes are always straying so far away from them. Even in this narrow circle there is more to be done than you can accomplish during the rest of your life. And there are many ways of helping the poor. You must work with them and show them how to work for themselves to raise themselves above the wretchedness of their condition."

So I tried to do what the fairy had pointed out, establishing all sorts of working societies, setting up soup kitchens and other charitable organizations. They were all very well, and they did much good in their way, but they had not the charm of my dear kaleidoscope, nor did they work so quickly.

And when I look out on the terrace where the fountain is playing, and see the sunbeams turned perpetually into rainbow colors as they are caught in it, then I am reminded of the wonderful gift I once possessed, and I think with a sigh of the lovely colors that went forth from it, and I wish that some enchantment again were mine that would enable me to rejoice so many hearts.

"Stand! Who Goes There?"

It was on the cold, dark, rainy night that followed the bloody battle of Grivitza. King Carol and his little army had together performed prodigies of valor. Three times the gallant rifle corps of Chasseurs and Dorobantzi had been repulsed by the deadly fire that poured down from the walls of Plevna. Unmoved under the heavy rain of bullets, the king kept his stand calmly, in the center of the battle, and his eagle eye never wavered, and his features were as impassive as if carved in marble. But when for the third time he saw his troops repulsed, leaving half their number on the field – two thousand of them already laid there – then the tears streamed down his cheeks. But his voice rang out loud and clear as he stopped the retreating column, exclaiming: "Where are you going? There lies the enemy!"

"Alas! So many have fallen! There are none left for a fresh attack!"

"How? None left? And you who speak? And he who comes hither? There are two of you! And here is a third! And yonder come others, four, five, six, seven, eight, nine, ten! Return, I say! The redoubt *must* be taken, I tell you! Forward! March!"

Thus did he collect his scattered forces and formed their ranks, and himself led them back into the thick of the fight. And the redoubt was taken, and what is more, the Romanians held it during the night, in spite of all the efforts of the Turks to drive them from it. From his tent the king listened to the shots that told a new attack was being made, and anxiously he asked himself how his young, untried army would hold out after the hard fighting of the day, that had thinned their ranks so cruelly. He had seen, also, that the redoubt of Grivitza was not Plevna itself; that a valley still lay between the fort and the beleaguered stronghold. His heart was heavy and full of care, and sleep would not come to him. Not a morsel had passed his lips that day, for he shared every privation with his soldiers. Many nights it had snowed so hard upon his camp bedstead, and the wind had blown with such violence that he had been compelled to place a little iron camp-stool across his feet, to prevent his cloak from being blown off.

Tonight before his tent a young soldier stood sentry, very ill-pleased at having to remain there while his comrades were engaged in action. Here was a fine opportunity gone in which he might have displayed his courage and have won for himself St. George's Cross, or the Virtutea Militara. He did not consider that he might have been among those who strewed the battlefield, the moaning of some of whom was more terrible than the silence of the rest as they lay there with their white faces calling heaven to witness how bravely they had fought. They had fought like lions indeed, but as they said themselves, their shots had all been directed against stone walls, while from behind these walls the Turks had living targets – human flesh and blood – to aim at. But of all that Stan did not think; he only thought how pleased his pretty sweetheart would have been to see him return home wearing the cross upon his breast. He could not know that the taking of Grivitza by no means meant the taking of Plevna. He little thought how many long and weary nights he would still spend in the trenches standing on sentry duty, with his feet half-frozen, before the fall of the town itself. He was all eagerness, all attention to the sounds that came over continuously from the fort, the almost incessant cannonade and the sharp volleys of musketry that seemed nevertheless always to keep the same distance, neither approaching nor going further off. Stan knew as well as the king himself that should the Turks succeed in forcing the lines they would be close upon the tent, and there would be small chance of protecting it. In that case, however, it mattered little to the king what became of his own person, for he could not afford to return home defeated. For him there was only the choice between victory and death, since if vanquished, Romania would have ceased to exist.

Suddenly the sentinel heard a step approaching, the tread of a tall powerful man, who the next moment stood before him. Except in very old pictures, Stan had never seen the uniform the stranger wore. It was not Russian, neither was it Cossack or Turkish. He was covered with a long blue cloak with gold cord, red breeches, and high yellow boots. A strange looking sword, neither rapier nor broadsword, hung at his side. The soldier knew not what to think of the remarkable looking man who stood before him, but after a momentary, involuntary hesitation he lowered his bayonet with the challenge: "Stand! Who goes there?"

"A Romanian," came the answer in a hollow voice.

"Do you know the password?"

"I know it."

"Romania," gave the soldier.

"Stephen the Great," answered the mysterious stranger without a trace of hesitation.

At that the sentinel stepped back, mechanically presenting arms, and the stranger raised his hand graciously in acknowledgment, with an imperious gesture, as of one accustomed always to be saluted thus.

"Is the prince awake?" he asked, preparing to enter the tent.

"He is, your Highness."

"Why do you call me Highness? Do you know me, then?"

"I could swear," the soldier stammered out; "I know you as I know my prayer-book – as I know the holy pictures on the wall, the cross in church. I could swear as truly as I stand here that you are Stephen the Great himself."

The stranger laid his hand on the young man's shoulder: "I knew that you would recognize me."

A thrill of pride and joy ran like fire through the soldier's veins, and he felt as if he could himself accomplish the most heroic exploits, for the hero's touch seemed to rest on him like a benediction lifting him above himself. He could not speak, his heart was so full. The other continued: "I am here to lead you Romanians to victory as I have done so often before. Whenever you see me stand beside your king upon the battle-field, then be sure that no harm will come to him, and that you will be victorious." And with these words Stephen passed into the tent. The sentinel stood gazing after him. Before his simple soul pictures out of his country's past seemed to rise around the figure of the great national hero. He called to mind the great battles Stephen had fought, in nearly all of which he had been wounded, but out of which he had nearly always come victorious, and had built forty churches to commemorate his victories – for every victory a church! Small wonder that his grateful people honored him as a saint – their noble Stephen, with his strong arm and his mighty heart, and his unfailing trust in God. Stan remembered the story of the terrible night, in which the Turks had driven Stephen back under the walls of his fortress of Neamtzu, and when the fugitive prince, spent with fatigue and bleeding from all his wounds, beat at the gates for admission no hand opened to him, but he heard his mother's voice asking: "Who is the stranger who knocks so loudly at my son's gate?"

"'Tis I, mother; open quickly! My army is defeated, and I am wounded sorely. Make haste to open, for the Turks are at my heels!"

"Who art thou, stranger, that thou dost dare to speak in my son's name and with his voice? Never did my son come home defeated. He is on the field of battle putting his enemies to flight! And shouldst thou do me the shame of being indeed my son, know this at least – defeated thou shalt never enter here."

Then Stephen sounded a blast upon his horn to collect his scattered troops, and when he had rallied them and revived their sinking courage he routed the Turks, driving them back over the Danube. After that he returned to Neamtzu and made his triumphal entry into the city, welcomed this time by his mother with tears of joy. Ah! She was of the stuff a hero's mother should be made of, that high-souled woman! Another time, when hard pressed by the enemy, he had fled to the mountains, fearing he could hold out no longer, Stephen found shelter in the house of a beautiful and stately woman. Worn out with all his fatigues he fell asleep, but was awakened at dawn by his hostess, leading in her nine sons whom she had sent out during the night to collect troops for him, and who now returned, each with a goodly following. With the army thus brought together Stephen was able to attack the Turks anew, and he was so successful, gaining victory on victory, that in the end he drove them completely out of the country. His brave deeds compelled the admiration of the whole of Europe, and the pope entered into an alliance with the Romanian prince, to whom he gave the title of "Defender of Christendom". Stephen and his little nation were indeed the bulwark holding back the tide of invasion.

All that passed through Stan's mind as he stood there, and he was quite sad when guard was relieved and he had to go away without seeing the noble visitor again. The other soldiers asked him what had happened, and he answered in awestruck tones: "Stephen the Great is there!" They looked at him thinking the horrors and hardships of these last days, together with the lonely night watch, had been too much for him and had unsettled his brain. But when Stan went on seriously telling them how they might expect to see Stephen beside the king in battle, since he had promised to be there to protect the country and its ruler, then they listened with more attention and crossed themselves, saying that after all it might be true, for signs and wonders have been sent ere now, as Holy Scripture tells us, especially when a little nation is fighting for its liberty against a powerful foe. When at cockcrow an officer came to report to the king that the night attack on the redoubt had been repulsed he was found fast asleep, leaning his head on his hand. Directly he awakened, he looked around as if his eyes sought someone, and he asked at once whether nobody had entered the tent during the night.

"Nobody," replied the attendants, "until the officer arrived bearing his dispatches."

"But I most certainly saw," the king began, and then he paused, telling himself it must have been a dream. He must have dreamed that Stephen the Great had come into his tent that night, and had talked for a long time with him, foretelling the victory, and giving him counsel how he might best dispose his little army. It had all seemed so real, the king could hardly believe that it had been only a dream; but if it were, then it must have been a dream sent to bring him hope and comfort in the hour of peril.

To Stan it was hardly a surprise next morning to see the strange guest of the night before riding the whole time close at the king's elbow, seeming, with his far-reaching eyes, to scan the battle-field in all directions, and ever and anon lifting his hand to ward off the shot that menaced the prince whom he had come to lead to victory. It was often said that King Carol exposed himself far more than a leader should on whose life so much depended, but Stan knew that there was no danger. Stan saw how the great Stephen's hand was always held protectingly above Carol's head to keep off all peril.

One terrible night in the trenches in the blinding snow and sleet, when many of the soldiers had their feet frostbitten from standing in the icy water, Stephen appeared again and spoke to Stan, telling him of the unsuccessful attack that would take place on the morrow, but that the Romanians must not lose courage, for in the end the victory would be theirs. Stan thought of this during the changeful fortune of the next day's fighting, and remained calm and hopeful throughout the worst moments. Once a bullet struck him, but his wound was only slight, though his cap was riddled in three places by other bullets.

On the night preceding December 10th, Stephen the Great appeared to Osman Pasha and told him of the hopelessness of further resistance. "'Tis all in vain you seek to prolong the struggle," spoke the vision to the brave Turkish commander. "Your sortie of the morrow will be unavailing. Plevna must fall; it is written that my people shall enter within its walls. Not all your valor can now retard the fatal moment. But you have held out like a hero; you will be honored as a hero in surrender, and old scores will be cleared off this day between thy people and mine. The task which I had to leave unfinished when death called me away, Carol now accomplishes after all these years."

And on the morrow Plevna fell, and King Carol rode forward to meet the wounded Osman, complimenting him on his magnificent defense, which had lasted far beyond the period any man could have expected. Had the siege lasted but a few days longer, had Stephen not been there to protect his brave Romanians, they must all have perished. For a snowstorm arose such as is only seen in our plains – a storm that neither men nor horses could live through, with twenty degrees below zero, and such huge blocks of floating ice upon the Danube that not a scrap of food could be brought across the river. The king left Plevna with his troops and set out upon the most awful ride of his whole life. The whole way from Plevna to Nicopolis was strewn with corpses alike of friends and foes, and the greatest numbers were the Turks who had come away from Plevna starving. Dead bodies were sitting, lying, standing everywhere – frozen so hard that they did not even fall over. Other poor wretches were to be seen stretching out their arms in mute appeal to heaven, and then falling down dead. The horses in the gun carriages were frozen in the shafts, the drivers frozen at their posts. In one place a little group had collected round a wheel, to which they had set fire, to have a little warmth, but all were dead. At every step King Carol's horses started and shied, trying to avoid treading on the corpses which lay everywhere beneath the snow. And overhead wheeled the ravens, disturbed in their hideous feast, to which they settled again as the advancing army passed on. It was a ghastly sight. But all the way Stephen the Great rode by King Carol's side. At last Nicopolis was reached. There in the trenches around the fortress the Turkish prisoners were crowded together, clamoring for bread. But bread was not to be obtained, because the passage of the Danube was still blocked with ice so that no boat could make its way across. Many almost perished that night from cold and hunger. But Stan, who had ridden in the king's escort, and had never lost sight of his leader, saw that Stephen was always there; it was he who rode by the king's side and kept his horse from stumbling on the steep incline that resembled a sheet of ice that led to the citadel. It was he who mounted guard at night before the king's door, and then went round among the ranks, speaking words of comfort and encouragement to all the weary, dispirited soldiers. Thanks to him, nearly all of the ten thousand who reached there survived the horrors of that cruel night. Next day the king contrived to cross the river in a small launch. The boat was constantly caught between blocks of ice that one minute almost tossed it in the air, and the next threatened to sink it utterly, but Stan, who was watching from the shore, saw a lofty form step out in front of it across the ice, and the boat seemed to follow where he beckoned, and to steer its way safely through that perilous passage. Then Stephen guided the little craft until it touched the shore, and the king could set his foot once more in safety on Romanian soil. It was he, too, Stan thought, who helped the other little boats to cross from the Romanian side, laden with provisions for those who were hungering. After that Stan saw him no more, and for a time he knew not what happened. For finally he had been compelled to go into a hospital. His feet had been frostbitten and were already turning black, and it was feared he might lose them, like so many a poor fellow in that campaign. But they were saved, thanks to good care and nursing; while the thought of him whom he had seen cheered and sustained him through those trying hours. He knew the cause they were fighting for must triumph, he knew that the king was destined to lead their nation to glory and prosperity, since the greatest it had ever brought forth stood by his side and blessed his undertaking. King Carol showed himself in all things the worthy continuator of his great predecessor's work; he, too, built beautiful churches throughout the whole land in thankfulness to God for the favor he had shown him.

The day the troops made their triumphant entry into Bucharest he saw Stephen the Great once more – a mere shadowy form, riding beside the king. Another shadow, that of Michael the Brave, came toward them, saluting his valiant brother-in-arms from afar. Stan bore the colors and on his breast shone both the cross of St. George and the medal of the Virtutea Militara. His hand shook with excitement as he recognized the heroes, and he wanted to point them out to others, but they saw nothing and only thought Stan still a little weak in the head from his wound. But to that he replied that it was only three toes he had lost, and that could only effect one in the feet and not in the head.

As long as he lives Stan will remember his "Stand! Who goes there?" of that night in Grivitza, and he tells it to his children and to his friends when they sit under the trees and smoke on holiday afternoons. And the older ones all laugh and say: "What a good story he tells!" but do not believe a word of it. But the children believe it, and are delighted, and feel sure that their country will become great and strong, since it is protected by the great men of old days, who have been seen giving aid to their king.

Queen Marie of Romania

The Sun-Child

> *The tears all told her whence they came and grew so heavy,*
> *that beneath the burden sore,*
> *The maiden died...*
>
> The Bard of the Dambovitza.

At her birth-hour the sun kissed her and made her his. The sun enwrapped her in a golden halo, and called her his child. The sun stole into her heart and took up his dwelling therein, he sent his rays to fill her wee hands and told her that forever they were hers, he left his reflection in the blue of her eyes, and buried his radiance within the thoughts of her brain – therefore was she the Sun-Child, the Sun-Child whom everyone loved.

Her hair was golden, because the sun had forgotten his light amongst her curls, her eyes had the color of deep summer seas that held captive his smile. Wee were the feet that carried her noiselessly into the dark lives of men, and her hands were two soft promises that had come down from purer climes. Not even the sound of water bubbling out of desert sands could equal the charm of her voice, and the words she spoke were like priceless pearls that some legendary queen might thread upon a silken string. When she smiled, it was as though all the buds of spring had suddenly opened, covering the world with blossoms after weary winter nights. The Sun-Child was beautiful with a beauty no other child possessed.

She lived with her parents in a humble street; both father and mother were simple and ignorant, little understanding what was the light their little one had brought down into their midst. But others understood, and flocked towards the Sun-Child's dwelling laying all their longing, their dreams, and their sorrows at her bare little feet. The Sun-Child was not afraid of their voices. Patiently she listened to their tales of woe; her small fingers gathered the tears from their eyes, gleaned the sighs from their lips; her heart, where the sun had his dwelling, became a beacon for weary wanderers, a sanctuary for souls that had lost their way, and so much light did the Sun-Child carry in her bosom, that it was as though she could have turned the whole world into gold. But human sorrow is a weight heavier far than all the gravestones that cover the dead, and little did the Sun-Child realize what she was doing when she gave herself up to all those who wept…

From far and wide they came to her, the weary, the heartbroken, the crushed, the humiliated, miserable outcasts flocking together from the four corners of the earth. In a long file they came, hoping to steal some of the light the great sun had left in her hands at her birth, and the rich came also, for they too carry many sorrows in their hearts... And the Sun-Child gave and gave, laying up no store for herself.

Her mother scolded her, telling her that she was foolish; her father was full of anger when he saw all the beggars and cripples and the haggard, tattered waifs collecting round his doorstep, talking to his little one, kissing her hands, listening to her words, as though she had belonged to the wise ones of this earth.

What had the Sun-Child to say to them? In what way did she console them, what power was hers, what magic, what tongue? I know not, for it is indeed a mystery that belongs to God.

But often at night her mother would awake from her sleep, and then it was to her as though out of the silence she could hear the Sun-Child's heart talking all alone in the dark, talking of all that it had felt and understood. And the mother would be filled with anguish, knowing that at night children should sleep, that their hearts also should sleep, forgetting for a while the toil of the day and its troubles and cares. But the Sun-Child's heart could not be silent nor could it rest, for full to overflowing was the Sun-Child's heart...

The heart was telling about the poor woman whose children had died one after the other, so that the bare mounds of their graves stood side by side like little heaps of sand blown up by the wind. It told about the old man who was so poor that he had naught to feed on but bread-crusts, that like a stray dog he picked out of the gutters in the streets; of the sister whose little brother died in her arms, although she had cried to the heavens to take her in his stead; of the bride who in vain waited for the bridegroom who never came back; of treachery, of vice, of poverty did the heart tell, of lost dreams, of shattered homes, of death, of pestilence and murder, of dark waters and darker streets; of creeping jealousies, of sordid sufferings, of hollow desires and of tongues that say untruths. All this did the Sun-Child's heart relate in the dead of night, when it ought to have been at rest, but strange it was: never matter how sad or how infamous were the tales the heart was remembering, in passing through the thoughts of the Sun-Child even the ugliest story became beautiful, even the darkest deed seemed forgivable, even the greatest sorrow appeared bearable. It was as though the sunshine had taken hold of them and turned them into light...

The mother marveled and trembled as she listened, but the mother could not understand...

One day the Sun-Child was sitting on its threshold in the ugly little street; upon the broken doorstep it had placed many little phials filled with the tears it had gathered from those that wept. The phials stood in a little row beside her and the sun, shining upon them, made them resemble giant diamonds of inestimable worth. With a rusty nail, the Sun-Child was gently striking against them, drawing from them marvelous melodies sweeter than the tunes which angels play on their harps. The sordid street was filled with harmonies so sweetly penetrating, that the dirty panes of the windows began to vibrate, echoing, like distant voices, the notes that float-ed through the air… And so much light had collected round the Sun-Child that she seemed to be seated upon golden steps…

"What are those bottles?" asked her mother, stepping out of the house.

"They are holy philters," answered the Sun-Child, "philters I have filled from human hearts."

"Why do they shine so brightly?" enquired the mother with a frown on her brow.

"Because I have changed them into diamonds," said the Sun-Child, "dia-monds that I am bringing to God."

"Give them to me," demanded the mother, "we are poor, and if they have become precious I can sell them, and turn them into golden coin."

"Do not touch them, oh, mother," cried the Sun-Child, "they are sacred, and I bought them with part of my life!"

"Thy talk is foolish," scolded the mother, "give me thy phials that I may carry them to the merchant at the far street corner, so that we may have wood for the winter and bread for our starving stomachs through the long, bitter months!"

"Do not touch them, my mother!" repeated the Sun-Child, "did I not tell thee that I bought them with part of my life!"

Looking down at her little daughter the mother suddenly became aware of her paleness, and seeing it, for a moment she hesitated, her foot quite close to the precious vials.

"Thou art not as other children," grumbled the mother, "thy ways are un-canny, and thine eyes are too large, they frighten me, they seem to be look-ing beyond the boundaries of this earth. Get thee hence with thy bottles, or verily I shall smash them, or sell them, I cannot bear the sound that they make!"

"They are the sound of tears, oh, my mother, of tears that I am carrying to God."

"Be still!" cried the mother, "enough of thy talk! Be off! Go to play with other children, sit not thus idle on my doorstep, for I am busy, and thou art sorely in my way."

So the Sun-Child gathered up her precious flasks, and carried them to an-other place. To a wood did the Sun-Child carry them, and setting them down on a stone, she played to the birds, to the leaves of the trees, to the sky above her, and to the small clouds that silently floated past. And the tears in the bottles talked a wonderful language, filling the little forest with music, relating of the long way they had come, remembering the eyes out of which they had fallen into the Sun-Child's heart. The forest became like a cathedral on the day of All Saints. The Sun-Child sat gazing up at the far-off heavens; but why was the Sun-Child's face so pale... so white?

It came to pass that the queen of the land heard talk of the Sun-Child, of the Sun-Child with the wonderful heart... And desiring to see her, the high lady had her brought to the palace where she dwelt. Through noble halls, up marble steps, over shining floors did the Sun-Child's feet carry her towards a garden where the royal woman sat in lonely grandeur, awaiting the strange little guest. Curious it was, but all the splendor through which the Sun-Child passed paled before her radiance – the Sun-Child was brighter than gold and precious stones, fairer than lilies, sweeter than the roses that bent towards her as she passed... But then, see ye, she was the Sun-Child, the Sun-Child whom everyone loved.

Now the queen hid a secret in her soul, a woe that filled her days with darkness, a woe that made her nights a torture, a torture of which no one ever knew; but when she saw the Sun-Child, it was to her as though the gates of heaven had suddenly opened, and stretching out her arms to the little stranger, she drew her within them, pressing her wildly to her aching heart. With her hands, in which the sun had left his rays, the little one caressed the weeping woman; from her heart, where the sun had confided his light, she drew forth such radiance that the sad queen's face began to shine like a star. Both arms round the lonely woman's neck, the Sun-Child whispered words into her ears, words that no other ever heard, but the queen's expression as she gazed up into the skies above was so marvelous, that those around instinctively folded their hands. What, however, no one noticed was the Sun-Child's paleness. When she walked back through the garden – verily she was whiter than moon-blossoms when they are very white.

The Sun-Child had become the pulse of the land, the heart of the town; more and more people came to her asking light from her hands... The Sun-Child gave and gave, but the collection of little tear-bottles near her bed became bigger and bigger, till they almost entirely encircled her miserable couch – somehow the Sun-Child felt that when the circuit of phials would be completed... But why speak of such things?...

The Sun-Child's mother was too busy to count the tears her little daughter gathered from human hearts into her own; besides, since she had been called to the palace, the simple woman looked upon her little one with a feeling of awe, rejoicing over the reputation she had won in the town.

Something, however, which the mother never knew, was that the Sun-Child felt a great pain in her heart, a pain as though the sun within her bosom were burning her up. Still, whenever anyone came to her doorstep the Sun-Child had always the same smile, and her hands were ever full of light... But the pain in her heart was becoming daily harder to bear, and the face of the Sun-Child was now pale as the moon on winter nights.

Often it happened that the Sun-Child came back from her wanderings very late at night; her parents, though anxious at first, soon got accustomed to her strange little ways, and would go to bed quite quietly without awaiting her return, for had not the Sun-Child a charmed life?

Thus it came to pass that one evening the Sun-Child stole softly home in through the door mother and father had left ajar, that she stole noiselessly, softly, to her poor small bed, carrying a wee flask in her hand. It was only a tiny glass bottle full of clear, shining tears, a tiny glass bottle that completed the almost closed ring... Softly, the Sun-Child lay down upon her pallet of rags; no noise did the Sun-Child make, for she did not wish to awake her parents from their well-earned sleep, but the Sun-Child was horribly tired – the little phial she had carried home was the heaviest her hands had ever held. Folding her arms over her aching bosom the Sun-Child closed her eyes and lay quite still, as though she had been dead...

As she lay there all the tears in the many little bottles began to relate their stories – to speak of all the griefs they had seen, and the Sun-Child's heart responded, answering their complaints, for verily the small heart understood them all too well... and, therefore… therefore, did the small heart break... Quite noiselessly did it break, never a sound did it make, but as it burst asunder all the light that the sun had hidden within it on the day of its birth, streamed forth, flooding the room with a radiance so great that it was as though all the glories of heaven had come down upon earth.

With the feeling that some miracle had taken place, the parents awoke, and staring around them they could not imagine what had happened, so overpowering indeed was the glare that filled the humble dwelling, that they had to shield their eyes with their hands. Never had the dawn shone thus into their hovel! Oh! What did it mean? What was it? Where was their child?

With trembling steps the man and the woman approached the pallet where the Sun-Child lay dead... There she rested, her hands still crossed over her heart, and the Sun-Child was now like an alabaster casket filled with light.

Falling on their knees, the father and mother stared in speechless wonder. And as they gazed at the wee corpse, there was a sound as of cracking glass, and the innumerable little flasks that stood in a closed ring around the bed splintered into a thousand pieces, but instead of tears a shower of diamonds scattered over the floor, a shower of shining, wonderful diamonds, of priceless worth... But the Sun-Child lay quite still, the Sun-Child made no movement, for the first time the Sun-Child did not rise to greet her parents with her sweet, sunny smile...

There is no more to relate... Only this quite little thing: When the moment came to lift up the Sun-Child, so as to lay her in her poor little coffin, the body crumbled into ashes, into tiny grey, soft little ashes, ashes that could be gathered into a single hand. For see ye, no one had ever guessed that the sun that had dwelt in the little child's heart had been so strong, that it had consumed it entirely, so that when its small soul flew back to God, the worn-out little shell fell to pieces, burnt up by a flame that had been too ardent, a flame that had been too strong to last.

The queen, on hearing what had happened, begged for the Sun-Child's ashes, and she buried them with her own royal hands, buried them in her palace garden, there where the shade was darkest, there where the birds sang most!...

But every day at dawn and at sunset the grave became golden, golden like a dream, for in spite of the shade at those hours, all the rays of heaven came there, quite naturally, came back to the heart of the Sun-Child, that had been their dwelling, to the heart of the Sun-Child, whom everyone had loved.

Conu Ilie's Rose Tree

Once upon a time, there lived a rich old *boier*.[38] He was very fat, and his house was squat and fat as he was, with a very big roof covered with wooden tiles. The house was all white, and from afar it looked like a huge mushroom with a grey head. A long thin poplar tree grew up beside it, making it look even squatter than it was. In front of it there was a covered porch upheld by six stout columns, as stout as their master, and under this porch the rich old fellow would sit on a seat all bolstered with cushions, and smoke in lazy content his *ciubuc*.[39] He wore a sort of Turkish dressing gown, in the brightest colors the East could weave, and was specially proud of his sashes, which were one and all heavily embroidered with gold. On his head, he wore a monstrous sort of hat, the shape of an onion, but as big as a pumpkin – it was really hard to understand what pleasure he could find in wearing such a hideous hat. *Conu*[40] Ilie had a very loud greasy voice, and he inordinately admired everything that he possessed. He also vastly enjoyed his own jokes, which he repeated constantly, and often he alone could understand. But as he was very rich, all his neighbors laughed with him when he laughed, as evidently it was what was expected of them. As a general rule it is wise to laugh with the rich man when he laughs, and to weep with him when he weeps – it is a safe rule to stick to, and you will never go far wrong if you do.

Everything old Conu Ilie possessed was not quite as wonderful as he imagined, his taste was at times grievously at fault, but this did not matter much, as no one told him. He was not married, but had in fact always been too much in love with himself to find time to fall in love with anyone else; now he was already getting on in age, and it were better not to ask how many inches he measured round his middle. He liked assembling many people about him, but especially men, being too lazy to care for ladies' society. Then leaning back with crossed legs amidst his innumerable cushions, he would hold forth on many subjects, understanding but little about any of them, but evidently gloriously enjoying the sound of his own voice. He had a sly look in his eye, and would often wink at one or another of his neighbors as though in secret understanding with him; this would flatter the neighbor, even if he did not clearly realize what they were in understanding about.

You and I would perhaps have said that Conu Ilie was a silly old fellow; perhaps some of his neighbors thought so too, but if they did, they only

---

[38] "Boier", nobleman [note in the first edition].
[39] "Ciubuc", oriental pipe [note in the first edition].
[40] "Conu", old-fashioned expression for "Sir" or "Mr." [note in the first edition].

told it to their wives, but never to Conu Ilie himself, so that he lived in a sort of fool's paradise in which he felt supremely at his ease.

One of the reasons why Conu Ilie liked to sit under the porch was that from there he could look out into his garden, which was a cool and delightful place where the butterflies loved to dance about. But being lazy and ponderous, he seldom walked in it, preferring to contemplate it from his cushioned seat through the enormous clouds of smoke he puffed from his pipe.

In this garden of his, Conu Ilie possessed something, which even you and I could admire without stint, even if we had thoroughly disapproved of the shape of his hideous hat – and this was a rose tree, with a single wonderful rose. Yes, I know you will ask why only a single rose. But if you had seen that rose, you would have been quite contented that it should be the only flower on the tree, for indeed it was a queen amongst roses, a perfect, perfect rose... Pale pink, its petals had the color of a babe flushed by sleep. It was of unusual size, much, much larger than ordinary roses, and so perfect of shape that the saints themselves might have modelled it for their joy. So exquisite was its perfume that it saturated the air with its sweetness so that its fragrance even penetrated under the porch where old Ilie sat enjoying his own self.

Fatigued at having to pretend to admire everything the *boier* possessed, as well as having to laugh at his rather stale wit, his guests felt real relief when it was the rose's turn to receive admiration; then their voices had a more natural sound and words flowed freely from their tongues. Ilie would send one friend after another down into the garden to admire the exquisite flower, whilst he broadened himself out more and more amongst his cushions, taking the superb attitudes of some sultan who, having bought a new slave, exhibits her charms before those less rich or less lucky than himself. He would blow out his cheeks, nod his head, whilst his fat fingers played about with the heavy golden chain and gaudy trinkets dangling in glittering magnificence upon his rotund person.

"Well, what do you say about my rose?" he would ask over and over again. "What do you say?" And even after each separate guest had answered this question he would still continue to ask, "Well, what do you say, what do you say?" and this finally was not particularly amusing for anybody. You will perhaps wonder why in spite of being such a perfect old nuisance, the *boier* was able to assemble so many guests around him. Well, the truth was that Conu Ilie's house was a center of material joys. His tobacco was first class, his rooms cool in summer, warm in winter, his chairs well bolstered, his carpets soft to the feet, wine was served at all hours of the day, but above all, Conu Ilie possessed a cook... a cook! An old gipsy he was, and a real culinary prodigy; his cooking was an art, not a trade, he could set a better dinner on the table than any king's cook. No one could roll *sarmale*[41] as he could, or make *placinte*[42] as light, or roast a sucking pig so crisply. As to his partridges fried in oil, wrapped in vine-leaves and succulent bacon, the very thought of them made your mouth water several days beforehand. Muddy-faced, with agile fingers, dark as a monkey's, was old Iancu the gipsy, and he received his betters with cringing back and servile gestures of welcome, kissing their hands and their shoulders, and always repeating "Health to you, health to you, may you enjoy my dishes without any heaviness to your stomach, or bad dreams to your sleep." Oh, but his *baclava*[43] was a marvel, and as to the cream of his *cataifs*[44], it was white and light as the foam of the sea. Yes, old Iancu was indeed a rare though ugly treasure to possess.

Conu Ilie's repasts lasted endlessly. He would sit in an armchair at the head of his heavily laden table, smacking his lips and announcing beforehand what dish was going to be set before them. And if by some fatal mischance it did not turn out according to his expectations, he would fly into a towering rage, and box the ears of whatever servant was unfortunate enough to be serving him at that moment. His language on these occasions was anything but elegant, so that even the little green frogs, croaking in the pond outside, would blush and dip their goggle-eyed heads under water so as to hear no more. Wine flowed freely at the *boier*'s table, and a troop of *lautars*[45] played all the time. After supper – (I am talking of the summertime) – the pompous old fellow and his guests would go out to sit down under the porch, where coffee was brought all fragrant and steaming, *ciubucs* were lighted, and although even the most elastic digestions had been already severely tried, fat-bellied flasks of strong liqueur were handed round in glasses none too small. Ilie would of course spread himself out upon the softest cushions and his language would become more unctuous and self-complacent than ever, punctuated by occasional hiccoughs, which were merely the outward expression of his stomach's perfect satisfaction.

One evening as these satiated gentlemen sat together digesting an unusually copious repast, an exquisite voice rose suddenly out of the darkness of the night. So extraordinarily lovely was it, that even these very material old gentlemen held their breaths to listen. Like a crystal-clear fountain mounting towards the skies, the rapturous notes rose higher and higher, filling the garden with a harmony such that all the leaves of the trees quivered,

---

[41] "Sarmale", chopped meat rolled into vine or spinach [sourkraut] leaves [note in the first edition].

[42] "Placinta", very thin leaf-like pastry [note in the first edition].

[43] "Baclava", very heavy cake mixed with almonds [note in the first edition].

[44] "Cataifs", cake fried in a particular way and covered with whipped cream [note in the first edition].

[45] "Lautar", gipsy minstrel [note in the first edition].

and that the tall lilies, standing in a circle round the pond, bent their heads to listen.

"Who can this human nightingale be?" asked someone.

"Indeed, it is the most glorious voice I have ever heard", said another.

"If I could only count a voice like that in my choir!" added *parintele*[46] Serafim, who was one of Conu Ilie's most assiduous visitors and whose tummy rivalled that of his host.

"It must be some damsel enamored of my person", declared Conu Ilie, passing both his hands up and down over his well-stretched waistcoat with a caressing movement. "Very probably she has perceived me on Sunday in my yellow-striped caftan and gold-embroidered sash, for only on that day do I move from the house."

"It is indeed a garment which would make a parrot turn green with envy", nodded Conu Ghitsa, Ilie's closest friend.

"What if the parrot were already green?" asked someone, and in answer a fat guttural voice chuckled from somewhere out of the dark.

"Hush, hush, listen, this is heavenly music", said Mitru, the youngest of the party, who could appreciate beauty as well as meat and drink.

Ever more beautiful became the song that was being sung out there in the dark, yet, peer about as they would, nowhere could Conu Ilie and his guests perceive vestige of a woman's dress, nor the faintest sound of a step. Some went down into the garden to search within the shade of the bushes, and all round by the hedge, but they came back completely baffled, nowhere was anyone to be seen. The sky was all full of stars, but the largest star of all stood straight above Conu Ilie's wonderful rose tree. So large it was and so bright, that it might have been a giant yellow diamond set in a vast dome of black enamel that had neither beginning nor end. All the other stars paled before this one, which was brighter and more beautiful than all the rest. The perfect pink rose seemed to be staring right up at it, opening wide her petals so as to receive its rays right into her heart.

Mitru, in passing, noticed how sweet was the rose's perfume, and tried to bend her towards him so as to inhale her fragrance, but the terrible thorns that protected her pricked his fingers so violently that the blood fell in warm red drops to the ground. And somehow it seemed to Mitru that the rose laughed ever so softly, but this was of course pure imagination, for how can a rose laugh?

For a while Conu Ilie and his guests sat in silence, hoping to hear the glorious voice once more – but all was still now, no more the faintest sound came from the garden, and at length, having exhausted every topic of conversation, the sleepy gentlemen dispersed for the night.

From then onwards, every evening, the wonderful voice was heard in the *boier*'s garden, and although no female figure could ever be discovered

---

[46] "Parintele", priest [note in the first edition].

156

anywhere, vain old Ilie continued to imagine that some enamored damsel haunted his premises in remembrance of the irresistible yellow-striped caftan he wore each Sunday in church. Greater airs than ever did he now give himself, and when sauntering through the village after the morning Mass, he would puff himself out like a strutting pigeon, benignly smiling to the right, to the left, stroking his glossy beard whilst he twirled his silver-nobbed cane round and round between his fingers. According to him, each handsome village wench might be the mysterious singer with the wondrous voice.

"But perhaps it was not only a peasant girl", said Ilie to himself, "but some lovely princess who has heard about me, and being adorably bashful, steals into my garden at night only, when she cannot be seen." And Ilie licked his lips, such dainty visions of enamored princesses did he conjure up to himself as he waddled along full of his own importance. There were tall ones and small ones, plump ones and slim ones, fair ones and dark ones, and princesses who looked at him with eyes all alight with passion, and others who veiled themselves in mystery like virgins in a temple. Ilie was supremely satisfied; this new illusion gave a special flavor to his already eminently agreeable life.

But someone else, who had nothing to do with Conu Ilie and his satellites, had fathomed the mystery of the wonderful voice. Each night when the *boier* and his guests had retired to bed, a little shepherd-lad with hare feet would steal through the hedge, which encircled Conu Ilie's garden, and with beating heart approach the rose tree where the single rose bloomed in all her lonely splendor, and would stand before it with clasped hands, in an ecstasy of adoration. Dinu the shepherd had discovered that the rose it was who sang, and sang only on nights when the great star stood straight above her, sending down its rays into her heart. Yes, Conu Ilie's rose was in love with the star which looked like a yellow diamond set in a black enamel dome that had neither beginning nor end, and being attached to the ground by roots which went deep, deep down, the rose could not move from the spot where she was planted. The star knowing this would remain suspended just above her, far off out of reach, alas, but adoring her with its light. The star gave its brightness, and because the rose loved so ardently, she had found a voice with which to express her passion, a voice which resembled a human voice.

Dinu, understanding the rose's secret and possessing none of Conu Ilie's vanity, did not imagine that the beautiful flower loved him, though his very soul was held captive by her divinely sweet voice.

And the rose ? Well, the rose... like many a woman, was not averse to being adored even by so humble a lad, though she had naught but her pity to offer in exchange for his devotion, for her love, all her love, was given to one far beyond her reach...

I know not how it came to pass, but one day Conu Ilie discovered that the rose it was who sang – his rose – the rose in his garden, and being Conu Ilie, he very naturally concluded that the rose was singing because of a hopeless passion for himself.

"This is very touching", he said to his circle of admirers, "very touching indeed."

But at the bottom of his vain old heart he was decidedly disappointed to have to give up his theory about the mysterious princess, who each day in his imagination had had another face.

"If that poor rose loves you so much", said his companions, "you must not make her pine in vain too long. Indeed, after supper you are none too agile, preferring your ease amongst your many cushions, but you will all the same one evening have to sacrifice yourself and go down to where she stands, and thank her for her songs."

"I shall go", said Conu Ilie, and each evening from the softness of his couch he would repeat, "I shall go", and still he sat on stroking his well-stretched, well-filled waistcoat.

Younger and shorter of temper than the other guests, Mitru one night lost all patience with him, and seizing him suddenly under his arms, set him on his feet, where he stood, all red and snorting with astonished indignation. But Mitru paid no attention. "Come along, get up", he said. "There are only four steps down into the garden, and the lovely rose is waiting for you", but under his breath he added, "Verily I cannot understand her taste!"

That night, Ilie descended from his porch into the garden, and under the light of the stars, like a peacock with spread tail, he strutted round and round his rose tree, hoping that the beautiful flower could see all the magnificence of his scarlet and gold-shot caftan sprinkled over with small bunches of embroidered tulips.

I know not if the rose saw old Ilie's splendor, but I know that she sang more rapturously than ever, and right above where she bloomed shone the wondrous luminous bright yellow star.

All of a sudden, a dark cloud passed over the star's face, and when the star was hidden, immediately the rose ceased to sing.

"She has stopped singing", said Conu Ilie, "a cloud has hidden the face of the stars, therefore she can see me no longer – and because I am now hidden from her sight, she has ceased singing; if ever I had doubted, I now know for certain that the poor dear little rose is pining away for the love of me."

But the barefooted shepherd-boy knew better; he also knew that one day, when the beautiful rose fell to pieces, shedding her marvelous petals like pale pink shells all over the lawn, that it was because her heart had broken, broken because the star had become faithless! Being attracted to a new love in another place, it no more shone down upon Conu Ilie's garden, and no new rose ever bloomed again upon that tree.

Conu Ilie, furious that one of the chief attractions should have disappeared, had the rose tree torn out by the roots and burnt. In its place he planted a magenta-colored dahlia.

"Dahlias are much more beautiful than roses", declared he complacently – and his satellites of course repeated his words: "Dahlias are much more beautiful than roses", and nodded their heads solemnly, as though their fat old host had uttered an important truth.

But Dinu the shepherd kept thinking of the rose, which had broken its heart. He was not vain, nor was he faithless, but poor and simple, and not clever at all. And at night when he went to bed, he would carefully draw the thin, faded little curtain over his tiny window so as not to see the great big, wonderful star shining so proudly right over there at the other end of the sky…

Baba Alba

She was as old as the hills – at least so said those of her village: as old as the hills! Though I do not think anybody really knew how old the hills were. Anyhow, she was old, very old, and tiny and wrinkled like a last year's apple, and she had only one tooth in her head. She lived just outside the village in a little mud-hut on the hillside, a quite crooked little hut with a big maize-thatched roof like a lid, but a lid which never really fitted its box. Of course she was a witch, you have guessed that I am sure – how could she be anything but a witch if she was as old as the hills, and bent nearly double, with a face wrinkled like a last year's apple, and with only one tooth in her head? But that was not all… She actually lived all alone with a rusty old raven who had only one eye. He was a horrid old bird, he looked sly and wise and very disagreeable, but old Baba Alba[47] seemed to like him. There was also a little green lizard who lived in a crack of the wall above her bed. I do not think there was anything particular to say against the lizard, but then people do not generally live with lizards, do they? So this was certainly another proof that Baba Alba was a witch…

She was very poor – dreadfully poor, her hut was but a hovel, her bed but a heap of rags, but all the same, Baba Alba was possessor of one treasure, and a strange treasure it was for an old witch to possess – a bell! Yes, of all things, a bell! A large bronze bell, hung on a pole, which had been fixed between two trees. Who fixed it there, no one ever knew; it had always been there, as old Baba Alba had also always been there, which proves how old, very old, both of them were. The rusty old raven would sit upon the pole above the bell, head cocked on one side, looking wise and cross and sad.

The bell was a very beautiful bell. It was so mildewed that it was almost turquoise blue, a lovely color! On one side, a cross had been cast upon it, and on the other, three arrows sticking into a heart; there was also an inscription upon it, but no one had ever deciphered the inscription – the villagers believed that even Baba Alba herself had no idea of what was inscribed on the bell. This may have been so, but I do not know, for Baba Alba was not at all communicative about her own affairs.

Naturally all the children of the village were irresistibly attracted to the old witch's hut, but they were also afraid of it, this greatly adding to its attraction! Once a day, old Baba Alba would limp off into the forest to fetch wood for her fire; she also fetched mushrooms and berries and other things… At least so goes the tale… Baba Alba always left the crooked little gate in the thorn hedge, which enclosed her meagre piece of ground, open

---

[47] "Baba Alba" means Old Mother White [note in the first edition].

when she was away; of course that would have made it very easy to explore her dwelling or give a pull to the shabby cord attached to the bell, but no child ever dared enter the witch's enclosure, however great their desire might be. The curious thing was that, also in winter, through mud or snow, the old woman would make her excursions into the forest, but except wood for her fire, I really do not know what she could find there in winter... And it must have been hard walking for such a very old body. Sometimes the children would call after her, or throw stones at her, or hard pieces of earth; they would also sing teasing little songs, but when the old woman turned round, threatening them with her crooked stick, they would scurry off like little cowards and hide behind the bushes or projecting rocks. This was the sort of song they sang at old Baba Alba:

Baba Alba, Baba Alba,
Who are you indeed?
With your crow and your bell
And the stories you tell,
And the wood you bring,
Like a low crawling thing,
Back to your muddy old hut.

Baba Alba, Baba Alba,
Who are you indeed?
With your nose like a hook,
And your shabby black crook,
And your hut with a roof
Which is not weatherproof,
And with only one tooth in your head!

Baba Alba, Baba Alba,
Oh! Tell us, I pray,
Did you come from the gnomes,
And the black one who roams?
Do you know him quite well?
And really can you tell
When the stars fall out of the skies?

Baba Alba, Baba Alba,
Oh! Tell us, I pray,
If the little bridge broke,
If the earth were all smoke,
If your hut tumbled down,
And cracked your old crown,
Baba Alba, oh! What would you do?

Or this one:

Hoo hoo! Hoo hoo! Hoo hoo!
Tell us, oh do!
Whoever made you?
Oh! Was it the goat,
Whose old ugly coat
Is grey as your hair
Or the rags that you wear?
Or was it the toad
Who sits in the road?
Or was it the storm,
That when you were born
Blew the old spider
Right over your way?

Hoo hoo! Hoo hoo! Hoo hoo!
Tell us, oh do!
What way do you take
To the secret lake,
Where you sit and sigh
Whilst the clouds roll by?
The lake where you see
The things that will be.
The lake where you grow
The herbs, that you throw
In the philters you brew
With gore and with dew
For the dark one, who comes
When the moon is quite new,
Hoo hoo! Hoo hoo! Hoo hoo!

They also sang much uglier songs, which I am not going to repeat, because no nice little children ever ought to sing such songs; but little children – alas! – are not always nice! Nor are little piggies, nor crocodiles, although they do not sing.

Sometimes Baba Alba did not raise her stick at all, but only looked at them with her red-rimmed eyes – and then the children slunk away home with a strange feeling of shame, and as they passed the old woman's little hut, it would seem to them that they heard the raven hooting at them with hoarse, croaking voice.

Exactly in what manner Baba Alba used her witchcraft could never be quite explained; but when a pig suddenly died in the village, when old Father Nicu broke his leg, when the tapers in front of the Virgin's image suddenly went out – all twelve of them at one go! – when neighbor Anna's house

163

burnt down, and when there was an eclipse of the sun, or when the hail destroyed Widow Zoe's maize – of course it was Baba Alba's fault. Even if you do not like to believe all this, you will have to admit that when *Popa*[48] Dionisie's cow had a calf with two heads, no one could be held responsible for it but Baba Alba, and her raven, and her bell, and perhaps also the little green lizard, who lived in the wall above her bed.

There was only one person in the village, and that was Vasile, who did not believe that Baba Alba was a witch – but he was of no importance at all, he was but a motherless, fatherless orphan, whom no one claimed and who lived by public charity. Popa Dionisie used him for guarding his pigs, and allowed him to sleep in the wood-shed, and share the *mamaliga*[49] which his old wife cooked. Popa Dionisie's wife was deaf, so she had never really understood who Vasile was, but she liked his eyes, which were round and bright, like blue stars, fringed by pitch-black lashes; this made them look still bluer, especially as his face was very pale and his hair very dark.

Vasile knew a few things about Baba Alba that nobody else knew and this was because he was not afraid of her at all. I will even tell you – but quite as a secret! – that sometimes he used to go to her at night... Yes! I am sure about what I am saying, because the old moon told me, and it was she who discovered all about it... I have quite forgotten to say that the villagers had never heard the sound of Baba Alba's bell – she never rang it; it was even believed that it had no tongue.

There was also something else very strange about that bell, but this only Vasile knew, because he had been up at the old woman's hut at late hours... On certain nights, Baba Alba's bell would radiate a faint blue light. Oh! Such a lovely soft light, phosphorescent as the trail ships sometimes leave on the ocean when they pass. Baba Alba would sit out amidst the dew which sparkled all around her like many tears, and watch the bell like a stargazer, and all the while she would mumble to herself words which seemed to have no sense. The light from the bell would fall on her old head, and make it look all frosty; it also imparted a strange radiance to her rags, till they looked almost silvery. The moon told me this, and Vasile saw it also!

One day Vasile, drawn by some power he could not resist, entered the witch's enclosure, and came and sat down beside her amongst the dew-drops. Above their heads, a stain against the sky, darker than the night, sat the old raven with ruffled plumes. The moonlight made his one eye shine like a bead.

Old Baba Alba did not scowl at the orphan, but neither did she give him any word of encouragement; she simply sat there staring at her bell, and mumbling her incantations.

---

[48] "Popa", village priest [note in the first edition].

[49] "Mamaliga", maize bread [note in the first edition].

164

"Do you never ring your bell?" whispered the boy.

"No," said the witch.

"Why?" asked the boy.

"I must not," answered the queer old being.

"Must not?" The boy's voice was full of enquiry.

"No," said the old woman again.

And that night Vasile did not ask any more questions.

"But it's strange that she never rings the bell," said Vasile to himself next day, as he sat out on the hillside guarding the old priest's pigs. He sat up amongst the autumn crocuses, that grew all over the hillside, like hundreds and thousands of pale mauve fairy-cups. Vasile had a little switch in his hand, and sometimes when he was not thinking, he would lash at one of the delicate flowers and break its neck; then he was sorry, because he hated to see things die... All the woods were ablaze with their autumn colors – the sun was shining on them, and they were very beautiful. Vasile raised his hand to protect his eyes from the glare – but he was not looking at the golden forests, nor at the ruby-red cherry trees, nor at the wondrous poplar which grew up straight and tall before him, its leaves all a-tremble with yellow light, its white trunk standing out like ivory against the incredibly blue sky – he was thinking about Baba Alba's bell...

"I am sure it must have a beautiful voice," thought Vasile, "but I do wonder why she lets it be dumb?"

A less dreamy child, a more adventurous one, would no doubt have conceived a plan to ring the mysterious bell, but this idea never came to Vasile – somehow it would have seemed like a sacrilege; all the same, Vasile had a sort of feeling that one day he would hear its voice.

Down below in the village, the bridge over the little brook had broken in two, just at the moment when Ioan Sirbu's cart was crossing it! The cart had been piled up with huge orange pumpkins, and all the pumpkins rolled into the water. There had also been potatoes at the bottom of the cart, and they had scampered all about the place as though they had been alive, and this of course was old Baba Alba's fault. At that moment, as it happened, she was up in the forest gathering fat mushrooms with grey, velvety heads and bulky stems. Her ragged apron was quite full of them and all around her the red berries on the bushes glowed like fairy-rubies – how she managed to make the bridge break down in the village I really do not know, but she did! Everybody said so, though the bridge was very old and shaky and Ioan Sirbu's cart very heavy.

The lumpy pumpkins lay about in the water like small orange rocks, the fussy little stream wanted to roll them down to the river, but they were too heavy. The sun shone down upon them, and seemed to laugh at Ioan Sirbu, who was scratching his head in bewilderment, swearing at his patient oxen and asking the saints in heaven and the devils in hell why such a disaster should happen just to his cart. – All the neighbors flocked together and after much talk made it clear to him that it was Baba Alba's fault – so Ioan Sirbu began cursing the old witch instead of his oxen, rather relieved, though, that he owed his disaster neither to the saints nor to the devil...

But what was Baba Alba searching for in the forest? She did not need any more mushrooms, her apron was quite full of them, yet she was standing there, shading her eyes with her shaky hands – it was more as though she were waiting for somebody – but who could Baba Alba be waiting for?

Twit, twit, chirped a little robin, hopping on to a twig. Twit! Twit! He was asking the old witch-woman who she was waiting for. The animals of the forest were not afraid of Baba Alba.

"I have not seen him for thirty years," said Baba Alba.

"Who?" asked the little robin. The old woman did not answer, but turned and limped away.

"Who, who?" called the little robin after her, and a bullfinch who was not far off also called out: "Who, who?" An impertinent little squirrel, almost orange in color, ran up to the top of a fir tree, and called at the top of his voice, "Who, who?" though he had no idea at all what it was all about.

On reaching her hut old Baba Alba let her bundle of dry sticks slip off her back on to the ground, and emptying her apron of its mushrooms on to the bank of hard-beaten earth in front of her hovel, sat down next to them, wiping the perspiration from her forehead with the back of her hand.

"Thirty years, thirty years," she continued to mumble, "and every day I go up into the forest to see if he is not coming along the mountain track."

She looked awfully old and forsaken as she sat there all alone amongst her mushrooms and dry sticks. The old raven with a hoarse croak flew suddenly down from his perch – flop! – straight on to her shoulder, and the little green lizard, guessing her return, came gliding out of the hut with quick, nervous movements, just to see if all was well, for these were her only companions!

Oh! Of course she must really have been a witch or she would have chosen other companions! Or do you think they had chosen her?

It was such a beautiful evening, and the sun, in going down, made the shabby maize-roof shine like gold; the lizard's green coat glittered, it might have been real enamel. But all that light only made old Baba Alba and her raven look still uglier and older and sadder; truly the moon suited them better... Well, it just happened to be full moon that night! And it was the moon who told me what Vasile heard, because Vasile, the moment he had driven Popa Dionisie's pigs home into their courtyard, had stolen up to the witch's dwelling. He had arrived in time to help the old woman light her fire. This he had done more than once. As he was a sad, lonely little boy, he liked to come and help the sad, lonely old woman; she hardly ever talked to him at all – but he could not really believe that she was a witch.

But once she had suddenly looked at him, and had murmured quite unexpectedly: "He also had blue eyes!"

"Who?"

But again he received no answer, and as he was not a very inquisitive little boy, and accustomed to be silent, he did not enquire any further. He was very fond of the little green lizard, and as Vasile could whistle beautifully, the lizard was also very fond of him, for lizards love music. The moment it heard Vasile it would poke its head out of its hole and then come zigzagging down the cracked wall, with rapid little runs. Vasile was less fond of the raven, and rather wished he had not been there; he certainly gave a witchy look to the place.

"Do you really brew philters and poisons?" asked Vasile, "and can you make the dead get up out of their graves, and the comet turn away from her trail?"

"Is that what they say about me?" enquired the old creature.

"Yes, and that at St. Dumitru you make the apples, which the peasants are carrying as offerings to the church, dance out of their hands and jump into your cooking-pot!"

"And what else?" asked the old woman.

"That you have a treasure hidden away under your *vatra*[50], from the time of the great Trajan – that it is cursed gold."

"Do you want some of my treasure?" asked the witch.

"What could I do with gold?" enquired Vasile.

"Well, generally people want gold," declared Alba.

"Have you got a treasure under your *vatra*?" insisted the boy.

"No," the old woman shook her head.

"And is your raven the devil's first cousin?"

Again the old woman shook her head. She was so very, very bent, that she seldom looked at you, in fact she could hardly lift her head, but now she tried to do so, and Vasile imagined that she was actually smiling.

"My poor old raven!" was all she said.

Now it was quite dark and the fire in the *vatra* threw a red glow over Vasile, who had a little dish on his lap – he was peeling the old woman's mushrooms.

"There was a time," said the old woman, "when I did not live with a raven."

"Who did you live with, then?" asked Vasile.

"The moon is rising," said Baba Alba, ignoring the boy's question. "I must go out to my bell."

She did not invite Vasile to go with her, but she knew that he would follow her. The little green lizard scurried back into its hole, but the old raven flew up upon the pole over the bell, which was his usual place.

But now I shall let the moon tell you what she saw:

---

[50] "Vatra", hearth [note in the first edition].

167

"Old Baba Alba," said the moon, "always comes out on nights when I am full – even when it is winter, the cold does not seem to disturb her much. I think she is always waiting for someone, in fact I know she is – but on this particular night I learnt for whom it was that she was waiting, because all of a sudden she told it to Vasile. I think she had become fond of Vasile – she too, like Popa Dionisie's old wife, loved his eyes. The Popa's old wife had had once, a very long time ago, a little boy of her own and his eyes had resembled Vasile's eyes – but whom did Vasile's eyes remind Baba Alba of, that is what I wanted to know! Well, I was at my brightest, and the night was still, and rather chilly, because it was October. I was flooding the world with silver. Against the sky the mountains looked very black, but the river in the valley beneath us gleamed like a dream vision. The bell was sending forth its fairy blue light, the old woman staring up at it in that rapt, trance-like way that was hers. Little Vasile sat beside her, and I could look straight into his eyes. Really, they were wonderful! No lake could have been deeper or more mysterious…

'Are you expecting something of that bell?' asked the orphan suddenly out of the silence.

'Yes, I am,' assented the witch.

'What?' asked the boy.

'That it should sound,' said the woman.

'But if it has a tongue it cannot be so difficult to make it sound,' observed the child.

'It must sound all by itself,' declared the queer old body.

'Why?' asked the boy again.

'Because then a soul will have been delivered, and a heart will have been washed of its sin,' answered solemnly the witch.

'What heart?' enquired the boy in an awed whisper.

'The heart of my son!'

Though Vasile was little given to showing any astonishment, this announcement all the same made him start, it seemed so very astonishing that this creature who was old as the hills should have a son!

'Where is he?' murmured the boy.

For a moment the old, old woman did not answer, silence had become the law of her being, words came to her like pain. The old and lonely find it hard to speak, but lifting with difficulty her trembling head, she stared into the small boy's eyes – then it was as though some ice which had long bound her tired heart suddenly melted, and hiding her withered old face in her hands, she broke into hoarse and terrible sobs. Vasile was frightened, and I found it difficult to keep my light quite steady – for Baba Alba, Baba Alba, was she not a witch! And how could a witch be overcome by human grief! Yes, her sobs were terrible, like a hurricane over a dried land – one felt that tears could not come to soften their agony.

'He had blue eyes like yours,' murmured the torn old soul at last, 'and he was the only one I had, but I was so poor I could give him no joy – and he became a bad boy and afterwards a bad man... and he... killed...' Here the old woman paused, and the uncanny raven suddenly cawed, which gave Vasile a terrible start. That old bird was really horrid!

'For many a month I kept him hidden away in the forest,' related the woman; 'I brought him food in secret places – but one day he was gone...' Another long pause. Vasile was staring up at the old woman; a breeze passed through the trees, making the dead leaves whisper together, as though they too were marveling over old Baba Alba's tale.

'I searched for him, searched for him,' pursued the poor woman at last, 'searched and searched till the bones in my body ached... Although I was not very old in those days – not so very old... Then I left the place where I had been living and I came here... I could not remain where he had been and was no more.'

'Had he been caught?' whispered the child anxiously.

'No,' said Baba Alba. 'No!' And again she was silent. The raven shifted his position on the pole above the bell, stretching one wing with his foot, for he was getting stiff.

'Then the old raven came to live with me,' said Baba Alba, folding her shaking hands in her lap as though to stop their trembling, 'and from the very first I was called *the witch*, perhaps because I was silent and shunned all humanity and never went to church... But now could I go to church?' –

'You might have gone to pray for your son,' suggested Vasile.

'Yes, I might have done that,' agreed Baba Alba humbly. 'Yes, I might have done that, but I no more believed in God!'

'Oh!' exclaimed the orphan as though in pain. 'Oh!'

'Twenty years passed,' resumed the old woman, 'and then suddenly one night...' She paused, and I had to open my ears very wide because her voice became but a whisper. Vasile drew as near to her as he dared.

'One night... I heard a strange sound at my door – it was a very dark night, and very windy, there was snow on the ground and my hut was cold. I sat up in my bed, not sure, if I was awake or dreaming, then I heard a sound like a bell, muffled – yet distinctly the sound of a bell... All trembling I rose from my pallet of rags and opened the door. Outside a man was standing, tall and dark and silent; the wind was tossing a black veil about his head. At his feet lay something darker than the night... 'Men's hearts are of stone, said a deep voice; the world is cold, mother, let me in...' Then I shrieked aloud: 'Tudor!' For indeed it was my son! I drew him into my hovel, shutting the door upon the storm outside, and also upon that dark object which had been laid upon my threshold. Oh, yes, especially upon that! For God forgive me, but I dared not to think upon what my son might have laid before my door... With trembling hands, I coaxed a flame back to life on my hearth, but I dared not look into the face of my son, there was something changed about him, something that I could not recognize, something that made my heart beat... But then I had not seen him for twenty years... And he would not sit down.'

'Had he chains on his hands or on his feet?' asked Vasile in a whisper.

'No, no!' protested the old woman – 'and after a terrible silence all of a sudden he burst out, like a sluice breaking: 'Mother, why turnest thou thy face away from mine?' Then for the first time I raised my head to look at him, and lo! He was garbed in the habit of a monk! A long cassock falling to his feet, a dark veil shrouding his head. His face shadowy, terrible, sinister. A wild, unkempt beard covered the lower part of it, and thick, unkempt hair fell from under his veil to his shoulders. But the coarse stuff on his left shoulder was worn through and I could see a deep wound from which the blood was dripping down over his heart... Then I gave a piercing shriek. Somehow I had felt certain that there would be blood about him, somewhere – but I had imagined it on his hands, not on his shoulder! For murderers generally have red hands... He saw that I was looking at his wound and a sort of awful smile came to his lips, but his eyes were fierce and anxious like those of a tracked beast. 'I am a monk, Mother, he said, 'but I am as yet unforgiven, for I have not confessed my sin – I cannot confess – I will not confess!' And he clenched his hands. I then understood that night still lived in his soul... 'My shoulder is bleeding, Mother, because I have carried towards thee, over seven hills and seven dales, a bell... A bell which is as heavy as the sin I carry about with me in my heart... And the weight of it has worn my flesh away to the bone... I shall hang up the bell for thee in front of thy hut. Thou must never sound it, Mother! It will sound by itself on the day when I am forgiven... But not till that day.' Then with an unexpected movement he bent down and kissed my forehead – his lips were icy cold – then I heard the door closing, it was all over... And I stood once more before my hearth... alone... and I had said no word of love to him, and I had not washed his wound! Outside the storm was raging, raging like souls in torment – I was so paralyzed with fear that I dared not open the door to look out into the night after him. Perhaps I had been dreaming – but no... There on the ground before me was a quite fresh stain of blood. I knelt down... as in church, I knelt down and touched that stain with my forehead... I cannot say what made me do this – but you see, the blood was of my son's shoulder, and not of his hands… And what he had laid down before my threshold was a bell... not... not...' and the old, old woman again hid her face in her hands... 'Next morning,' she said at length, taking up her tale again, 'I found the bell hanging on the pole between the two trees, as you see it now – the storm had passed away with the darkness, but everywhere there were scarlet stains splashed about on the white, white snow. That was thirty years ago,' added the sad soul. 'I am nearly ninety; my grave is waiting for me, dearly do I long for rest, but I dare not die before the bell rings... I must not, I will not die… till I hear its voice...' Vasile had stolen a small cold hand into the old woman's dry, horny palm. No, Baba Alba was not a witch..."

That was how the moon told me her tale.

Winter had come on. The mountainside, so lovely in summer, was now visited by icy-cold winds. The little village huddled away at its foot felt all shivery, and the peasants moved about with blue noses, beating their hands under their armpits to keep their fingers warm. It was a very poor village, and beneath it, in the valley, the turbulent river tossed its impatience.

Things were going wrong in the village. The schoolmaster's wife had lost her wedding ring, nearly all the children had measles, and the hens had some sort of malady which made them die by the dozen. The mayor had taken to drinking and old Mother Safta had gone mad – but there was even worse: the bell in the village church had suddenly cracked – right through! And now its voice was cracked also and discordant, so that it rather discouraged than invited people to prayer. The good peasant-folk put their heads together, discussing and deploring these misfortunes, and the name of Baba Alba came back again and again.

I cannot remember who first suggested it, but the idea was suddenly circulated that, as of course Baba Alba was as usual responsible for all the ill luck which fell upon the community, she ought to be made to pay for it. One had had patience long enough, but the crack in the bell was the limit, it was beyond what any Christian could tolerate – and so... here many heads were put together, and there was much whispering... Baba Alba has a bell... Yes, but... Well, it's only fair!... Yes, of course it was fair, but... But what?... Well, who would like to go and fetch her bell? Go inside her enclosure! Face her spells and her black arts!... Ah! Indeed, there was the hitch! Certainly, there were hours when she left her hut to wander in the forest, those mysterious, suspicious wanderings... But all the same... And the old raven, was he not the devil's first cousin? – And there was the lizard. Of course, a lizard is a very small animal, but if you look at it attentively, you can see that it has quite the shape of a crocodile... And who could know how far a witch's power went... She could perhaps turn you to stone, or smite you with blindness, or steal your reason from you... Or even turn you into a hare, which all the dogs would chase... Oh! Certainly, whatever one undertook must be undertaken with precautions... And all the wise men of the village rubbed their scrubby chins, and scratched the back of their heads in perplexity. "Why not in the night?" suggested someone... Splendid! That was the way – in the night, when everything was dark; but it must be before Christmas, so that the new bell could be hung up for the holy feast-days... No one had ever heard its voice – but all of them were dead certain that the bell must long to be freed from the terrible old woman's black arts – so not only was it not stealing, but a blessed deed... A real Christian deed, almost a crusade in fact!.. This last idea was very pleasant to the ardent churchgoers; it set their consciences at rest! To free the bell, that really would be a fine thing. A Christian bell in such hands!

And so it was decided that on the night before Christmas Eve, a whole band of strong and decided young fellows should steal up to old Baba Alba's enclosure and carry off the bell – deliver it, they said, and no one admitted that such an heroic deed could be called theft...

But this is how it all came to pass. Listen well, for it is rather wonderful what I am going to relate:

The days crept by, no faster or slower than usual, although a smoldering excitement could be felt everywhere in the village. Only Vasile, who even in winter-time guarded the priest's pigs, knew nothing about what had been planned against his old friend, and on the very same evening that the deed was to be done, he climbed up the steep path to Baba Alba's cottage; he had visited her more often than ever since that night when she had told him all about Tudor, her son. Her hope had now become his; ardently, ardently he desired to hear the voice of the bell, which would mean that the murderer had found at last mercy in the sight of the Lord. Tudor must be also a very old man now, nigh upon seventy, Vasile had calculated in his slow way, because although Baba Alba was not as old as the hills, she was very, very old, cruelly, sadly old and worn-out. That one frail hope alone kept her from laying down to die... Vasile understood instinctively that she was longing for eternal rest. When he reached the old woman's hut, he found his lonely friend just stepping out into the cold moonlight, closing the door behind her so that the heat of her *vatra* should not escape into the night. She was a queer figure indeed, for she had heaped all the old rags she possessed upon her body, and over the whole she had hung a rough sheepskin coat. An old white cloth was on her head and fingerless gloves of felt on her hands. She looked very tiny and frail, and limped along painfully with the aid of a thick crooked stick.

"Come with me," she said to the orphan. "But it will be cold, very cold, and perhaps we shall sit there in vain – I do not know why, I have a curious presentiment that this night something will happen..." And as she said this, her old raven croaked three times. "He feels something in the air, I am sure," she added. The strange companions sat down in their usual place. Yes, certainly it was very cold, and all about them the snow sparkled crisply – the stars were out in myriads, and the moon was almost full. There was no wind. Above the bell, which glimmered faintly, sat the old raven, darker and gaunter than ever, a shadow to which Vasile had grown quite accustomed. In fact, he knew he would have missed it, had it no more been there.

At first all was quite still. The old woman was mumbling something under her breath, rocking herself slowly backwards and forwards with an almost unconscious movement. "Something is going to happen, something is going to happen," was the thought that was rolling about in Vasile's head.

172

And, indeed, steps were coming stealthily up the hill – many steps, but Vasile did not hear them, they were deadened by the thick, hard snow.

All at once the light on the bell began to brighten visibly – yes, it really did! Or was Vasile only imagining it to himself? – But Baba Alba must have seen it also, for she suddenly laid hold of the little boy's hand. Both of them stared and stared – and as they stared, the bell before them became brighter and brighter, till finally their eyes could hardly bear the glare… But it was not only Vasile and his old companion who were perceiving this astonishing phenomenon; the band of strong young fellows, who had come up so stealthily, to do a deed they had tried to convince themselves was heroic, had halted at the old witch's thorn hedge, and were gazing with all their eyes at the extraordinary sight.

Brighter, brighter grew the bell, till it danced before their eyes like a living flame – and then, oh, dear! A marvelous note rose clear into the air, vibrant, musical, heavenly, with a sound of ecstasy in it, a sound of longing – a sound of deliverance…

And all those looking on saw how old Baba Alba rose to her feet, how age seemed to fall from her, her shoulders to straighten, how she seemed to grow beneath the marvelous light which inundated her with a radiance which could be naught but heavenly! But the most extraordinary thing of all was that out of the dark a tall figure was seen advancing towards her with outstretched arms, the figure of a man, and the same light, which transfigured the despised old outcast, threw an astonishing radiance upon the man's face… And all saw that it was the face of a quite young, a very beautiful stripling – and his eyes were blue and star-like as the eyes of Vasile the orphan.

And all the while the bell was ringing, ringing, ringing, like a voice full of an ecstasy too great for this earth… Then, as suddenly as the vision had risen before their eyes, it began to dissolve, and with it the light on the bell vanished. Everything became pale and ghostly once more in a world where the moon alone shed its radiance over the indifferent, hard-frozen silent earth…

On the ground beneath the bell lay Baba Alba, her arms outstretched like the arms of a cross, her poor old face buried in the snow, and above her the ink-black raven croaked and croaked, as though he could never stop croaking any more. Vasile sank on his knees beside the old woman he had learned to love, and very gently, as one who wants to express his sympathy, he began stroking the white cloth, which covered Baba Alba's head…

But those who had come to do a brave deed slunk away one by one, not looking behind them – shamefacedly, without finding a word to say – and as they silently descended the steep mountain path, the bell began to sound again – but this time mournfully, tolling a knell for the dead.

On the day after Christmas, old Baba Alba was buried in the old cemetery on the hillside. No one discussed her right to be laid in holy ground. Those who had contemplated the marvelous vision of that night, when they had stolen up the hill with evil thoughts in their hearts, ever afterwards crossed themselves when they remembered what they had seen; and the villagers never doubted their tale, for had not everyone heard the wondrous voice of the bell, as it suddenly tolled out into the night?

It was even decided that it was sacrilege to move the bell from where it hung. The spot became a blessed spot, and because Vasile alone had recognized that Baba Alba was not a witch, he was appointed as guardian of the bell. He was even given a very small pittance by the community, so that he could inhabit Baba Alba's crooked little cottage with the over-large maize-roof. Popa Dionisie's pigs were fetched up by him each day to graze in the enclosure, which in former days Vasile alone had dared to enter.

But only on feast-days and days of fasts and mourning did Vasile ever sound the bell. Its voice was always beautiful, but never, never again did it sing as it had done on that night when Baba Alba's son had found forgiveness.

The old raven kept his place on the pole above the bell, till the first *viorele*[51] poked their blue heads through their winter covering of dead leaves; then it flew away, and was never more seen. But the little green lizard lived with Vasile. They loved each other very much, and no one any more feared that he would turn into a crocodile...

On the same day that Baba Alba was buried, it came to pass that a far-off monastery, hidden away amongst high mountains and night-black fir trees, a very old monk was laid to rest in the solitary forest curchyard, which faced the rising sun. Two nights before, the very old monk had called the *staritz*[52] to his death-bed and had confessed a crime committed in his youth, nearly threescore years ago... He had been a silent man and none of the other brothers had ever guessed that a murderer had been living in their midst – but when he was dead they missed him, because, although he was old, old and taciturn, he had had eyes as blue as mountain lakes.

"You remember," said one old monk to another, "how thirty years ago he decided, as penance, to carry our old castaway bell over seven hills and seven dales to the poorest house in the farthest village he could reach?... Indeed he was a strange, but a holy man." And the *staritz*, passing that way, heard them – but he said nothing, although three days ago he knew to whose hut the bell had been brought. Confession is sacred – the *staritz* was the sole guardian now of the secret, which had remained fifty years locked away in the impenitent heart of old Baba Alba's son…

---

[51] "Viorele", blue scylla [note in the first edition].
[52] "Staritz" [stareț], abbot [note in the first edition].

174

The Snake Island

Somewhere in the middle of the sea lies a small island, called the Island of Snakes. It looks like an enormous rock which has been dropped there, nobody knows why, nobody knows when. Nobody knows either why the island is called the Island of Snakes, nobody has ever seen any snakes upon it, but I know why, and I am going to tell you all about it; it is a very curious story, and I am sure it will interest you very much.

Right in the center of the island stands a lighthouse. Snow-white its tower rises like a mysterious giant column towards the skies. An old Turk with a white beard guards it. He is a lonesome old fellow, who has almost forgotten the human tongue, so long has he lived there in utter solitude, and when anyone visits him, he mostly talks in gestures, nods his head, shrugs his shoulders, moves his hands about, winks with his eyes, so that you can understand him even if you do not talk Turkish.

One day his granddaughter came to live with him, because people were getting afraid that the old man might go mad with loneliness, with no company except that of the white seagulls which lived by hundreds and thousands amongst the rocks, filling the air with their weird, melancholy cries – just like distressed little children calling for their mothers.

"He might go mad and forget to light the lamp," people declared, "and so he must have a companion."

The old Turk had too few words to explain that he did not mind his solitude, but that it might be too much for such a very young girl. Nobody seemed to understand his objections, so he gave up trying to explain, nodded his old head and accepted a situation, which, after all, had its advantages. Now he need no more cook his own meals, nor tidy up the house; there was something in that, yes, indeed, there was something in that! He would make long, lazy mornings of it, lying in bed, puffing at his old pipe and thinking of I know not what, whilst his granddaughter cooked and tidied up. What do you think that a lonely old Turk on a rock in the middle of the sea can think of? Perhaps of the light which he lights every evening, perhaps of the ships, which might pass that way, perhaps of his youth? Perhaps of his Turkish paradise, or perhaps only of his supper? Who knows?

Zuleika, his granddaughter, was a very beautiful girl with extraordinary red hair; so beautiful was she, in fact, that it really seemed a pity that she should live all alone on a desert island with an old man who only talked in gestures. But Zuleika had a happy nature, and sang all day long as she went about her work. She loved the blue sky and the deep, restless sea, which encircled her; she loved the screeching, twirling, restless seagulls, so white that their wings were like flashes of silver in the moonlight; she loved the smell of camomile flowers, the only plant which grew amongst the rocks, she even loved the storms and the furious winds which tried to tear her red hair from her head. She did not mind the solitude; there was so much joy and youth in her heart that it brightened all things for her, even her mute old grandfather whom she dearly cherished. "His beard is as white as the walls of his tower," she would declare, "and I like things that harmonize. Also the seagulls seem to have brushed their wings against the whitewash, but I do wonder what they have lost, so as to screech like that all day long!" Zuleika, as you see, was not to be pitied, and I know that you would have loved the smile of her lips, and the flash of her fine white teeth. She could take her work easily, because there was never any hurry in this desolate place, no visits to prepare for, no fuss, no worry, no distraction; of course, it could have been called dull, but Zuleika's heart was too merry ever to feel dull; besides she had a vivid imagination, and that is almost like a companion. Zuleika felt sure that one day something wonderful would happen to her. She dreamed of adventures of all sorts. Beautiful princes generally appeared in these dreams; they had golden curls, and their rich clothing was always of the brightest hue. "If the sky and the sea are so beautiful," argued Zuleika with herself, "there must be also other beautiful things on earth – so why not also beautiful princes with golden locks?" Then she would laugh, and her glorious teeth would flash in the sunshine, white as her grandfather's lighthouse, white as the seagulls' wings. "It's a glorious thing to be young," she cried, "and to have a heart that laughs within you, just because you are alive."

She was standing on a high rock on the very edge of the sea. The wind had got hold of her fiery tresses, and was tossing them about like flames. Circling above her against the bright blue sky were a thousand, thousand seagulls, filling the air with their shrieks. The sea was blue as a dark sapphire, and foam, white as snow, dashed up against the foot of the rock where she stood. All of a sudden, her eye was attracted by something extraordinarily shiny, which was gliding towards her over the ground. It was green and gold and blue, really it had beautiful colors. What could it be? The sun made it shine and flash, then suddenly, when it dipped into a piece of uneven ground, it would become shadowy, then flash again. Zuleika stood quite still, her hair tossed all around her head by the wind. The wind knew how beautiful she was, also the laughing blue sky overhead knew it, and the white foam beneath seemed to long to kiss her feet.

All at once, Zuleika understood that what was gliding towards her was a large glittering snake! She stood quite still, overcome by fear at the sight. "What shall I do?" she said to herself. "I do not want to have to pass the creature, and yet I cannot retreat, because I am quite on the edge of the rock!" And she began to tremble all over, and the seagulls circling above her head shrieked louder than ever.

Once, in very ancient times, Mother Eve was fascinated by a serpent who led her into really bad trouble, and ever since its aspect has had a curious effect upon the daughters of man; they are attracted and repelled all in one. This is just what was happening to red-haired Zuleika. The serpent had ceased moving, and was staring at the beautiful girl with luminous eyes. The longer it stared, the more completely without will did Zuleika feel; her blood seemed to be turning to water in her veins, she was no more Zuleika at all, only a very submissive being, entirely fascinated by those two eyes which were staring at her.

All at once the snake turned and began sliding off in the opposite direction, and the young girl, as though it were the most natural thing in the world, followed it obediently, just as if an order had been given to her. The sea-gulls shrieked their warning, but Zuleika had no ears for their calls; the sea beneath dashed up against the rocks, imploring her to turn back, but Zuleika, with a smile on her lips, followed the serpent over the whole island's length.

That evening the old Turk waited in vain for his granddaughter. She did not come. His supper was uncooked, and with much grumbling he scraped together the cold remains of his midday meal, then with stiff legs climbed the long stairs to light his lamp. When he came down again Zuleika had not yet returned. Of course the old fellow ought to have been very anxious, but he was calm by nature and old age, and the solitude he had for so many years lived in had made him quite unemotional. He simply took his pipe and went to sit outside, watching the stars come out one by one.

"Ah! But that was a nasty supper I ate this evening," he murmured. "It's a pity indeed the lass did not return, I don't want to have to begin my own cooking all over again," and he sighed, rubbing his forehead with his trembling old hand as one who would like to think and cannot.

It became darker and darker, and still he sat there puffing at his pipe. The wind made his white beard tremble, but the stars paid no attention to him at all. All about him was the sound of the sea, the sound he had lived with for so many years.

"The island is not very big," murmured the old man, "one can scarcely get lost upon it, and if the child has fallen into the sea, it's not I who'll be able to fish her out again – but a rare pity it would be!"

And two visions kept rising in his stiff old brain, that of cold suppers and of Zuleika's beautiful red hair floating upon the waves like prodigious seaweed.

"And certainly it would be a pity," he murmured, "such young blood," but more than that he would not worry, except that instead of going inside, he sat there all night under the stars, with his back against the white wall of his lighthouse, even after his pipe had gone out.

And Zuleika, what had happened to Zuleika? Of course, you will be wondering, and having a more lively brain than the lighthouse keeper, you will be impatient to know. The truth is that what happened to Zuleika is so extraordinary, that I am sure it will be difficult for you to believe!

She continued to follow the uncanny but beautiful reptile as though it had been the most natural thing in the world. Right across the island did the serpent lead her, till they reached the further side, where the rocks were very rough and uneven. Zuleika had generally bare feet, or they were stuck into loose *papuci*[53], for you must not forget that Zuleika was a Turkish girl, and that she wore large baggy trousers of faded blue cotton, a very attractive color, which made a pleasant harmony with her red hair, and over these trousers she wore a sort of wide cloak of the same material, covering head and shoulders. This cloak she held together under her eyes if she was in male company, but here on the desert island it was not necessary, her grandfather was too old to count as a man; besides, he was her grandfather. All at once, the serpent began gliding down between two rocks, down, down, until it paused before the narrow entry to a cave. Never had the girl, though she had thoroughly explored the island, discovered this cave. This was really most exciting! And so entirely under the snake's spell was Zuleika, that not for a moment did she hesitate to enter the dark tunnel in its wake. Phew! But it was dark! Zuleika kept stumbling and bumping her head and arms. In places, the passage was quite low, so that Zuleika had almost to bend in two. Her strange companion had become faintly phosphorescent, so that she could see it in the dark like a phantom streak of light. The passage seemed endless, and the girl was beginning to like her adventure no more when suddenly the passage opened out and...

Oh, dear, what a sight! Zuleika stood as though frozen to the spot. A shudder of fear ran through her body, but she could not move, her feet seemed rooted to the ground, she simply stood still and stared. She found herself in a sort of cave, and in the middle of it sat the most terrifying old hag you can possibly imagine. She looked hundreds of years old, and was squatting all of a heap, surrounded by a circle of glittering snakes. Two dripping candles burned on each side of her. Like streaks of mildew her grey-green locks hung down over her withered cheeks. Her eyes were deep-sunken and red-rimmed, her lower lip hung loosely, and her head had a trembling movement, as though mounted on wires. I cannot tell you what she was dressed in, there was no shape about her at all, her body looked like a thrown-away heap of filthy rags. She certainly was a frightening and horrible sight, and no less frightening were her uncanny companions – really, poor Zuleika had been lured into a terrible place!

The horrible old witch had a sort of tom-tom in her hands. This does not sound as though it were a very attractive instrument, but the strange thing was that each time the old horror struck it, a most enchanting melody rose from beneath her skeleton fingers, and it was this music which fascinated

---

[53] "Papuci", heelless slippers [note in the first edition].

178

the snakes as well as the girl, who never in her life had heard sound more beautiful. It was a strange mixture of harps, bells, and violins, so sweet and alluring that she felt her heart become quite soft within her, and a warm, glorious feeling flow through her veins, as though sunshine had entered her blood. The old hag kept staring at Zuleika as she beat on her tom-tom. Her horrible red-rimmed eyes seemed to have the same power as that of the serpent who had led her to this place, and the girl felt that she was being irresistibly drawn within the circle of snakes, till at last she found herself seated by the side of the old monster, quite near her, and in a dazed way she saw how all the serpents were staring at her, whilst the magic music held her completely under its spell.

All at once, the witch stopped playing, and the snakes glided away, rolling themselves up into uncanny coils against the walls of the cave.

"I've been waiting many years for you!" declared the old hag to Zuleika.

"What are you?" asked the girl with quaking voice.

"I'm Zampura, the snake charmer and guardian of treasures and secrets. My years have never been numbered, my wisdom has never been fathomed. All knowledge of things on the earth and under the earth is mine."

"What do you want with me?" asked the frightened girl.

"That you will learn in good time," said the witch, with a toothless grin.

With a shudder, Zuleika moved away a little.

"Oh, no one cares much for me," chuckled the old horror, "except when I play on my tom-tom," and again Zampura touched her wonderful instrument.

Immediately Zuleika felt that extraordinary sensation of wellbeing, as though the music were sunshine running through her veins.

Putting down her tom-tom, Zampura suddenly called out, "Turo, Turo!" and the serpent who had been Zuleika's leader came gliding towards them from somewhere out of the shade.

"Lead this earth-born with the fiery locks there where thou knowest, and when thou hast reached the last door, there shalt thou leave her. Go!" said the witch, turning to her captive. "Go there where my servant shall lead thee."

"Oh, but I must get back to my grandfather," protested Zuleika, "besides, I would rather go home!"

"Follow my servant," commanded the terrible woman, and as the girl still hesitated between her fear of the witch and her desire to escape, she was suddenly enwrapped again in waves of irresistible harmony, so that tamely she rose to her feet and without further protest followed the serpent, who led her away past its coiled companions, down another tunnel, where there were many doors. These doors opened one after another as Zuleika passed, revealing unheard-of treasures of gold and precious stones. In each room lay different colored gems stored up in glittering heaps which dazzled the eye – red, blue, green, violet, flame-colored – as well as pearls and diamonds; so brilliant were the diamonds that sparks flew out of them like small flashes of lightning. "Oh, oh, oh!" exclaimed the girl, and she found no other word but "oh!" so dazzled and fascinated was she by these extraordinary riches. She quite forgot to be frightened, it was all like some wonderful dream. Who did this treasure belong to? How in the world had it come there? But the serpent said nothing, nor did it pause; it simply glided on and Zuleika had to follow it. At last it stopped before a closed door, and hit its head against it three times, like a miniature battering ram. The door opened and Zuleika drew back with a gasp... She was looking into a small domed cave all of glittering stones, as though the rock were shot through and through with gold. On the floor a rare Persian carpet all blue, green, and brown had been spread, and coiled in the center lay a huge, huge serpent... But what made this serpent so distinctive from any other was that it had the color of old ivory, white with yellow shades, and upon its head was a small golden crown, each spike of which was tipped with a pear-shaped pearl! Repulsive and yet beautiful was the terrible creature, and when it raised its head, Zuleika had the uncanny sensation that it was looking at her with human eyes.

Almost without knowing that she was moving, Zuleika stepped into the cave, and as she did so the door shut behind her, and with a shudder she realized that she had been left all alone face to face with the ghostly reptile.

Slowly the creature uncoiled itself and came sliding noiselessly towards the frightened girl's feet. She flattened herself against the wall, tried to scream, but no sound came from her blanched lips. Nearer, nearer came the sliding, gliding monster! Zuleika had lost her slippers long ago, her feet were quite bare; now she could feel the serpent's cold coils passing over her toes; again, she tried to scream, but she seemed to have quite lost her voice. With a gesture of instinctive self-protection, she folded her arms over her face, and began to sob convulsively.

All at once, the same soft sounds of sweet music, which already twice had charmed her, came floating through the air, enwrapping her in its waves of irresistible harmony. What happened then she never quite realized, but as the music died down, becoming fainter and fainter, she found herself seated upon the beauteous Persian carpet and coiled in white rings around her was the giant serpent, its head resting upon her knees, looking up at her with its human eyes so full of pain.

This cave also was lighted by two tall, thick candles, stuck into queer-shaped bronze holders. Softly, softly the wax dripped; a faint odor of incense rose from their flames, pervading the place.

"I'm dreaming," said Zuleika to herself, and quite unconsciously she began stroking the great snake's head. "It's no good struggling against a dream, one just has to let oneself live through it, and the happy moment will come when I'll wake up. Now I won't be a bit astonished if this gruesome creature suddenly begins talking to me, it would be well in keeping with all the

180

rest." And hardly had this thought come to the girl, than the serpent lifted its head and actually did speak.

"I'm sad, fair maiden," it said; "sad, so sad, for indeed I am not really a snake at all, but an unfortunate prince under a dreadful spell!"

"A prince!" cried Zuleika. Had she not always dreamed of meeting a prince? – But oh, not in this form! She shuddered.

"I make you shudder!" pursued the sad voice, "yet so long have I yearned for human companionship! But it has always been refused me. Lately the burden of my captivity has weighed so heavily upon me that I began to pine away. Old Zampura became anxious, afraid that I should die, therefore has she lured you into my cave, so that I should not mope so much, but I know that I disgust you, and yet I can only be saved through a maiden's love."

Yes, the strange dream was continuing – did ever human maid have so queer a dream! She had always desired adventure, now she was in the middle of adventure so strange that her wildest imagination had never even pictured it – or was it a dream? Was it?

The soft voice continued: "All those treasures have been gathered by the terrible old woman through centuries; she is old, old, no one can calculate how old! They are all the treasures gathered in from ships which used to be wrecked upon these rocks, but since the lighthouse has burned upon it there are no more wrecks. This enrages old Zampura, and she hates your grandfather. In hopes of making him forget to light his lamp she has lured you into her caves – and she has sent you to me because she knows I am pining for human company, but she does not know that you could save me!"

"How could I save you?" whispered Zuleika – the serpent's head was now lying on her shoulder.

"You must love me," murmured the creature.

"Oh, but how can I love you!" cried the unfortunate girl.

"Look into my eyes and perhaps you will be able to," implored the poor serpent.

"Oh no, oh no, I want to wake up, I want to go home!" sobbed Zuleika like a little child.

The serpent coiled itself a little nearer and began relating in a whisper: "I am in reality a prince; I belong to a country where the flowers bloom all the year round, where soft silken stuffs are woven, and carpets thick as freshly fallen snow. I possess a palace built of sea-green marble, with ten tall towers, which overlook all the land. Birds of paradise fly in and out of the trees in my gardens, where silver fountains tell their secrets to the lovers who stroll 'neath the light of the moon! Fifty milk-white stallions stand in my stables, their hoofs are of polished gold. Peacocks strut over the twenty terraces, and when the sun sets, each evening a silver bell sounds from the highest tower, and its voice is like a prayer which is heard all over my land..." the serpent paused.

"Go on," murmured Zuleika – her eyes were closed – "go on speaking, it's like a wondrous fairy tale."

"Within the palace," continued the snake, "there are seven different halls in seven different-colored stones. One is blue as hills seen at a distance, one is pink as the first almond blossom kissed by spring. One is golden as the sun's first greeting, one is green as paradise meadows, one is white as the North Pole's ice fields, one is purple as an emperor's mantle, and the last is black as a starless night. In the center of its floor splashes a magic fountain, throwing up blue, shining bubbles to the ceiling, which is so high that the eye can hardly see it, and one wonders if it is but the dark sky overhead – the palace floors are each day strewn with the heads of freshly cut roses, red as bleeding hearts. Sweet music sounds from every corner, and in the royal bed-chamber is a couch all covered with silken draperies the color of the moon..." For a moment, the serpent paused, then very gently it said: "And all this can be thine, oh, sweet, sweet maiden, if thou couldst but love a snake!" and now the serpent's head lay under Zuleika's cheek, and Zuleika did not shudder. Indeed, indeed it was a wondrous dream.

The old lighthouse keeper was standing beneath his tower. The light of the sun shining on rocks and sea dazzled his tired eyes; he had raised his hand to shade them as he gazed out towards the horizon. What was he expecting? What was he waiting for? Really, the old man hardly knew. Something uncomfortable was stirring in his heart, something was wrong with the world. Solitude had never weighed upon him before, but now somehow everything seemed horribly still. He had hardly held converse with his granddaughter, had never realized that her glorious youth had gladdened his days. Oh, if only she had never come here! Formerly he had not felt his loneliness, but now he could have cried aloud with the desire to see the red-haired maiden once more come towards him with that wondrous smile on her lips.

With a weary sigh the old Turk let his hand sink to his side; no ship gladdened the horizon, no figure of youth came striding towards him over the blooming camomile flowers, crushing their heads 'neath her bare brown feet till the air was full of their pungent perfume. With dragging steps the lonely man crept back to his small white room. Lighting his pipe he sat down upon his bed, head bent, his hands hanging between his knees. He was not hungry, nothing tasted good anymore; even his pipe brought little comfort, and the sea seemed to be sobbing – never before had he noticed how it sobbed.

Suddenly a little sound made him look up, and there stood Zuleika on the doorstep – all the sunshine seemed to stream into the room with her, her head was a blaze of fiery red. But was it really Zuleika, that pale-faced girl! And where was the smile on her lips?

"Zuleika," said the old man, "Zuleika," and with a little cry Zuleika ran towards him, and throwing herself down on the ground, hid her face on his knees and sobbed.

"Zuleika, Zuleika," no word but her name came to the old Turk's lips, who had quite forgotten how to talk or to express any emotion.

And it was better so; Zuleika did not want to talk. A week had she been absent, and now she knew that what she had lived through had not been a dream; she had returned different from what she was when she had gone away, a lifetime seemed to have been lived through since then.

It was the ivory-colored serpent who had helped her to escape; it knew the old witch's habits, and had been able to tell her when the cave's entry was unguarded, and thus had she this morning managed to steal away. But though free, Zuleika was not happy. Something cruelly heavy weighed on her heart. Something like a regret, or more truly, something like a remorse. The bewitched prince had asked for her love, had implored her to kiss him, once, only once, declaring that thus would the spell, which held him captive, be broken. But Zuleika had shuddered at the thought, again and again had she tried to overcome her repulsion, and had failed. With eyes as sad as human eyes when filled with grief, the great serpent had looked at her – but even those looks which made the tears start to her eyes had not been able to overcome her repulsion – she could not, could not kiss a snake…

Silently Zuleika went about her work. But how changed she was! The old Turk watched her, and his heart was sad. Zuleika sang no more, laughed no more, Zuleika was like a pale ghost of herself.

Is that the end of Zuleika's adventure, you will be wondering? No, oh no, for this, as I told you, is a very curious story. When the sun went down, and the old Turk had gone up the long stairs to light his lamp, a great unrest came over the red-haired maiden. She had prepared and laid out her grandfather's supper, tidied up the room, set things in order; now her work was done, so she sat down on the bed. Everything seemed strange to her, unreal, or was it she who had become unreal? The last rays of the sun were filling the white little room till it became all golden yellow, and then gradually turned rosy-red. And as she sat there a vision rose suddenly before her eyes, the vision of a great palace somewhere in a far-distant land. She was treading on marble floors, which changed color beneath her feet, till her steps directed her towards a hall all black, so black, that it was as though all at once she had stepped from day into night...

Something was gliding towards her over the marble slabs, something ghostly, and although all around her was dark, impenetrable night, two eyes were gazing at her, two great sad eyes with a look so pleading that Zuleika rose from the bed with a cry, clutching at her red locks with both hands in a wild gesture of fear. An intolerable longing had stolen into her heart, something that seemed to torture the very soul within her, filling her with aching, pulsing pain. What was it? Something was driving her, forcing her to leave the small white room. And was that music? Oh, yes, well did she know that tune – she could not resist, it was calling her, calling her away... Zuleika sprang towards the door; her face was ghastly, pale and trembling were her half-open lips. But on the threshold she met her grandfather, who stared at her with a puzzled look, then laying his hand on her arm, he quietly led her back into the house.

"Zuleika, Zuleika," he repeated many times, "Zuleika!" and patted her head gently, as we sometimes pat a restive, frightened horse – and that night Zuleika lay all huddled up on the floor beside her grandfather's bed, her head nestling close to his rough old hand.

Four days running, at the hour of sunset, did the same strange unrest come over Zuleika, and each time it was her mute old grandfather who brought some sort of quiet back to her troubled spirit; but the fifth evening the old Turk lingered somewhat longer up there with the lighting of his lamp, and when he came back, the little white room was empty, quite empty, except for the last golden rays of the dying sun, which made it gloriously bright.

„Zuleika, Zuleika," cried the old man, quite distracted, „Zuleika, Zuleika! Don't leave me quite alone!"

But his voice received no answer, gradually the golden glow faded quite away, and the old Turk was left all alone, shivering in the gathering shadows of night...

Yes, Zuleika had stolen back to the cave of snakes! She too had been bewitched! When the hour of sunset came she could remain no more in the lighthouse, a thousand threads seemed drawing soul and body towards the dark place whence she had so desired to escape. Was it old Zampura's charmed music, which was drawing her, or was it... was it something else...? Zuleika did not know, did not argue with herself; she was unaccustomed to complicated soul-problems, she only knew that her heart was aching with almost physical pain, tears were in her throat, and her arms felt empty, she knew not of what!

Oh, it could not be that she had really come to love the gruesome ivory-white snake? Yet she saw its eyes everywhere, in all things; their pleading was always with her, and with it an overwhelming yearning to hear once more the dreaded reptile's soft, tender voice. Its fate had lain in her hands, hers had been the power to release it from captivity, from the deadly power Zampura had over it, and she had failed. Now peace fled from her, her once quiet life sufficed her no more, all the time she was longing, longing she knew not for what! Was love really stirring within her heart?

As Zuleika reached the cave's entry, she found Turo the snake waiting for her there, as though it had been the most natural thing in the world. Unhesitatingly, she followed him as she had done the first time... And there in the center of the first grotto sat the fearful witch, her wobbly old head shaking and trembling more than ever; her awful red-rimmed eyes staring at her victim, whilst a grin of triumph rendered still more hideous her repulsive mouth.

"Ah, ha, ah, ha!" she chuckled, "so you have come back, have you? And at last some sort of emotion is shaking the half-witted old grandfather of yours, and now when you won't go back at all any more, then perhaps he'll become distracted, and at last forget to light his lamp, which may cause new treasures to find their way to my dwelling; it's already too long since we've had any wrecks!" and the monster laughed a gruesome, sinister laugh.

Zuleika stood quite still, she could not move. Pale as death was she.

"I'm going to make it quite impossible for you ever to go back to your grandfather," continued the tormentor. "Drink this, then you'll be mine, for all time mine!" and with a skeleton hand the witch held out to her captive a small white-jade bowl, filled with some unknown beverage.

Still Zuleika did not move; fascinated as she was by the sorceress, some vestige of will still remained in her; she would not, oh no, she would not swallow that philter which would change her, God knows into what!

"How dare you disobey me!" screamed the hag, "drink this immediately, or I shall have you stung to death by my snakes!"

But still Zuleika did not budge, it was as though some secret power were urging her to resist.

"Rise up, all my followers," cried the terrible woman, clapping her hands together with a sound of rattling bones; and oh, horror! From all corners of the cave snakes began sliding towards her, a gruesome company, which seemed to rise out of the shadows to destroy this unruly child of man.

Zuleika began to tremble, all her flesh shivered, every drop of blood was turning to ice in her veins, and yet something, something within her urged her to resist. Now the serpents had formed a circle around her. Their beady eyes were fixed upon her; their forked tongues were darting in and out of their mouths, as though ready at any moment, nay, eager, to strike.

"Once more I call upon you either to drink the draught I offer you, and to become a snake among snakes, or to die by a thousand stings, which those into whose ranks you refuse to enter will inflict upon you with a thousand pains!"

Just as Zuleika was stepping forward to accept the fatal cup, overcome with horror no words can describe, there was a flash like white light, and suddenly she felt that something appallingly powerful was clasping her body in an iron grip! A scream of terror escaped her lips; now, indeed, death was upon her, there was no escape! No escape...!

Then all at once, amidst sounds of deadly sweet music, she heard a voice whispering into her ear, "Kiss me, kiss me, and with that one kiss save us both!" and there on her shoulder lay the great white serpent's head, imploring her with its eyes so human in their pain.

Without hesitating, as one who feels death quite near, Zuleika bent down and pressed her warm young lips to the cold, repulsive head of the snake...

A wild cry! The hissing of many furious reptiles... flashes of light, magic strains of music... then a sensation of relief, oh, what exquisite relief, and looking up, Zuleika saw smiling down upon her the face of the fairy prince, which had haunted the dreams of her youth.

Yes! She was in his arms, her head lay against his heart, he was kissing her eyes, her cheeks, her lips. Golden were his curls as she had always seen them in her visions, upon his head he wore a crown tipped by pear-shaped pearls, and his eyes, his wonderful eyes, were those which had called her so irresistibly back to this gruesome place...

"Thou hast delivered me, oh, Zuleika!" he said, pressing her passionately against his breast. "With thy kiss of pity and love thou hast given me back life and hope. Now thou art mine, and I shall carry thee off to that enchanted sea-green palace, with its ten tall towers, which overlook the whole land. Thou shalt hear my fountains splash, my fifty white stallions will neigh when they hear thee approaching, and all the birds of paradise will follow wherever thou goest!"

Zuleika said nothing, she only knew that this was reality, that now she was not dreaming, and that her heart, her young heart, was bursting with love.

Crouched in a horrible heap, all-livid with fear, sat the evil witch. It was her turn to shudder and tremble.

"Look not upon the deed I must now do, my Zuleika," spoke the prince, "but justice has to be done; I have been delivered, and now it is my turn to deliver others as unfortunate as I!" And drawing his sword, with one mighty stroke he severed the wicked woman's head from her body, so that it rolled like a horrid ball all over the floor of the cave!

As he did so, a great cry of joy was heard echoing through the place, and a crowd of eager young faces pressed round the lovers, who were clasped in each other's arms.

"We are delivered, we are delivered!" they cried, for all the other snakes had also once been human beings who had fallen into Zampura's hands. Now their former shapes had been given back to them, and therefore mightily did they rejoice.

"Now all is well, thanks to thee," said the prince, "come with me; we shall go to thy grandfather to receive his blessing, then away together over the blue sea towards joy shall we sail!" and taking his bride by the hand, the prince, followed by the happy throng of those who had been delivered, led his beloved out of the fatal cave – but as she passed the terrible head of Zampura, Zuleika hid her face in her hands, for there it lay grinning, a ghastly, harmless thing.

The light of the moon was vying with the old Turk's lamp, for in spite of his pain and anxiety he had not forgotten to light the signal, which shone far out to sea. All lonely he sat, propped up against the whitewashed wall.

His pipe had gone out, and his hands were trembling, he hardly knew why. All at once, it seemed to him that he espied a great white sail, floating o'er the dark sea towards his rocky isle. And what was that? The sound of many voices all singing together in chorus a song which sounded like a hymn of thanksgiving! Who could be singing on this lonely, lonely night? Nearer and nearer it came and so beautiful it was that involuntarily the old man folded his hands.

And there stood Zuleika, the moonshine streaming down upon her fiery head, making it look all silvery. By the hand she was holding a young man in costly raiment; so costly, indeed, was his raiment, and so beautiful was his countenance, that naught else could he be but the son of a king. Behind them in long file were other couples, singing, singing a happy chant, which rejoiced both the moon and the stars. Or were they all but ghostly apparitions? Was he dreaming, was he dreaming? Oh! What had come to pass?

I know not if the old lighthouse keeper ever quite understood what had happened; although Zuleika tried to explain it to him, you must also admit that it was asking rather much of his stiff old brains. But this he knew: that the ship he had seen sailing towards him 'neath the face of the moon had been no phantom ship, but a costly vessel, such as never before had anchored near his isle, and that next morning it had sailed away with his red-haired Zuleika, sailed away for a far-off shore. Wrapped in her old faded blue cloak had she stood, holding its worn folds together under her eyes, whilst sacks and sacks of treasure were being heaped about her upon the deck. Oh! What did it all mean, what did it mean?

But one thing was certain: it was a king's son who was standing beside her, and love, ardent love, was shining in both their eyes. Behind them those who had come with them yesterday were once more singing that song which sounded like a hymn of thanksgiving...

Then the ship had begun moving away, slowly, slowly, like a stately swan who knows naught of haste. Zuleika had waved her hand, waved and waved it till he could distinguish her figure no more.

Sadly had the old man wandered back to his lighthouse; never before had the way seemed so long, never had his legs felt so weary, so heavy the weight of years... A small sack full of something very heavy had the beautiful prince pressed into his hands as he went... The old man sat down on his usual seat, his back to the whitewashed walls of his tower, face turned towards the heaving, sailless sea. Without curiosity, he opened the sack and, diving his hand deep into it, he drew out a number of shining precious stones – blue, green, red, white, violet, they lay sparkling in his palm. Oh, what were they? Whence did they come? What did it all mean?

The old Turk shook his head: "I really do not understand anything anymore," he sighed. "It's all too confusing; such things ought not to happen to a solitary old man on a rock in the middle of the sea, because his brain simply cannot comprehend what it is all about! But Zuleika? Why did Zuleika leave me? If she meant to leave me, why did Zuleika come here at all?" and again he shook his head.

Round about his tower the seagulls sailed and screeched; there were thousands and thousands of them, and all of them seemed to want to explain to him the things he did not understand, but it was too complicated; then, really they ought not all to talk at once. But none of them really told him why Zuleika had gone!

"Zuleika," murmured the old man, "Zuleika," and a great shining tear rolled down on to his palm, amongst the precious, many-colored gems... What did he need with gems? He was old, he was old, and if the seagulls wanted him to understand what they were saying, then why did they all talk at once?

Parintele Simeon's Wonder Book. A Very Moral Story

Once upon a time, there was a monastery. Such a tiny, white little monastery, nestling at the foot of high, high mountains, the peaks of which stuck right up into the clouds. Like a flock of gigantic birds, the little white houses clustered round their white church, against a background of dark fir trees, so dark and thick that they made the houses look all the whiter by contrast. At daybreak and at sunset, a bell with a rather shrill voice would go dingle, dingle, dingle... and the doors of the many little houses would open all at once and black-frocked monks with their dark-veiled head-dresses would troop into the church for prayers. On Sundays and on feast-days, the little bell would go dingle, dingle, dingle, much more often, and the monks would seem to be saying their prayers all day long. But worst of all it was in time of Lent; then the little bell left the monks no peace at all, and as they were all very old, I think their knees must often have felt stiff and sore.

In the tiniest and whitest and cleanest little house of all lived *Parintele*[54] Simeon, the tiniest of little monks; so small was he that he almost looked like a dwarf. He was a dear old fellow, with very few teeth left in his head, so that he mumbled when he talked. His beard was as white as his white-washed walls. His black frock was so long that he stumbled over it. Suffering from gout, he wore huge felt shoes so that he shuffled more than he walked. He had a kindly smile and children and dogs loved him.

Once I saw Parintele Simeon inside his dear little white house. He had taken off his dark cassock, and was sitting in the tiniest of tiny little rooms upon the tiniest of three-legged stools. His under-robe was as white as his beard, as white as his walls, and as white as the boiled potatoes, which he was eating with a white wooden spoon.

Half of the tiny little room was filled up by a huge whitewashed oven, all twisty and strange of shape. I never saw anything as white as Father Simeon's dwelling; the only dark spots in it were the black bowl he ate his potatoes out of, and a huge dark leather volume, which lay upon a wooden bench.

Now there was something very mysterious and wonderful about this book, which was Father Simeon's most cherished treasure – all the monastery stood in awe of and envied this precious book... It was fat... fat... and tremendously heavy, and had so many pages in it that it would have taken you a whole day to count them – a whole day!

The children of the village nearby knew about this book. In fact it was the pride of all the countryside, and it was said that no other monk in any other

---

[54] The word means a monk, as well as an ordinary priest [note in the first edition].

convent in the country possessed such a book. On Sundays after the church service was over, Parintele Simeon would sometimes allow a few of the village children to come into his tiny white little dwelling to look at his book. This was the greatest, greatest pleasure, which could be given them, but as Simeon's house was so teeny-weeny, he could take but very few children into it at a time, and so greatly did he prize his old volume, that never for a moment would he allow that it should be moved elsewhere, nor that anyone should turn over the leaves when he was not there.

If, of an evening, you had peeped in through Parintele Simeon's tiny window, you would have probably seen him seated on his low three-legged stool and, in front of him on the bench, the precious volume. A single candle stuck into a black earthenware jar would be burning beside him, throwing a flickering light over the pages and over his thick, snowy beard, which would shine as though frosted. On those occasions, Parintele Simeon wore enormous round horn spectacles on his nose, which made his eyes huge, huge, giving him the appearance of a wise old owl.

Not all the monks of this community were as clean and tidy as Parintele Simeon, who could have stood as model for all the monks of all the monasteries all over the country. There were especially three old monks, which were quite a shame to the place. They were called Pamfil, Trofim, and Tihon; they seemed to find a special satisfaction in being dirty, as though they had made a vow never to wash, and you won't believe it, but moss actually grew amongst the hairs of their grimy beards, which had never known the teeth of a comb! They lived in dilapidated hovels, which hid, as though ashamed, behind the white little houses of the other monks. You would not at all have liked to go into these dwellings, which were anything but clean, and which had an unpleasant fusty odor. Their windows had been stuck down with brown paper, so that even in summer they could not be opened. Flies filled the place, buzzing everywhere, covering everything with ugly black spots and even getting into the food.

When it was very warm these three old shadows would crawl out of their dark, smoke-filled dwellings and sit upon a very rickety wooden bench under the apple trees, blinking at the sun. This was about all they did, except of course go twice a day to the church, where they would stand in dark corners against the walls, uncanny old mummies, mumbling prayers as they slipped the worn beads of their rosaries one by one through their trembling fingers. In their own somewhat nebulous way, brothers Pamfil, Trofim, and Tihon were jealous of old Simeon, because the *staritz* praised him, saying that he was a model monk – but more especially were they jealous of his wonderful book. Why should he possess such a book, and they not? Thus argued Pamfil, Trofim, and Tihon, and there are, I am afraid, a good many people in this world who argue that way – although to my mind it is not logic, because, after all, what is yours is yours, and what is mine is mine, and that ought to be the end of it; yet sometimes it isn't, but only the beginning, as you'll see by this sad little tale I'm going to tell you.

Down in the village beneath the monastery lived a woodcutter's family. There were many children in that family, in fact, there seemed to be a new baby every year, so that Mother Zetta had a terrible time of it keeping them all tidy and out of trouble, cooking for them and putting them to bed or tumbling them out of the house at daybreak. Occasionally, when she had time, they would have their faces and hands washed, but this was not very often, for Mother Zetta was really too busy, and also too poor, and soap was scarce. But for Easter Saturday's midnight Mass the good woman would dress them in their best clothes, tying red, white-spotted handkerchiefs upon the little girls' heads, which made them look like a row of toadstools. The boys would have their noses wiped, their whitest shirts put on, and their hair brushed down over their foreheads right into their eyes, with a hard, wet brush, a proceeding they quite particularly disliked, but accepted as a sort of finishing up of the long Lenten fasts. Then taper in hand, they would be marshalled off in long file to the monastery church, Mother Zetta with their father bringing up the rear; and it had never happened yet that Mother Zetta was not carrying a newborn baby in her arms.

The Mass lasted till daybreak, and after it was over the tired family would trudge home again through the pine forest, each child guarding its taper so that it should not be blown out. The hands shielding the trembling flames would glow transparent red, and the big pines would be partially lit up as the small procession hurried through their ranks.

After all these ceremonies, the Easter breakfast would be a great feast. Eggs dyed red were its principal feature, with a flat bread like a thick plait of hair twisted into a ring, and best of all, a white cheese made of sheep's milk; this the children liked inordinately, and they would sit on the cottage threshold consuming great hunches of it, which they held in their hands like huge slices of white cake.

The middle part of this worthy family consisted of Ghitsa and Stanca, a couple of twins. They were six years old, and were always getting into trouble. No well-deserved chastisement ever seemed to have any effect upon them, they always ran into fresh adventures, for which they were afterwards liberally spanked... The monastery was their great attraction, and more especially Father Simeon's little cottage, Father Simeon himself, who looked like a dwarf out of a fairy story, and above all, Father Simeon's wonderful book! One Sunday, after Mass, it had been Ghitsa and Stanca's turn to be allowed to go into the old monk's sanctuary, and to turn over the leaves of the book.

But now it is time that I should tell you why this book was so different from other books, why it really and truly was a wonder-book. Well, now you will hear...

There were beautiful legends printed on its parchment leaves, and whilst you read the stories the personages would actually all appear before you, all the saints and martyrs, the kings and queens, knights and soldiers, the beggars and dogs, horses and birds, the flowers, palaces and castles, even the sea and mountains and landscapes of the Holy Land, and even sometimes visions of heaven, but these only showed themselves to those quite worthy of such heavenly manifestation, as for instance the venerable *staritz*, or the *metropolitan*[55] when he came to visit the monastery, or worthy Parintele Simeon himself.

Ghitsa and Stanca, who that day were on their best behavior, had seen wonderful things: all about a beautiful saint, with a sky-blue mantle and a luminous halo round her head – a saint who had divided her riches amongst the dumb, the blind, and the lame, giving all she had to the poor, finally even her beautiful sky-blue cloak. Never, oh, never, had the twins seen or even dreamed of anything so beautiful, and their greatest, greatest desire was to see more, if possible to see all that the book contained. But as there were many little children in the village, Ghitsa and Stanca would have to wait a long time till their turn would come again. Now Ghitsa and Stanca were not fond of waiting, patience was not one of their virtues. Each Sunday they would come up to the monastery in hopes of getting another peep at the wonder-book; they would hang about the big grass courtyard of the monastery – and not leave till they were quite sure they could no more get into Parintele Simeon's cottage. It was on one of these occasions that Ghitsa and Stanca made the acquaintance of Pamfil, Trofim, and Tihon, and it was this acquaintance which brought about their misfortune, as you will shortly hear.

These three not very interesting old fossils had also been allowed a look into the book. Once in their presence the *staritz* had spoken of a beautiful vision of the Golden City which he had seen in Simeon's book, and the three shabby, grimy old fellows, perhaps just because of their griminess and because of the abominable little holes they lived in, longed to get a glimpse of the Golden City and had asked old Simeon to open the book at that page. Simeon had immediately complied with their desire, but the visions would not rise before the eyes of these three dingy old beings. Much upset, and feeling as though adverse spirits had entered his snow-white cell with the three shabby brothers, Simeon had folded his hands and prayed, but the visions had remained amongst the leaves of the book, although the kind old monk began reading the legend all over again with his most suave voice. Finally, much upset, he had turned to a page of minor importance, a page of lesser visions, and these had risen up before Trofim, Pamfil, and Tihon, taking precise shape. But the three monks had set their hearts upon seeing the Golden City; some dim yearning had entered their

---

[55] "Metropolitan", head of the Romanian Church [note in the first edition].

souls which they were loath to give up, and as it had not appeared they kept a dull feeling of resentment against Simeon, as though he had purposely despoiled them of something. Father Simeon would never have despoiled anybody of anything, he had the biggest, kindest heart in his little body; besides he was really a holy man.

Now it came to pass that, one Sunday afternoon, Ghitsa and Stanca were hovering about the convent enclosure, up to all sorts of tricks, playing all sorts of games, one eye, however, always watching Father Simeon's house, hoping that the dear old man would step out of his door and invite them inside, just as in a fairy story. But Father Simeon, holy man, was having his Sunday afternoon siesta – this was his Sunday's treat – and he had no idea that such an anxious couple were waiting outside.

Stanca was a pretty little girl. From afar, she curiously resembled a diminutive woman with her much-worn red *catrintsa*[56] wrapped tightly round her skinny little hips over a long white shirt, which came far below her knees. From beneath a discolored kerchief two brown plaits peeped out, much bleached by the sun, so that in places they were almost straw-colored. Her face was thin, her eyes large, grey, and solemn, surrounded by long black lashes. Ghitsa was more cheerful of countenance, chubby-cheeked, with sparkling black eyes and an untidy mop of dark curls; he smiled readily, showing two rows of brilliantly white teeth. His hemp shirt was much darned, and there was a little tear at the back of his trousers, which allowed a comic little piece of shirt to protrude in an impudent sort of way.

It was warm, and the sun shone so brightly that the three old fossils, Pamfil, Trofim, and Tihon, crawled out of their hovels and settled down upon their rickety bench, like three rusty old crows on a perch. With vague, bleared eyes, they stared at nothing, but out of long habit their beads were always slipping, click-click, through their palsied fingers.

Ghitsa, tired of waiting for Simeon's door to open, went up to the shadowy figures on the seat and asked: "When will he be coming out?"

"Who?" asked Pamfil.

"Father Simeon," said the boy.

"He is sleeping," said Trofim, in his quivering old voice.

"How long will he sleep?"

"That's his business," grumbled Tihon.

"Have you seen his book?" asked Ghitsa in a whisper.

The three old brothers nodded.

"We want to see it again," confided the child, simply because he wanted to confide in someone.

---

[56] "Catrintsa", a piece of straight cloth, often in bright colors and heavily embroidered, which peasant women wear as a skirt wrapped round their hips, over their shirts [note in the first edition].

"Everybody wants to see it, always," complained Trofim, "but Simeon is a sly old hypocrite, and selfish too."

"You think he won't let us look at his book again?" asked Stanca timidly. She did not quite like the look of the three old fossils.

"He probably won't," mumbled old Tihon.

"But what can we do then?" asked Ghitsa disappointedly, and Stanca stuck her finger into her mouth, anxiously awaiting the answer. Her eyes were very round and questioning.

"Go home," said Tihon crossly.

"I've a better idea than that," declared Pamfil, and his toothless mouth had a sort of grin.

"What is it?" asked Ghitsa eagerly.

"You must steal into Simeon's house when he is not there, and take a long, long look at the book, all by yourselves."

"Oh!" gasped Stanca in a shocked voice.

"Oh!" mimicked Pamfil, "and, pray, why not?"

"But he would be very angry," explained the boy.

"Does that matter?" asked one of the monks.

"Yes, I think so, don't you?" asked Ghitsa.

"No," said Trofim.

"But how could we get into his house?" enquired Ghitsa, temptation already stealing into his heart. Stanca still had her finger in her mouth, but her eyes were anxious.

"If he goes out, I suppose he locks his door?" Ghitsa insisted.

"Yes, but he does not take his key with him," said Pamfil mysteriously.

"Where does he keep it?" whispered Ghitsa, his eyes sparkling.

"Will you relate to me what you see in the book if I tell you?" asked Pamfil.

"Of course!" promised the child.

"Well, he keeps it in a little hole under the threshold," explained Pamfil's quivering, cracked voice.

The other two old fellows grinned a toothless grin, they looked like three horrid old gargoyles; Ghitsa did not like them at all, they were too ugly, but they could impart useful information.

"But when will he be out?" asked Ghitsa, almost under his breath.

"What do you ask?" enquired Tihon, holding his hand to his ear.

"When will he be out?" repeated the child, clearing his throat.

"Tomorrow, from early morning till late at night," said Pamfil; "he has something to do in town. That's your chance, but remember, we want to hear all about what you see!"

Ghitsa nodded his head, as he had become quite speechless; then, suddenly taking hold of his sister's hand, he scampered away as quickly as his legs could carry him, the little escaped corner of his shirt sticking out behind in a more comic way than ever.

"Stupid little idiots," grumbled Trofim.

"But I would be pleased if they played a trick upon Simeon," mumbled Tihon. "It would serve him right" – Tihon had still a vague feeling as though he had been despoiled of seeing a vision of the Golden City.

"We'll go in now," decided Pamfil, and obeying him as though they were all wound up with the same key, the three nasty old fellows shuffled back into the shade of their hovels.

It was towards evening next day that Ghitsa, dragging a rather reluctant Stanca by the hand, stole into the convent enclosure. The sun was setting, and the tall fir tree standing like a sentinel before the church door, that fir tree which had such a high, bare trunk, threw a long, long dark shadow right over the grass to Father Simeon's gate. It was like a giant black finger pointing out the way. Was it a sign? Ghitsa was superstitious, and would much rather it had been a ray of light; but for all that, he was not going to give up his adventure now at the eleventh hour, when he was so near his goal! He had spent an uncomfortable enough day thinking of it, and planning it all out, till it had actually given him a pain in his stomach, yes, right in the middle, something that hurt when he gulped. Stanca had only come with him because as a matter of course she always followed Ghitsa wherever he went. Ghitsa was quite trembling; even the piece of shirt sticking out of the tear in his trousers at the back seemed limper and less sure of itself... Here was the threshold. "Under the threshold," the uncanny old monk had said... Ghitsa was so excited that he fumbled about awkwardly. The perspiration stood in large drops on his forehead. A little gust of wind sweeping through old Simeon's apple tree gave him a start, it sounded like a warning whisper...

"Help me!" begged Ghitsa of Stanca – his voice was quite unlike his own. Stanca crouched down on her heels beside her brother, and putting her hand into a small crevice in the stone immediately drew out the key...

"Oh," gasped Ghitsa, "we've got it; what luck!" his eyes sparkled with a mixture of fear and pleasure.

The lock was stiff, and a fellow with a bad conscience is generally awkward; his heart beats too quickly, too loudly, which is both disturbing and confusing, it robs him of his faculties. Ghitsa was realizing this just now. But after a great effort he was able to turn the key, and the children found themselves in Father Simeon's snow-white little dwelling... How neat it was, so tidy, so clean, and so white; it actually seemed to shine. There was a faint smell of cold smoke in the room, but no other smell at all, which is rare in a monk's cell.

"Look," whispered Stanca, taking her finger out of her mouth to point at something... And there lay the book! Huge, dark, and important-looking – a weighty thing indeed, full of meaning, full of possibilities...

Father Simeon's great horn spectacles lay on the volume; a sort of bleareyed guardian, they somehow seemed to be looking at the children. Not only the spectacles were looking at the children but, out of the dark corner, the painted eyes of Father Simeon's icon where it hung on the wall. St. Nicholas it was, and his eyes were huge and staring and very watchful. Stanca suddenly felt them fixed upon her, and a little cold shiver ran down her back. Being in everyday life a pious little girl, she promptly, as was proper, went up to the holy picture, crossed herself and kissed it. In doing so, she made the little branch of *busuioc*[57] stuck behind it fall. This gave Stanca a fright. She tried to put it back in place, but it would not hold; she tried several times, but each time it slipped and fell on the floor – was that a bad sign?

"I wish St. Nicholas would not stare so!" whispered Stanca to her brother.

"It's rather uncomfortable," admitted Ghitsa, "but don't look at him, then perhaps you'll forget that he is there. But come now, we must make haste and open the book, so as to get away again before old Parintele Simeon returns."

The spectacles *had* to be taken off the volume; Ghitsa had a sort of feeling as if they would bite him or defend themselves in some way. Very gingerly, he took them up between thumb and first finger; the spectacles did not resist or do anything unexpected. But how dark it was getting. They certainly would need a light... Oh! But there! Pushed back into the corner was the candle in its black jar, and beside it a very old box of matches...

Ghitsa lit the candle. Immediately his and Stanca's shadows were thrown against the white wall, big and uncomfortable, prominent. They were like two huge black beings, mimicking the children's movements. It is really disagreeable to have a bad conscience, and when you have, your heartbeats are such a confusing and sickening company.

But now the great moment had come! The children's heads were close together, bent over the book. Ghitsa was seated on the little three-legged stool, Stanca kneeling at his side.

"You open first," whispered Ghitsa, who was not feeling very brave.

"No, you, you!" insisted Stanca. It really was only fair that Ghitsa, the instigator, should take the risks...

Behind the children the door had opened silently – but they had no idea of this, nor that three hideous old faces framed in rusty black veils were peeping in upon them; the three fusty old monks, who had been the tempters, had come to profit by the children's sin, for was it not a sin to cheat such a good and holy man as Father Simeon?

Ghitsa, with trembling fingers and terribly noisy heart inside him, now proceeded to open the book and turn over the first pages... Nothing appeared before the children's eyes except hundreds and thousands of little black letters, which to their unlearned eyes had no sense whatever. No vi-

---

[57] "Busuioc", basil-plant. The peasants decorate their holy pictures in church and at home with it. Young women put it under their pillow, believing that it will bring them a husband within the year [note in the first edition].

sion arose to delight them, they saw nothing at all, no beautiful saints in blue mantles, no kings, no queens, no angels... Then all at once... Fizz... Bang! Poof! Ha-ha-ha! Oh! Goodness, goodness! What was that! Something dreadful was happening – Ghitsa had just turned over another page – fizz – bang! poof! ha-ha-ha! – and red lights and flames suddenly filled the room! Dear old Father Simeon's snow-white room! There was a smell of sulphur and now the place was alive with grinning evil faces, the air full of horrible laughter, and long claw-like hands clutched at the children's hair and clothes...

What had happened? Oh! Oh! Had hell opened its doors and let all its devils out? Well, yes! Incredible as it may seem to you, it was just exactly what had happened. Only hell, in this case, had been old Simeon's wonder-book. Instead of angels and saints and martyrs, a dozen horrible red devils with long tails and pointed little horns on their heads had jumped out of the precious volume. This was the children's awful punishment for wanting to deceive such a kind-hearted, holy little man as Parintele Simeon!

"Come along," cried the devils, "this is really a fine piece of luck. It's years since we had such a catch! And ha-ha-ha, there are also those three old black fellows, they'll be rather tough but they'll all the same help to pepper our hotch-potch – come along now, hurry up! You tender little morsels, quick, quick, come along!" And the devils, seizing Stanca by her pigtails and Ghitsa by his curls, twirled the terrified children out of the little white house. Old Pamfil, Trofim, and Tihon tried to escape, but their shaky old limbs would not obey them; besides they were quite paralyzed with fright. One devil got hold of Pamfil's beard, another of Trofim's veil, a third of old Tihon's nose, and with cackling screams and atrocious laughter, hurried their victims off into the wood...

I am sure you are dreadfully anxious wondering what is going to happen to poor Ghitsa and Stanca, and you are right to be anxious, for, indeed, they had fallen into terrible hands! That was an appalling way the children passed into the thick forest, pushed and tugged, pinched and punched, ill-treated in every way by the odious red devils till at last they reached a clearing surrounded by fir trees so dark and high that they seemed to shut out the whole sky. And in that clearing there was a big fire over which an enormous black pot was hanging, suspended from the branch of a withered oak tree. Two black devils with red eyes were stirring the pot with long, three-spiked pitchforks. "Ha-ha-ha! Ha-ha-ha!" laughed the two black devils, and their voices were even more evil than those of the red devils.

"So you have got hold of the two little rascals, have you? Bravo, bravo! And of the three ugly old crows as well – what a good supper we'll have! But first let us dance, let us dance!" And all the devils, red and black, joining hands, began capering and dancing round the fire, brandishing their pitchforks, whisking their horrid tails, and singing disgusting songs.

Like two lost lambs, Ghitsa and Stanca stood trembling, tears of despair coursing down their cheeks.

"Oh! Oh! Oh!" they sobbed, "we did not mean to, really, we did not mean to – we thought that we would see saints and martyrs and angels with white wings..."

"And have seen red devils instead, ha-ha-ha!" laughed the capering fiends. "It is all very well to say that you did not mean to! Did not mean to what? Did not mean to go into Parintele Simeon's house, perhaps? But then why were you there? Did not mean to conjure up devils out of his holy book? That we well believe! Ha-ha-ha! Ha-ha-ha! But now it is our turn to have a good time," and suddenly one of the devils lunged forward and hooked his horrible pitchfork just into the little piece of shirt which hung from the tear in Ghitsa's trousers, and lifted him right off the ground, up, up, till he held him dangling, head downwards, just over the terrible black pot.

"Oh, oh!" screamed Stanca. "It's my brother! My poor dear little brother! Save him, save him, oh! Blessed Virgin Mary, oh! Dear St. Nicholas, oh! Good St. Dumitre, oh! Merciful St. Paraschiva, oh! Mother of God and all the blessed martyrs in heaven, save my poor brother, save him, save him!" And the little girl threw herself upon her knees, crossing herself and touching the ground many times with her forehead. "Oh! Dear Virgin Mary, oh! Holy Mother of God..." But the devils only laughed all the louder and continued to dangle poor Ghitsa by that frail scrap of shirt, right over the gaping, steaming pot. Oh! Oh! At any moment the shirt might tear, and then what would be the fate of Ghitsa, poor little Ghitsa?

Stanca lay now face downwards, her head hidden amongst the moss on the ground. The three old monks had been tied by the devils to three trees. Fright seemed to have melted the bones in their bodies, and they hung quite limp, like three empty cassocks, their grimy, moss-grown beards almost sweeping the ground.

Now it was quite night and one big star, having managed to rise above the fir trees, peeped down with an astonished eye of light upon the tragic scene below... All at once the sound of a voice chanting... Far away, but distinct, and certainly, it was coming nearer... Stanca raised her head and a quiver ran through the old monks' bodies. Ghitsa kicked about, and made frantic movements with arms and legs, as though trying to swim in mid-air; from time to time he uttered lamentable howls, but each time the devils drowned his complaints with their laughter.

The chant came nearer, nearer. Now, even the devils were listening; their hideous laughter had stopped. Nearer, nearer came the singing; certainly, it was a holy chant, not particularly melodious, and the voice was shaky, but it was a holy chant, a church chant... A light flickered through the trees... Now the chant was quite near – a dry branch cracked, then another... There was a shuffling step... and... there stood Parintele Simeon, a faint halo shining round his high, saintly forehead, his two old hands clasped as though for prayer. Aghast he stood still, retaining his attitude of prayer – the halo round his forehead flickered as though sharing his emotions.

Stanca with a sob of relief ran up to him and seized hold of his cassock. But Parintele Simeon's eyes were fixed upon poor Ghitsa and the hateful red fiends which had him in their grasp, fiends such as his saintly spirit had only dreamed of on nights of indigestion, and those I can assure you were few, in Father Simeon's holy and frugal life.

With hanging tails, like dogs afraid of a whipping, the devils were crouching round the fire. Only the one who was dangling poor Ghitsa over the black pot was still standing, though he too had his tail between his legs.

Old Simeon realized the danger of poor Ghitsa's position. If he ordered the devil to put him down, he naturally would drop him into the boiling soup, and what then of poor Ghitsa? Then an inspiration came to old Simeon. Of course it was given to him by God, because God loved old Simeon, and in His great mercy He is ever ready to pardon little children and sinners when they repent, and I assure you, hanging there over the pot, so near a tragic end, Ghitsa was repenting for all he was worth. – Well, as I said, Simeon had an inspiration. With a stride you would not have imagined possible for such a small fellow, more like a soldier striding to battle, Simeon cut his way through the circle of devils, which dared not molest a man so holy, and with God's own strength lent him for the occasion, regardless of the flames leaping about him, the tiny monk gave one tremendous push… sh!... to the sinister black pot, overturned it, so that the broth went hissing and spluttering into the fire, covering the red devils with scalding spray and steam... There was a ghastly scream... A child's voice mingling with the hideous, devilish voices – turmoil – consternation...

What really happened I do not know; it all came about with such bewildering rapidity – but the devils, red and black, fled shrieking fearfully into the forest darkness, and a poor little Ghitsa, all black and singed, and very much the worse for wear, lay sobbing in Parintele Simeon's short arms, lay against his holy, kindly bosom, lay with his face buried in the saintly man's white beard, comforting, but prickly for all its belonging to so holy a man; like an erring little lamb he lay there, a lamb that after cruel misadventure finds his shepherd at last...

It was a moving spectacle, indeed, I hope you all appreciate how touching it was: old Parintele Simeon seated on the ground, the halo round his forehead, now quite steady, clasping the repentant sinner to his kindly heart; Stanca with her arms around both of them, the fire smoking behind them like a huge funeral pyre, and staring through its wavering fumes, the three old monks, their bones still soft as cotton-wool, but some sort of life coming back to their soulless eyes – and some sort of repentance to their envious hearts.

"I'll never do it again, I'll never do it again," sobbed Ghitsa, "I only wanted to see saints and angels; I never thought that devils could live in such a holy book. Oh! Oh! All my skin is aching, I am black and burnt and a very, very unhappy little boy. Kiss me, Stanca, kiss me! I'll never do it again!" And of course Stanca kissed her brother with the effusion of a mother who has been given back her child.

Father Simeon was beginning to grasp the situation, for Ghitsa, in confused sentences, broken by sobs, confessed all his sin.

"The good God will forgive you," he said solemnly, making the sign of the cross over the children's foreheads. "But brothers Pamfil, Trofim, and Tihon will have to fast and pray many a day before they can again find favor in the face of the Lord, for a grievous sin it is indeed to lead little white lambs astray!"

Ghitsa did not feel very white, but all the same, it was comforting to be likened unto such an innocent animal, it gave you back some of your self-respect. So he wiped his eyes.

Simeon, full of the Christian spirit of forgiveness, rose from the ground and went to each of the old monks in turn and untied the cords, which held them captive. In contrast to the blessed glow round Simeon's head, the faces of the three culprits looked particularly sinister and dark, but the moment they were unbound, all three fell with their faces to the ground and kissed the little monk's felt shoes, for indeed after their deplorable adventure with the devils, the monk veritably appeared to them as a savior. Father Simeon did not much care for their groveling gratitude, nor for their whining praises, but being filled with the spirit of Christian forbearance he surrendered his felt slippers without outward show of impatience to the insistent kisses of their loose-lipped mouths.

There is not much more to relate. By the light of his halo, Father Simeon led the two children back through the dark forest to the monastery, the three fusty old brothers following in their wake, like three shadows that have been whipped.

"And next Sunday," said the holy little man as they stood before his house, "next Sunday my door will be open to you, and if God is willing and your hearts contrite, your spirits purified, perchance new visions will be revealed to you from the sacred pages of my book." Then lifting his hands in blessing: "Now be off, my little lambs", he said; "depart in peace!" And like two small models of virtue, hand in hand the twins ran back through the dark forest to the arms of their anxious parents, who had quite thought that they were lost.

It seems that the next Sunday "God was willing," for I have been told that on that day, when the pages of the wonder-book were turned, Stanca and Ghitsa saw not only saints and martyrs, but also many, many angels with snow-white wings... Therefore, we may presumably admit that they came to Parintele Simeon's snow-white dwelling in the right Christian spirit and with contrite hearts... I, for one, like to think of the God-fearing Simeon seated on his tiny three-legged stool, his horn spectacles on his nose, a child

200

kneeling on each side of him, all three absorbed in the heavenly visions of his sacred wonder-book. Stanca had not forgotten to bring a fresh twig of *busuioc* to stick behind the icon in the corner to replace the dry twig that on that tragic night had fallen to the ground, and I can assure you that St. Nicholas's eyes had no more a disapproving look...

But what of the devils? you may ask. Well, the devils... The devils had been driven away...

A Christmas Tale

This is a very strange tale I have got to tell you today. It is about a mysterious well – a deep, deep well which lay in the center of a dark forest. It is also a Christmas tale.

No one knew why that well was there, nor who had dug it, nor how old it was. The peasants from the villages around stood in great awe of this well, because from its depth a weird sound could be heard, a sort of moan, half sob, half gurgle, and sometimes a sound as though someone were knocking against its sides, which made you think of a lost soul in distress, perhaps held captive down there and unable to get out.

The village nearest the forest was called Galea. It was a very poor little village, its cottages small and miserable, with tiny gardens in which the flowers always looked sad and anemic, for the ground was stony and unfruitful. In the center of the village stood a little wooden church. It was ancient and rather shaky, its huge roof looked too big for it, but the passing seasons had toned it down to a rich brown with a grey shimmer, which was pleasant to the eye. Old stunted lilac bushes clustered round it, protecting the humble graves, which lay scattered about beneath their shade, like a forlorn flock of sheep. The peasants were rather ashamed of their tiny dilapidated church, and dreamed of building a fine edifice, all white with a tin roof, that would shine like silver in the sun, and not let the rain nor the snow through in the bad seasons, a church with stout columns in front, all decorated in bright colors, and with God's eye painted over the door.

You and I would probably have infinitely preferred the crooked little wooden church with its over-large roof, but then you see, each community has its ambition and its pride, and does not want to stand behind other communities. Bostea, the village on the other side of the forest, had a beautiful new big church of the kind that Galea coveted. But Galea was a much, much poorer village than Bostea, and it sadly felt its inferiority.

But it was about the mysterious well I was going to tell you, was it not?

The villagers for some reason had conceived the idea that the unknown being who was held captive in that well, could become a danger to the countryside if it ever managed to get out, and that the only way to keep it contented was by throwing small offerings down into its depth. The poor often think that they must make sacrifices to God or to any power greater than themselves, it is a sort of way of keeping off ill luck from their thresholds. And yet God knows their lives are full enough of sacrifices from beginning to end. There were certain feast-days on which the villagers had the habit of taking their offerings to the dreaded well, and these were especially St. Maria Mare[58] and St. Dumitru[59]. The moment Mass was over, before any dancing or drinking could begin, they would collect in groups and start off into the forest with their queer little offerings. Some brought flowers or colored eggs, others flat breads sprinkled with poppy seeds; some brought bunches of corn tied with bright ribbons. Little children would sacrifice their first ripe plums, cherries, or nuts, also the precious little pebbles picked up in the riverbed, and which became a lovely bright pink when you licked them. The maidens made sacrifice of beads from their girdles and little painted cards with pictures of the saints or small holy medals, or of trinkets bought at the *moshi*.[60] The young men would throw down small coins, buttons from their military tunics, or the bright red carnation they so fondly wore stuck behind their left ear. Even quite old women would go limping through the sunshine, distaff in hand. Quite exhausted they would sink down on the well's edge and pronounce strange wishes over the water, throwing in wisps of wool or flax, whilst they murmured prayers, watching the while with one eye what the young ones were doing, always ready to criticize or to disapprove. But in winter the well was almost quite forsaken, for no one particularly cared to go through the forest in that season.

Right on the outskirts of Galea, lived a widow in a cottage so small and humble that it was really hardly more than a hut. In all the village she was known as poor Maria, and she had but one little boy, Petru, who had large grey eyes set in a pale, anxious small face. Petru had had two little sisters, but both of them lay under the lilac bushes of the churchyard, and so poor was Maria that she had not even been able to mark the spot with crosses, and this made Petru very sad. Petru was pious and an ardent believer. He faithfully observed all the precepts of the Church; he was a conscientious faster, though verily at all times Petru had but little to eat. He would devoutly listen to all that old *Popa*[61] Toader had to say, though sometimes he did not properly understand what it meant, and certain scraps of his exhortations would remain sticking in his mind, taking undue proportions. Amongst others, Petru had conceived an uncomfortable belief that because the church of Bostea was larger and newer than their poor little wooden church, it was, therefore, also a holier place. This idea had come to him because, on Easter Sunday, Popa Toader had spoken about collecting money for building a new church, and had held up as example the Bostea church, which God would surely bless, as it had been erected by sacrifices

---

[58] "Mare" (Romanian): great. The Christian feast day of the Assumption of Mary is commonly celebrated on 15 August.

[59] Saint Demetrius of Thessaloniki: his feast day is celebrated on 26 October in the Eastern Orthodox Church.

[60] "Moşi", fair [note in the first edition].

[61] Priest.

made by every inhabitant, who each year had offered part of his hard-earned economies for the honor of God. Petru of course had no money, not even the poorest little farthing; certainly, if he had, he would have gladly given it for the building of the new church. Petru had never been to Bostea, and just because of that, he had created in his imagination a wonderful vision of its church, which must have all the beauties and qualities Galea's poor little sanctuary never possessed.

Petru was about seven years old when his mother fell very ill indeed; it was just at the beginning of winter, which that year had set in with unusual severity. Petru loved his mother beyond all things on earth, and his poor little heart was wrung with terrible grief, seeing her thus pining away, and he so utterly helpless before her suffering.

Maria was a very patient woman, she never complained; it was from her that Petru had his big grey eyes and pathetic face. There was no real bed in Maria's hovel; she lay on a sort of wooden bench over which a few ragged rugs had been spread, and upon this miserable pallet she lay all shaken by fever, her lips blue and cracked. A large earthen oven took up part of the hut; it had all sorts of shapes so as to fit into the crooked little room. Maria lay behind this oven, which Petru tried to keep as warm as he could by going each day to fetch wood on the outskirts of the forest, whence he would wearily return carrying on his back as many dry branches as he could. Petru was small, so that the weight was almost too much for him, and would quite bend him in two until he looked like a giant porcupine crawling home through the snow. Petru would also try to cook. A few strings of dry onions hung against the wall behind the oven, and in a wooden bowl on the floor was their meagre provision of *malai*.[62] Probably Petru was not a very successful cook; anyhow Maria turned away with a weary sigh from the daily mess he so anxiously offered her. This made Petru terribly unhappy and great round tears would roll down his pinched little face. He would hide away in a corner and say his prayers over and over again, all the prayers Popa Toader had ever taught him, even if they had no connexion with his trouble – but they were prayers, therefore of course acceptable to God. After that the little boy would crawl on to the wooden pallet beside his mother, nestling close up to her, hoping to keep her warm with the embrace of his skinny little arms.

Alas, God did not seem to listen to Petru's prayers, because his mother grew worse and worse instead of better, till Petru began tormenting himself, imagining that he must have displeased God in some way. Yet worry his head as he would, he could not remember a single occasion upon which he had broken the law, for Petru was an almost painfully well-behaved little boy, who never had any time to enjoy life or to be naughty, having had to work and make himself useful, ever since he had been able to stand

---

[62] "Mălai", meal, maize [note in the first edition].

on his feet. He had always been an anxious little soul, ever ready to carry burdens too heavy for his frail shoulders.

It was Christmas Eve, and still poor Maria lay on her pallet, sick unto death, when an idea came into Petru's head. Petru had ideas sometimes, but they would not always work out, because no one had ever time to bother about his mind, nor to help it to expand. But this idea had grown and grown till it had become a fixture, and then, when it was quite ripe, Petru set about carrying it out, and this is what it was: He knew that when one desires something very, very much, one must offer a taper to some blessed image, more especially to that of the Mother of God. Those little lights have a wonderful way of reinforcing prayer. Now Petru had obtained one of these little tapers from the old village chanter, as recompense for small services rendered last Sunday during Mass. It was certainly a very thin, fragile-looking little taper, a thing to be treated with infinite care, but the old man had also given him a smashed old match-box, in which there were still five unused matches, and if he could keep them from the damp, they certainly would light his little taper for him when he placed it before the icon of his choice.

All might have been quite simple, had not Petru been possessed with the idea that he must carry his candle to the Bostea church, for, with the other villagers, he shared the mistaken idea that their own old wooden church was not quite an entirely worthy House of God – poor dear crooked little church.

Now to get to Bostea, you had either to make a very, very long road, or you had to take the shortcut through the dark forest where the mysterious well stood. Even in summer time Petru dreaded the groaning, moaning well; how much more, therefore, in winter, when the forest was all black and when wolves might be prowling about. Yet he dare not remain away too long from his mother's bedside, so in spite of his fear he made up his mind that he must face that grim path through the wood.

Petru put on his rough, well-used *suman*[63] and the old *caciula*[64] which had once been his father's, and which gave him the quaint appearance of a wandering fungus, slipped on his fingerless gloves, which were so much darned that there was more darn about them than glove, and having hidden the precious taper and matches in his pocket, he was ready to start. Before slipping outside, however, he did not forget to pile all the reserve of dried sticks upon the fire, and to place a small mug of water beside his mother, who lay with her face turned to the wall, mumbling all sorts of strange things which had no sense and which filled poor little Petru's soul with dread.

---

[63] "Suman", cape, overcoat [note in the first edition].
[64] "Căciula", peasant's fur cap or bonnet [note in the first edition].

Dusk was already gathering, but Petru had not been able to get off sooner. He felt nervous, but now that his mind was made up, he meant to carry out his plan, never matter what the effort might cost him. Soon he reached the edge of the forest and bravely plunged into its shade, but his heart beat like a heavy hammer in his breast.

"Perhaps I shall be able to avoid the well," thought the boy. "I know there are two paths – one is a little longer, but it does not go past the well..."

The wind was howling through the branches; in the stillness of the forest it sounded like an angry voice. Petru shivered, it was terribly cold. But luckily the snow was not very deep, except in places where it lay in drifts. Hurry as he would, night seemed to be pursuing him, gaining on him, catching him up. His breath came in hard gasps, which hurt him at the bottom of his throat. What a terribly big forest, and how tall the trees were! Never had poor Petru felt so small.

"I hope, oh, I do hope I am on the right road," said the child almost aloud, "I do not want to come past that terrible old well."

And just as he said this, thump, thump, he heard an uncanny sound that made his heart jump into his mouth. Thump – thump, and then came another sound more like a moan rising from the very bosom of the earth.

Perspiration broke out on poor Petru's forehead in spite of the cold. How dark it was getting, the trees had become walls of darkness shutting him in on all sides... Thump, thump... Oh, dear, oh, dear, that certainly was the sound of the well.

As though hypnotized, Petru advanced. He might have turned away, have slipped through the trees avoiding the place of dread, but he somehow never thought of this but advanced steadily, fascinated by the horror of the thing!

Yes, there stood the well, a dark, sinister object that he could not avoid. In his anxiety Petru stumbled, tried to recover his footing, but fell with a little gasp at the very edge of the well! For a moment, he lay there, his face buried in the cold snow whilst great dry sobs tore his breast. But what was that? Someone else was weeping? He was not alone in his solitude, someone besides himself was in distress, and – could he be mistaken? It seemed to be a child's voice, weeping, weeping. Petru picked himself up. He was feeling less afraid now – why should he be afraid of a little child crying in the dark? But then came again the sound he dreaded – thump, thump. Oh! That dreadful well! His knees shook beneath him, and yet he must look over the edge – some force stronger than himself seemed to oblige him to do so. Petru had always hated looking down into the well, even in the daytime, when his mother had held his hand; for nights afterwards he could not sleep, always imagining that he was falling down that terrible black shaft. Now he was quite alone, it was almost night, nevertheless he *must* look over the edge. Who could be down there? What secret could be hidden in that unknown depth? Thump-thump – was it Petru's heart beating, or did the sound really come from the well?

Then suddenly a shrill child's voice cried: "Oh, let me out, let me out, throw me down your little taper – I am all alone here in the dark, and so cold, so cold."

"My little taper!" gasped Petru, forgetting his astonishment, his fear and everything else in the one desire of guarding that most precious of possessions. "Oh, I cannot throw you down my little taper that I really cannot, cannot do."

"But I am cold down here," cried the child's voice, "I am cold and frightened, it is Christmas Eve, and I am all alone down here, and it is so dark."

"But my mother's ill, she is dying," answered Petru, now quite fearlessly leaning over the shaft. He did not pause to ponder about the extraordinary thing that was happening to him; instinctively his one thought was to cling to that precious taper which was to buy back his mother's health. "I cannot give you my taper" – there was anguish in his voice – "I must go to Bostea to light it in front of the Virgin's image, so that mother may get well."

"There are many tapers lit before that image on Christmas Eve," answered the voice. "The Blessed One would not miss your poor little light, whilst down here I am cold and lost and forsaken; give me, give me your light."

"But all the other lights burning before the Queen of Heaven would not be my light," sobbed Petru, now entirely overcome by grief. "I'll never be able to get another taper, I am quite a poor little boy, and if mother dies, I am alone upon earth, and I am too small to know how to live all alone!" and the little fellow sank to his knees, resting his forehead against the well's edge.

"In the name of the Holy Virgin's blessed Child, give me your taper," pleaded the voice. "This is the night of His Birth, can any prayer be refused if asked in His Name tonight?"

Still Petru wavered, soul torn in two – what was his duty? Both ways his religious convictions stood up to confront him, he had put all his hope in the lighting of this taper in the Bostea church.

"In the name of the Holy Child," repeated the voice, which was becoming fainter. "On this night of His Birth, and in the name of His Mother – oh, I am so cold, so lonely, and I too am a child, a little child – oh, give me your light."

Petru was sobbing now; his soul seemed to be dissolving in the bitter grief. Grief for the captive child down there, grief for his mother, grief for himself, grief for the whole sad world where everything was sordid and miserable and poor – poor like their hut and like the little old wooden church with the over-large roof, and as he leaned there, all bent in two by grief, a vision of the Bostea church rose before him, that church he would now never reach. An impossible glory surrounded it, the glory of things one cannot touch, for now Petru knew that he would sacrifice his little taper –

had it not been asked for in the name of the Blessed One whose birthday it was tonight? Somehow Petru never paused to consider how his one poor little taper could save the captive down there. In the confusion of his thoughts that one small candle had taken enormous proportions, had become the one important thing upon earth.

"Here is my little taper," he sobbed; "take it. And here are the five only matches I have – be sure and catch them before the water can damp them," he added with childish anxiety, "because if they get wet they will not light." And leaning over the shaft of the hated well, little Petru made sacrifice of all he possessed.

After that he fell with his forehead against the frozen edge, his face hidden in his hands, weeping as though his heart would break.

Suddenly he raised his head. What was that? Music? Was he dreaming? A sound of harps seemed to be throbbing in the air around him, the sound of many, many harps. And whence did that light come! That wonderful golden light? Petru stumbled to his feet, his *caciula* falling from his head as he did so. Both the light and the rapturous music were mounting out of the well, out of that dreaded dark shaft. What was it? What was happening? Why had he suddenly the feeling that his heart was filled to overflowing with joy, with infinite joy?

"Oh!" gasped Petru, and as in church, when the Holy Mystery is being fulfilled, the ragged little fellow fell to his knees. For now a wondrous child had stepped out of the well and stood before him, a child with golden curls and a beautiful face, a child who seemed all made of light.

"Thank you," said the bright vision to Petru. "You had pity on me, delivering me from the dark, you sacrificed to me what seemed your only hope, but see what glory your one little taper can shed around," and the child held up his hand and Petru saw how his one little taper had become as a light which could light the whole world!

"Go home to your mother, she is waiting for you," said the Wondrous One; "I am going to carry your taper to the little old wooden church, for verily it is just as holy as any great church ever built."

With trembling hands Petru picked up his *caciula*, but he did not put it on his head, which he could not cover in a presence so holy, and as one walking in a dream he followed the Child of Light whose radiance filled the whole forest.

Petru felt neither cold nor fear, nor fatigue, and it was as though wings had grown on his feet. When the village was reached, the Child of Light stood still for a moment, and with his hand pointed towards poor Maria's hut.

"She is waiting for you," he repeated; "then after you've seen her go to the old, old church."

Of course Petru obeyed the Wondrous One's bidding, and with beating heart hurried to his mother's dwelling. Tearing open the door and bursting into the room, "Mother! Mother!" he cried. And there stood poor Maria with a smile on her face, all trace of illness wiped from her; she seemed suddenly to have become very beautiful, even the rags she wore had become lovely, so young did she look. Her arms were wide open, those arms that were the only soft place Petru had ever known upon earth. And into those arms did Petru take refuge, hiding his face upon her bosom, too overcome for speech. Maria did not ask what had happened, she only knew that all sickness had gone from her, that it was Christmas Eve, and that Petru, her only child, was lying against her heart.

Later, Petru stole out of the hut towards the old wooden church as the Child of Light had bidden him do. The stars were all out, but the village was fast asleep, everything was quite silent, the houses were but dark shadows on the white snow. Generally, the church was but a darker shadow amidst shadows, hardly more dignified than the peasants' dwellings, except that it possessed a small belfry. But tonight! Oh! Tonight, it had suddenly turned into a casket full of light! Light streamed out through its windows, through the cracks of its beam-walls, through the chinks of the great roof. The much-despised little building had become a thing of radiance, casting long rays of light towards the heavens, and long rays of light over the frozen snow.

Hands folded, with faltering step, Petru approached God's House, like a pilgrim come from afar; with bent head he stepped over the threshold and there fell on his knees, overcome by wonder and joy. The three doors of the altar-screen stood wide open, and on the altar itself burned Petru's little taper; no other candle had been lit in all the church, and yet the light of that one little taper was strong enough to turn the lowly little sanctuary into a thing of beauty, a thing of radiance, a thing of peace and joy. Surely even the church of Bostea could not be more beautiful than Galea's church was tonight! Petru understood that a miracle had come to pass: his mother had been cured, the old well delivered of its curse, and although the Holy Child was nowhere to be seen, the Holy Child's hand it was which had placed Petru's humble offering upon the altar of God.

But one thing Petru had not realized: that it was his love which had brought about the miracle – his love and his faith. And this strange thing came to pass one Christmas Eve – on the Birthday of Christ.

The Magic Doll of Romania (fragments)

A Wonder Story in Which East and West Do Meet. Written for American Children

"To you, the boys and girls of America, I dedicate this book. A token that I have not forgotten, your welcome – your friendship. Romance joins together all people who are young in heart – whatever their ages, wherever their homes. Marie."

A Letter to You

Dear children of America:

All too quickly did I pass through your country! It was like a dream which flashed into my life, and was gone. But not out of my mind, nor out of my heart! And I remember your faces – your many eager, healthy, happy faces, so full of life, of interest, of hope for all that is still to be. I could speak to so few of you, I had no time to enter your homes, nor to sit at your tables and listen to your talk. But for all that, I have the happy feeling that we could have been friends.

But what could I do for all of you, when I was passing by so swiftly, leaving nothing behind me but a memory which – all too soon – will fade and be gone? None of us like to be forgotten, and I am no exception to this rule. So I began to wonder what I could do in order that you should remember me. And so it was that I decided to write this story for you – a simple story, with songs and verses in it, which I hope all of you will enjoy. And because I am queen of a far-away country which I know will interest you – a country full of poetry and pictures, of old customs and quaint habits handed down through long generations from father to son, from mother to daughter – I have placed my story in Romania and among the peasants, for it is they who guard the past. I have said that mine is a story in which "East and West *do* meet", because I bring a small American girl – little Nancy – with me over the seas. I hope that she will become your friend, as she is mine. May Nancy's wanderings from plain to mountain, from mountain to sea, become a pleasant wandering to you also. The songs and verses are my own, but they are inspired by the songs of my country. They are not stately poetry, but they may give you a better idea of the people of this poetical realm. So take them with the rest, for what they are worth!

And you, child of America, in whose home this book has found a place, remember that I have written it with warm love and with a sincere desire that if East and West cannot really meet, they shall at least become acquainted with each other, and grow to become friends – brought closer together by the pen of one who knows how to love and appreciate both. Therefore, with all of my best wishes, with my blessings also, I send this little book to you. Receive it kindly, and let it keep the memory of my friendship always fresh in your heart.

Marie
Bucharest, 1929.

***

She was called Nancy. Nancy is a friendly name – don't you think so? And in an American town she lived in a neat little bungalow with a mottled green roof and a broad front window, into which, in summertime, a rose-bush thrust its long branches heavily laden with red blossoms. Nancy would lean toward the crimson roses and speak to them, for she loved to speak to all things smiling beneath God's sky. And all things answered Nancy, because her heart was full of love. […]

***

And when Christmas Eve had come, under the lighted tree Granny had seated the strangest little person that Nancy had ever seen! It was a doll, wearing a white shirt all embroidered with red. Instead of a skirt, she wore a woven cloth of black and gold, simply folded around her and held to-gether by a long, brightly colored girdle. This girdle was wound around and around her waist. The ends of the girdle were little golden tassels. On her feet were queerly shaped sandals. And just imagine! Instead of wearing stockings, her legs were wrapped in narrow linen cloths which were wound with black strings that fastened under her knees. On her head, in-stead of a hat, she had a many-colored handkerchief. And her black hair was plaited in two long braids. She was the cunningest creature you ever saw! And so pretty! Her large brown eyes stared at Nancy, and her lashes were long and feather-like.

"Oh! Granny!" And Nancy had stood there, hands clasped, a look of de-light on her face. "Who is she?"

"She is a Romanian doll!" Granny was chuckling delightedly. "Isn't she charming?"

"Romanian?" Nancy's face was a blank.

"Yes, from Romania."

"Where's Romania?" asked Nancy.

"Romania?…" Granny had repeated the word. Then she had smiled a rather shy smile, which made a thousand little lines run all over her face. "Roma-nia! Well, dearie, to tell you the truth, I don't know. I did not learn about Romania when I was young, and you do not yet go to school – as you should have done long ago, and as you will have to do this season, my little girl!"

"But, Granny, she's lovely!"

Granny looked pleased. "Yes, Nancy, that's what I thought. And at the shop they told me that they are becoming quite the fashion. 'Those Romanian dolls are the newest thing we have,' they said. So I took the prettiest of all – for my little Nancy!"

***

It was night, but Nancy was not yet asleep. Drawn close up to her little white bed was a chair. And on the chair sat her new treasure, the Romanian doll. Nancy had not yet turned out her light. She was sleepy, but she must still stare awhile longer at this strange little maiden from that far country about which Granny knew nothing. She was lovely, but what a strange way of dressing! Just a shirt and a gold and black cloth wrapped round her! And those queer shoes! And no stockings – only strips of linen! And yet she really was too sweet in that funny costume! And what large eyes she had!
"If only she could speak," thought Nancy. "If only she could…" I think that it was just then that Nancy fell asleep.
But she awoke with a start. Was someone singing? Nancy sat up. Yes! And what a weird little song! Nancy listened with beating heart:

> *"Little leaf in the snow, I am lonely*
> *For the land where the carts slowly plod*
> *Through the dust, and the bells call my people*
> *From their work, to the worship of God.*
>
> *Where the long corn-leaf blows in the sunshine,*
> *Sits my hut at the edge of the wood.*
> *I could see the tall sunflowers' faces*
> *From the place in the door where I stood."*

Nancy rubbed her eyes. Was she dreaming? […]
No! Indeed she was not sleeping: for there sat the Romanian doll, and actually… Was it possible? Great tears were running down her cheeks! Nancy was mute with astonishment! She had never heard of dolls crying real, great, wet tears. Perhaps there was something quite special about Romanian dolls! […]

***

"What are you called?" inquired Nancy, leaning tenderly over the living doll.
"Florica," said the small voice.
"How beautiful! Florica! None of us are called Florica here."
"It means little flower."
"That's sweet!" said Nancy. "What sort of flower are you?"
"A red carnation," promptly answered Florica, "because that's our national flower, you know."
"Is it?" Nancy was much interested. "But where is Romania?"

"There... Where the sun rises... Near the Black Sea..."

"Is it very black?"

"No. Only when it's stormy. It can be as blue as a turquoise or as a sapphire. And sometimes it's emerald green."

"Why are you so queerly dressed, Florica?"

"Queerly?" The doll raised her long lashes, and stared with puzzled eyes into Nancy's face. There was a slightly offended tone in her voice. "Queerly dressed? Why, I am a little peasant girl. All our peasant girls are dressed as I am."

"It is a lovely dress," said Nancy hurriedly.

"Yes," agreed Florica. "We maidens always embroider the waists in which we are to be married."

"But you are not married!" exclaimed Nancy, quite aghast.

"No, no!" Florica laughed a silvery little laugh. "I am a small girl like you."

"I am very happy to have you," said Nancy, with a deep, satisfied sigh. "I am rather lonely sometimes. But now we must sleep; it's the middle of the night. I must turn out my light. Granny always says little girls must sleep in the night."

"I, too, have an old granny – over there, in our village," sighed Florica. "She is very old, but the flax which she spins is whiter than her hair. In the village they call her Baba Zoe. She knows many things..."

"You will tell me all about them tomorrow," murmured Nancy. "Tomorrow we'll..."

And Nancy fell asleep. The moon, peeping through the curtains a little later, saw Nancy lying in her cozy bed. And, tucked into the hollow of her arm, lay Florica – Florica, the magic doll of Romania.

Florica's eyes were also closed. But when the moon sent her rays hovering over the bed, they fell on a great tear which shone like a diamond on her cheek. Poor little Florica! [...]

***

What had happened to Nancy? It is not so easy to explain what *had* happened to her. That sort of thing doesn't happen to everybody in everyday life. I know it has never happened to me – nor has it happened to you, either, I imagine. But I'll try to make you understand it, although it was rather extraordinary!

You see, the night before, Florica had been telling Nancy so many interesting things about Romania that finally Nancy had asked: "But can't I get there?" And Florica had answered: "Yes, you can if you will do as I tell you."

"Of course I will," said Nancy – because, you remember, she was always so eager to know what the rest of the world was like.

"Then listen!" And Florica had whispered something into Nancy's ear. I really don't know what she told her! But it was on the next day that Nancy, as you will remember, had asked permission to go to the woods; and that

Granny, who was a kind Granny, had said, "Yes". And... well!... Nancy never came back! If you ask me, I think that it was all schemed, arranged, and carried out by that little rascal of a doll, Florica! Anyway, this remains a fact: On the morning when old Sue had come back quite desperate, after having searched all night for Nancy – on that self-same morning, you see, Nancy awoke to something quite unexpected. Just listen!

Nancy awoke in a wee white room upon which her eyes had never before rested! A ray of light was dancing in through the smallest window that she had ever seen, and on the sill of that tiny window stood a flowerpot, with a red geranium growing in it. In the farthest corner of the room was a huge, bulging hearth which touched the ceiling, but the ceiling was so low that the hearth had no need to stretch very high to reach it.

Nancy felt rather stiff. What was she lying on? It certainly was not her own soft little bed! She raised herself on one elbow, and peered around. She was lying on a sort of wooden bench, and under her head was a pillow of rather rough linen with an edge of embroidery. She was covered with a thick kind of carpet-blanket, striped with many colors: orange, green, blue, black, red, yellow, and a sort of terra-cotta brown. Never had Nancy seen so many colors together. And none of the colors seemed to clash with the others. It was certainly an attractive rug – but where were the sheets? Really, this was very strange! There lay Florica, close beside her. But Florica had turned into a real little girl of about her own size! And beside Florica lay two smaller children, and also an animal of some sort. It was not a dog. What was it? What, indeed, could it be?

This time Nancy sat up and peered over the three sleepers to discover what sort of animal it was. It was all curly, and a sort of orangy-brown in color. Its curls were not silky, but rough and hard-looking, and among them were caught pieces of dead leaves. Nancy rubbed her eyes. All this was indeed very strange! And how prettily that inquisitive sunbeam pushed its way through the scarlet geranium: the flower was a flame! But Nancy must find out what that fuzzy, curly animal was! Suddenly it stirred, sat up on its haunches, grunted, and turned toward the stranger a long head with flopping ears, tiny eyes, and moist snout. A pig! Did you ever hear of such a thing! A chestnut colored piggy-wiggy, with bristly curls, and with shy little eyes, half hidden in the fat of its face. "Well, I never!" This time Nancy made as though to quit this so-called bed, upon which children and piggies slept together. She dangled her legs over the side, the palms of her two hands pressed down on the boards, and made ready to spring to the floor. She had a feeling that the pig was laughing at her. He had more expression than ordinary pigs. And Nancy, although she highly disapproved of the position which he occupied beside the sleeping children, could not help comparing him, to his advantage, with the American pigs which she had seen. This one was much nicer. He did not look so naked. And instead of having, as other pigs have, hard straight bristles which would hardly cover a scaly skin, he had curls. In fact, this pig was all rust-colored curls.

"I hate the idea of having you sleep on one bed with us, if this hard thing can be called a bed," said Nancy to the pig. "But I think that you're a great improvement upon American-English pigs."

The pig looked pleased. He flopped his long ears, made a funny, jerky motion, grunted, and then, head high in air, moved the flat front part of his snout in the most amusing way. Nancy felt that she was going to laugh out loud, but she put her hand over her mouth. She did not want to wake up the others.

But somebody was opening the crooked little door in the wall near the hearth! Nancy, suddenly feeling almost frightened, lay down again as quickly as she could, and pulled up the striped rug until there was little of her left uncovered. But she kept a close watch on the door, forgetting, for the moment, all about Master Piggy-Wiggy.

The door opened slowly, and the first thing that Nancy saw was a large bundle of dry branches. Could a bundle of sticks walk all by itself? But no, the sticks were on somebody's back! Whose? Nancy stared with all her might. The person – whoever it was – was quite hidden by the faggots. Bump! Now the bundle was on the ground. And there stood a very, very old woman. Nancy caught her breath and pulled the cover still further over her. A witch!... Yes, there could be no doubt of it whatsoever! That old woman could be nothing but a witch! And she, Nancy, was caught in the witch's hut! And the fuzzy piggy-wiggy was a bewitched prince. And the red flower in the window had no doubt been, once upon a time, a princess – a real princess in a silk dress, with pearls round her throat. And now the princess was a geranium in a pot! Of course she would rather be a geranium than a pig, but all the same...

Nancy shuddered, but decided to have another good look at the witch. What was she doing? Nancy peeped from beneath her cover. The witch was leaning over the hearth, breaking bits of branches, and poking them into the furnace door. Of course it *was* a furnace! That was the right word for a witch's hearth. What was she going to cook in her furnace? Nancy stared hard at the witch. She was very, very old and quite bent. She could not straighten out. She was dressed rather differently from ordinary witches: she had a white shirt of very coarse linen with an edge of black embroidery, and around the lower part of her body was a skirt – or rather, a black piece of stuff, which had been wrapped around her. And this cloth had a red edge. There was also a broad girdle of thick red cloth around the witch's waist, which seemed to hold her shirt and skirt together. On her head she wore a black and red handkerchief, tied under her chin; very little of her hair was to be seen, but that was muddy gray in color. She had a long nose, and her chin seemed to be trying to reach up to meet it. The eyes under her bushy eyebrows were dark, and reminded Nancy of polished

216

black cherries. Curiously enough, the witch did not look wicked at all. She had a face, which was kindly. And certainly she was quick about lighting the fire, which almost immediately began to crackle with a cheerful sound, filling the small room with a pleasant odor of wood smoke. What would the witch do now? She drew a small three-legged stool out from a corner behind the hearth, sat down on it, and began stirring something in a black pot, which she placed on the burning sticks. Of course, that was exactly what a witch would do: cook something in a black pot. And then the witch began to sing. Yes, witches always sang over their black pots. "Incantations" – wasn't that what they called their songs? And they cooked toads, and serpents, and strange herbs. And then they mixed them with nasty things, although, of course, snakes and toads were nasty enough without anything nastier! But stretch her neck as she would, Nancy could not manage to see into the pot. The witch was not singing in English and yet Nancy could understand what she sang! That was queer, indeed!

> *"White frost on my head,*
> *White flowers for the dead!*
> *Bright flame burn,*
> *Old earth turn!*
> *Bitter the bread,*
> *Restless the bed,*
> *Of those grown old!*
>
> *Dim mist on my hair,*
> *Dim eyes which stare*
> *At days gone by*
> *And hopes which die!*
> *God keeps the gate*
> *To homes which wait*
> *For those grown old!"*

Then the witch turned her head and looked at Nancy. Nancy felt her heart give a great jump, yet... The witch was smiling at her! She had no teeth, but her smile was as kindly as Granny's smile at home!

***

"So Florica has brought you here, has she? Did you sleep well, little chicken?"

"Funny old creature!" thought Nancy. "Evidently she knows all about Florica, but I wonder if she knows that Florica is really a doll? Why does she call me 'little chicken'? And why can I understand what she says, although I'm quite sure that it's not English that she is speaking?"

"I was not here yesterday," said Nancy. And she felt sure that it was a rather silly thing to say.

"No, you certainly weren't. But our bed is large enough for many, and Ghitsa keeps the children warm."

"I suppose that's the pig," concluded Nancy. "But probably the old witch knows nothing about hot-water bottles, or she would not use Ghitsa." There certainly were not many things in this whitewashed room. It was much too small to hold more than the wooden bed – which was really only a large seat – the huge hearth, a table, and that heavy painted chest against the wall. It was a decorative chest: green, with red tulips and red carnations painted on it. Nancy wondered what was inside.

"I just wonder, how came you here?" asked the old witch.

"I'm rather confused about it myself," confessed Nancy. "Florica simply said that I must go to sleep, and wake up somewhere else."

"That sounds easy enough," nodded the witch.

"And Romania is far away, isn't it?" asked Nancy.

"Far from where?" inquired the old woman.

"Far from America."

"*Vai!*" exclaimed the witch. "Is that where Florica brought you from?"

"Yes," nodded Nancy. "But what have you to do with Florica?"

"I'm her granny," said the witch.

"You!"

"Yes. Don't you like the looks of me?"

"Then you are Baba Zoe! And you are not a witch?" Nancy was not quite sure whether she was disappointed or relieved.

"A witch! *Vai*! No! Although I do know many a little thing."

"Then Ghitsa is not a bewitched prince?"

"God preserve us, and the good Virgin Mary!" And the old woman devoutly crossed herself, half turning toward a small icon hanging close up to the ceiling in one of the corners. "So Ghitsa is a bewitched prince, is he? And what else have I bewitched in this house?"

"I thought that perhaps the geranium…"

"That the geranium... what?"

"Perhaps had been a princess!"

"*Vai*! *Vai*!" The old woman clapped her hands together. "But, little chicken, there aren't so many princes and princesses wandering about the roads nowadays!"

"We've none in America, and we don't really want any," declared Nancy democratically. "But we don't mind *seeing* them!"

I think that Nancy felt just a shade of disappointment. No witches, no princes, no princesses! Only a pig sleeping beside the children to keep them warm!

"I wish that Florica would wake up," she said. For she was beginning to feel rather uncomfortable.

"Poke her! She is as lazy as sleeping waters," declared Baba Zoe.

Nancy leaned over the doll of yesterday, and shook her gently. "Florica!"

Florica sat up with a start, and in waking she also awoke the children – a small boy and a small girl – who started up, and stared at Nancy out of enormous, round, brown eyes which were encircled by unusually long lashes. Ghitsa, with a grunt, jumped from the bed, and scurried across the floor, taking shelter between the painted chest and the wall.

"Well!" cried Florica, with sparkling eyes. "Here we are!"

"How did you do it?" queried Nancy.

"Sent you to sleep in the forest! You remember the yellow crocuses, don't you?"

"Yes, and the first violet which we found."

"Then we sat down, you remember?"

"Yes."

"And do you remember an old crow which was sitting on a branch over-head?"

"Yes, and you began saying funny things to him."

"Quite right! But what do you remember after that?"

Nancy drew her brows together. She was making a great effort to think.

"I can't quite remember anything else..."

"No, of course you can't. I did all the rest!"

"With the help of the crow?" asked Nancy.

"Perhaps," teased Florica. "But I don't give away all my secrets."

"But how could we get here all in one night?"

"Perhaps *she's* the witch," grinned old Zoe.

"Can Romanians do such things?" asked simple little Nancy.

"But we don't know as much as you do," declared Florica. "Anyway, not about machines, and electricity, and power plants, and concrete roads! And not every one of us has an automobile and a refrigerator. Nor can we have radios, which bring concerts, and speeches, and sermons right into our houses. And we don't have telephones all over the place."

"What's the child speaking about?" asked her granny, putting her fingers to her ear, as if her hand were a trumpet.

"But she has not explained how we came here!" complained Nancy.

"Florica was always a wise one," declared Baba Zoe, looking tenderly at her grandchild.

"And how did you become a real little girl?" was Nancy's next question.

"I'm so confused that I don't know whether I'm standing on my head or on my feet. And poor old Granny, waiting for me for supper! However shall I let her know where I am?" And suddenly our little American had large tears in her eyes.

"Come, Nancy!" cried Florica. "I'll show you the cherry-tree in full bloom, just outside of our house. And Radu and Anica will come also while *Buni-ca*[65] prepares the *mamaliga* for breakfast."

---

[65] Grandmother.

And she threw her arms around her friend's neck.

„*Mamaliga*?" said Nancy. "What's that?" But as she spoke, a great tear rolled down her cheek and splashed the floor.

"Come and see the cherry-tree!" insisted Florica.

And so, hand in hand, the two small friends ran out into the sunshine.

* * *

And what sunshine it was! Like melted gold, flooding all things! Nancy stood on the threshold, drawing in the pure morning air in great gulps, as if she were thirsty. Quite close to the door stood a cherry-tree in full bloom. Its blossoms were so thick and so white that they seemed to give out light. At its foot grew little groups of light pink and periwinkle-blue hyacinths. They were not at all show hyacinths. But for all that, their perfume was so intense that it filled the air. And there were a few daffodils of the simple double kind, which were proudly yellow, though they were small and their stalks were thin. There was no real garden around this house, which in fact was nothing more than a hut. There was no neatly cropped lawn, no tidy stone path leading to the door. Everything was crooked and disheveled. Even the grass grew only in tufts, and certainly it had never known a mowing machine. But there was something attractive about it all – as well as something unkempt. Picturesque would have been the word for it, had Nancy known it. Nancy turned around to look at the cottage. It was a funny, square little box of a thing, and like everything else, it was somewhat crooked. There were no sharp angles anywhere. It looked as if a child had modelled it with chubby, awkward hands. Its roof was too large for it, and looked top-heavy. It was thatched with dry corn-leaves, and a lean, gray cow was comfortably chewing the overlapping leaves – which proves to you that the cottage was not very high. Smoke was actually curling out through the thatched roof itself, because – strange as it may seem – the house had no chimney anywhere! On one side of the house there was that which may once have imagined itself to be a garden, and which still had the remnant of a fence. But garden and enclosure had both crumbled away, only to add to the picturesque untidiness of the place as a whole. All around the base of the hut was a beaten earth ledge which somewhat resembled a seat, and upon which stood pots and dishes of various shapes. A somewhat meager company of very fussy hens were picking among these pots, and strutting in and out of the front door, which ridiculously resembled an open mouth too much on one side of a face. Nancy continued to consider this the front door, but the truth was that the modest hut did not boast of a second door.

Baba Zoe's house could not in any way be compared with Granny's bungalow. There was no kitchen, no bathroom, no refrigerator, and no shed for a Ford. It was the queerest, dearest little house that Nancy had ever seen. In fact, it was more like a toy house than a real one. But how exactly the right thing that cherry-tree was, tickling the shaggy maize roof with its bloom-laden branches! That was a perfect picture.

"I like it," said Nancy, with a deep sigh of contentment. "But I suppose it's not the season for sunflowers?"

"No, no!" protested Florica. "The sunflowers come in late summer or autumn. See, none of the trees are green yet, except the willow."

"Would Granny like it, do you think?"

Florica put her head on one side, in the way so peculiar to her. "Somehow, I'm not quite sure that she would."

"There's no arm-chair," suggested Nancy.

"And no shiny electric stove," added Florica.

"And no bedrooms upstairs," said the little American.

"There is no upstairs at all!" confessed Florica.

"And then, Granny would hardly like to have Ghitsa sleeping with us," mused Nancy.

"No, I don't think that she would," agreed the ex-doll. "And she would not approve of having only one bed for everybody together. Nor would she care for the idea of having no sheets, even for that one bed. Nor would she approve of cooking in the bedroom. Nor would she hang her supply of onions in the room which you call – I think – the living-room or the parlor."

"It's the living-room when it's large," said Nancy, somewhat pompously.

"Neither would she approve of our rough grass, would she? And she would think it all wrong that the cow should feed upon the thatch," added Florica.

"Tell me," asked Nancy, "how did you really get me here? And how is it that I understand all that you and your granny say, and that you understand me?"

"There are mysteries in the world," teased Florica, "and even if Bunica – that's my granny, you know – isn't a witch, I might be one!"

"That doesn't explain how I crossed the ocean in one night, to wake up in Romania."

"No, it doesn't," agreed Florica provokingly.

"Are you never going to explain?" asked Nancy.

"Perhaps not!" laughed Florica. And she began dancing about until the black braids of her hair went flying about her face as if they were alive. She tucked up a corner of her black skirt, in order that she might be unhindered, and her legs flew about almost as much as her braids. Her small brother and sister, the twins, who had been solemnly sitting upon the beaten earth ledge among the hens and the pots, sucking their thumbs, jumped up and joined in the fun. Suddenly Nancy felt that her legs could not resist that gay circle, and so in a moment she, too, had joined hands with the others in the ring.

From somewhere came the sound of a flute playing the queerest dance music that you ever did hear; but they were all whirling around so quickly that Nancy could not see who was playing. Everything was a blur, and the irrepressible Florica was singing at the top of her voice – which was much louder ever since she had ceased to be a doll. And this was her song:

"Wake, Mother Earth!
Awake, awake!
Thy sleep is done;
Comes now the sun
That beams with mirth:
Awake!

See, Mother Earth!
Behold, behold!
Love's bow is bended!
The Spring has ended
Gray Winter's dearth:
Behold!

Hush, Mother Earth!
Be calm! Be glad!
The buds now break!
The dead awake!
'Tis Spring's rebirth:
Be glad!"

"That's a spring song!" cried Florica. And so suddenly did she let go the hands of the others who were swinging with her in the round dance, that little Radu and Anica went flying to right and to left, as if they were a couple of bundles. And Nancy, before she realized what was happening, found herself caught up in the arms of someone whom she had not even noticed while she was dancing. And that sudden embrace saved her from the undignified fate of the twins.
"Oh, goodness!" gasped Nancy. "I beg your pardon!"
"No pardon needed," exclaimed a pleasant voice. And Nancy found herself looking up into two large, blue-gray eyes, shaded by ink-black lashes.
"Oh, I didn't see you!" cried Nancy.
"But I saw *you*," said the one who held her in his arms.
"Don't be so horrified, Nancy! That's my big brother, Dobre, the shepherd", cried Florica. And teasingly she sang:

"Dobre! Oh, Dobre!
Where are your sheep?
Earth is wide and
Waters are deep!

I can hear how they bleat by the pond
On the rim of the far and beyond!"

"Yes, that is Dobre! And his sheep love him. And so do the girls, because he has the finest eyes in the village, and because he knows how to play such beautiful tunes on his flute."

Nancy stared up at Dobre. She had never seen anyone like him before. He wore a shirt of coarse linen, gray-white in color, with trousers to match. On his feet were the same queer sort of sandal-shoes as those, which Florica wore, and horsehair thongs were wound about his legs up to his knees. A very broad leather belt, encrusted with brass buttons, encircled his waist. On his head was a high sheepskin cap, and over one shoulder hung a sheep-skin cloak. He really looked as if he had stepped out of a storybook, and as if he were exactly the sort of shepherd boy who might follow the Star of Bethlehem, or fall in love with a princess – with a *real* princess.

Suddenly Nancy felt very shy and self-conscious. Never before in her life had she seen anyone so good-looking as Florica's older brother.

"Those were father's sheep," explained Florica. "He was killed in the war. Mother went to look for him, and died on the way back from Moldavia, without having found his grave. We stayed with Bunica. The twins had only just been born before mother left, but they did not die as so many babies in the village did. But they've never been very gay, little Radu and Anica. However, they are no trouble."

There stood Radu and Anica, two diminutive reproductions of their elders, staring with overlarge eyes and solemn faces, as if they did not know how to laugh. Even while they were whirling about in the dance, their faces had been solemn little masks.

"What are you called?" asked Dobre, pointing at the little American with his rough wooden flute.

"Nancy," said the little girl.

"When I go into the hills with my sheep, will you come too, Nancy?"

Nancy really did not know what answer to give. She turned to Florica, and seized her hand.

"Would you like to go, Nancy?" asked Florica.

"Not alone," whispered Nancy.

"I, too, would go with you," said Florica. "Our hills are wonderful, you know. And no one plays more lively *doine* than Dobre."

"What does *doine* mean?" asked Nancy.

"Love-songs," explained Florica.

"Love-songs?" Nancy looked puzzled. "Are they nice?"

"They are the nicest songs we have," declared the shepherd boy. And his beautiful teeth flashed in a gay laugh. "Come along to the river's edge this evening when the sun is low, and I'll play you some. And Florica will sing.

Goodbye!" But Dobre did not really say "Goodbye!" What he really said was, "*La revedere!*" – which means the same thing.

Dobre moved off, turning once or twice to look back and wave his large fur cap.

"He is going to fetch his staff and his sheep," explained Florica.

"Has he had his breakfast?" anxiously inquired Nancy.

Florica laughed. "He has a lump of *mamaliga* and an onion in his pocket, and there is plenty of water down in the little stream under the willow trees."

Nancy had no idea what *mamaliga* was, but somehow she did not think that an onion was exactly the food for anyone with such beautiful teeth and eyes as those of Dobre, Florica's brother. […]

***

The apple-trees were in flower and the swallows, by hundreds, were returning from the south. Dobre, Florica and Nancy had been wandering toward the hills for several days. It had been a slow advance, for sheep do not move quickly, and all of the long, long journey had been made on foot. This was a wonderful experience, although it was tiring at first. And it was all part of the strange dream in which Nancy seemed to be living.

First, they had traveled over endless roads, which cut across the plains as if they were gray bands holding the earth together. Then the little party had quitted the high roads for the narrower ways leading toward the highlands, and the roads had become less broad and more twisting, and there were fruit-trees in full bloom growing along their sides.

It was a long, long wandering, and it might have been dull, had it not been for the many quaint and sometimes wonderful things which Florica had to relate, and had it not been for Dobre's flute. There was a spell about Dobre's music that took hold of you. Nancy felt that she could follow him and his music to the very ends of the earth.

And one day they came to a lovely spot. Never had Nancy seen a place more mysterious – nor one more full of romance. There stood a wondrous white building encircled by high walls. It had almost the appearance of a fortress, but there was no feeling of war about it, only one of peace – of deep, white peace, surrounded by God's green. This was a convent, which nestled like a great white bird at the foot of wonderfully wooded hills. The beeches were just breaking into leaf, and so luminous and transparent was their opening foliage that they seemed to give forth light instead of shade. Dobre had gone somewhat out of his usual course to lead the little girls to this spot.

"Nancy must pay a visit to our nuns," he had said. "She must enter the white convent walls and step into the wondrously painted church where the ancient tombs lie in eternal sleep amid dust which the sun turns to gold."

224

But the flock had been left outside. It was not proper for the sheep to enter the holy enclosure. Dobre, leading the way, passed under the vaulted passage of the belfry. The pair of heavy doors were wide open, as if they were two outstretched arms; they were heavy oaken doors, studded with huge rusty nails. Underfoot were rounded cobblestones, with which the entire courtyard was paved. Nancy found them somewhat hard on her tired feet. But what peace! White peace, indeed! Never had Nancy seen anything as white as that lovely building with its many columns – a double row of them, one above the other – forming a spacious square around the church. A bell was ringing, not insistently, but as a voice, which was calling together those who, even without its reminding, would have come from long habit. Nancy felt awed. Never before had she been in a place such as this. Her voice was suddenly hushed, and she stood still, staring about her.

"We must go into the church," said Dobre. "It is one of the most beautiful of our country. It is very, very old, and was built by one of our princes, who was very pious and who had many beautiful churches built in all parts of the country. You will see his portrait painted on the wall, when we enter."

Nancy listened attentively to all that her companion had to tell her. This was all very wonderful, indeed. She slipped her hand into Dobre's, and I believe that Dobre liked the feeling of that little hand in his. He had taken off his fur cap, and had stuck it under his armpit. Florica took Nancy's other hand. And it was thus that the three comrades passed under the columned and painted porch, into the dim sanctuary.

How lovely it was! So old, so mellow, so fairylike! Such a mysterious light! And how quaint those paintings on the walls, and how graceful those silver lamps which, on their long chains, seemed to have just emerged from the dark void above! And there was a curious thing. The altar was hidden behind a high, shadowy, screen-like wall. It was entirely carved, and in it were three doors. Numberless icons were set into the old and intricate gilt carving. And quite at the top rose a large cross. There was a curious odor about the church: a mixture of incense, and the smell of dust, and a faint scent of damp earth. It well suited the ancient, dusk-filled place. The more you looked at the walls, the more paintings did you see: just as, when you gaze at the night sky, the stars seem to multiply endlessly. The whole church was covered with paintings: up, up, until at the very top of the dome, an enormous Christ gazed at you with eyes which seemed to be of the size of small blue lakes.

"Now we must show her the princes," whispered Florica, dragging her friend back to the part of the church through which they had first come, which was the part farthest from the altar.

"Look!" she whispered.

And at these paintings Nancy gazed up in wonder. Upon a background of dull gold stood famous kings of legend, watching the years roll by, their queens and their children, beside them.

"You see," whispered Florica, "they had many children: their daughters stand in a row on one side, their sons on the other. And all of them have crowns on their heads."

"They don't seem to enjoy their crowns," whispered Nancy.

"But they needn't," explained Florica. "They must be satisfied with the honor, you see."

"No, I don't see," murmured Nancy. "They don't look happy at all."

"But they need not be happy!" protested Florica.

"But why?" insisted Nancy.

"Because they are princes and princesses; that's enough."

"It isn't," firmly declared Nancy. "And why are the king and queen holding a church in their hands?"

"That's because they built it."

"Well, it is all very strange and wonderful, and not at all as at home," sighed Nancy, as they emerged from the old church. "But I love the shuddery feeling that it gives me: it's like living in a time with which you have nothing to do. But see how cheerful the sun is here, outside!"

And so it was! For after the dim church, the sunlight on the white outer walls was fairly glaring. […]

***

That was a long road which the three companions traveled that day, and yet they did not reach *Matusa*[66] Daria's house, but had to sleep another night under the stars. The stars were beautiful, but owing to the mountain air the night was very cold, and more than once Nancy gave a longing thought to her little white bed under the snug green roof of Granny's house. Once, even, Dobre heard something like a muffled sob, and drew his sheepskin more closely around his precious charges. But morning was so beautiful that all the homesickness was forgotten. And just before sunset the children reached a high point whence there was a marvelous view over the hills toward the plains. Here they rested, and Nancy, seated on a heap of stones, folded her hands in ecstasy; almost solemn did she feel, so astoundingly beautiful, so worldwide and glorious was that view.

"And that stone building, like a wee fairy-castle over there on a rock – what is it?" asked she, pointing with her finger.

"That is the Queen's Castle," said Dobre.

"A real queen?"

"Our Queen!"

"She lives there?"

"Sometimes," said Florica, "when she wants to rest."

---

[66] "Mătuşa": aunt.

226

"Is she resting now?"

"Let me see if a flag is waving from the highest tower," said Dobre. "That's the sign that she's there."

"Oh! I do hope that she's there!"

Nancy almost gasped. This was more and more like a fairy-story; Florica's and Dobre's queen! That was almost too good to be true!

"It is too far, I cannot see whether there is a flag there or not. Let us hurry down. When we are nearer, we shall see if there is."

And hurry they did. Even the sheep tripped along more briskly, as if even they felt excited. What a beautiful descent that was! At each turn the view was different, and each view seemed more marvelous than the last. There were deep green valleys with almost virgin forest tumbling down into them – stupendous beech woods which were bursting into leaf; and further back, ink-black spruce, like armies standing on guard, protecting the rocky mountains beyond. How impressive it was!

"Will she have her crown on?"

"Are you still thinking of the Queen?" asked Dobre.

Nancy nodded.

"When she is here, the Queen usually wears a simple dress like ours," explained Florica, "but because she is married and has many children, she wears a white veil instead of a colored handkerchief."

"I thought that she would wear a crown," said Nancy. There was disappointment in her voice.

"But a crown is heavy," said Florica wisely.

"How can she look like a queen without a crown?" insisted the little American.

"A white veil looks almost like a crown," said Dobre.

"Is she fond of her people?"

"Yes," pronounced the shepherd, almost solemnly. "She cared for our wounded during the war, and fed the hungry children, and went into the widows' huts."

"Is she beautiful?" asked Nancy, gazing up into the peasant's face.

"Her eyes have wept as have the eyes of our mothers," said Florica. "They say that she, too, laid a little son to rest under the ground, and that she had to leave him alone in the old church, because the enemy came and drove her and the King out from their royal palace. They also drove out all of the royal children – except the baby Prince, who lay sleeping in the church, keeping vigil until their return."

"Then perhaps she is too old to be beautiful?" And now there was anxiety in Nancy's voice.

"They say," explained Florica, "that when she came into the country, she was fair as are the ripe cornfields, and that her eyes were blue, and that she was as lovely as Ileana Cosinzeana of our fairy-tales. But she was a stranger then."

227

"But now she is no longer a stranger?"

"No," said Dobre, "she has cried with us and she has laughed with us; she has sung our songs and broken our bread. She has sat before our hearths and held our little ones in her arms. And the poorest come up to her castle, and never does she send them away."

"And the King?"

"He drew his sword to liberate our people, so that all of us within our frontier should be brothers once more. He is brave and good, and he always thinks of us before he thinks of himself."

"How do you know all that?" asked the little stranger.

"We all know it," said Dobre. And as if someone higher than he were present, he took his cap from his head.

"They've lived for us," said Dobre, and his sister nodded her head.

"I hope that the Queen will be there!" cried Nancy, clasping her hands.

"See, there's the flag!" cried Florica. "Red with the orange eagle upon it, and with a blue border."

"Let's hurry!" begged Nancy.

And off they started again, down, down the steep descent, as fast as their feet could carry them. Once Nancy exclaimed, seizing Florica's hand:

"To think that you were a doll in a shop and that Granny bought you!"

"And now perhaps I'll show you a real, live queen," laughed the little peasant.

"It sounds like a story-book," said Nancy.

***

Matusa Daria's cottage lay a little above the highroad on a green meadow, and was surrounded by huge apple-trees in full bloom. It was certainly a more prosperous dwelling than Baba Zoc's hut. It had actually two stories and a small wooden gallery, which was reached by half a dozen wooden steps. But what made it wonderful was, that from its wee windows you could see the Queen's Castle, as if it were a beautiful picture painted against the sky.

"It's like the fortresses in my Book of Legends!" cried Nancy.

"It was a fortress," explained Matusa Daria. "They say some Teuton knights built it long ago to protect this valley against the Turks."

"The Turks?" Nancy looked bewildered.

"We were always trying to protect ourselves against the Turks," explained Dobre, somewhat vaguely.

"And against other enemies also," added Daria.

"We always had enemies on every side and we were continually invaded. Romania is a land of tears."

"Very lately we were invaded from three sides. My father died during the last invasion; mother died soon after, and left the twins."

"She left you also," sighed Matusa Daria. "Many wee children were left, but most of them died."

"The twins were the smallest," murmured Florica, who probably had a motherly feeling toward her younger brother and sister, because peasant girls are motherly at an early age, in that land near the Rising Sun. Work begins early, and even childhood is not free from toil – the toil of those who till the land.

"Do you know," said Nancy quaintly, turning toward Florica's aunt, "Florica was a doll in America, and she magicked me over to Romania. And now, out of your windows I can see the Queen's Castle."

"*Vai*!" exclaimed Daria, who was a comfortable, motherly person, without much imagination. She had always been the prosperous member of an otherwise poor family; but there was no pride in her on that account; she was all kindness and hospitality.

"*Vai, Vai*! But it's a real fairy-story! And who would have imagined that Florica would be as clever as all that – our Florica! And all the way from America! *Vai, Vai*! How did you do it, Florica? And how did you get over to America, and as a doll into the bargain? God Almighty, protect us!" And the good woman crossed herself several times.

"Yes, and see my shoes – they are beginning to wear out because we've walked so far," continued practical Nancy, "and please, may I have some hot water? I haven't had a bath for a long time, and the nuns gave me a piece of soap."

"From Bucharest," added Florica; but she gave no explanation of the way in which she had done her great trick.

"A bath!" exclaimed the peasant woman. "Does the little chicken want to get right into the water?"

"Yes, if you please," insisted the little American. Decidedly she was destined to be called "little chicken" by all these kindly people; *puiule*[67] was the word they really used. "I'd like to get right in it and I'd like it to be hot, because that takes the dirt off better, Granny always said."

"Did she? Your old granny in America, I suppose? But here, wouldn't the river do?"

"No, please!" Nancy was quite positive. "I've had rivers and streams all along the road, and mighty chilly they were, too! But if you don't mind, today I'd like a real bath."

"Listen to the child!" exclaimed the peasant woman. "Today if you don't mind, I'd like a real bath! And she all the way from America and after so much travel that her shoes are nearly worn out! I'm beginning to wonder if my head is screwed on the right way. A bath! That reminds me of a story that an old nun told me. She came from our mountain convent, and slept a night in my house. She says that the Queen, who was then a young princess, had once spent a few days at their convent – such an honor! But just think! Every day she wanted a bath! And of course there was no bathtub –

_____

[67] Romanian for: chick, little one, darling.

229

nothing which she could use except the wooden tub in which the nuns washed their linen. So that had to do, and from all sides the nuns carried hot water, which they heated on their little stoves for the Princess' bath. But they brought such boiling water – to make sure that it would really be a hot bath – that when it was ready, the Princess could not get into it!" And old Daria laughed, holding her sides. And the three children laughed with her, while a little star peeped in at the window to see what the joke was. For evening had come suddenly, and the Queen's Castle was now but a shadow against the darkening sky.

"But the little chicken shall have her bath! I, too, have a tub, in which I do my washing. It's in the shed – but that will be all right, I suppose. And I'll see that you are not scalded as the poor Princess was."

"Yes, you see, if I visit the Queen tomorrow, I must be as clean as I am when I am in America," explained Nancy. "She would get a wrong idea of little American girls if I had not had a bath. Granny would feel very badly about it, and so would black Sue. And the Queen..."

Up went Daria's hands again. "The Queen! And she talks quietly of visiting the Queen in her castle – as if everybody could go up and knock at the Queen's door, and ask to come in! And she, poor dear, there for a rest. And sometimes, they say, she wants to be alone; for she loves her gardens and her plants. She has such beautiful flowers that when we pass them we cross ourselves, because the colors are like those in paradise."

Daria's words came rushing out in a torrent; she was quite shocked that anyone could talk so lightly of seeing the Queen.

"But she is our mother," said Florica simply. "She is our mother."

"That's true! May the Holy Virgin give her many days." And old Daria crossed herself again.

"And I know that she's fond of American," added Nancy. "So I'm sure that when she hears that there is a little American girl here, she'll let me come to see her. Yes, I'm sure of that! But please, may I have my bath now?"

"You know," related Daria, ignoring for the moment Nancy's insistence upon her bath, "before the Queen came here, the castle was a melancholy, forsaken place – a dead thing. Then after the war, the people gave it to the Queen, because they love her. And the Queen made the ancient little fortress wake up and live. It was as if it were a blind thing opening its eyes to see. And our village blesses her. We used to be on enemy's ground; but since the war, we belong again to the Old Country and the Queen's little castle is like a symbol; it was a new and blessed awakening in every way."

"Does she love her castle?" inquired Nancy.

"She does! She's given it a soul, so of course she loves it. And we are happy when we see the flag being hoisted – and look! There is the first light beginning to shine."

Nancy, her face close to that of the peasant woman, peeped through the small window at the now shadowy castle, and truly, there was something like an eye of light looking down upon them.

"Oh, please, I must have a hot bath!" urged Nancy again. "I must be as clean as Granny would like me to be, when I go up there!"

"Well, well! You know what you want at any rate, little chicken, so let's heat the water. But you, Dobre, must go and fetch it up from the river. And I suppose you are hungry, too?"

So Nancy had a bath in Matusa Daria's washtub. The water was delightfully hot, although it was not scalding, as the Princess' bath in the convent had been. The nun's beautiful piece of soap proved a great blessing, although more for show than for use, and with the help of the hot water Nancy made it do wonders. Florica looked on with her large peasant eyes which never showed any astonishment; but when she was invited to take part in the little American's bath, she slipped off her clothes, stepped without ado into the steaming tub and seated herself beside her traveling companion.

"Do you think that she will receive us tomorrow?" asked Nancy.

"Who? The Queen?"

"Yes!"

"I hope that she will," said Florica.

"Shall we tell her that you were a doll?" asked Nancy.

"She believes in fairy-stories, I know," said Florica with a wise nod of her head, "so I think that we can tell her."

"Here, let me soap your back," proposed Nancy, "because we must be clean!"

So it was that two well-scrubbed little girls went to sleep side by side that night under Matusa Daria's roof. Once Nancy awoke, and giving her bedfellow a little nudge, asked in a sleepy voice: "Do you think that she has ever met *Haiduc*[68]?"

"Who?" Florica's voice was heavy with sleep.

"The Queen," murmured Nancy.

But Florica merely said "Huh!" and turned over on her side.

Beyond, on the high rock, stood the small castle, its light looking down as if it were a giant star upon the village beneath – or as if it were a beacon, towering aloft to guide any wanderer who might pass that way.

***

What an awakening that was for Nancy! The sun peeped into the cottage. The children were still fast asleep – it was many a day since they had slept under a roof. But the sun had no intention of being ignored. He lengthened his rays as if they were searchlights, and played them about over the

---

[68] In folkloric tradition of the Balkans the hajduk (Romanian: "haiduc") is a romanticized hero figure who steals from the rich and gives to the poor. Hajduks were mostly highwaymen, but among them were also also freedom fighters from the 17th to mid 19th centuries.

wooden bed in which the two girls slept, closely cuddled one against the other. Finally the beams were so warm on Nancy's face that she sat up and rubbed her eyes, yawned, winked several times, yawned again, and then gave a sudden exclamation: "Oh! The Queen!"

"What?" murmured Florica.

"But it's today that we'll see her!"

Florica opened large eyes, and a slow smile came to her lips.

"And over in America I was a doll," was what she said.

Nancy passed her hands over her hair.

"I'm afraid it's grown awfully long!" she said anxiously.

"What's grown long?"

"My hair's grown long – I feel it. But do get up quickly, Florica."

"It has dear little curly ends, your hair. I am sure that the Queen will like its honey color!"

"Do you think that she will?" Nancy's voice was eager, excited.

"Yes, she'll like it," declared the peasant child with conviction.

About an hour later, the three traveling companions were climbing up the steep path leading to the castle. Up, up – and still up; it was like climbing toward an eagle's nest. What wonderful places men of olden times chose on which to build! Nancy was rather out of breath. Besides, excitement and other emotions almost choked her.

"Suppose she won't let us come in?"

"She is our mother," pronounced Florica, with the simplicity of perfect faith.

Florica and Dobre were quite calm, but there was an expression on their faces which they might have worn if they had been going to church. Matusa Daria had seen to it that Dobre had on a spotlessly clean shirt. He had laid off his heavy sheepskin coat, and he looked tall and slim – all in white, with the high fur bonnet on his head.

"There's an old white-haired man, it seems, who guards the door. He's a sort of wizard who helped the Queen to make the castle come to life. They told me about him yesterday in the village – because I did not go to bed as early as you two did. But he has a kind heart, they say! And he tells the Queen which peasants are the poorest. He stays there when the Queen is away and looks after the place." Dobre paused for a moment, and took off his bonnet. "We're nearly there!" he said.

A steep flight of stone steps – hundreds of them! And at the top, a door of oak, with an iron hinge, was framed in rough stone. That was the front door. In fact, the castle had only one door, because it was a fortress, built hundreds of years ago to defend the village. But despite these ancient precautions against intruders, the children mounted the long stone stairs without delay, for there was no one there to prevent them. Finally, they reached the closed door. A statue of the Virgin, carved in stone, stood above it, against the wall. She held the Christ child in her arms, but her eyes were gazing far over the valley.

"You must knock!" whispered Florica.

Dobre raised the heavy bronze knocker and knocked once, twice, thrice! At first there was no sound. The children waited, holding their breaths. Their hearts were pounding like hammers. Ah! Someone was coming! The door opened slowly; it was very heavy. A door such as this could only open slowly. A white head, a kindly face! "Children!" The old man smiled. Dobre looking up from the step where he stood, twisting his *caciula* bonnet shyly backward and forward between his fingers, said: "This is a little foreigner and she'd like to see the Queen."

"I've come all the way from America with Florica, who was a Romanian doll," explained Nancy. "And in America we, too, know of your Queen –"

"Well, this is interesting!" exclaimed the old man. "I must go and call the Princess."

"He's going to call the Princess," whispered Nancy in an awed voice. "So there's also a princess!"

"Yes, yes; she's the Queen's daughter. And she's very fond of small children. And she can ride like the Haiduc!"

"Oh!" exclaimed the little American. "I can't wait to see her!"

A light step – and a bright voice, young and happy, called out: "Where are they?" And there stood a real princess! The sun shone on her, and her eyes were large and dark violet, her teeth very white. She was dressed as the peasants dress on Sundays and feast-days. Her shirt was heavy with embroidery; her pleated red skirt had a silver border. She wore a dark orange scarf on her head, and a scarlet geranium over one ear. She was lovely!

"Come in!" she cried. "Mother is upstairs; I'll call her. She'll be so interested when she hears that there's a small American girl here. We loved America – but how far away it is! Aren't you tired? What's your name?"

"Nancy! And these are Florica and Dobre. Florica was a doll, but she brought me here."

The Princess clapped her hands. "You must tell that to mother! She is fond of fairy-stories. Nancy! Such a darling name. And Florica and Dobre!"

The Princess turned to the little peasants and stretched out both of her hands – which they kissed.

"You're a *cioban*[69], Dobre! Where have you left your sheep?"

"At Matusa Daria's," explained Dobre.

"Ah! That's the dear little house on the hill with the large apple-trees, I know. But now you must follow me up to mother."

Fleet-footed as a deer, the Princess turned and, hurrying on before them, led the three wanderers into a marvelous, fairylike little courtyard, which was one blaze of sunlight and of red geraniums. At least, that was how it

_____

[69] Shepherd.

appeared at first sight to Nancy. It was the most wonderful little courtyard the child had ever seen!

Imagine a small square enclosure, shut in by high fortress walls as thick as six ordinary walls! On the outer side were loopholes – small, unglassed windows, hewn out through the deep walls. Through these you could look out over the valley below, where a slender river flowed along beneath shady trees. But the river was so far, far down that it seemed to be a silver ribbon of several shades. One part of the courtyard was higher than the rest, and this was walled off into a wee garden which was gay with flowers – red, violet and orange!

Looking up, Nancy saw a medley of towers, galleries, windows, piled up one above the other. No two of the windows had the same shape – and such ducky little windows they were! Just the sort for bewitched princesses, hobgoblins, or wizards to peep out of. Scarlet and fire-colored flowers hung in bright cascades from every window and gallery, and so warmly did the sun stream down upon them that they seemed to glow like fire! Chimneys of different sizes grew out of the brownish red tiles of the roof, and from one of these a wisp of smoke curled up toward the blue sky, as if it were a swirl of mist which the morning had forgotten to call away.

Oh, indeed, indeed, it was an enchanted castle! Nancy had to rub her eyes and pinch her arms to make sure that it was not all a dream, that she was truly here, that she had spoken to a real princess, and that the crooked little flight of steps before her actually led up to the part of the castle in which the Queen lived. Not a queen in a fairy-story, but a real queen of flesh and blood, whom the peasants so quaintly called "Our Mother".

***

The Princess had disappeared up the crooked little stairs. How quickly she moved! Her feet seemed to have wings. And the little stairs were just the sort of stairs to lead one into fairyland. But here was the Princess again! What lovely eyes she had, like great dark violet flowers! And when she ran, the silver border of her skirt glittered like star dust.

"Come," she cried gladly, "Mother's thrilled that a small American girl has found her way up to her castle. She's waiting in her room."

And so, with beating heart, Nancy mounted those stairs, her hand firmly clasped in that of the Princess. Dobre and Florica followed close on their heels. On the staircase was a blue carpet with quaint designs of brown, black and green. And when they reached the top, there was a tiny door, so low that the Princess, who was tall, had to bend her head. Through this door, they entered a small entrance hall. Such a quaint little place it was! All white, with vaulted ceiling and with wee windows set in incredibly thick walls! And everywhere, sunshine and flowers!

Never had Nancy dreamed that there could be so many flowers. They stood in great jars on the old carved chests and tables, on the windowsills, on the floor; they even shone from shiny copper vessels which hung by old chains from the ceiling. There were irises, tulips, lilacs, apple-blossoms and all sorts of flowering branches. The air was sweet with their fragrance, and the sun, streaming in through the windows, made their colors blaze. Underfoot, mellow-tinted rugs of many shades spread over a dark floor. Queer, solemn-faced saints peeped down upon you from gilded backgrounds. They seemed curiously at home, on those plain white walls.

Certainly this was not Nancy's idea of a royal palace, but it was ever so much pleasanter and more homelike – although it was entirely different from anything which she had ever seen before. She had imagined a palace full of golden chairs, gorgeous silk hangings, and portraits of ancestors in heavily carved frames – and, everywhere, tall footmen in bright liveries. But this was an enchanted little castle, guarded by an old wizard with white hair – a flowery retreat to which a queen came to rest.

"Here they are, mother!" cried the Princess. "Look at her! Isn't she darling – and she's called Nancy!"

And there, by a plain white hearth, stood the Queen. A bright woodfire was burning behind her, casting over her a radiant glow. Was she old or young? Plain or beautiful? These questions seemed all at once to have no importance. What Nancy saw was a smile of welcome and a pair of blue eyes, which were kind, although strangely sad. "Nancy!" It was a mother's voice. The Queen bent down and kissed the little American stranger, and she also kissed Dobre and Florica – although Dobre was a real boy! But as Nancy looked at the Queen, it seemed quite natural that she should kiss Dobre. For was she not "their mother", as they themselves had proclaimed? Her hands, too, were a mother's hands. Nancy had never known her own mother, but when the Queen passed her hands over her head, gently but firmly, Nancy knew that this was done as her own mother would have done it.

"So you are called Nancy! Let me look at you! You know, I am fond of Americans, large and small. In some way, I believe that we've always understood each other. And these are Florica and Dobre, your companions? You have a frank, affectionate face, Nancy. And I'm pleased that you have made friends with my little Romanians. I always want all people of all countries to be friends!"

"And, mother", exclaimed the Princess, "imagine, Florica came to America as a doll! It was Florica who managed to bring Nancy here!"

"That's a real fairy-story," said the Queen. "Tell me about it, Nancy."

The Queen seated herself in a large armchair near the blazing hearth, and Nancy found herself on a low stool at her feet, with her hand in that of the Queen. For some reason she did not feel shy. The Queen's eyes and smile made her feel quite at home. She was dressed very much as was the Princess – whom she called Ileana – but on her head was a long white veil, as white as the walls of her room.

Here also, the ceiling was vaulted, and there were even more flowers than in the little reception hall outside – especially yellow, heliotrope and bronze-colored tulips. And there was one huge old silver jar, full of white, gray and lavender tinted irises. On the windowsill stood a peasant's jug, full of apple-blossom branches which were of the delicate color of snow when the dawn paints it pink! There was peace in this small white room, and the song of many birds in the trees made fitting music for it – as if they were a soft accompaniment which you dreamed of, rather than heard. The floor had been stained black. Yellow rugs, blue-bordered, were spread over it. There were touches of yellow about the cushions, curtains and chairs. Over the couch, hung three old silver church-lamps filled with white flowers, which took the place of the lights. Their shadows on the white walls took queer shapes. A dream-room in a dream-castle! And there sat Nancy, the little American girl, her hand quite at home in that of the Queen, who listened to her as she told of Granny, and of old Sue, and of the Romanian doll which had come to life and conjured her across the sea...

***

"And your poor old granny-isn't she very lonely and sad?" asked the Queen, when Nancy had finished her tale.

"Florica is so clever, and she promised to let Granny know that I am safe and sound," explained Nancy.

The Queen stretched out her hand to Florica, who shyly came nearer and kissed it.

"Are you a little witch, Florica?" she asked.

"I was sad in a foreign country," murmured Florica. "I could not remain a doll; so I brought Nancy over here to see our beloved country. For I love her, and since I had to come back, I wanted her to come with me."

"You were too full of *dor*[70] to remain in a foreign land, weren't you, Florica?"

"Yes", said Florica, with her eyes on the ground.

"And do you know, Nancy, when I first came here from England, I was very young and I, too, was full of *dor* for the country which I had left? But now I belong to this country, because I have shared all of its joys and sorrows."

Nancy did not quite understand, but she liked to hear the Queen. "Don't you have any *dor* for England now?" she asked.

"Yes, sometimes," said the Queen, "but I have learned this, little Nancy: all lands and all people are lovable if we know them well enough. Our hearts are where our work is. 'That which thy hand findeth to do, do with all thy might.' I tried to live up to that ideal, little Nancy."

"Did you like America?" asked the child.

---

[70] Great longing, yearning.

236

"Ah, yes, I surely did, Nancy. But I was not there long enough! I did not see all of it – it's a world in itself! But I loved it, and your people were very kind. I have known how kind-hearted the Americans are, ever since the war. They helped us then, and even afterwards, with the sick and the wounded – and also with the hungry, orphaned children, of whom there were thousands and thousands! The Americans are generous; their hearts are warm. Ileana also knows how good and kind they can be!"

"Indeed I do!" exclaimed the Princess. "Mother, Nicky and I want to go to America again!"

"Then will you go and see Granny and old black Sue?" pleaded Nancy.

"Of course we will!" declared Ileana. "And has your house perchance a green roof?"

"Yes, it has!" exclaimed Nancy, clapping her hands. "How did you guess?"

"Because I especially remember a wee cottage with a green roof, in America, which was so ducky that I would have liked to carry it off with me!"

"Perhaps it was Granny's house!"

"And if we had knocked at the door, would old black Sue have let us in?" teased the Princess.

"Of course!" declared Nancy.

At this everybody laughed, even Dobre and Florica – and they seldom laughed, they were such solemn little people.

"And when you go back again to America, you must tell everybody about Romania," said the Queen. "About our wonderful forests, rivers and plains, and about our peasants in their lovely costumes – our dear, patient, faithful peasants whose men were such good soldiers during the war. Don't you love their darling huts, Nancy – and their many songs?"

"Yes," nodded Nancy. "But I don't think that Granny would like me to sleep in the same bed with a pig!"

Again the Queen and the Princess laughed.

"I hope that it was a chestnut-colored pig?" said Ileana.

"With a coppery shine on its curls?" added the Queen.

"Yes, yes, it was!" assented Nancy.

"And you must see the Black Sea," declared the Queen. "Dobre, are you going to take our little stranger down to our seashore?"

"I hope to," said Dobre, "if her legs are not too short for such a long journey."

"Nancy must not imagine that we have no trains in Romania!" said the Queen. "We are not so efficient as you are in America, but it's only our dear *ciobans* who always travel on foot! But if you've plenty of time to spare, wandering slowly – as the shepherds do – is a wonderful way to see the heart of the country. If you don't hurry, perhaps you'll find me near the Black Sea when you reach there. You must come and see my little white house at Balcic – when the lilies are in bloom."

"Do you also count the seasons by their flowers?" asked the little American.

The Queen laughed. "It's a Romanian custom which I've fallen into," she declared. "Besides, I'm such an ardent flower-lover that I plant gardens wherever I go, and the seasons become precious to me according to what flowers are in bloom. Ileana, you must show Nancy our gardens below the castle. The irises are lovely just now – seas of violet, yellow and blue."

"May I first ask you something?" said Nancy as if most of her conversation had not been made up of questions.

"Anything you like," smiled the Queen.

"Do you ever wear a crown?"

Peals of laughter from the violet-eyed Princess. "You are disappointed not to see mother in her crown? She is lovely in her crown, and on the day of father's and mother's coronation she wore such a wonderful robe of gold with a red shimmer woven in it! It seemed like dawn and sunset blended into one! And she wore a great mantle of the same shiny fabric. She really was a legendary queen on that day!"

The Queen's eyes had a far-away look. "Yes," she said, "I suppose that one always thinks of a queen as having a crown on her head; and when one sees her so, one always thinks of the beauty of the crown, but never of its weight. A crown is a heavy thing, Nancy. It has become a symbol of servitude rather than one of glory."

"But I should like to see you in a robe of gold and a golden crown," said Nancy, not at all understanding what the Queen had meant.

Again the Princess laughed. "A queen's first duty is to be lovely, isn't it?"

"I could not imagine an ugly queen!" said Nancy.

"We are much simpler people than little Americans imagine," smiled the woman in the white veil. "Our joys and sorrows are much like your own. But we kings and queens have not only our own griefs to bear: we must bear the griefs of our people as well. And we always have anxiety about their welfare. That anxiety is sometimes heavy. So we need hearts which are large, patient and understanding – and they must be forgiving, too, Nancy, because sometimes we are cruelly misunderstood."

Nancy stared with wide-open eyes. "Are you sad?" she asked.

The Queen leaned down and kissed the little stranger. "I try never to be sad," she said. "People need to be consoled, not to be saddened. My message must always be a message of hope. There is so much sadness in the world, so much poverty and suffering, that when the people come to a queen, they must be met with smiles and not tears, brave words and not sighs!"

Nancy pondered over this for a moment. Then: "It's true," she said, "that I cannot imagine a weeping queen!"

"Except when the Knave of Hearts steals her tarts, all on a summer's day!" teased the Princess.

"But the Queen of Hearts wore *her* crown even when she was baking pies," declared Nancy.

"So we're back again at my crown, are we?" laughed the Queen. "I'll give you a picture of myself with my crown on, Nancy, and you can take it back to America with you. But you must tell them that it is not my crown that makes me a queen, but my love and my work, and whatever human understanding I have of the joys and sorrows of others."

The white veiled woman rose from her chair: "Never forget that you've been here, Nancy. And when you go home, take a message of my love with you – won't you, little girl?"

"But I'll see you again by the Black Sea, shan't I?" There was a sound of pleading in the child's voice.

"Yes, I hope so, Nancy. But now I must go back to the city. I am anxious and the King needs me; he is not well." And in the Queen's voice was a sound of tears.

"I'll pray that he may be better," said Nancy.

"We, too, will pray – night and morning," said Dobre and Florica. And turning to one of the saints on the walls, they bowed their heads, and crossed themselves several times.

"Then goodbye for today, Nancy. God bless you, and keep you safe!"

Again that mother's touch of gentle hands on her head. And as if she were in a dream, Nancy allowed herself to be led from the room.

***

The old man with the white hair was waiting outside the Queen's room, and he it was who showed the children all over the castle. Never was there such a wonderful little castle as this one at Brana! Up and down many winding stairs they went, along open galleries which actually hung over the courtyard, into heavily beamed or vaulted rooms, each one shaped differently from the last, and all with such mysterious, unexpected little corners, and such wonderful, huge fireplaces. One fireplace was so large that there was a little seat inside of it, on which you could sit close to the flame. There were enchanting tower-rooms, with wee windows so high up that it made you giddy to look down from them upon the world beneath. There was even – oh, wonder of wonders! – a narrow secret staircase hewn out in the thickness of the wall, in which the only light came from the baby flame of a tiny earthenware lamp which resembled those of the ancient catacombs. And there were flowers in every corner, on every landing, in every window, on every table and chest, and beside every bed – as well as in great jars standing about the floors. The beds were large and low, like couches, and they had wonderful colored covers and many soft cushions. Every object was so rare and curious that one wondered from what distant land it had been brought. A wonder castle indeed!

But it was Ileana, the star-eyed Princess, who showed them over the gardens. They were blue, yellow and violet with irises, as the Queen had said.

The largest of the gardens was a large orchard meadow, full of old apple-trees in glorious bloom. In and out between the trees wound grass paths, bordered on both sides with irises, tulips and lupins – and with lovely creeping phlox running out into the paths in tumbled masses of pale mauve. Wherever you lifted your head, there was the castle looking down upon you, a dream vision painted against the sky.

"Later, the gardens will be full of roses, white lilies and delphiniums," explained Ileana, "and those are followed by fire-lilies, dahlias, asters, hollyhocks, marigolds, gladiolas and many other flowers. Mother knows their names better than I do. She brings back so many bulbs, roots and seeds from all her journeys that she calls these her 'gardens of memory,' because they remind her of so many people and places she loves. I forgot to show you a tiny ivy plant in the courtyard which she brought from Washington's grave!"

The Princess then said goodbye to them, expressing many wishes for their well-being, and the hope of meeting them again on the shores of the Black Sea. So charming was she, that the children were sad to leave her.

And now they started on their wanderings again after Matusa Daria had blessed them profusely, and filled their pockets and pouches with a plentiful supply of food.

"And to think that you are going to drag that dear little foreign chicken all over the high mountains, and down through the plains to the sea!" she exclaimed. "And look out for the Haiduc. He is hiding somewhere in the deep forests. If you ever reach the Black Sea, I hope that Florica will send you back to your granny. If she doesn't, there'll be nothing left of you after more wandering."

"But we hope to see the Queen again by the Black Sea!" was Nancy's reply. "She says that she may be there when the lilies are in bloom!"

"Well, be careful that the Haiduc doesn't catch you first!"

And as they began climbing the steep mountainside up toward the dark fir forest, Nancy kept thinking of this warning. Were they really to have the thrill of meeting the Haiduc? First the Queen, then the Haiduc! It would be too wonderful! But a trace of a shudder passed over her. An exciting adventure, but it might also be a very dangerous one! And vaguely the words of all the wild songs about the Haiduc came back to her – snatches floating through her mind as cloudlets drift through a summer sky.

> "Oh, mother, my mother,
> When the Haiduc is calling,
> Restrain me from going –
> I cannot resist him!"

And she remembered another verse which Florica had once sung to her of his coming. How did it go?

"O'er seven deep valleys,
And seven dark seas,
With seven black ravens,
As swift as the breeze –"

And indeed the woods up there were black, almost sinister – full of shadows – as they frowned down upon her. If a raven had suddenly flown over the sky just then, I think that Nancy's heart would have popped out of her mouth! Higher and higher they climbed. The forest was coming nearer, like a tremendous army marching down upon the deep valleys – which seemed to be secret passages cut into the mountainside. Evening found them seated around a large fire of dead branches which Dobre had built for them. Above their heads towered the tall firs, enormous, dusky, shutting out the inquisitive stars. The sheep lay, mere shadows, in a wide circle around them. A faint wind whispered in the branches, a strange voice speaking of things, which the children could not understand. A little shiver ran down Nancy's back.

"I wonder if she is sleeping!" said Nancy.

"Who?" asked Florica.

"The Queen," whispered Nancy. "I can still feel the touch of her hands on my head. But her eyes are sad. I suppose that by this time there's a light in her castle window."

"Her eyes are sad because she's thinking of her little boy lying in the old church and of all the other children who died during the years of war and famine. You see, she is our mother; and she saw all of those sorrows with her own eyes. And then, too, did she not say that our dear King is sick?" explained Florica in her solemn voice.

"And I forgot to ask her if she had ever seen the Haiduc!" said Nancy. "There were many more things about which I wanted to ask her. She did not seem to mind answering questions."

"It seems to me that, as it was, you asked her more questions than one person could answer in a day," laughed Dobre.

"But, of course, she must know everything, because she's queen," said Florica.

"Of course," assented the big brother. And then there was silence except for the sound of the branches whispering overhead. The children had fallen asleep.

But there was another sound, coming nearer and nearer, although the children did not hear it, for it was still too far away. The sound of a horse galloping... The fire crackled. The flames spurted up toward the frowning trees above. The pine needles rustled. Occasionally there came the faint sighing of Dobre's sheep, breathing in their sleep. A flutter of wings! A dark shadow – another – and yet another! What was it – the wind? Or was it really the beating of wings – of many, many ravens' wings? Ink-black, hushed, mysterious, sinister "messengers, flown o'er seven valleys and seven silent seas". The Haiduc's ravens! A dark cloud of softly whispering, gently flapping, shadowy, stealthy wings! The Haiduc's outrunners! And now, ever so much more distinctly, the sound of a horse's hoofs...

***

Nancy awoke with a start. What was it? A fluttering of wings! The air was full of them! A tardy moon had risen above the trees, and was pouring a silver light down through their branches into the glade where the wanderers had been sleeping. Dobre leaped to his feet, and stood like a ghost, white and pale, with a hundred dark wings fluttering above his head.

"Ravens!" he cried. "The Haiduc's ravens!"

"And hark! The sound of galloping hoofs!" came an answering cry from Florica.

The two girls scuttled like frightened rabbits to the shepherd's side. Yes! That was the sound of galloping hoofs coming nearer and nearer. How on earth could a horse gallop so fast through the woods at night? "Oh!" cried Nancy. In her voice was mingled ecstasy and fear. Dobre's sheep, awakened by fright, began bleating. Huddled together in a dark mass, their voices were as piteous as those of children lost in the night. The wild neigh of a horse! A cracking of broken branches! A tremendous plunge through the dark! A rider on a coal-black charger crashed suddenly into their midst! The Haiduc!

Nancy clapped her hands, while Dobre raised his staff as if in defense. With quivering legs and wide-open nostrils, his unkempt mane and tail blown hither and thither by the wind, the horse seemed enormous in the pale moonlight. The man on his back was young and handsome, but there was something wild about his appearance. And the expression of his face was far from reassuring. His belt bristled with daggers, and a gun was slung over one of his shoulders. Full of hostility, the white-clad shepherd and the dark intruder faced each other as rivals.

"What are you doing in my realm?" shouted the rider.

"I'm a peaceful shepherd, crossing the hills with my sheep. Mountain and forest are mine as well as yours!" Dobre retorted angrily.

"We'll see about that!" declared the Haiduc. And as he spoke, his eyes suddenly discovered the two maidens. "One of them seems to be a stranger." He laughed wildly. "I, too, have a liking for such fair company!"

Dobre swung his staff, as if to ward off a blow. As he did so, the Haiduc swooped by, leaned down in his saddle with hawk-like rapidity, caught the frightened Nancy up in his arms, and with a cry of triumph, dashed off with her into the forest. It seemed to Nancy that the whole forest was laughing – horribly – that every tree was in league with the Haiduc, wild Lord of the Hills.

***

Nancy heard Florica give a piercing shriek, saw her stretch out desperate arms. After that she heard nothing more except the rush of the air through the trees, as the robber galloped furiously away, bearing her into the thickest forest.

Nancy had no idea how long that race lasted. She was firmly clasped in the man's arms, half smothered under his cloak. All of the forest was zebraed with dark and light stripes by the moon. But the pace was too swift for her to see anything else – besides, the Haiduc's mantle kept flapping backward and forward over her eyes.

A sudden jerk! The horse, rearing on his hind legs, seemed to rise into the air. Nancy screamed. Her scream was answered by a shout of many voices. And this shout was caught up, and echoed again more faintly – probably by the hills. Where was she? Laughter, shouts, excited running hither and thither, and Nancy felt that she was standing on her feet, very shaky and bewildered. There were tears in her eyes, but she was unharmed. Timidly she looked about her. What a wonderful place! Rocks in a circle, high, dark, unscalable; a gorge into which there appeared to be no opening. It might have been a stage setting for a den of robbers and criminals. The little girl shuddered. Why had she not stayed home with Granny and old Sue, under the safe green roof of their bungalow?

"Come here!" It was the Haiduc's voice. Nancy was too afraid to disobey. Despising herself for not making a braver resistance, she advanced toward her captor. All that she could do to save her pride, was to hold her head stiffly and to glare at the armed man with angry, defiant eyes.

But the Haiduc was dreadfully handsome! He looked exactly as he should have looked – fearful but magnificent – with his dark cloak, his daggers, his gun. In a half-circle, his band stood around him. They were not so splendid as their master, but one and all they were imposing – a stalwart crew of ruffians, armed to the teeth.

"You're a stranger, my girl," said the Haiduc. "Who are you?"

Nancy resented his masterful tone, and this gave her courage to reply proudly – although her voice sounded small in this great vastness: "I'm a free American, and in America no one has ever been troubled on the highroads, except by Red Indians – and even that was long ago, for they are well-behaved nowadays!"

"Which means that we are not! Thank you, small maiden! But in the first place, you are not in America; and in the second place, you were not on the highroad. The mountain passes are mine!"

"You are not as noble as you look," declared Nancy with spirit.

"So I look noble, do I?" laughed the desperado. "That, at least, is good to hear. But come, little guest, let me offer you a bit of food. Our ride was a trifle violent!"

"I don't want your food." Nancy's voice trembled. "I want Florica and Dobre!"

"I suppose Dobre was that fine ghost of a fellow, all in white?"

"He's not a ghost. He's just as much alive as you are – and far kinder." This with a fine little snort from Nancy.

"Oho! I like your spirit, little one. But come along with me, even if you are not hungry. I have a surprise for you. You are taking a high tone with the Lord of the Wilderness. But when you see who is my guest, you'll open your eyes, I promise you."

"What sort of guest can *you* have?" Nancy was now so angry that she felt very brave. Also, in spite of herself, she could not help admiring the Haiduc, who was so exactly her idea of a real ruffian hero – the sort of hero whom you never meet nowadays. This would be a wonderful adventure to relate at home – but of course it would still have to end well, for all good stories do.

"What sort of guest? Just wait till you see! You seem to forget who I am!"

"A robber!" snorted Nancy. "A thief who steals maiden's hearts and tosses them away when he is tired of them! Oh, I know about you!"

The Haiduc threw back his head, and filled the night with peals of laughter. Rude of him, thought Nancy. But she could not help remarking what splendid white teeth he had, and how his eyes flashed like black diamonds in the moonlight.

"Enough talk! Come along – or do you want me to carry you?" And her captor advanced toward her with a threatening gesture, although his lips were still smiling.

"No, I'm coming!" Nancy tried to speak without undignified haste.

"I like you," declared the stalwart man. "Follow me, and you'll not regret it!"

And so Nancy followed the terrible Haiduc through the moonlight, toward the dark wall of rocks. Really, it was all like a dream!

***

Suddenly Nancy cried out with astonishment. And who do you think was sitting there on a rock – as if it were a throne? The Queen, you guess? Yes! There she was! And – most astounding! – she was wearing the golden robe and mantle which Ileana had described. And this time she had her crown on her head! Such a massive crown it was! It differed from other crowns because a round pendant hung down from each side of it – like wee shields over the Queen's ears.

"Tonight," thought Nancy, "she looks like a picture-book queen. Even the Queen of Hearts might envy her that crown."

Rocks formed the background for the regal picture. They were dark and forbidding, and rose as if they were the mighty walls of some great hall in which the Queen was enthroned. In dusky rows upon a ledge above her head, sat the Haiduc's ravens, a black frieze silvered by the moon.

How had the Queen come there? How could she have climbed the mountains, and picked her way through the thick forest, in such gorgeous attire?

Leaning from her high seat, she smiled down upon the bewildered child: "So it's you, little Nancy! You never imagined, did you, that we would meet again so soon?"

"But, you see, I shouldn't be here at all," explained Nancy; "I was stolen by the Haiduc."

"Oh, is that how it happened?" exclaimed the Queen.

"Yes. It was so rude of him that I wish you would scold him. Of course," she added hastily, "I am glad to see you again! But really, it was not fair to carry me off in the middle of the night."

"But the Haiduc is one of Romania's favorite heroes, you know," said Her Majesty.

"That may be," conceded Nancy, "but in America we have our own ideas about liberty!"

"Yes, I know. The first thing that I saw when we steamed into New York harbor, was your Statue of Liberty. I'm happy to hear that all of you so loyally respect what she stands for."

Nancy did not quite understand this, but it sounded well, and at least the Queen admired the Statue of Liberty.

"But why are you here?" asked the child. "If we had a queen in America, she wouldn't visit robbers – especially when she was wearing her crown and her coronation robes."

"Ah! You see," explained the Queen, "the Haiduc is very much like Robin Hood. And although an outlaw, Robin Hood was a gentleman, you know."

"But you can't pretend that the Haiduc is a gentleman, can you?" Nancy was shocked.

"That's what I mean!"

"But he stole me!" cried Nancy with indignation. "He stole me away from my friends, and half smothered me under his cloak to keep me from seeing anything."

"That *was* awkward of him," admitted the royal lady, "because on moonlight nights the forest is truly beautiful. He should have allowed you to see it."

"But you don't seem to be shocked at the way in which he carried me off," cried Nancy.

"What if I had asked him to bring you here?"

"You!" Nancy's voice was an exclamation of horrified protest.

"Yes, I!" Her Majesty was smiling. "Suppose that I wanted to have you taken back into olden times?"

"Into olden times?" Nancy stared. What on earth did the Queen mean?

"Yes. Because there is no Haiduc today except in song," explained the Queen.

"Then why are you and I here? And all those ravens... and the moonlight... and your voice...?"

"And the Haiduc?" It was that bold brigand himself who spoke these words. Nancy stared at him. How handsome he was! What black eyes, what white teeth he had! And the silver hilts of his daggers and pistols gleamed like so many lights under the moon. Was he better looking than Dobre, the shepherd. Was he...? But as she stared, the Haiduc's face seemed to become less distinct. A mist passed before it. And the Queen...? Was a mist rising? The Queen's face also had become blurred. Her voice sounded far away.

"Suppose that I had taken you back into olden times, Nancy. The Haiduc, you know, was always a protector of the poor. Therefore he is the Queen's friend. The Haiduc, like Robin Hood, steals only from those who have much and give little. The Haiduc..." There was a sudden rush of wings! All the ravens had risen into the air! Their blackness was shutting out the light of the moon, was screening the glittering vision of the Queen from the bewildered child's gaze. "The Haiduc is the Queen's ally. In olden times, the Queen..." – the voice was growing fainter and fainter – "always wore her crown. And when the Haiduc had collected great treasures..." Nancy had a last luminous vision of the crowned woman, and for a moment her voice was distinct again: "…he gave his wealth to the Queen to divide among the poor. And she herself came to honor him. The Haiduc…"

"Nancy! Wake up!"

What was that?

"Nancy, hurry! We must start again!"

That was surely Florica's voice. How had she found the Haiduc's lair?

"Wake up, Nancy!"

"But the Haiduc!" murmured Nancy, "and the Queen!"

"Nancy, you're dreaming."

"Dreaming?" cried Nancy. Relief and regret mingled in her voice.

"You've quite forgotten where we are!" said Florica.

"Where we are?" Nancy was now wide-awake, rubbing her eyes. "But the ravens? The black horse? The moonlight? And the Queen's golden gown?"

"Come, Nancy!" It was Dobre's voice. "Our *mamaliga* is ready. We must be off!"

And there stood Dobre, with his flock about him and it was not the moon, but the sun, which was making him gleam like a candle!

"Dobre, didn't you hear the Haiduc?"

"The Haiduc, little stranger? How should I have heard him?"

"But you stood there with your staff, ready to fight him – when the air was full of the ravens' wings!"

"Little girl, you've been dreaming!"

"Dreaming! But I saw the Queen! She was wearing her crown and her coronation mantle. She sat on a rock, with the ravens perched above her, as if they were on guard!"

"Dreaming, dreaming!" Dobre shook his head. "Your mind was so full of the Queen and the Haiduc that you *had* to dream about them, I suppose."

"But the Haiduc's great black horse, with the long mane and tail! Didn't you see him leap, hear him neigh?"

"Nancy," said Florica, "sit down. We must eat our *mamaliga* and be off!"

Nancy sat down. The sun was filtering shyly through the trees.

"But I felt the Haiduc's cloak smothering me," insisted Nancy, her mouth full of *mamaliga.*

"I hope that he was as good-looking as our songs make him!" said Florica, and she laughed.

"Does he really exist only in song?" asked Nancy. There was real disappointment in her voice.

"Well," confessed Florica, "I've never seen him, nor has anyone else whom I know. They've only *heard* about him, as one hears of Moses or Trajan or the Fairy Godmother."

"But she told me that he was good to the poor, and that he stole only from the rich!" insisted Nancy.

"Who told you?"

"The Queen!"

"Well, well!" exclaimed Dobre. His mouth, too, was full of *mamaliga*. "It's quite true. The Haiduc is a friend of the poor and of the defenseless."

"But then he *does* exist?" Nancy asked anxiously.

"Does or did. Did or does?" laughed Florica.

"Well, I'm all muddled up!" sighed Nancy. "I really did see her there on her throne of rocks, gleaming in the moonlight. And the Haiduc was handsome!"

"That's as it should be," said Florica, and again she laughed. Sometimes solemn Florica laughed like any other little girl, but not often. Perhaps she lived too near to the Rising Sun?

***

For many, many days the three friends wandered through hills and forests. Dobre had been eager to meet an old shepherd whom he expected to find on the mountaintop, even at this early season. Sherban Scurtu was always one of the first to return from the plains and climb back to the mountains, after the long winter's rest. Dobre meant to leave his sheep under the care of that dependable guardian. Being eager to escort their little guest as far as the shores of the Black Sea, he knew that they could travel more rapidly, if they were not trammeled by the slow-moving flock. Sherban Scurtu proved to be all that the boy had expected. Gruff but kindly, he made no objection to shepherding Dobre's fold as well as his own.

"Go ahead, youngster! Scurtu will look after your flock. I'm old and you're young – and it's not every day that one is host to such a sweet little guest from beyond the blue."

And the old man gave a low, kindly laugh. Nancy was delighted with old Sherban. With his shaggy beard and long gray locks, he looked like one of the twelve apostles grown old in the wilderness. He had many yarns to spin, and as the children rested with him for three days, Nancy had ample time to listen to all of them.

From the spot where he had erected his shelter of earth and sticks, there was a wide-sweeping view of hills and valleys, and plains beneath. A magic view! It was so limitless, hazy and dreamlike that you wondered whether it was imagination or reality. It filled you with a sense of peace and comfort; life seemed natural and easy up here, so far above the world.

However, old Scurtu knew nothing at all about certain things of which Nancy spoke. Nor was there any use in trying to make him understand them; such things, for instance, as skyscrapers, elevators, wireless telegraphs and radios. He would shake his head, smiling like a wise child who is willing to *listen* to fairy-tales but who does not mean to believe them.

"No, little one. It sounds very wonderful! Houses forty stories high! Boxes which shoot you up to the top as if by magic! Voices which you can hear from any distance! No, no, my child, don't muddle my poor old brain with them, for it is accustomed to small huts, corn-thatched and cozy; they are large enough for me. And the only voice which I need is that of God – and I hear it in the church bells, in the wind..."

"But I assure you," insisted Nancy, "that we use other wonderful inventions. They save trouble and they save time."

"Time?" A slow smile came to the shepherd's lips. "What's time? We don't need to hurry, my sheep and I. We know by the lengthening or shortening of the days what season it is, and whether wintertime, when we must quit our hills, is far away or close at hand."

Listening to him, Nancy had the drowsy sensation that, indeed, nothing did matter at all, and that a view such as Scurtu had daily before his eyes, could fill heart and brain to the exclusion of all sense of haste.

"But I don't want to feel that way,", said Nancy to herself; for the East and West were quarreling within her, the present and the past, today and yesterday. But there was such charm in that yesterday that she had to make an effort to prevent it from putting her to sleep. She told Scurtu her dream of the Haiduc, and Scurtu declared that perhaps it was not a dream at all. He had never seen the Haiduc, but that did not prove that he did not exist!

"But the Queen was there, wearing her crown and a golden robe!" cried Nancy.

"God bless her, and give her health and long life," said Sherban. "It's right that she should wear her crown."

No, decidedly Nancy could not astonish old Sherban Scurtu. He knew of things eternal, such as stars, sun, moon, rain and wind – he needed neither radios, nor elevators, nor any other machines.

"I am fond of him," sighed Nancy, when the time came for moving on. And she was truly sad to leave the old man who had the face of an apostle grown old in the wilderness.

***

Old Scurtu had replenished the children's pouches with a new supply of *mamaliga.* He had also given them some white sheep-cheese which he had made himself, and even some onions – although he had little to give, and although he knew that the children would soon reach the plains beneath, where it was easy to get food, while he, on his mountain, had to be sparing, since there were few occasions when he could renew his meager store. Nancy was no longer particular about what she ate. Everything tasted good in this keen mountain air, and their continual walking sharpened her appetite astonishingly. Nancy's shoes were in a sad state. Good, stout American shoes although they were, they were all but wrecked!

"We must get some *opinci*[71]," declared Florica. "And when your dress is in rags, we'll get you one like mine."

"Then I'll look like the magic doll of Romania that you were, when you came to our bungalow!" laughed Nancy.

I do not think that Granny or old Sue would have been very proud of Nancy's appearance at that moment. She certainly looked healthy, but with ragged dress, battered shoes, unkempt hair, sunburned face and grimy hands, she was far from being what a neat, freshly washed little American girl should be. It must be confessed that by this time Nancy had all the appearance of the little tramp that she had become. She resembled her companions in another way, also: she no longer kept count of time. But the days were growing longer, and although they still waded through occasional drifts of old snow in the mountain gorges, when they reached the flat land, they found the fruit-trees far past their bloom, many meadows full of flowers, and hay already being cut. Although Nancy had become as hard as a nail, she was grateful when one or another of the slow moving carts offered them a lift. There was something delightfully dreamy in this slow advance along a straight, white road which spread endlessly before them like a broad ribbon, unwinding as they went. The springless carts creaked, moaned and bumped, and nothing seemed to hurry the placid, slow-moving, large-eyed, widehorned oxen. Sometimes, perched high upon a stack of wood, Nancy would contemplate the world from her exalted but uneasy seat; or deep in soft, fragrant hay, she would lie on her back and gaze up at the gentian-blue sky until, shading her eyes with her arm, she would finally fall asleep. When they journeyed in carts, they were hidden by a haze of dust which rose from the wheels and the oxen's feet. They seemed to see everything through a veil which turned from gray to gold as the sun sank in the west. But whenever an automobile dashed by, the dust

---

[71] Peasant leather footwear.

became intolerable, and stifling clouds hung in its wake long after – leaving a gritty feeling between Nancy's teeth.

"Horrid things!" she would exclaim. "Why must they go so fast?" And she would indignantly bury her face in her hands.

"Nearly all of them come from America, you know. That's your progress, little stranger," teased the shepherd.

"But the dust is not American," retorted the indignant Nancy.

Yet strangely enough Nancy never felt sorry that she was in the groaning cart instead of being in the wind-quick motor, so accustomed had she become to this slow, dreamy form of travel. Never had she felt so near the earth, so much a part of the whole of nature.

Florica had proposed that on their way toward the sea, they should pass through Bucharest, Romania's capital city, but Dobre had protested.

"It's out of our way," he said. "And if Nancy wanted to see sky-scrapers and such things, Bucharest would disappoint her. Of course it has some large shops and finely dressed people, a palace and many churches, but it has none of the beauty of our plains, and forests and mountains. They are the *real* Romania. Nancy has cities enough in her own huge country. Let's show her what she does not have at home!"

So they avoided the towns, and continued their slow way along highroads which ran through villages, through vast fields in which wheat and corn barley were ripening to gold; past lost-looking wells, with long poles pointing to the skies; and past lonely stone crosses, quaintly carved with strange devices – sacred monuments of the days of yore, which were now old, scarred and forgotten. They trudged along the banks of willow-bordered rivers, whose shallow waters flowed sluggishly over broad beds of sand or stones; they crossed rickety bridges which trembled under their feet; they passed gypsy fires of an evening, when the day's toil was done. And generally the stars watched over their sleep. On, on they went, not counting the days. They were hospitably received at every cottage at which they stopped, and kindly answered by every peasant from whom they asked advice – everywhere they saw friendly faces. Even the poorest was always ready to share his last morsel of food, and no hut was too small to shelter them – even overnight, if necessary. On, on, till they came to wide, willow-grown swamps – the forerunners of the broad Danube – which they must cross before reaching their final goal. In these swamps Nancy saw hundreds of black and white storks, marching about. Stiff-legged and important-looking, they had an air of birds, which could at any moment be called upon to fulfill the important mission of their kind. Their long red legs gave them the appearance of being dressed in livery. For some reason, they seemed to be something more than mere birds, and entitled to respect.

"Many babies must be born in your land to keep so many storks busy," observed Nancy.

"I've never seen them carrying babies," said Florica, "but I *have* seen them gobbling frogs. I am sure about the frogs, but not so certain about the babies. At any rate, storks or no storks, we *do* have many babies in our villages, although not all of them live to grow up."

"Don't you look after them?" asked Nancy.

"Well, most of them look after themselves. Their mothers, you see, work. Often their elder sisters look after them; I looked after the twins. But when there's no elder sister..." Florica left her sentence unfinished.

"What then?" persisted Nancy.

Florica shrugged her shoulders, and made a vague gesture with her hands – which might have meant anything.

"Have you no Child Welfare and that sort of thing?"

Florica's face was a blank.

"Don't ladies and district-nurses and doctors come to give you help and advice?"

"Our villages are far away," said Florica vaguely.

"But the Queen?" demanded Nancy.

"She's our mother," was Florica's fervent reply.

"But a mother usually helps," insisted the little American.

"Of course she helps when we ask her to. But we only ask her when we need something."

Nancy shook her head. She loved her little friend, and she had a warm feeling for Dobre, but when she tried to be practical with them, they seemed to become vague and to evade her. There was no sense of progress in them, no "push", no vigor. They were contented with things as they were – although really Baba Zoe's hut, for instance, while delightful to look at, left plenty of room for improvement. "When I'm grown up," thought Nancy, "I'll come back here and teach them to be progressive." Young as she was, Nancy had heard a great deal at home about being "progressive". But these friends of hers did not seem even to know the meaning of the word!

Yet how lovely it was here, among the willow-trees! How calm, how restful, how dreamy! Yes, this was a dreamy land. Then Nancy remembered how Florica had said that this was a country near the Rising Sun. Probably that had something to do with their lack of progress! Nancy drew a deep sigh of contentment. She was glad that she was not grown up, and that she did not have to begin yet to be progressive. It was so delightful to sit here and watch the sun going down; no hurry, no pressure, no noise. Peace and quiet – and over there stood Dobre, his back against a spreading poplar, playing on his flute. Decidedly, the sunsets loved Dobre and his flute!

***

Nancy was duly impressed by the great bridge over the Danube: "King Carol's bridge," Dobre called it, because it had been built during the reign of King Carol, who was King Ferdinand's uncle.

"Ferdinand became our second King, because King Carol had no children – except a little girl who died when she was very young," explained Dobre.

"And Ferdinand married Marie, who came from over the seas when she was young," was Florica's addition to her brother's history lesson.

"Is she the Queen?" asked Nancy.

"Yes, the Queen whom we saw in her castle and whom we hope to meet again by the Black Sea. She began by being a princess."

"And our first Queen was a very good mother," said the shepherd boy. "But her hair was gray instead of golden. She wrote beautiful verses, and was a poet whom the whole world loved. Her name was Carmen Sylva."

"And Queen Marie, my Queen?" asked Nancy. "Does she write poetry?"

"I don't know," confessed Dobre. "They say she's written a book about our brave soldiers, and many stories for children – and a book about Romania. She wants the whole world to love Romania."

"She's laughed with us and wept with us; she has known good days and bad." Florica had said this before. It was a picture to which she seemed to cling, as the reason that they loved Regina Maria and her brave King.

"But she said that the King was very sick, didn't she?"

"Yes. We must pray for him." And Dobre took off his bonnet.

"And King Carol, the old King, built this bridge!" Nancy's voice was full of wonder. "It's a very large bridge for one man to build!"

"I don't think that he built it with his own hands," explained Dobre. "He ordered it to be built – for until that time it was a long way around to the sea. Now we can go to it from Bucharest, in a straight line."

As the children were speaking, and looking up at the huge Danube bridge, a train rushed over the high viaduct. Up there, far above their heads, it looked like a caterpillar – at least it would have if a caterpillar could go at such a pace.

"We also have great bridges in America," said Nancy.

"Have you seen them?"

"No; but we have many books with pictures."

"I'd love to have books," sighed Dobre.

"We have our songs," said Florica.

"And my flute," added Dobre.

"And our sunrises and sunsets," said Florica.

"And our rivers and mountains," added Dobre.

"And the Black Sea," laughed Nancy. "And you live near the Rising Sun."

Thus, chattering busily, the children crossed the great bridge. And on and on they still walked, until at last they reached the Sea. The Black Sea!

It was not black at the time when Nancy had her first glimpse of it. It was a deep indigo blue, and small white clouds were floating over it. It looked calm and reassuring. It filled you with a longing to sail out over it – far, far away...

"I'm not facing America, am I?" asked Nancy.

"No, no! Over there on the other side of the Black Sea is Russia, I believe."

"And there's also a city somewhere called Constantinople," added his sister.

"Geography is so hard," sighed Nancy.

"But we've taught you all about Romania in a pleasant way, haven't we?"

"Ah! yes!" agreed the little American. "I wish that all geography lessons were like that – even if they wore out my shoes!"

"Over there, do you see a town?" Dobre pointed with his hand.

"Yes!"

"That's our port. It's called Constantza."

"Why didn't you take me there?"

"We'd be lost in a town," said the shepherd.

"Do many ships come to your port?"

"I suppose so," Dobre was rather vague. He knew more about sheep than about ships.

"If you were an American boy, you'd probably know how many ships came to your port every year, and what they brought and what they took away."

"Would he?" Florica was much impressed.

"But you don't seem to care much about such things," said Nancy.

"I don't expect ever to cross the sea," explained Dobre, rather lamely.

"Don't you want to come to America?"

"They say that people go to America when their own countries are too full. Ours is not too full," replied Dobre.

"And we're nearer the Rising Sun here," added Florica, who had a quaint way of repeating certain sentences.

Nancy was seated on a mound of earth near the edge of a cliff, which overhung the sea. She looked up at her two friends. How different they were from anyone she had ever seen in America! They were like a picture, standing side by side in their quaint costumes. Vaguely she felt that she would never really understand them – they were so calm, they asked so few questions, they were so little interested in the whys and wherefores of things. And when they spoke, all their words were pictures – as they themselves were pictures, which impressed themselves on your mind, and remained with you always. America was as beautiful as Romania, but it did not make such pictures. Nancy thought of how much she loved Florica and Dobre – but there was a touch of sadness about her love. You always feel a little tinge of sadness when you don't quite understand people; it gives you a feeling of loneliness – a sense of trying to grasp a mist with your hands.

Dobre, with his large eyes wide open, was gazing over the water. With both hands clasped on the top of his shepherd's staff, he was resting his chin upon them. What was he thinking? And beside him stood Florica. She, too, resembled a painting. You can hardly imagine how slim she was, in her tightly folded skirt, which she called a *catrintsa*. She, also, was able to remain absolutely still – as still as a statue – with her eyes fixed upon the distance. What did she see? How flat the land was – as flat as the sea below! There seemed to be two seas, one above the other. And what masses of wild flowers! They were a real garden! What gorgeous violet splashes those pea-flowers made! And never had Florica seen such enormous thistles; their prickly leaves drew strange, intricate green patterns against the blue of the sky. Nancy felt a sort of drowsiness stealing over her. The perfect stillness of her companions seemed to throw her into a trance. Nothing seemed real any more. The world was becoming a vast, never-ending vision – a very quiet dream, lovely and enormous, in which rich colors, pleasant sensations, and a harmony of sounds, blended into one – until she began to feel that never again would she need to ask questions, or wonder at anything, or hurry, or fuss, or learn, or progress. Blue sky. Blue Sea. Green world of flowers. And, painted against the horizon, Florica and Dobre – two dream-figures in this land near the Rising Sun. Two friends! The land near the Rising Sun!

I am not quite sure, but I *think* that just then Nancy fell asleep.

***

"This point is called Caliacra," said Dobre. The three children were standing on a narrow tongue of land, which jutted out into the sea. It was a wild, lonely place. But what colors! The ground upon which they stood was a wilderness of scattered stones, but it was marvelous because hundreds and thousands of poppies had sprung up between the stones, as if sown by some magic hand, and had covered the waste with a carpet of brilliant scarlet. The ground seemed to be flaming – and the more so because it was the hour of sunset. Romania seemed to love this hour as an artist might love colors which he had invented and which no other painter had ever before even imagined.

Nancy, with Dobre firmly holding her hand, advanced carefully to the very edge of the cliff, which overhung the water. How steep they were! They were jagged, giant walls, bright Indian red in color, and at their base began the sea's blue-green expanse. It looked wickedly, secretly deep. And, as the sun sank lower and lower, the red of the rocks, as if it were dye, began to tint the surface of the sea, until it turned into seething copper – over which ripples of sapphires, emeralds and turquoises glittered continually. Finally the entire water took on the colors of a peacock's tail. It was so bright and so fascinating that, as Nancy gazed down upon it, she felt as if some force, which she could not resist, were pulling at her from below.

"Don't go too near the edge, little stranger. The mermaids might beckon to you, and then you would not be able to stay on the land."

"Are they down there?"

"Yes; and when they are lonely, they rise from the water, and sing such rapturous songs that no human being can resist them."

"What happens to you then?"

"Then comes a mad desire to throw yourself into the sea."

Nancy drew back with a shudder; and Dobre felt her hand tremble in his.

"And what else is down there?" Her eyes were full of inquiry, and, despite a sense of dread, she felt that she must peep once more into the depths beneath.

"Shells and fishes, and a thousand living creatures which are half-animals and half-plants."

Here Florica's voice chimed in: "Not only living things, but also lost treasures from sunken ships, and the bleached bones of sailors and fishermen who never returned to their homes."

"And see those many sea gulls, skimming over the water with melancholy cries," added Dobre. "They are the souls of those who died without an opportunity to say farewell to their loved ones."

Then, for a time, the children stopped talking. A great hush fell over the world. The flaming colors were paling. The sea gulls' wings were becoming whiter and whiter. Dusk was beginning to creep over the world. For a moment the sun hung suspended, a fiery ball over the horizon. Then, suddenly, it dipped into the sea, and was gone. Hand in hand stood the three children, while the shadows thickened around them. How still it was! How strangely still! Suddenly a voice disturbed the silence. They turned and saw an old man standing beside them – an old man with a white beard and a head of snow-white hair.

"Have you come to say a prayer on Saint Nicholas' grave?" he asked.

"Saint Nicholas!" three astonished voices exclaimed.

"Yes. Don't you know that he is buried here among our rocks?"

"Who are you?" asked Nancy in an awed whisper.

"Oh! I'm only the old keeper of the Caliacra lighthouse. I've lived here for so many years that I have stopped counting them."

"I'm an American," volunteered Nancy.

"Dear, dear! You must have come in a ship?"

"I – I don't exactly know," stammered Nancy.

"Well, that's queer." But the old man did not seem much interested or surprised. "Shall I take you to Saint Nicholas?"

"Is he the one with the white beard, who brings children presents in a sack?"

The old fellow shook his head. "No, no! He is our own special Saint Nicholas. Some say that he was a hermit, and others say that he was a pirate who was up to all sorts of trick."

"A fine sort of saint!" Nancy sniffed.

"And what do *you* think he was?" asked Florica.

"Well, well!" The old man scratched his head. "He may have begun as a pirate and ended as a saint. Stranger things have happened. The fact remains that he's Saint Nicholas now, and that he's buried here, and that he has a superb view out over the sea! Come along, before it gets too dark.

And you'll see the little silver lamp which the Queen has hung over his grave."

"The Queen!" There was a thrill in Nancy's voice.

"Yes, the Queen. She loves this place, and comes here often. So does the Princess, who runs all about over the rocks, barefooted, like a mountain sheep. The Queen never forgets to visit me in my lighthouse! 'And, Costica,' she once said to me, 'you must always keep Saint Nicholas' grave tidy. And I'll bring him a silver lamp, if you will plant some of the wild Dobrugea irises on his tomb!' She has time even for dead saints in desert places. And she knew that I would not have far to go to find those little irises. She would not have told me to plant roses, because she knows that no roses grow here – and that I am old and my legs are shaky! She's fond of gardening, the Queen is!"

Thus chatting, white-haired Costica led the way, down between steep and broken rocks, to a small promontory which was half shut in by overhanging cliffs. It was almost a grotto, open toward the sea. Here, in the half-dark, the children discerned a small white stone cross, which stood at the head of a narrow grave that was thickly covered with the pointed leaves of dwarf irises, now past their bloom.

"The whole grave is blue and violet when they are in flower," said the old guardian proudly.

Behind the cross, a low niche had been hewn out of the rock near the ground, and in it hung a small lamp of chased silver. Below the lamp was the painted image of a very old saint. His beard was long. His widely opened eyes seemed to be gazing past them, toward the sea.

"He doesn't look like a pirate!" Nancy was leaning over the icon in order to see it better. There was disappointment in her voice. Old Costica, a little shocked at so irreverent a remark, explained that even if he *had* been a pirate to begin with, he certainly would have had to look like a saint when he became one. That was the least that he could do – or that a painter could do for him! Nancy, looking up at the white-bearded face above her, could not help thinking that perhaps Saint Nicholas had looked much like Costica in real life. What a pity that Saint Nicholas was dead! Nancy would have enjoyed making the acquaintance of a live saint. And perhaps he would have told her whether he really had been a pirate first – and whether it was pleasanter to be a pirate or a saint. "At any rate, he must have had more fun as a pirate," she said to herself.

"But now, my little chickens, you'd better come and share a solitary old man's supper, and sleep this night at the foot of the lighthouse under his roof."

Bending down over the sacred picture, Dobre and Florica crossed themselves. Then all four together slowly climbed the hill toward the lighthouse. Turning back for a last glimpse of the saint's grave, the children could still see the Queen's lamp, a twinkling speck in the vastness of the night.

"See," said Florica, "it is as if the smallest star of the heavens had come down to watch over Saint Nicholas' grave."

"Yes. He would have been lonely otherwise," added Dobre.

"I wonder if the Queen knows that it looks like a star," mused Nancy.

"I light it every evening," explained old Costica, "every single evening, when I light the beacon."

"But it does look like a star – a wee, lonely star," insisted Florica. "And I shall always be glad to think that Saint Nicholas has a light burning for him all through the night."

***

Two days later, three sunburned, dust-covered, weary little waifs arrived at the small sea-town of Balcic. What a queer little place it was! After a long tramp over a plain as flat as the back of a man's hand, the children had come quite suddenly upon a deep gorge. Here the earth was torn asunder, as if by some tremendous convulsion, and a widening valley dipped steeply downward toward the sea. What a curious, gray-white world! Gray-white cliffs, which shone like silver in the sun! Gray-white houses of clay, wood or stone, tumbling down the hillsides one on top of the other, as if they found it a hard task to keep a firm footing upon such bare slopes! Here and there a slim minaret painted a white column against the sky. Now and again solemn, mouse-gray donkeys picked their slow way down toward the harbor, over steep and stony paths, which wound between crumbling walls. And everywhere were Turks, as slow, solemn and patient as the donkeys which they drove before them! At how many quaint fountains and wells of Eastern design, did whole flocks of sheep come to drink – as did also those tame but savage-looking buffaloes, with curved horns and absentminded faces! How brightly the copper and pewter vessels, which the Tartar women were carrying over their shoulders upon wooden yokes, shone in the glittering light! And what picturesque, gay-colored groups these women formed, in their baggy cotton trousers of old greens, blues and mauves. Their hair was tightly braided into many little plaits; their henna-dyed eyebrows drew straight lines over their foreheads. They chattered and laughed, showing extraordinarily white teeth. Very different from these noisy groups were the Turkish women, in their sober black caftans, with their white head-cloths drawn half over their faces. They looked as if they were on their way to a funeral, and they flitted past as noiselessly as shadows.

The water that flowed from the many fountains looked deliciously fresh and cool. Beyond, the sea shone like a turquoise carpet woven with threads of light.

The children had reached the principal street; the pavement was rough and uneven – which made Nancy realize how tired were her feet.

"Look," cried Florica suddenly, "there are flags everywhere! The Queen must be here! In every village, our people always raise the flag when the King or Queen comes."

"But see!" chimed in Dobre. "Every flag has a large black veil fastened to it! What can it mean?"

"Let's stop and ask," proposed Nancy, the practical one.

It was no use to ask a Turk, since he would hardly understand Romanian, but over there was a dark fellow who would probably be able to tell them. He was sitting before his door, among his pots and pans, his rugs and stuffs, and his other wares – which overflowed from his shop onto the pavement. The dark fellow talked very poor Romanian. He was probably a Bulgarian, or perhaps an Armenian. For Balcic had once been a Bulgarian town, and its population was very mixed.[72] At any rate, the shopman did not seem to understand Dobre's question – and this may have been partly because he was an extraordinary sleepy chap. He was amiable, however, and he pointed with a lazy hand toward a brown-coated policeman, who was lolling in the middle of the street. It seemed to Nancy that nobody here had anything to do. Removing his bonnet, Dobre politely asked this casual-looking representative of the law, why the flags were all flying and why they were veiled with black.

"Don't you know?" exclaimed the policeman, shaken for a moment from his comfortable calm.

"Our good King is dead[73], and the Queen has come here to rest!"

"Ah! Our kind, brave King, who brought all the Romanians together and made our Unity. This is terrible news!" cried Dobre, full of grief.

A few loiterers, lolling in front of the houses and shops, joined the small group in the middle of the street, and one after another spoke of the sad event.

"Such a worthy King!" said one voice.

"We'll never have such another!" said an old man.

"And to die thus, so long before his time – and when his country needed him so greatly!" said a third voice.

"May God rest his soul and give comfort to our Queen! She has suffered much. It has been enough to test her patience."

---

[72] Balcic (Balchik), an old Bulgarian town, belonged from 1913 until 1940 to the Kingdom of Romania, when it was ceded by Romania to Bulgaria again. The Balchik Palace, a summer residence of Queen Marie called by her "Tenha Yuvah" (Turkish for: Solitary Nest), is a museum now.

[73] King Ferdinand of Romania died on 20 July 1927.

258

"And now there's a child on the throne – little Michael!"[74]

"May God give him health and a long life in which to serve his people!" cried many voices together.

"Poor little chicken, may he be blessed – and his poor mother with him!" It was a woman's voice who said this. Shaking her head, she added: "They say that on the night after the King's death the blue-eyed little fellow put a small lamp in the window, so that his grandfather could see from heaven that he was thinking of him!"

"Bless his little heart!" exclaimed a fat old mother, who also had stopped to listen.

"And the Queen?" asked Nancy anxiously.

"She loves our Balcic!" proclaimed a villager, who evidently felt that this was a matter of no small importance for this humble seaport.

"And the Queen finds rest here, near our sea!" said the motherly woman. "She has turned her gardens from a waste place into a paradise."

"May God give her many days! She is our mother and now that our good father is dead, there will be more things than ever to appeal to the mercy of her heart."

"She has loved us," said another voice, "as she loved her own family. But her own first-born[75] broke her heart."

The fat old woman crossed herself. "His father, who has gone to heaven, will plead for him. Up there he knows how much his son must regret what he has done!"

"Those who tear themselves away from Romania always regret."

"Where is the Queen?" asked Florica. Her voice was full of emotion.

"Over there!" The brown-coated policeman pointed with a small stick toward a spot beyond the town which looked like an oasis – a green garden in a silver waste.

"We'll go to her," said Dobre. He spoke very quietly, as if it were the most natural thing in the world for them to go to the Queen. But Nancy noticed that his eyes, too, were full of tears.

**

"How could it be called the Black Sea!" With clasped hands, Nancy stood gazing out over a sheet of shimmering, glittering blue. What light, what

---

[74] King Michael (1921-2017) was the last king of Romania. He ascended to the throne in 1927, while he was only five years old and his father, Crown Prince Carol had renounced his succession rights. In 1930 his father, King Carol II, returned to Romania and ruled until 1940, when he was forced to abdicate. King Michael ruled until 1947, when the communist government abolished the monarchy and replaced it by the so-called "People's Republic". King Michael lived in exile until 1990, when he first visited Romania again. In 1997, he was finally allowed to return to his country.

[75] King Carol II (1893-1953) renounced his succession rights in 1925 in favour of his son Michael, but returned in 1930 and reigned again until his forced abdication in 1940. He then lived in exile in Portugal, where he died in 1953.

color, what sunshine! And what a refreshing sea breeze fanned her heated cheeks! And there stood the Queen's home. As white as if it were a dream, and quaintly Eastern in shape, it rose unexpectedly. It was a snowy picture against a green background. Its tall minaret seemed to be a watchtower to overlook the sea. The Queen had named her little house "Tenha Yuvah", which meant, in Turkish, "Solitary Nest". It was, indeed, a corner to come to for rest, for health, joy or peace. And there, proudly waving from a small squat tower, was the same flag which Nancy had seen flying on the little old fortress in the Transylvanian hills; red, with a blue border, and bearing an orange eagle in the center.

The children were walking across a long paved terrace which overlooked the sea, and which had a narrow canal of fresh, cool water running down the middle of it. Overhead was a pergola of rough beams, with roses, glycines and vines running riot over it; beneath, the sea, lapping against the base of the wall. And flowers everywhere! A blaze of color! Tall hollyhocks of every conceivable hue, giant Canterbury bells, flaming poppies, late irises – and what wonderful roses! A paradise of flowers!

The three wanderers timidly advanced, with fast-beating hearts, but unchallenged by any guardian. Presently they reached some steps leading down to a second terrace. Here the water of the canal splashed in a tiny cascade to the lower level. The principal feature of this second flagged terrace was a giant poplar, which leaned out over the water as if its rustling leaves were constantly talking with the waves. So low did this poplar lean, that Nancy almost feared that it would lose its balance and topple over into the sea.

And the children were near the white house. Would anyone stop them? Or were they, perhaps, moving in a dream over enchanted ground? The sea made a sing-song, whispering a chant both sad and sweet. Then something happened which took them by surprise. A door on the lower terrace opened, and a woman dressed in black stepped out into the blazing sunshine. Her gown trailed in long folds behind her, and on her head she wore a veil, which fell over her shoulders to the ground. Slowly she advanced across the terrace. Then, seating herself on the low stone parapet toward the sea, she gazed wistfully over the water, as one might do who was waiting for someone to return.

The Queen! All in black! How sad she looked! And how lovely, Nancy thought. Would they dare to approach her as they had done in the quaint old castle in the hills? Would she ever see them? And, wondered Nancy, would she recognize them? If only the Princess with the great blue eyes were there, she would tell them what to do! As if their thoughts had called her thither, there was Ileana descending a flight of stone steps from one of the upper terraces! She, too, was all in black, but her dress was cut Turkishwise. And just imagine! She was barefooted, as were all of the Tartar girls whom Nancy had seen in the neighborhood. Imagine Nancy's surprise at finding a princess barefooted!

"Mother," exclaimed Ileana, "here are our three little friends from Brana. Isn't it wonderful that they have made the journey and arrived safely?"

And hurrying gracefully toward them, she welcomed them with a radiant smile and with friendly outstretched hands. The Queen turned her head, and raised her hand to shade her eyes against the sun.

"Bring them here," she said. "What a pleasure it is to see them again."

Ileana led the three wanderers toward her.

"So you've come all of that long journey on foot! What wonderful children you are! I should never have been able to walk such a long, long journey."

And when the Queen said, "Such a long journey," Nancy had the feeling that she was thinking of another journey which had been long, long... to this day of mourning.

"We saw the black on the flags," said Nancy, almost in a whisper.

"And you understood what it meant?" The Queen's voice was sad.

"The people told us."

"He earned his rest," said the Queen, simply. "He worked long for his country, and he was very tired at the end. He, too, had traveled a long way."

"The people are sad," whispered Nancy. She hardly knew why she said this, but her heart went out to the Queen, who looked strangely lonely.

"They loved him," the Queen nodded. "I am sure that they loved him – and that was his reward!"

"But I think that they love you, too!" said Nancy.

"Yes, I think that they do," said the Queen. "But I am still here... and one never knows where a road may end."

"But you are happy to be here, aren't you?" Nancy could not imagine that the Queen would not be happy to have a long way yet before her. Life was so wonderful, and it held so much to see and to discover. Besides, the Queen must be happy when she had both this cozy white house by the sea, and that splendid castle in the hills – and such a winsome daughter as Ileana! A smile came to the Queen's face, and illumined it as with sunshine.

"Yes, little Nancy, I am happy to be here. How ungrateful I should be if I did not love all this beauty: the sea, my little white house, and all these flowers. I am happy, too, for every kind word said to me, for every smile given to me – and grateful for the sympathy shown me in my grief. From America, little Nancy, I have received countless tokens of love and understanding. Americans are warm-hearted."

The Queen turned her head to look over the sea. Her eyes were sad, but there was something peaceful about her. There was no revolt in her grief.

"I longed to bring him here to rest. He had never seen my little house after it was finished, nor did he ever see how beautifully my flowers have blossomed. He was fond of flowers. But I suppose that the peace that our dear

King has found in heaven is greater than any rest which we could have given him here."

Dobre's and Florica's great eyes were fixed on the Queen. They stood silent and reverent. Each time that the Queen mentioned the name of the King, they crossed themselves, and murmured: "May God rest his soul in peace!"

"Yes," echoed the Queen, "in peace! It was that which he needed. There had been but little of tranquility in his life of late. The beautiful words of our burial service say: 'In a green place to rest.' It makes me see deep green meadows, full of shade and flowers." And again she said wistfully, "He was fond of flowers."

"Mother," exclaimed Ileana, "you must show them your lily walk. It is beautiful just now. Mother has given a name to each of her gardens – and she has used our names! There were six of us once, you know!"

"What did you name this terrace, on which the house is built?"

In a low voice the Queen answered: "This is called the Carol Terrace. He was my eldest child, and our great hope. He left us... to live in a far country. But I often think that he must have great *dor* for the land of his birth – and I named this terrace after him." Then, the Queen pointed to a wee, fairy-like garden, full of white lilies, which hung suspended above a high stonewall. "That is the Mircea garden. He was a tiny boy with fair hair and brown eyes. God took him from us during the war. Neither Carol nor Mircea ever saw this beloved corner near the sea."

Ileana bent toward the Queen, and spoke tenderly. "Mother," she said, "do show them your lilies, which you call 'a dream come true'."

The Queen turned with a smile, and looked up into her daughter's face. Nancy thought that she could read an affectionate understanding in their eyes.

"Ileana knows what to say to her mother when she looks back instead of forward." The Queen had risen to her feet, and she stood tall and black against the blue sea. "But we must not hark back. It is weakness to do so. At this hour when my heart is heavy, I must remember the motto, which the King adopted during the war – my saying that 'Tomorrow is yours if you have strength to grasp it.' He lived up to it. I must try to do the same." The Queen spoke solemnly.

Fascinated, with wide-open eyes, the three children stared at her. And Nancy thought, "Her dress is blacker than the blue Black Sea."

"But come," said the Queen, taking Nancy's hand in her own, "let me show you my lilies – my lovely dream come true."

***

A lovely dream come true! Indeed, what could have been more beautiful than the Queen's lily walk! Imagine two rows of milk-white columns used as a pergola! Staves of wood were stretched from one capital to the other, and over them roses were climbing. On both sides of the columns were long beds of white Madonna lilies. So shiningly pure were these flowers that they stood as if they were tall silver lights against the shining blue of the sea. The whole length of this lily walk was paved with huge, round millstones, one beside the other. At the very end was a round stone seat against a wall which enclosed the garden; and here one of the millstone slabs had been used as the top for a table. A cluster of bright flowers grew in the center of the table, in the round hole in the millstone. The idea delighted Nancy.

How white the lilies looked in contrast to the Queen's somber veils. She was like a nun in a cloister garden. Nancy had once seen a picture of something like this, but this scene, she thought to herself, was more beautiful than the picture.

"How do you like 'my dream come true'?" asked the Queen, when they reached the end of the walk. "And my walk of millstones? You see, I had a collection of them – although you may be amused at my making it. But I bought several old Turkish mills because they were so picturesque that I did not want them to be pulled down. And then I had all of the old millstones! They were useful for my lily walk!"

Nancy was speechless with rapture. Hands clasped in ecstasy, she looked at the lilies, at the sea, at the white pillars – and at the picture of the black-robed woman who was outlined against this luminous setting.

"Mother calls this the Sandro Terrace," explained Ileana, "because the King of Serbia gave her the white columns. They came all the way from Dalmatia. Sandro, who is really called Alexander, is my sister Mignon's husband. Her garden is just above this terrace. And above that is my garden! Then comes little Michael's garden. And then Peter's – he is my sister Mignon's little boy. And above Peter's garden is the Ferdinand Terrace – my father's terrace. The two terraces which you passed were the Nicholas and Elizabeth Terraces. And everywhere mother has planted flowers which remind her of someone!"

"These white lilies were given to me by a good American friend," explained the Queen. "When they came up so magnificently, I wrote to him to say that his lilies were three hundred shouts of thanksgiving."

"Mother has so many ideas," exclaimed Ileana, "that we often seem to be running to catch up with them. On the fountain of water, which flows from beneath our large trees, mother has carved:

> 'For those who thirst: water!
> For the weary: rest!
> Peace unto the heavy-laden!
> Hope unto the beginners of life!'"

"Ileana will show you our home and the spacious white room which looks out over the sea," said the Queen. "And she will show you more about these many-named gardens – especially the Mircea garden, which is my

263

favorite. Then she will give you all sorts of good things to eat. And this evening you must see the lily walk, for in the moonlight it becomes a fairy-land – a dream-picture which is almost too full of beauty for this sad world."

Ileana clasped her mother's hand. "Mother," she said, "you'll make many another dream come true! That is the reward of one who sows seeds."

"Ileana is my most ardent follower," smiled the Queen. "We dream togeth-er and build together. She 'carries on.' One day, she will leave me to 'carry on' in a far land, for that is the destiny of princesses. I, too, came from afar. And, little Nancy – strange as it may seem – whenever I bend down to in-hale the perfume of my lilies by the Black Sea, their fragrance reminds me of a little garden I loved when I was a child – a garden which belonged to old Queen Victoria. Each time that I smell my own lilies here, I see that other little garden. Human feelings are hard to explain, but with the poet[76], I say:

> 'I will not shut me from my kind;
> And, lest I stiffen into stone,
> I will not ease[77] my heart alone,
> Nor feed with sighs the passing wind.'"

Seeing a blank look on Nancy's face, the Queen smiled, bent down and kissed her. "Go, little girl, or I'll confuse you. I've too many thoughts today. Ileana will be better company for way-weary wanderers, who must be hungry and thirsty. If I were you, Ileana, I would feed and rest them first, and show them the gardens afterward."

"And I'll take them out in my boat," cried Ileana. "I'm sure that they'll like that!"

"Ileana is a sort of mermaid," laughed the Queen. "I'm surprised that she doesn't take you out for a swim!"

***

That was perhaps the most wonderful of all the days, which Nancy spent in Romania – that day at Tenha Yuvah, the Queen's White House on the Black Sea. And Nancy has never forgotten that the Black Sea was not black at all but blue – ah, so blue! And, although she did not know it at the time, this was to be Nancy's last day in the Land of the Rising Sun.

The charming Princess with the pansy eyes and the bare feet made it a day of wonder for the three children. What a delightful companion she was! First of all, as her mother had advised, she fed them with all sorts of good things. Cakes, biscuits, jams of every variety, and delicious, hot little rolls, thickly buttered. They sat on a covered balcony, looking out over the sea,

---

[76] Queen Marie is quoting verses from the poem "In Memoriam" by the English poet Lord Alfred Tennyson (1809-1892).

[77] The original verse by Tennyson was: "I will not eat my heart alone".

"where mother and I sleep – out of doors, American-wise," explained Ileana. The china from which they ate was as yellow as buttercups, and each piece had a border of peacock-colored leaves, which shone in the sunlight as do the wings of Brazilian butterflies. Nancy was entranced by the bright silver coffeepots; each of which had a small silver parrot on the top instead of a knob! There was also a fat earthenware pot in the form of an orange pumpkin – and in that pot there was honey! And some of the heavy silver spoons had tiny ships as handles, while others had queer little sea horses. What amusing spoons! The flat silver bowl, which stood in the center of the table, was filled with the most wonderfully colored roses that Nancy had ever seen – roses of a red, coppery orange, difficult to describe.

"These," Ileana said, "were father's favorite roses."

All the cushions and chair coverings were bright orange to match the roses – and so, also, were the curtains of the dining room. The dining room had a huge, white, Turkish fireplace of the quaintest shape, which was unlike anything to be seen in any other place. Everything was quaint, original, enchanting – and everything was different from what Nancy had seen at the little castle at Brana, although no less delightful.

"Mother is eager to have her surroundings beautiful in every detail," explained Ileana. "She says that they need not be rich or costly, but that each object must be suitable to its setting."

In Tenha Yuvah this was true. Everything suited its surroundings. Perhaps it was this, which gave Nancy such a sense of contentment of body and soul. Dobre and Florica, with their great, solemn eyes, were drinking in all that they saw, but they asked fewer questions than Nancy; and, in their peasant way, they never seemed to be astonished by anything. They were more shy than Nancy at being invited to sit down to table with a princess. But perhaps that was because this table was so different from the low "*mamaliga* table" in Baba Zoe's hut!

The princess was as good as her word, and really did take them for a sail in her small boat. She handled the sails cleverly. To help her, there was only a Turkish boy, who wore a fez on his head, and was called Hassan. He had very white teeth and a freckled nose. He and the Princess joked together as true friends.

The Queen's white house was still whiter when seen from the sea. From afar it was as white as the lilies in the Sandro colonnade, and it seemed to shine with light. Nancy felt that it was keeping guard over them.

Tenha Yuvah, the Solitary Nest!

Nancy gazed and gazed. She wanted to remember every detail, so that she could describe it all to Granny, when she went home. How wonderful to possess two such enchanting dwellings: the little castle of Brana in the mountains, and this white Turkish house on the Black Sea!

"But you must not imagine," explained Ileana, "that we always live in such small houses. At Bucharest, mother has a large palace with many rooms and with many servants – with soldiers on guard, who blow a trumpet whenever we go out, or whenever we come home from a drive. And it has a great park around it. But mother runs away to her small homes as often as she can, because we love to live where we can be outdoors all day long. In palaces, life is not like that. Mother says that you should be able to step out of your home on every side and on every level – for then you are really free! But around our palace home, mother has planted more roses than have ever been planted in any other place. She wants it to be like Sleeping Beauty's castle, which had so many roses that one could hardly get through them. But if we can't get through them, we can get around them!"

How the Princess could laugh! And then her eyes sparkled, and the Turkish boy laughed with her even when he did not understand what the joke was about. No wonder that Ileana was a joy to the Queen in her sorrow.

After landing, when their boat trip was over, Ileana and her little guests went up to the Carol Terrace. At one end of it, stood an ancient stone cross, sternly outlined against the sea; and by the side of this cross grew a rosebush with roses which seemed to Nancy as red as those which grew by her little bungalow at home. Suddenly she stood still, as if she were turned to stone; then she darted to the rosebush and exclaimed: "Are you, my friend, come to bloom here by the Black Sea?" And can you believe it? The bush actually answered, singing ever so softly, in a queer little voice:

> "Little Nancy, return to your home!
> Your mysterious journey is done:
> Return from the Queen, and the Land
> At the verge of the bright Rising Sun!
>
> My roots lie deep,
> Nor do they sleep
> As mortals think. I know
> What I have spied
> Where secrets hide
> Beneath the silent snow.
>
> If go you must,
> Oh, ever trust
>
> The red, red rose – your friend:
> For she'll be near
> To guard you, dear,
> Where'er your steps may trend."

There was a pause, and then Nancy once more heard the red rose singing:

"With your friends you have trudged through the dust
Of the roads which have led to the sea,
You have slept in the light of the stars
With the land of the Turk in the lee.

To your far away home you must go,
Where your granny is waiting for you.
Bid farewell to the friends you have made,
And return to the arms of old Sue!

Fare east, fare west –
Home's ever best!"

"They're calling me home!" cried Nancy, aghast. "The rose-bush is calling me home! Florica, what shall I do?" Tears of distress stood in her eyes, for Nancy's heart was torn between East and West.

Florica stood quite still. Her gaze was fixed upon the sea. It seemed to Nancy that no one else in the world could stand as still as Florica, the little peasant who once had been a doll. At length she said: "I'll do the trick again." But her voice was very low, and it trembled – because Florica had become so very fond of Nancy!

Nancy turned and looked at Dobre, but he would not face the little stranger. He did not want her to see that there were tears in his eyes.

"What is it, children?" It was Ileana who asked this question, for she had seen that something was amiss.

"This is my friend, the red rose," explained Nancy. "She tells me that I must go home to Granny. She says that Granny hasn't slept a wink since I left home."

The Princess did not seem at all astonished that the red rose should have given Nancy such a message. I suppose that the Queen had taught Ileana how to speak with roses and lilies, with the waves, and the sea gulls, and with the four winds which howl around the towers of the Castle of Brana.

"If the red rose says that your poor grandmother hasn't slept since you left her, I'm afraid that you must hurry back to her as quickly as you can!"

"Florica can do the trick," said Nancy; "but the Queen said that I must see the lilies in the moonlight." The little girl was close on the verge of tears.

"I don't imagine that it will matter much if you spend a few more hours here. We'll keep you until the moon comes, and the lily garden turns to a dream – and then we will ask the clever Florica to conjure you back to your grandmother. If she can do that, you can wake up tomorrow morning in your own little bed! What fun!"

How did Ileana understand so well about such things? Florica looked up at her, and a knowing smile passed between the princess and the peasant child. They did not seem to need words. Then Ileana noticed that the shepherd boy was silent. She took his hand kindly: "You are sad, Dobre?"

Dobre looked at her with large eyes. "Yes, I am sad. I am fond of the little stranger. We've walked many a long mile together. I've played my sweetest tunes to her. And for many a day and many a night, I have protected her."

"And we've broken bread together," added Florica.

"We have quenched our thirst with refreshing water from the same wells," sighed the shepherd. "And, sitting hand in hand, we have watched more than one moon rise."

"Together, you will see the moon rise tonight," said the Princess.

"But after that?" asked the boy.

"After that, you will have a fond memory to cherish: memory to give new beauty to your sheep and your flute, to your plains and your hills, to your dreams, Dobre."

How wise Ileana was! Almost as wise as the peasants themselves!

"But come with me now," she added, "and rest in our great room, among its masses of flowers of every color. And I will show you the many silver lamps which hang near my mother's bed, and I will tell you a story which she once told to me, when my heart was sad!"

Yes Ileana was wise. And her heart had taught her the way in which to talk to these three children, who felt the hour of parting creeping toward them, as if it were a shadow of blackness.

***

That night, on the Queen's terrace, the three companions watched the moon rise. Hand in hand, they stood for the last time, and allowed the mystery and the wonder of the silvery night to sink into their souls. And it was under the white colonnade that Nancy said goodbye to the Queen. The air was full of the fragrance of the lilies – that sweet, heavy fragrance which reminded the Queen of a garden that she had loved as a child. The white pillars, with the white flowers beneath them, stood like ghosts against the water, which was now a really truly Black Sea – but a Black Sea shot through with silver, as if it were a magic tissue woven by fairy hands. The moon hung low in the sky, an enormous shining shield tracing a silver path on the dark waters. It dwarfed the stars, and humbled them. There, among the lilies, the Queen bent down, kissed the little stranger, and slipped into her hand a small golden locket.

"Forget my black veils, Nancy, and think of me, as a queen with a golden crown, and without grief! Goodbye, little stranger. Perhaps the day will come when I will return to America. And when I do, I will truly stop at your door, and ask old Black Sue to let me in. Goodbye, my dear, goodbye..."

There remained in Nancy's memory a fleeting vision of Ileana's lustrous eyes, and the picture of Dobre, as white as the pillars and as the lilies beneath them – of dear Dobre who had been so kind and so protective. He, too, had bent down and kissed the little stranger. And, as he did so, he had pressed his precious wooden flute into her hand – a parting gift! And in Nancy's memory will also linger, as long as she lives, that last glimpse of Florica – her magic doll of Romania, who had whisked her across the seas. There she stood, so wise in life and its mysteries, holding the red rose in her hand – the red, red rose – which Nancy now knew was growing in two places at the same time! But now there were nowhere to be seen any of those somber birds of mystery which Nancy had seen in her dream of the Haiduc. But afterward she seemed to remember having seen a sea gull with silver wings. But of this she was not quite sure. And – was that the red rose's voice? For she could hear a song which she had already heard once before!

> "My roots lie deep,
> Nor do they sleep
> As mortals think. I know
> What I have spied
> Where secrets hide
> Beneath the silent snow."

There was a pause, and then Nancy once more heard the red rose singing:

> "If go you must,
> Oh, ever trust
> The red, red rose – your friend:
> For she'll be near
> To guard you, dear,
> Where'er your steps may trend."

The singing stopped, and Nancy gave a start. "Florica!" she gasped, "Florica ! Where are you?"

***

"Granny!"

"Oh, my child! What a fright you have given me!" And there sat Granny, almost speechless with surprise. Her spectacles had fallen, unnoticed, into her lap. Granny! And behind her, old Sue – hands in air, and teeth as white as the Queen's lilies! Tears like great dewdrops were running down her ebony cheeks. "Law bless you, honey! My young un has come back! You li'l rascal! Ole Sue's heart done cracked right in two! And now it's whole again! Lawzie, Lawzie!"

"Granny – I've come back."

"But what's done happen to you, chile?" Old Sue was horrified. And in truth Nancy was a surprising sight! Bronzed by the sun hardened by the wind, with tattered dress and worn-out shoes, and with her fair hair an unkempt, tousled mass which hung about her face, she was indeed a grimy and ragged urchin as she stood before them. But for all that, she was clutching in one hand a small golden locket, which carried, within, the miniature of a queen, if you please! And Nancy knew that it was a real queen, with a real crown of gold upon her head! And clutched in her other hand was a little wooden flute – an absurd little ten-cent wooden flute!

"Nancy, Nancy!" Granny could say nothing else! Tears choked her voice. And again she repeated "Nancy!"

"And I've come back without Florica!" exclaimed the ragged little girl. "The red rose told me that it was time to come home. I found her growing near the Black Sea, too."

Granny was understanding less and less. "The red rose?"

"Yes. And the Princess said that it would be best for me to listen to the rose, for it told me that you hadn't slept since I left home."

"Lawzie, Lawzie, what's de chile sayin'?"

"And, Granny, I left the Queen among her lilies by the Black Sea – and it isn't black at all; it's blue! And the moon was shining, and the fragrance of the lilies reminded the Queen of a garden which she had loved when she was a little girl – and it belonged to Queen Victoria, the garden did! And her lilies – the Queen's lilies, I mean – are a dream come true! And Ileana sails her own little boat – with a Turkish boy who has freckles on his nose! And the silver coffeepots have tiny parrots for knobs. And the Queen's little castle has a staircase in it! And, Granny! The Haiduc is not a real person; it's only in the songs that he steals the maiden's hearts. But I dreamed about him; he was very bold and handsome – and the Queen was visiting him with her crown on! And, Granny – do you know? – Romania is near the Rising Sun, and that's why even the small girls sing songs which are so strange that we American girls can't understand them!"

"Nancy, Nancy! Wait a minute! Don't try to tell me so much all at once! You'll drive me crazy, my dear! And how you do look! I've never seen such a little scarecrow. I would scarcely have recognized you, if I'd met you in the street!"

"But I *am* Nancy – your own little Nancy!" She earnestly assured her. Certainly those were Nancy's eyes which were staring up out of her grimy, sunburned face. And they might have been two small pieces torn from the sky. "But, Granny!" And now there was a pathetic tremble in her granddaughter's chin – a wee tremble which would have made your eyes a trifle moist to see. "Florica wouldn't come back with me. She is no longer a doll. And she says that Romanians cannot live away from their own country, for if they did, their hearts would break with *dor*."

"*Dor!* Whatever does the precious child mean? And why are there tears in her eyes? Come here, Nancy, my child, and let me kiss you!"

270

Then Nancy threw herself into her grandmother's arms. And as she did so, she burst into tears! "It's because –" she sobbed, "because my heart is so full of *dor* for Florica, for Dobre – and for the Queen – and for Ileana! Granny, Romania really *is* the land near the Rising Sun! And truly the Black Sea is not black at all, but blue – ever so blue! And the setting sun there turns everything to pink and orange! Oh, it is beautiful! And the Queen – !"

"Well, I have never heard such a thing before! Never!" Granny's cap was askew. This was all very perplexing, she thought to herself, and really, Nancy *must* have a bath – and how her hair needed to be cut! Never before had the child been so untidy. Granny shook her head. "It will take me a month to understand all this! It's too confusing! What queer ideas are these that the child is chattering about? And when she comes home so suddenly – and in such a state – it takes my breath away! But at any rate, thank heaven! That uncanny doll – which was not a doll – has stayed where she belonged, in the land of the Rising Sun, by the Black Sea, which is blue! I have never heard such nonsense! But this experience has taught me something! No more foreigners for me, if you please! It's never safe to let one of them into your house – not even a foreign doll!"

Then Granny's eyes fell upon the small golden locket. She took it gently from Nancy's hand, and opening it, looked at the picture of the Queen.

"Well," she observed, grudging, "she is a real queen anyway – see her crown! It's very handsome, my dear! But still, as for foreigners – no, I thank you! No more of them for me!"

But in spite of Granny's objections to foreigners, Nancy knew one fact:

EAST AND WEST *had* MET!

Selected Essays about Romania

Note

The selected autobiographical writings about Romania were published in the following editions during the lifetime of the queens of Romania:

Queen Elisabeth of Romania (Carmen Sylva): *Bucharest*, in: Harper's Weekly. A Journal of Civilization, Saturday, February 4, 1893, New York, vol. XXXVII, No. 1885, p. 107-111.

Queen Marie of Romania: *My Country*, London: Hodder & Stoughton, 1916, p. 5-16.

Queen Marie of Romania: *The Country that I Love. An Exile's Memories,* London: Duckworth, 1925: Preface ["Why this book was written"], p. 9-13; Chapter XII [Jassy], p. 128-147; Chapter XV [Bran], p. 162-175.

Queen Elisabeth of Romania (Carmen Sylva): Bucharest

For three long days, on a vessel dressed with flags, I had been floating down the wide, brown waters of the Danube, which rapidly increased in volume like the final movement of a symphony. Everywhere, whether in town or village, a brilliant reception was accorded me; and yet my eye was not satiated with the richness of coloring beneath the Oriental sky, which in the daytime was of a turquoise blue, melting at sunset, when the orb of day was magnified to double its ordinary size, into a gleaming yellow, strewn with golden dust. In the pure light of the end of November, on the lovely undulating fields, on the black soil, which had yielded riches without effort, and was prepared, on demand, to give yet more, on the thick white dust of the wide roads, marked out by the reckless driving of chariots, the bright colors of the costumes of the peasants trooping forth to receive me, stood out in vivid relief – bodices of dazzling whiteness, richly embroidered with red, black, and gold; floating veils of white linen, or of ivory – white or sulphur-colored silk, and petticoats of peony red or claret-color. Men were galloping on their small and thin but swift horses, their goatskin cloaks floating behind them and looking like a second mane on the necks of their steeds. An embroidered *sayon*, or outer coat, covered their chests, resembling a many-colored tattooing above the sash, which was twelve inches wide, and held a perfect arsenal of pistols and knives. The shirt, also embroidered, fell over their white felt pantaloons; and on their heads were large caps, looking like white furs, beneath which curls of raven-black hair hung down to their shoulders.

As I approached these picturesque groups, I noticed some men of noble stature, with faces of rare beauty, whose grave expression was but seldom varied by a smile, showing rows of pearly-white teeth. And these faces, of a type so new to me, with the aquiline noses, the delicate quivering nostrils, the marvelously large black or greenish-gray eyes gleaming with a somber fire, deep-sunk within their sockets, and over-shadowed by thick straight eyebrows, the bronzed complexions, the sonorous language, sounding now harsh, now almost guttural, spoken with such ease, indeed with such extraordinary eloquence, by these grave Romanian men and matrons, and by children whose expression was as soft as the gleam of a star, all combined to produce on me an impression of an intensity and passion unknown in our northwestern climate. And then I noted, with admiration, that the handsome face, of southern type, of my young consort, was in perfect harmony alike with the men and with the country he has conquered for himself by his own unaided effort.

This, then, was my new country! This was Romania, of which so far I had seen nothing but the vast melancholy plains, the shores of the wide river, and the all but uninhabitable marshes in which the frogs croak amongst the reeds and the wild hemp.

Every now and then a picket of Dorobantzi presented arms, or sounded a flourish of trumpets which was heard on the other side of the water and died away amongst the opposite mountains of Serbia and Bulgaria, districts less fertile, it is true, but of brighter aspect and with more inhabitants than Romania. On a daughter of the Rhine, that Rhine which leaps happily along like a flash of lightning between bright villages nestling amongst trees, the wide, silent, mighty river flowing through uninterrupted solitudes produced an impression of melancholy, and added to that *serrement de cœur* with which I approached the unknown possibilities of my new destiny.

If there be a difficult position in this world it is surely that of a young foreign princess making her entry into her capital. The faces about you express nothing but a cold curiosity, whereas but a few days before every eye that looked on you was dim with tears, and every lip trembled, in spite of the shouts of "Hurrah!" and "God bless you, our dear child; our little princess!" You are no longer a child to anyone, and you are astonished to find yourself married; you are afraid of displeasing, and convinced of your incapacity to cope with the grandeur of the mission, which will weigh upon your shoulders like a too heavy mantle.

I carried with me, however, one consolation, which I concealed with a kind of shame, and that was my pen. But I should have been as much astonished at being called a poet as a bird would at being called a singer. Can the soul of your soul have a name?

In those days, I realized, painfully, that it is not enough to have a soul, however big, full of love, rich in good intentions and overflowing with affection that soul may be. One must *seem* everywhere – for everywhere it is one's duty to please. Now, for the first time in my life, I thought of my appearance. I had never had time to do so before, for my youth had been passed by the bedsides of the dying, or in the midst of most intellectual society, and my eyes had wept too much to see anything in life but its sadness. With profound melancholy, then, I gazed on the ever-increasing crowds, which bore witness to our approach to the capital; and I wondered how often I should find myself powerless to assuage the misery doubtless hidden amongst those gathered here.

With my heart beating against my side as an imprisoned butterfly beats against a glass, with dry lips, cold hands, and trembling knees, with a roar in my ears louder than the boom of the cannon, the clash of the bells, and the military bands playing the national hymn, I tried to smile at my husband, who was explaining what I saw about me, and was rejoicing at the thought of taking his young wife over the first part of the railway he had laid down himself to connect his capital with the Danube. I had to wrestle with the anguish, which made my throat contract, the inexplicable uneasiness which had oppressed me for several days, as I descended from the train to speak to all the people grouped upon the quays. But as I left the station to get into the carriage, a cry of admiration escaped me; above the waving plumes, the glittering uniforms, the horses, and the flags, beyond the sea of human beads, I bad caught sight of the town nestling between the hills and amongst the green valleys. With its gleaming roofs, its hundreds of little churches, its green, yellow, and blue houses, all bathed in the dazzling sunshine, which made even the wood scintillate like zinc, it reminded me vaguely of Moscow.[78]

Once in the carriage I had to bow perpetually, which is too exhausting to allow one to look about at one's ease, especially when the faintest smile becomes an effort, and every movement of the eyes causes a pain to shoot right through one's head. However, in the long drive from the station to the capital, and then from the capital to the palace, I saw some houses which seemed too small for their inhabitants, men who seemed to touch the roofs of their dwellings with their foreheads, and women wearing green and blue petticoats, and bodices as white as snow, with white handkerchiefs bordered with lace fastened on their heads, and a carnation stuck behind one ear. On first arrival this prevalence of white in country and in town strikes one with surprise; but one soon learns to wear it one's self in preference to anything else, as it is the only thing which stands the sun and dust.

It seems astonishing that each church should have but two bells, and that the effect of a carillon is only produced by the ringing of the bells of a great number of churches; on the day of my arrival, especially these churches of Bucharest appeared simply innumerable…

The court of the capital where I was to alight was completely covered with a red dais, which seemed to cast a fantastic light upon the people assembled to meet me, on the red togas of the lawyers, and on the sacerdotal robes of the Metropolitan and the bishops, all of whom had long gray or while beards. Forty couples were married on this occasion, all the brides wearing a veil of gold net...

"There is the palace," said the King to me. – "Where?" I replied. – "We are entering it now," he answered, with a smile. Then I understood that it is "the sovereign who makes the palace, as a stone in a field may become an altar". The palace of Bucharest is an old mansion that had belonged to a boyar[79], hastily got ready for our reception. The young sovereign had not had time to think of making it comfortable, for his nights were passed in preparing the overwhelming work of the day; and on the very day of our

---

[78] In her youth, in Spring 1864, Princess Elisabeth of Wied (later Queen of Romania) had visited Moscow and spent some weeks at the Mikhailovsky Palace, invited by her aunt and godmother, Grand Duchess Elena Pavlovna, the consort of Grand Duke Michael Pavlovich of Russia.

[79] A boyar is a member of a privileged class in Romania [note in first edition].

arrival, I found on his writing-table the first plan of the bridge over the Danube, which is to be built at last, after twenty years of patient waiting. Not a window would shut in this palace, and the damp ascended to the first floor. Even now, twenty years afterwards, I suffer from the fever I contracted in it, and we lost many servants and many horses from the damp with which the walls were saturated. There is no resemblance between the Bucharest of today and that at which we were now arriving. Since that time one thousand houses are built, on an average, every year, and slabs of pavement are now laid down in the streets, taking the place of the old flagstones and ruts. The palace, too, has gone through a complete transformation. The original building has, it is true, been utilized, giving to the exterior a certain appearance of patch-work; but the inside has a look of home about it, and an altogether individual character. A sculptor, a true *cinquecento* master, named Stöhr, who has worked for us for twenty-five years, presided at this transformation, and has decorated our rooms with wainscots and furniture of rare beauty. The throne-room has become a library in the German Renaissance style. The King's private study is a little museum, whilst my apartments contain several valuable old pictures of first rank, on which the light falls from above as in a gallery of paintings.

What was my astonishment on receiving the ladies of Bucharest, the day after my arrival, at discovering that there was no resemblance whatever between the members of the upper classes and the peasant women! No more matrons of solemn mien and sober veils, but dainty and graceful creatures, reminding me at once of the society of St. Petersburg and Naples. As for the men, they had a French air, at least that is how they struck me when I saw them the next day in the Chamber of Legislature, whither I was conducted in grand state. On that occasion, I was very much amused at the contrast between the elegance of our equipage and the streets we passed through, bordered by little houses irregularly built, and paved with huge stones of different sizes, causing me and my diadem to make a good many involuntary bows. On the evening of the same day there was a general illumination... Never in my life had I seen anything like it; in the very streets where now one big hotel touches another, and gas and electric light struggle for the mastery, nothing was then known but petroleum lamps and candles; and as none of the houses were more than one story high, between the court and the garden, there was often a break in the continuity of the illuminations, and more shadow than light... I could hardly help smiling, but I soon found this mode of lighting up, this true *lucus a non lucendo*, very characteristic; and then the pathetic side of it all struck me, for each one had done his best in his little house, however humble his means. I learned, moreover, that every Romanian makes a point of living in his own house, if it be but of mud, with no floor, with the four walls falling apart, and a thatched roof. Ask the humblest petitioner where she lives, and she will reply, "*In casele mele*" (In my houses!).

The day after this entry into my capital, I had fever. To be ill without knowing anyone, neither my husband, nor my maids of honor, nor the doctors, nor even my chambermaid, was really rather hard. It seemed, too, particularly trying to hear myself spoken of as nervous by people who knew nothing of my past, after the Spartan education I had had, too; nervous and badly brought up appear to me synonymous expressions. Many proud but silent tears did I shed in secret on my pillow at that time.

My first excursions were one series of surprises. In the town, there were some picturesque streets, where all the doorways were encumbered with many-colored stuffs, old iron, and green and brown pottery. Other quarters resembled a medley of dolls' houses, so singularly small were the dwellings, hidden beneath the trees, those luckless willows, which are being more thoroughly despoiled of their branches every year, or the acacias, which fill the whole town with their perfume in the spring. Open to the street were the shops of bakers, shoemakers, blacksmiths, with innumerable wine shops, where brandy made from plums, called *tzuica*, was sold, dingy little places, from the gloomy depths of which looked out men with brigand-like figures, but mild eyes and a melancholy smile. The nearer we approached the river Dimbovitza, which name signifies oak leaf, the more closely packed were the houses, with their projecting balconies and small pierced columns surmounted by carved trefoils, giving them something of a Moorish appearance.

And then the Dimbovitza itself – now reduced to subjection, supplemented by canals, lined with quays, markets, slaughter-houses, schools, hospitals, barracks, and beautiful churches (too beautiful, perhaps, because too new) – was very different in those days, and presented animated scenes on its banks such as would have delighted poets and artists. People bathed in the beautiful mud in pell-mell fashion, the children splashed about with shouts of delight, the water-carriers led their animals into the stream, wading knee-deep themselves as they filled their barrels. And in the deepest part of the ooze you could see huge forms moving about in confusion; grayish bodies with patches bald of hair, looking like hippopotami in the distance, though the massive horns, curving near the nape of the neck, and the black muzzles shining in the sun, proved them to be buffaloes.

As time went on I was to make close acquaintance with this clumsy, sluggish, antediluvian beast, so common in Romania. The cow yields quantities of rich milk, from which excellent cream is obtained, and of which very white but tasteless butter is made. For the buffalo to thrive it must be fed on the dried leaves of maize, and have a bed of mud to wallow in. It would die in the summer without marshes, and in winter if it did not have a subterranean retreat and a woolen covering. In the streets of the town, and in the open country, you see numerous buffaloes harnessed, in single file, to countless heavily laden vehicles, the animals' hoofs sinking deep in the dust in dry weather, and in the mud when it rains... Speaking of mud, what was my amusement the first time I was splashed with it, and that was in one of the principal roads, at finding that it made grease spots on my clothes! And when I saw ploughing! A plough drawn by from four to six oxen, just scratching over the earth with the branch of a tree serving as harrow... This is what they call ploughing here! More than that, the soil is so fertile that it is really all that is needed.

Romanian carriages are often drawn by horses, eight, twelve, or even sixteen little horses being yoked together in a helter-skelter manner with a kind of packthread. A boy astride on one of them guides them all with one hand, and in the other brandishes a long whip with a short handle. Thus do they cross the wide plains, standing out larger than life against the wide-stretching horizon. The driver, as he goes, sings a melancholy melody, and now and then he halts beside some well to water his cattle. The structures protecting the wells look rather like gallows rising solitary from the midst of the fields. Every man who has sunk a well is blessed, and many are the sins forgiven him. Whosoever drinks, after blowing in the water to drive away evil spirits, is bound to say, "May God pardon him!" Sometimes the charioteer falls asleep amongst the maize, his limbs relaxed, and abandoned to careless repose...

If we suddenly hear in the distance the ringing of small bells and long sustained cries like the whistles on the railways, we know we may expect to see appear eight horses and two postilions belonging to some wealthy man going to his country-seat at a rate of twenty kilometers an hour. The postilions wear embroidered leather garments, moccasins like those of Indians, hats with long fluttering ribbons, and shirts with wide sleeves that swell out like sails in the wind as they go. Like demons, they double themselves up, scream, crack their whips, talk to their horses, or fling you a greeting as they dash by, disappearing in a cloud of dust.

In the streets of Bucharest there is a perpetual going and coming of carriages, countless hackney-coaches, all open, with just a hood to protect the hirer from the cold, the sun, or the rain. The coachmen are extraordinary-looking creatures, beardless Russians of the Lipovan sect, wearing long black velvet robes, pulled in at the waist with a colored sash. They drive very rapidly, with the arm stretched out, as in St. Petersburg. They are clean, steady, and honest. I amused myself sometimes by counting them; no matter what the weather, from 120 to 150 carriages an hour passed the windows of the palace; only between two and four o'clock in the morning was there comparative quiet.

In addition to the noise of the carriages, peddlers and porters on foot make the streets reverberate with their long, melancholy cries. These walkers are mostly Bulgarians, wearing long white mantles with wide red woolen sashes, and a red or white fez on the head. They hawk milk, oranges, bonbons, a horrible drink of fermented millet, and sheep from which the skins have been taken, the still bleeding bodies hung upon poles. To our streets, which are an imitation of those of Paris, they give a quaint touch of the Oriental.

There is a good deal of amusement going on in Bucharest, and the people are very sociable and hospitable. No one would sit down to table without two or three extra covers in case of unexpected guests arriving. The peasant invites you to share his meal, if it be but a couple of onions, a few boiled beans, and half a melon. But for all that there is no real gayety, or rather no joy. Never did I see people so sad at heart as are the Romanians. The very children have a gravity about them unnatural to their years. Their little faces are pinched and pale; their great eyes, fringed with long curling lashes, gleam with intelligence; but their expression is so melancholy that it breaks one's heart to look at them.

The Romanian is never surprised at anything. The *nil admirari* is in his blood: he is born *blasé*. Enthusiasm is to him a thing unknown. The Moldavian peasants who had been bitten by mad wolves, and were sent to Pasteur in Paris, were no more surprised at what they saw in that city than if it had been their native village. Death has no terrors for them. The Romanian peasant dies, with his taper in his hand, with perfect indifference, and with a dignity which is quite Oriental.

At the ball given at the palace on New Year's day I asked a peasant deputy: "Does this please you?" – "Well enough," he replied; "but I have seen it before. Here is my wife, though, who sees it now for the first time." I turned to her: "You think it beautiful, do you not?" I said. – "It's not bad," was her reply, which she gave without a smile. Neither the floods of electric light, nor the jewels, nor the size of the room impressed them; it was the peasant woman who looked like a queen – cold and disdainful, wrapped to the chin in the severe folds of her veil, gazing with contempt upon all the Parisian costumes and bare shoulders.

On my arrival in the country, no lady ever set her foot in the streets. It was not only indecorous to do so, it was impossible, the middle of the thoroughfare being occupied by the drain. Now all the women walk on pavements bordered by shops and cafes, where people eat strawberries, with champagne and ices, seated at little tables, and trying to imitate Parisian ways. Now nothing is spoken in the town but French, whereas forty years ago Greek was the only language. We know now what will be played tomorrow at the Porte St. Martin; we criticize the new books and the latest fashions; we cut the reviews as if we lived in one of the *faubourgs* of Paris, and yet we are divided from Paris by the whole of Europe.

Mothers of families retire from the world, and deprive themselves of everything for the sake of being able to send their children to Paris, and the wealthier parents, after having had some little experience of the deplorable results of the absence of surveillance, now accompany their daughters.

Great fortunes have disappeared in Romania; the large houses where a hundred sat down to table every day, and as many poor were fed, are closed, and those bearing the grand old names are trying to make a living. A few ancient dames alone still remember the old days, and tell you tales of the time when the boyar received at his levee, sealed on his divan, whilst his shaved head and long beard were washed (an operation which took at least an hour), his sons and his whole court standing motionless before him, waiting to know if he would deign to address them. Not even a son ever dared to sit down or to smoke in the presence of his father. Now we are more democratic than the freest of republics, and can take very high rank in setting good manners at defiance!

Education abroad is fatal to family life, and young people do not know that confession to the mother at the end of each day is a better thing than either the École Centrale or the Lycée Louis le Grand of Paris can give. But nowadays everybody must study, and every young girl, whether rich or poor, must take her bachelor's degree.

No mother is fuller of solicitude than the Romanian; she is a perfect slave to her children. During the war, the devotion of the women of our country greatly astonished the foreign doctors. Some of these women never left the hospital, not even at night; they cared for the poor young soldiers as if they had been their own children, saying to themselves that perhaps tomorrow their own boys might be wrestling with the horrors of death among strangers.

Unfortunately, the sudden changes of climate, and the pestilential marshes which surround Bucharest, are a cause of perpetual anxiety to mothers. Words are powerless to describe the time of the epidemic of diphtheria, when as many as three children were buried in one coffin, when whole streets were depopulated, the inhabitants all dead; families of five or seven children swept away in one week – the poor mothers going out of their minds. It was like the last plague of Egypt, and the people called this scourge the *white pest*. Not one house was spared...[80]

It was after this terrible lime that taking the dead through the streets in open coffins was put a stop to. Previously a funeral was a kind of public fête; on a funereal car covered with gilded angels, garlands, and ribbons, the dead maiden was carried forth in her last ball dress, with hair dressed by the barber, and decked with flowers, and often even with her face rouged so as to look better! A military band playing Chopin's funeral march followed the corpse. It was like looking on at a "Dance of Death" to see the head of the deceased rolling from one side to the other of the satin pillow, whilst women shrieked, tore their hair, and smote upon their breasts. Now the loss of all this is made up for by crowds assembling in the

---

[80] Pathos is added to this account by the fact that the writer herself [Queen Elisabeth of Romania] lost her only child, a lovely girl of four years old, from diphtheria. [Note of the translator in the first edition].

churches, where the dead lie in state, the people jostling each other in their struggles to look on the face of the corpse or to kiss its hand. In the country the dead are still buried in accordance with the ancient rites; the obolus for Charon, the ferryman of hell, is placed in the mouth of the corpse, corn is put into the coffin, and the body is drenched with wine before it is lowered into the earth. On All-Saints day the so-called *colivo*, a kind of cake made of corn and sugar, is placed on the graves of the departed. "I shall eat of thy *colivo*", is an ordinary form of oath, an imprecation often heard.

On Sundays and *fête*-days the people of Romania[81] take their rest in a very peculiar manner; they dance from morning till evening with a perfectly solemn air, holding each others' hands, and shaking a handkerchief; they turn round slowly, of course, as they keep up the dance for twelve hours. Gypsies so dark that they look almost like negroes stand in the middle of the circle, scraping in melancholy fashion on their violins or mandolins, beating their dulcimers, and blowing on their shepherds' flutes till their lungs are quite exhausted. Round and round and round again go the dancers to the monotonous sound of this sad but exquisite music, the steps only changing with the rhythm of the melody, which is of Arabic character. At the end of the long monotonous day the performers are quite giddy and stupefied, and sink into a kind of dreamy, confused state of mind.

The people of Bucharest are very fond of flowers; there is not a window in the town without a few pots of geraniums, carnations, or mignonette. On the other hand, trees have anything but a good time of it here; the summer heat parches them up, and the winter kills them; men strip them of branches or chop them down, so that there is not a beautiful park, scarcely even a shady garden, to be seen. The difference of temperature between winter and summer is seventy degrees Centigrade. The plants from the north succumb beneath the torrid sunshine of August; those from the south to the snowstorms of January. The quantity of snow that falls, however, protects the soil from the intense cold, and makes Romania a country of vineyards *par excellence*. There are three seasons in Romania, of which one only – autumn – is fine. There is no such thing as spring. The two sledging months are a rest to the ears. As soon as the first snow falls, nothing but sledges are seen in the town; even the carriages are mounted on skates, and the houses are no longer shaken by the perpetual passing of traffic. Sometimes a snowstorm buries the low houses of the *faubourgs*, and eleven people once perished in a single night at the gates of Bucharest. It is no rare thing for wolves to come into the town. At such times the snow no longer seems to fall, but to be performing a tumultuous whirling, up-and-down dance, so that men and beasts are blinded, and merely go round and round when they think they are advancing.

---

[81] The original American translation holds an error here by mentioning "Bulgaria" instead of Romania (*Bucharest*, Harper's Weekley, 1893, p. 110).

The great cemetery of Bucharest is worthy of a visit. It commands a view of the whole town, a view which is especially grand in the evening, when the sunset bathes houses, churches, clouds, and dust in a glow of purple and violet tints, with here and there gleaming, scintillating points of light from the roofs and windows. Very touching, very naive, too, are the inscriptions on the picturesque tombs, which are adorned with photographs and locks of hair framed in the marble of the crosses. Food is even sometimes placed on the graves, as in the days of the Romans. In fact, the dead are never abandoned, never forgotten. One feels that they are constantly visited; and as night falls, the little lamps, which shine out on every side, give one an impression of restless, wandering, floating souls, over which one must keep watch.

I once passed half a night with an orphan at the grave of her father, who had just been buried amongst the strange scents peculiar to a cemetery after the great heat of the day, in the silence eloquent with the presence of the countless sleepers beneath the soil. The town shone as if illuminated, and its sounds came muffled by the distance like waves breaking behind the dunes. One's tears are stanched in the solemnity of the immutable peace – at least this is generally the case; but I remember once seeing an official of high rank, generally cold and impassible enough, fling himself upon the grave of his children, and tear up the ground with his fingers, calling his lost dear ones by name.

One poetic time at Bucharest is Easter week, when nearly two hundred churches are illuminated every evening. The bells are all clashing together; the people are crowding to offer fresh flowers to the images of the saints. On Good-Friday processions carrying torches walk round all the churches, and then take tapers from them to the cemetery with which to deck the graves, even the most neglected receiving each a little light placed on it by charitable hands.

On Easter eve, the King kisses the manuscript gospel whilst it is being read aloud. Then he takes the crucifix and the taper, and everyone comes to kiss the cross, and to light his taper at that of the King. When it strikes midnight all leave the church, to celebrate the resurrection in the open air.

Some of these churches are scarcely larger than a room; they are surmounted by a mushroom-shaped bell tower, and painted inside in the most fantastic manner. There are some "Last Judgments," with a kind of red serpent, in which struggle devils and condemned souls, whilst the redeemed look on with serene and unmoved countenances. There, too, we see founders holding up a church on the points of their fingers, and with their numerous progeny grouped about them, the sons on one side, the daughters on the other, all exactly alike in face, and differing only in height. Every church has its own tradition, and special facilities for granting certain petitions. In one you can secure the marriage of your daughter, in another the death of your enemy, in this you can bring discord into the house of your neighbor, in that you can secure the cure of a malady, in yet another the detection of thieves. There are men who are slowly killed by the offering in certain churches of tapers exactly their height; as these tapers burn, the persons indicated feel themselves wasting away, and when the tapers go out they die. One of our old servants imagined himself doomed to death in this manner. I said to myself, "To children we must offer the consolations of children," and I sent another taper of his height to another church, persuading him that the prayer of the just is more efficacious than that of the wicked. What was my horror when the person who had wished for his death died herself three days afterwards!... He himself, however, has been very well ever since, and is now quite plump.

A certain church was built by three young girls who loved the same man. They agreed that the one who still loved him when the building was finished should be the one to marry him. But, alas! When the whole thing was done, the girls all loved him as much as on the first day. Then they all went into a convent together.

Another chapel was built by a woman who had lifted her hand against her husband. (It is considered quite natural that a husband should beat his wife; a young wife, indeed, once wished for a divorce because her husband did not beat her, and she thought it proved he did not love her. But for a woman to beat her husband is considered such an enormity that the guilty one is accursed, and condemned for life to spin at her distaff day and night without rest or break.) The woman who had struck her husband had long been walking about in road and field, never ceasing to ply her spindle; at last she vowed that where the spindle fell, exhausted from fatigue, she would build a church. It fell at last for the first time, but a plum-tree immediately sprung up on the spot. She did not think she ought to pull it up to build, so she went on her way. A second time the spindle fell, but up sprung an apple-tree, so on she went with her ceaseless toil. When the spindle fell a third time, a spring of water gushed forth from the ground, and the girl said: "There must I build beside the living water," and from that day she had rest.

Another woman had been visited by every possible misfortune; she had lost her husband and all her children, and yet her hair had not turned white. Now the Romanians are afraid of women whose hair does not turn while, and they looked upon her as accursed and uncanny. She prayed day and night, but her hair remained black. Then she thought she would build a church; but it did no good, her hair was as black as ever. At last, one night, she dreamt that a voice told her to climb on the roof of her church when the first snow fell, to catch the falling flakes and cover her head with them. So she climbed on the roof, and covered her head with undriven snow; one by one the hairs turned white. When the poor creature came down she was all white, but tired – so tired that she laid her down and died!

A barren woman had prayed for a child in all the churches. She dreamt that if she stole a stone from every church already built, and with the collected stones erected yet another, she would become a mother. So one by one she carried the stones, making pilgrimages all over the country. When she had a good big pile she began to build, and the day the new church was finished she found a deserted child upon her threshold. This child she adopted!

The large church of Sarindar (the name of which comes from the Neo-Greek word signifying "fortieth") was built by Prince Matei Basarab[82], to atone for the assassination of his brother-in-law. He had gone to Constantinople to ask for the absolution of the patriarch, who had ordered him to build forty churches. This, the finest of all, was the fortieth. The same prince introduced the Romanian language into public worship and into schools, in place of the Slavonian, which he did not understand.

The exercise of benevolence is fraught with great difficulties in Romania; work must be found for the poor to do at home, for no one will go out to service: the cooks are Tziganes, the domestic servants Transylvanians or Hungarians, and everyone must have state employment. There is one society for distributing wood in winter, another for giving work, yet another to protect the village industry of making embroideries, which are as fine as any Oriental work, and have a character all their own. I have seen poems written, I have seen painting done, compositions made, lives lived, but never did I see real embroidery produced till I came to Romania. On the bodice of a young peasant girl I one day noticed that the embroidery on one of the sleeves on one side only crossed the embroidery of the shoulder piece. I asked the girl the reason of this, and she replied, "That is called a wandering stream." The language of our peasants is as flowery as nature herself; they never speak but in fanciful images. "How are you getting on at home?" I asked one day. "Like a racking cough," was the reply. "How are you today?" – "Like a dog in a cart," "You have a son?" – "I have had two pines, but the storm has laid them low." Now hear the cry from a mother's heart to her daughter: "Thy child is crying, thou hast let it fall; dost thou not know that thou should hold it like a little carnation?" "How is thy sweetheart?" – "Like the young corn in a field of maize." No Romanian will ever admit that he is quite well. "Deh!" he cries, "not so bad." Nor will he acknowledge that things are at the worst. Another peculiarity is that a Romanian will never assent fully to anything or make a positive assertion. You tell him something of which you are absolutely convinced, and, after listening to you in silence, he says, "It is possible, perhaps." Or you ask him where he is going, and he says, "I am about to go to the fields." And for centuries past the peasants never knew when they went to the fields whether they would return alive. When, during the war, I asked the

---

82 Matei Basarab was Prince of Wallachia between 1632 and 1654.

wounded how they were, they invariably replied, "Well enough, but I have a pain in my chest, and in the bone of my wounded leg, and in my arm." And perhaps the next day the poor fellow who had thus answered me was dead.

Many were the heart-rending and touching scenes I witnessed during the war which were to me a revelation of the strange nature of the Romanian people. With their superstitions, their childlike piety, they combined melancholy and fun. I have seen a devoted wife, after seeking her husband all along the shores of the Danube and in all the hospitals, finding him at last, broken down and disfigured, to greet him with a mere nod of the head before taking up her post at his bedside, there to nurse him day and night. I have heard some brave hero crying out in his agony for his mother, and covering the hands of that mother with kisses.

One poor wounded fellow, with the lower jaw destroyed, and hideous to look upon, wanted to dictate a letter to one of my ladies in waiting. This letter was to his wife, and he began with the usual formula: "I hope this letter will reach you in the happiest moment of your life. As for me," he went on, "I wish to tell you that I am very well off here, and that I am wounded in the chest." At this the young girl who was writing paused in astonishment. "But, Nicolas," she exclaimed, "that is not true." – "Do you think," he answered, "that she would remain faithful to me if she saw me looking so dreadful?"

Once I was sent for to the town to a young man whose leg had been amputated, and who was in inconsolable despair. Not having been present at the operation, I did not know which leg had been taken off. I sat down on the side of the bed, and remained talking to the poor fellow for a quarter of an hour, he smiling sweetly at me all the time. When I arose, my ladies of honor discovered that I had been sitting on the stump of the lost leg. I still shudder whenever I think of my stupidity. "You poor fellow!" I cried; "it must have hurt you terribly." – "I would have borne it many hours for the sake of listening to your voice," he replied.

A handsome young man had died in a tent opposite to mine, and the next morning dawned cold and dreary, for it was November. The fog shut us in like a wall, and the ground was like an oozy bog. All of a sudden, a man and a woman came forth from the fog like specters. The woman wore nothing but an old gray chemise, scarcely reaching to her knees, and about her worn old face hung the rags of what had once been a white linen wrap. She came forward on her bare feet through the deep mud, her arms clasping a bundle of linen for her son. She asked for him, and before I could get to her she fell on her knees with a heart-rending cry. A soldier with brutal haste had said to her, "Your son died in that tent yesterday". The clean white shirts she had so lovingly brought for him slipped from her hands into the mud, and tearing her hair and smiting her breast, she cried again and again, "Radu, my son! Radu! Radu! Radu!" She would listen to no comfort, accept no food, no shelter, but rose at last and went away through the fog, turning back at every step to cry again the name of her lost son. Her figure assumed immense proportions in the heavy air, and her voice rang out strangely through the damp gloom; and when she was out of sight, we could still hear the cry of "Radu! Radu!" The scene haunts me often now.

For four months I had been trying – alas! in vain – to save the life of a young man. About a quarter of an hour before his death someone spoke to me in rather a loud voice near his bed. I leaned over him, and said, "We are making too much noise, are we not?" – "What does that matter," he replied, "if only I can look at you?" When the end came, his mother began to sob and cry; but the people about asked her to be quiet, as they did not want me to know of his death till the next day. And she had the self-control and grandeur of soul to be silent.

On Christmas Eve, after a long severe frost, a thaw rendered the streets of Bucharest impassable. I was to go and meet the King, who was returning as a victorious hero after five months' absence. I thought it would have been a delirium of joy to me. But I had suffered too much; I had lost the power of rejoicing; I did not know how to be glad.[83] The last days before Plevna had all but destroyed all three armies at once. After a terrible snowstorm, the cold had been twenty degrees below zero. The Danube was so encumbered with ice that not a loaf of bread could be sent over it. If Osman Pasha had held out three days longer every soul would have perished. And now the road between Plevna and Nicopolis was covered with famished crowds. I know not how many left Plevna, but only ten thousand arrived at Nicopolis! The King started the next day on the same road on his way home to his capital. He had to leave his sledge, for it jolted over corpses. Horror-struck, he mounted a horse, and pressed on along this pathway of death, the horse starting and rearing at every step. There were groups of the dead sitting round the last fire they had lit in some deep rut, carts overturned, driver and buffaloes alike frozen in their places, standing up stiff as statues. There were the dying, their arms upraised to heaven in a final petition before they sank back with a last sigh and expired. At the battle of Grivitza sixteen thousand men had fallen; one battalion of cavalry had lost one-half its numbers; and for three days the enemy's fire made it impossible to pause for a moment for food or to bury the dead in the trenches. But all these horrors sunk into insignificance before those of the journey from Plevna to Nicopolis. By paths as slippery as glass the King climbed up to the fortress amidst the terrible clamor of the voices of ten thousand prisoners lying in the ditches, for whom not a scrap of food could be obtained. But as he gained the strong hold, the perils of the ice-path passed, the sun lit up Romania with a rosy light, and the heart of the young monarch was warmed

[83] During the war months in 1877, Queen Elisabeth of Romania had suffered an early pregnancy-loss.

within him at seeing his adopted land once more. The next day the King seemed to be exposed to such peril amongst the raging prisoners, who numbered many more than our troops, that the bold scheme was decided on of sending him away in a little iron-clad vessel, which cut its way through the ice, breaking it where it was thin, and literally springing over it where it was impenetrable, returning safely to port at last, and bringing bread to starving Nicopolis. When at Turno-Magurelli the King found himself, for the first time for five months, in a warmed and furnished room, with a bed to sleep on: he thought he was in an enchanted palace. Another snowstorm endangered his life between Magurelli and Craiova, where the train awaited to take him to his capital – draped with flags, decorated with garlands, to welcome back the hero and conqueror – and to his wife, whose hair had turned white with the anguish through which she had passed, and whose joy resembled grief, so weary was her heart.

Could one but go amongst them, the Tziganes would be a most interesting and curious study. They are still, and ever will be, pariahs, beggars and thieves, musicians and poets, cowards and complainers, wanderers and heathen, but, oh, so picturesque! Their camp, no matter where it is pitched in the wide plain, is always in charming disorder, and of a marvelous color, especially in the evening, when the huge red sun of Romania sets upon the violet horizon beneath the mighty green dome of heaven. The women of the camp wear garments of every imaginable hue, from tender green to brick red and orange yellow. Their nut-brown children run about half-naked, their little shirts just covering their shoulders and a bit of their necks. There sit the men, with tangled hair and soft velvety eyes, grouped about the fire, their naked feet against the copper kettles they are tinkering; or we see them gathered about the timber-yards or buildings where they are employed, running about the scaffoldings with the suppleness of Indians, in attitudes and positions that are always charming. Their language is as sonorous as beaten brass, and their songs are most beautiful; but it is only with reluctance that they will let anyone hear them.

One of the most interesting sights of Bucharest is the great Fair, to which all flock to buy, amongst other things, everything that is needed to celebrate the Fête of the Dead. This week is one long delight to children. In spite of the broiling sun, in spite of the smothering dust, thousands of carriages succeed each other in the long street (Calea Moshilor[84]) leading to the Fair, which is held in a place called Moshi, in memory of a great battle fought on this spot between Matei Basarab and Radu, who tried to take Bucharest with an army of Moldavians and Tartars. "And the women and children", says the chronicler, "climbed upon the flowering hedges to see the war wage." Tramway cars and carriages overflow with people, every window is packed with gaily decked heads, some very pretty faces amongst them,

---

[84] Calea Moşilor, a historic street in Bucharest.

and, once at the Fair, one wanders round in a labyrinth of little stalls, where terracotta pots, wooden pitchers, and glass necklaces are sold. One sees wagon-loads of handsome peasant women and pretty children driving off laden with purchases, and in the midst of the noise and confusion, the shouts, the brilliant colors, the bears and the giants, and the ever-thickening clouds of dust, you suddenly see the *calushar* dance begin. This is an old Romanian dance, derived from the ancient Saturnalia, or dance of Saturn, in which the herdsmen tried to hide that they had stolen away Jupiter to prevent Saturn from devouring him, as he had his other children. The dancers, dressed in white, with little bells on their legs, behave in the wildest way. They are in training long before, so as to be able to bear the fatigue of dancing in this way from Easter to Pentecost. They are led by a violinist, and one of them, his finger on his lips, maintains silence amongst the rest, threatening them with his staff if they speak. Saturn must not know from them where to find his son.

The Romanians express everything by dancing; men dance together, and women together. The soldiers in the barracks always manage to get a violin, a flute, or a bagpipe, on which someone plays a dance of some kind for them. On a campaign, in war, after the most fatiguing marches, in showers of shot and shell, they still dance, defying the projectiles, until one of the dancers is struck down. Then good-humor never fails, even in the hospital. The wounded amuse themselves by composing comedies to make those still in bed laugh, and act them with an animation, spirit, and power of imitation, which is perfectly marvelous.

Among the finest institutions of Bucharest are the hospitals. They have been so liberally endowed by former rulers that they have at the present time an income of three or four millions, and everyone is received and cared for gratis as long as he remains in bed. They have been partly rebuilt, and the new military hospital is constructed in accordance with all the latest scientific principles. A circle of military hospitals and barracks now surrounds the series of heights overlooking the royal countryseat, the old Cotroceni convent, and the cupola of the large orphanage sheltering four hundred orphans. Further off is a second *enceinte*, that of the fortifications, for from time immemorial Bucharest has always been a citadel – a strategic post of great importance.

The transformation of Bucharest into a fine modern town in the style of modern taste is now complete. It is now a town intersected with canals, well irrigated, adorned with grand buildings, such as the Athenaeum, the new Ministries, the Bank, the State Printing-Press, the Town-Hall, the Houses of Parliament, etc. The foundation of the Bacteriological Institute raises us to the level of the other scientific centers of Europe. But the picturesque Oriental Bucharest, the Bucharest, as big as Vienna, but with only 220,000 inhabitants, made up of little houses nestling in verdure, the Bucharest in which one could point out the houses of Monsieur this and Madame that (giving the *noms de guerre* of the persons indicated), has disappeared, to give place to a town just like any other. It only appears Oriental to those who come from the West. Those who come from Asia give a sigh of satisfaction as they cross the Danube. "Ah!" they say to themselves, "here we are in Europe."

Truly, we are remarkable sovereigns, for we have managed to accomplish in twenty-five years what it has taken others several centuries to achieve. We have created an army; on the arrival of the King[85] there was but one battery of artillery, now we have 700 cannons. Our first cruiser is the nucleus of a fleet. The State Budget, which before the arrival of the King was 38 millions, is now 150 millions. Political life has become comparatively calm and serious, and long periods elapse without changes in the Ministry or the dissolution of the Chambers. Railways intersect the country in every direction, taking grain to the sea, cattle to Italy, wood to Panama. There are schools everywhere, and we seem likely to suffer from having hastened our development so much, the upsetting of the equilibrium being especially felt in family life. We even make an attempt at socialism, so as to be quite abreast with modern civilization. But socialism takes root with difficulty in a country purely agricultural, where there are no industries, and where the farmers come quite naturally to consult their landlord, asking him whether it would be well for them to revolt – if they would really get more land by doing so, as the agitators tell them they would.

Romania bids fair to become what King Carol dreamt she might – a living artery of Europe. When the crown of the country, of the very existence of which he was ignorant, was offered to a young Hohenzollern prince, he opened the atlas, took a pencil, and seeing that a line drawn from London to Bombay passed through the principality which called him to be its head, he accepted the crown with these words:

"This is a country of the future!"

---

[85] King Carol I of Romania (1839-1914), the consort of Queen Elisabeth of Romania (Carmen Sylva), ruled as Prince of Romania from 1866 to 1881 and then as the first king of Romania until his death on 10 October 1914. His was the longest reign of a sovereign in Romanian history.

Queen Marie of Romania: My Country (fragments)

The Queen of a small Country! Those who are accustomed to see rulers of greater lands can little understand what it means. It means work and anxiety and hope, and great toiling for small results. But the field is large, and, if the heart be willing, great is the work. When young I thought it all work, uphill work; but the passing years brought another knowledge, a blessed knowledge, and now I know. This is a small country, a new country, but it is a country I love. I want others to love it also; therefore listen to a few words about it. Let me paint a few pictures, draw a few sketches as I have seen them, first with my eyes, then with my heart.

***

Once I was a stranger to this people; now I am one of them, and, because I came from so far, better was I able to see them with their good qualities and with their defects. Their country is a fruitful country, a country of vast plains, of waving corn, of deep forests, of rocky mountains, of rivers that in springtime are turbulent with foaming waters, that in summer are but sluggish streams lost amongst stones. A country where peasants toil 'neath scorching suns, a country untouched by the squalor of manufactories, a country of extremes where the winters are icy and the summers burning hot.

A link between East and West.

At first it was an alien country, its roads too dusty, too endless its plains. I had to learn to see its beauties – to feel its needs with my heart. Little by little the stranger became one of them, and now she would like the country of her birth to see this other country through the eyes of its Queen. Yes, little by little I learnt to understand this people, and little by little it learned to understand me. Now we trust each other, and so, if God wills, together we shall go towards a greater future!

My love of freedom and vast horizons, my love of open air and unexplored paths led to many a discovery. Alone I would ride for hours to reach a forlorn village, to see a crumbling church standing amongst its rustic crosses at a river's edge, or to be at a certain spot at sunset when sky and earth would be drenched with flaming red. Oh! The Romanian sunsets, how wondrous they are!

Once I was riding slowly homewards. The day had been torrid; the air was heavy with dust. In oceans of burnished gold, the cornfields spread before me. No breath of wind stirred their ripeness; they seemed waiting for the hour of harvest, proud of being the wealth of the land. As far as my eye could reach, cornfields, cornfields, dwindling away towards the horizon in a vapoury line. A blue haze lay over the world, and with it a smell of dew and ripening seed was slowly rising out of the ground. At the end of the road stood a well, its long pole like a giant finger pointing eternally to the sky. Beside it an old stone cross leaning on one side as though tired, a cross erected with the well in remembrance of someone who was dead... Peace enveloped me—my horse made no movement, it also was under the evening spell. From afar a herd of buffaloes came slowly towards me over the long straight road: an ungainly procession of beasts that might have belonged to antediluvian times. One by one they advance – mud-covered, patient, swinging their ugly bodies, carrying stiffly their heavily horned heads, their vacant eyes staring at nothing, though here and there with raised faces they seemed to be seeking something from the skies. From under their hoofs rose clouds of dust accompanying their every stride. The sinking sun caught hold of it, turning it into fiery smoke. It was as a veil of light spread over these beasts of burden, a glorious radiance advancing with them towards their rest. I stood quite still and looked upon them as they passed me one by one... And that evening a curtain seemed to have been drawn away from many a mystery. I had understood the meaning of the vast and fertile plain.

***

Twenty-three years have I now spent in this country, each day bringing its joy or its sorrow, its light or its shade; with each year my interests widened, my understanding deepened; I knew where I was needed to help.

I am not going to talk of my country's institutions, of its politics, of names known to the world. Others have done this more cleverly than I ever could. I want only to speak of its soul, of its atmosphere, of its peasants and soldiers, of things that made me love this country, that made my heart beat with its heart.

I have moved amongst the most humble. I have entered their cottages, asked them questions, taken their newborn in my arms. I talked their language awkwardly, making many a mistake; but, although a stranger, nowhere amongst the peasants did I meet with distrust or suspicion. They were ready to converse with me, ready to let me enter their cottages, and especially ready to speak of their woes. It is always of their woes that the poor have to relate, but these did it with singular dignity, speaking of death and misery with stoic resignation, counting the graves of their children as another would count the trees planted round his house. They are poor, they are ignorant, these peasants. They are neglected and superstitious, but there is a grand nobility in their race. They are frugal and sober, their wants are few, their desires limited; but one great dream each man cherishes in the depth of his heart: he wishes to be a landowner, to possess the ground that he tills; he wishes to call it his own. This they one and all told me; it was the monotonous refrain of all their talk.

***

When first I saw a Romanian village, with its tiny huts hidden amongst trees, the only green spots on the immense plains, I could hardly believe that families could inhabit houses so small. They resembled the houses we used to draw as children, with a door in the middle, a tiny window on each side, and smoke curling somewhere out of the heavily thatched roof. Often these roofs seem too heavy for the cottages; they seem to crush them, and the wide-open doors make them look as if they were screaming for help. In the evening the women sit with their distaffs spinning on the doorsteps, whilst the herds come tramping home through the dust, and the dogs bark furiously, filling the air with their clamor. Nowhere have I seen so many dogs as in a Romanian village – a sore trial to the rider on a frisky horse. All night long, the dogs bark, answering each other. They are never still; it is a sound inseparable from the Romanian night.

I always loved to wander through these villages. I have done so at each season, and every month has its charm. In springtime, they are half-buried in fruit-trees, a foamy ocean of blossoms out of which the round roofs of the huts rise like large grey clouds. Chickens, geese, and newly born pigs sport hither and thither over the doorsteps; early hyacinths and golden daffodils run loose in the untidy courtyards, where strangely shaped pots and bright rags of carpets lie about in picturesque disorder. Amongst all this the half-naked black-eyed children crawl about in happy freedom. Never was I able to understand how such large families, without counting fowls and many a four-footed friend, could find room in the two-minute chambers of which these huts are composed. In winter these villages are covered with snow; each hut is a white padded heap; all corners are rounded off so that every cottage has the aspect of being packed in cotton-wool. No efforts are made to clear away the drifts. The snow lies there where it has fallen; the small sledges bump over its inequalities, forming roads as wavy as a storm-beaten sea!

The Romanian peasant is never in a hurry. Time plays no part in his scheme of life. Accustomed to limitless horizons, he does not expect to reach the end of his way in a day. In summer the carts, in winter the sledges, move along those endless roads, slowly, resignedly, with untiring patience. Drawn by tiny, lean horses, the wooden sledges bump over the uneven snow, the peasant sits half-hidden amongst his stacks of wood, hay, or maize-stalks, according to the freight he may be transporting from place to place. Picturesque in his rough sheepskin coat, he is just as picturesque in summer in his white shirt and broad felt hat, contentedly lying upon his stacked-up corn, whilst his long-suffering oxen trudge away, seemingly as indifferent as their master to the length of the road. They are stone-grey, these oxen – lean, strong, with large-spread horns; their eyes are beautiful, with almost human look.

The Romanian road is a characteristic feature of the country. It is wide, it is dusty, generally it is straight, few trees shading its borders; mostly it is badly kept. But, like all things upon which civilization has not yet laid too heavy a hand, it has an indefinite charm – the charm of immensity, something dreamy, something infinite, something that need never come to an end... And along these roads the peasants' carts crawl, one after another in an endless file, enveloped in clouds of dust. If night overtake them on the way, the oxen are unyoked, the carts are drawn up beside the ditch, till the rising dawn reminds them that there are still many miles to their goal... When it rains the dust turns to mud; the road becomes then a river of mud! Romania is not a country of violent colors. There is a curious unity in its large horizons, its dusty roads, its white-clad peasants, its rough wooden carts. Even oxen and horses seem to have toned down to grey or dun, so as to become one with a sort of dreamy haziness that lies over the whole. It is only the sunsets that turn all these shadowy tints into a sudden marvel of color, flooding earth and sky with wondrous gold. I have seen haystacks change into fiery pyramids, rivers into burning ribbons, and pale, tired faces light up with a marvelous glow. A fleeting hour this hour of sunset, but each time it bursts upon me as an eternally renewed promise sent by God above. Perchance 'tis in winter and autumn that these sunsets are most glorious, when the earth is tired, when its year's labor is done, or when it is sleeping 'neath its shimmering shroud of snow, guarding in its bosom the harvest that is to come.

***

Very different are the mountain villages from those of the plain. The cottages are less miserable, less small, the thatched roofs are replaced by roofs of shingle that shine like silver in the sun. Richer and more varied are the peasants' costumes; the colors are brighter, and often a tiny flower-filled garden surrounds the house. Autumn is the season to visit these villages amongst the hills; autumn, when the trees are a flaming glory, when the dying year sends out a last effort of beauty before being vanquished by frost and snow.

Many a hearty welcome has been given me in these little villages, the peasants receiving me with flower-filled hands. At the first sign of my carriage, troops of rustic riders gallop out to meet me, scampering helter-skelter on their shaggy little horses, bearing banners or flowering branches, shouting with delight. Full tilt they fly after my carriage, raising clouds of dust. Like their masters, the ponies are wild with excitement; all is noise, color, movement; joy runs wild over the earth. The bells of the village ring, their voices are full of gladness, they too cry out their welcome. Crowds of gaily-clad women and children flock out of the houses, having plundered their gardens so as to strew flowers before the feet of their queen.

The church generally stands in the middle of the village; here the sovereign must leave her carriage, and, surrounded by an eager, happy crowd, she is led towards the sanctuary, where the priest receives her at the door, cross in hand. Wherever she moves the crowd moves with her; there is no awkwardness, no shyness, but neither is there any pushing or crushing. The Romanian peasants remain dignified; they are seldom rowdy in their joy.

They want to look at one, to touch one, to hear one's voice; but they show no astonishment and little curiosity. Mostly their expression remains serious, and their children stare at one with grave faces and huge, impressive eyes. It is only the galloping riders who become loud in their joy.

There are some strange customs amongst the peasants, curious superstitions. Romania being a dry country, it is lucky to arrive with rain: it means abundance, fertility, the hope of a fine harvest – wealth. Sometimes as I went through the villages, the peasant women would put large wooden buckets full of water before their threshold; a full vessel is a sign of good luck. They will even sprinkle water before one's feet, always because of that strange superstition, that water is abundance, and, when the great one comes amongst them, honor must be done unto her in every way. I have seen tall, handsome girls step out of their houses to meet me with overflowing water-jars on their heads; on my approach, they stood quite still, the drops splashing over their faces so as well to prove that their pitchers were full. It is lucky to meet a cart full of corn or straw coming towards one; but an empty cart is a sure sign of ill luck!

Many a time, in places I came to, the inhabitants have crowded around me, kissing my hands, the hem of my dress, falling down to kiss my feet, and more than once have they brought me their children, who made the sign of the cross before me as though I had been the holy image in a church. At first it was difficult unblushingly to accept such homage, but little by little I got accustomed to these loyal manifestations; half humble, half proud, I would advance amongst them, happy to be in their midst.

Queen Marie of Romania: The Country That I Love. An Exile's Memories (fragments)

"Why This Book Was Written" (Preface)

I feel that a few words are necessary to explain when and why this book was written. At one time I thought of modifying it, but reading it through again, as its author, I well realized that that throbbing note of suppressed anguish running through the whole was the real thread holding its pages together; if changed, much of their meaning, may I even say of their charm, would be lost.

At Jassy, after our retreat, and all the grief and misery attached to it, we lived through a time of intensest and most demoralizing depression. We had been hard hit, very hard; three quarters of our country had had to be surrendered; winter was upon us, and with it famine, want, and pestilence. Spirits were at lowest ebb, and confusion reigned in our midst.

I stood in the center of it all, myself a refugee, a queen with empty hands, a mother who had just buried her youngest child[86], one of the first victims of the epidemics raging around us – I felt this depression at first, as one too broken by personal grief to be able to help others. Little by little, however, the intense suffering around me tore me away from my own sorrow, gave me the ardent and intense desire to be of use to my people, and through them to my country, at a moment when all hope seemed to be abandoning us.

There was something within me which told me that my voice above all others was now necessary to them; we had become so small, so shivering, so helpless; and in our more primitive countries the idea of "a mother" nearby, to whom all can turn, is a great comfort, I might even say the great-est comfort. But how get into nearer and direct contact with the masses? How, as queen, raise my voice, so that it could be heard by thousands and thousands…?

Then, one day, an old professor[87] came to me, himself a writer – a friend. He too had lost everything; but, like his queen, he felt that some reaction must be brought about, some effort, some outward sign that faithful hearts were watching over those too broken, too poor, too miserable to lift their heads and struggle on. This old friend had just read *My Country*, published in England; he approved of it, said I must write more, that – this was a

---

[86] The youngest son of Queen Marie, Prince Mircea, had died aged three on 2 November 1916, shortly before the occupation of Bucharest by the enemy troops in the First World War.

[87] Nicolae Iorga (1871-1940) was a Romanian historian and politician. He translated several writings of Queen Marie into Romanian.

good beginning, but that there were many beauties left to describe – that the Romanians were happy, flattered that I, their queen, the princess born in a far-off land, should have so deeply absorbed the charm of my adopted country as to be able to describe it so accurately. "I shall translate it," he said, "but you must add to it; so many have left their homes, have been torn away from what they loved, that you will reach their hearts by speaking to them about the cherished regions they had to abandon. Chapter by chapter we shall publish it in the most popular newspaper, the one which finds its way into the trenches, into the villages even. In that way your voice will reach those who have never even seen you; you will become a reality to them, they will feel your heart beating with theirs, your soul suffering with theirs, and it will be a wonderful thing for them and for you. Not many sovereigns are given your gift, use it; you must come forward now, put aside all hesitation, all diffidence, all self-consciousness; I shall translate what you write as you write it, and if you vary the places you describe, you will always be sure to touch one or the other of your readers who come from that part – believe me, it is your duty to use that power of expression given to you – it may be an unusual thing for a queen to do, but is not our situation tragically unusual? Is it not the duty of each to help when he can, as he can...?"

That was what the old patriot had to say, and considering his arguments sufficient, I put all timidity on one side and began talking to my people. At first I wrote a few short pages telling them how my heart was with them, how I shared their sorrow, their anxiety, their humiliation; encouraging them to face the adversity of today in the firm intention of remaining steadfast, of not giving way to despair; and when I had stirred up their emotions and made them listen, I kept their interest alive by publishing every other week a chapter describing one or another of the parts torn from us. They got accustomed to wait impatiently for the appearance of these chapters, which later were printed in a small volume, upon atrocious war-paper, with still more atrocious ink. Fifteen thousand of these ugly little volumes were snapped up in no time, and when I wandered amongst the sick and wounded, through hundreds of hospitals, they kept asking for "the Queen's little book," which each sufferer wanted to lay under his pillow as a precious possession.

These pages have never yet been published in English; in which language they were written, as I can write in no other. Of course, I cannot expect that, in our more unemotional after-war days, they should awaken one quarter of the interest which they then aroused in the hearts of my stricken Romanians; but, perhaps, even today, they may please some. There are no war-pictures amongst them – those I collected in another volume – but the anguish of that time rings through them, and that is what makes them poignant to the one who wrote them, and I hope to be forgiven for not purging them of that underlying note of tragedy felt through every line. The original volume ends after the chapter about Jassy; but as it is being published so many years later, I felt that perhaps it would add to the book's interest if I wrote a few after-war pages, speaking of the joy of return, a joy mixed with much pain, as can well be imagined; but, all the same, it is a story that ends well, and there is something in that…

The illustrations were made by my daughter, the Queen of Greece, then quite a girl; they may be faulty, but they have the right atmosphere, the right feeling, for she too loves her country well!

Marie, Queen of Romania

Jassy

Patiently have you followed me in my many wanderings through the country I love; I have led you from plain to mountain, from mountain to sea, from the broad Danube to the hills of Vâlcea, where I lingered in the quiet monasteries so dear to my heart, and now I feel that so as not to weary you with too many pictures, I must close these pages, although still many visions float before my eyes. Indefinitely could I go on writing, for rich and wonderful is this country, picturesque, poetical, full of penetrating charm, and doubly precious at its hour of distress; yet I feel that for a while I must lay down my pen, guarding within my soul other pictures that one day, perchance, I shall paint for you, but not now… not now…

All the places that I have spoken about in this volume are places from which we are now separated by a cruel fate, places we are yearning to get back to, homes we had to forsake, fields that the invader is reaping, regions we have had to give up; but before I quite leave you, I would talk of the town which opened out her arms to us when we were wanderers, having had to quit our hearths, not knowing where to take shelter. We asked much of her, but she was generous; she took us up into her bosom, although many of us had neglected her in the days of prosperity and peace.

Jassy! The name has a special sound in our ears! Particularly at a moment when new and unheard-of dangers stare us in the face. When we had to flee from Bucharest, Jassy was the town we all flocked to; Jassy[88], once herself a proud capital, who had been sacrificed to another's glory, and who had suddenly to harbor those who had ignored her for so many years. She did her best to receive us, but her slender resources were sorely tried! Jassy! Town of shifting fates, town dear to every Moldavian heart, once a cherished and blooming center, in later years much neglected, much forsaken, living alone by her remembrances, abandoned even of those who loved her best. Her name has retained the sweetness of things once cherished, as the

---

[88] When Cuza Voda, in 1859, united Moldavia and Walachia, Bucharest was chosen as capital, much to Jassy's distress. She always has kept a feeling of resentment against Bucarest ever since. [Note in the first edition].

name of a woman formerly loved for her beauty, but whom the passing years have handed over to oblivion with so much else.

Situated upon several hills, amidst verdure and gardens, surrounded by fertile regions, Jassy has every reason to be proud of her position, a position that many a town might envy. Her churches are not to be counted, and seen from afar at dusk, when mist floats like a veil above her imperfections, Jassy has the air of an enchanted city, out of which her sanctuaries' many-shaped towers and cupolas rise like ghosts of past glories that nothing can efface.

But, through all ages, Jassy's geographical situation has been unlucky, therefore has she known invasion in every form, and with invasion, change and disaster, fire, famine and fear. So varied have been the phases of her destiny, so manifold the masters who claimed her, succeeding each other with such bewildering rapidity, that in reading the old chronicles, the mind gets confused, and it is difficult for the uninitiated to follow so intricate a tale. Standing, however, as we are before events great and fearful, I can but cast a look backwards, comparing today with yesterday, marveling how this unfortunate town has again and again been subjected to every form of disaster. Yet she stands and lives, undaunted by misfortune, no vicissitude having been able to tear her from the people to whom she belongs. I have tried to live in her past, so as better to understand her present, but today it would lead me too far were I to relate her whole history.

At the entrance of the town, on the road of Nicolina, stands a tall stone cross. Old, grey and venerable, it appears to be a guardian watching over the city's safety, a guardian in whose heart some ancient tale lies dormant. Often I wondered what event it recalled – now I know – only for a few days have I known! And I can but consider it a good omen that its story was revealed to me just now... The cross goes by the name of Ferenz, and marks a place where fallen foes lie buried... Between the years 1716-1717, during the reign of Mihai Vodă Racoviță, the Austrian-Germans, who were fighting the Turks near our frontiers, made incursions into Moldavia, taking possession for a time of Caşin and Neamţ. Some of their troops, led by traitors through the valley of Oituz, penetrated even into Jassy, but they were beaten back, and many were made prisoners in a bloody skirmish between the fortress of Cetăţuia and the convent of Frumoasa. The bodies of the fallen, with their leader, Ferenz, were buried at Nicolina, "the earth being heaped high above them", so says the chronicle; "and those also who tried to betray their country were killed and buried with the foe." And now the old cross stands on guard, high up above the town, its timeworn face turned towards the rising sun... Thus even at the gates of a city can the foe be turned back in shame!

Foes also of another kind has Jassy known: During the reign of Miron-Vodă Barnovski (1626-1629) there was a terrible winter, which now still goes by the name of Barnovski's winter; people died in the streets of cold and hunger, and wolves were supposed to have come as far as the outskirts of the town. Some years later, under the reign of Ștefăniță-Vodă Lupu, famine raged in the city, and the story goes that the population, having nothing to eat, fed upon reeds from the swamps about the town, so that the prince received the nickname of Papură-Vodă, "Reed Prince". Also in the winter 1684-85 there was famine, and dark tales are still told by the people about those times.

The reign of Mihail Grigore Sturdza (1834-1849) was marked by more than one misfortune. Twice Jassy was nearly burnt to the ground; in 1849 cholera made cruel ravages amongst her people, and the fearful epidemic was followed by a winter of deadly frost, by famine and misery of every sort, for it is a well-known saying that "misfortune never comes alone!"

But guests less lugubrious have also been known within Jassy's walls. In the year 1711 Peter the Great was received here with great ceremony and many honors by Dimitrie-Vodă Cantemir, who was known to the world at large for his erudition. "On this occasion," says the chronicle, "the Moldavian noblemen tasted 'French wine' for the first time," that is to say, champagne!

Stanislaus Leszynski, King of Poland, was also once a guest within Jassy's walls; having come with the intention of meeting King Charles XII of Sweden, he lived for a while in a private house. "When the Prince of the Land got wind of his presence, he showed the king all honor, and installed him grandly within the palace of Trei Ierarhi (Three Saints)".

"At an earlier date, the Sultan Mohammed IV, who was fighting the Poles, entered Jassy, where he promenaded about in great state, welcomed with much honor by Gheorghe Vodă Duca, who treated him royally; but the town was greatly shocked by the Sultan's having ordered a 'muezzin' to chant Turkish prayers from the belfry of St. Nicolai, one of Jassy's most cherished churches. Thereafter, for a long time the church was considered desecrated, and could no more be used before being sanctified anew."

In the year 1769 the Great Catherine took possession of Moldavia, and General Rumianzow was established as Governor. The Russian occupation lasted five years. Catherine's best known favorite, Patiomkine, died in Jassy, and it is said that his body lay in state in the beautiful old church of Golia.

Under the reign of Grigore Alexandru Ghica, Austria suddenly laid hands upon Bucovina, the port raising no protest; on the contrary, Turkey made a convention with Austria, in which it ceded these provinces over which it had but a protective right. All protest on the part of Moldavia was in vain, Grigore Vodă paying with his head for the efforts he made to uphold his country's interest.

From the year 1828 to 1834 the Russians once more occupied Moldavia, and Jassy was governed by Count Kiseleff, an able organizer, whose final departure the town had many reasons to regret. Between the years 1849-1856

Jassy was taken possession of in turns by the Russians, Turks and Austrians. Her vicissitudes, as may be seen, were without end, till finally, on the fifth of January (old style) 1859, Alexandru Ioan Cuza was unanimously elected Prince of Moldavia, and in the same month became Prince of Walachia, thus at last uniting both parts of the country under one scepter. Once, in the year 1600, the great national hero, Michael the Brave, had realized this dream, but only for the short period of five months. Cuza Vodă reigned at first with two governments, one in Jassy, one in Bucharest. Finally Bucharest was chosen as capital, prince and government establishing themselves definitely in the town. Henceforward Jassy had to look on at another's growing importance, whilst she was left to mourn past glories! Cuza Vodă's reign lasted seven years.

I have but roughly sketched some of Jassy's changing fortunes, picking out a tale here and there, without any effort at sequence or order, these being but lightly sketched pages – a picture-book, full of visions of places we love, without any larger pretensions; therefore would I now move away from the past to the Jassy of today.

The sad events of last autumn suddenly tore Jassy from her somnolent dreams of the past. Her streets, for many years so desolate and silent, teemed again with eager crowds; her houses, many of which had long since been shut up, had to open wide their doors to receive more guests than they could hold. Her dusty peace was scattered to the four winds by the inflow of all those who, having had to quit the capital, had come to take refuge within the walls of the town they had handed over to oblivion and regret. Almost brutal was this invasion, of which Jassy did not wholly approve – she would have preferred a less violent monopolizing of her solitude. Her wishes, however, were not consulted; she was simply obliged to strain her slender means to the utmost to try and harbor those who had no more homes of their own.

A certain aggrieved bitterness did the quiet town feel at first; why should she thus be taken possession of, after having been neglected so long? Why should her fragile pavements be shaken by a thousand motors? Why should those who had left her to crumble away suddenly establish themselves here as masters, when in the days of prosperity she had been ignored? Into the bargain, those who had quit the capital felt like exiles in this other town, and but slowly resigned themselves to what fate had decreed!

I, also, at first found it hard to settle down in a new center, under such circumstances, with so overwhelming a grief in my heart. Had I not left one of my own over there – where I could return no more! And then, the danger was not at an end; the enemy was on our heels, our army was retreating, our allies an unknown quantity; was it worth while working, beginning all over again? Would what we built stand? Or would our renewed efforts have to be surrendered into the invader's hands? Tragic hours! Hours of doubt and suffering, hours of cruel suspense, when effort seemed vain, when we all stood straining our ears, listening for the advancing feet of disaster – our hearts beating, our souls heavy with dread!

And yet, those in trouble could not wait; the hungry clamored for food, the naked for clothing, the wounded for care, the homeless for a roof over their heads! With the grim boom of cannon in our ears, we had to set about our labor, regardless of difficulties, never matter if what we built up was not destined to stand; it had to be done! Thus, little by little, did hard work help each man to overcome his sorrow, to strain his nerves to an effort that every day anew seemed far beyond his strength.

I will not enumerate all that was missing, all that had to be created under circumstances I hardly find words to describe. The fearfulness of our last winter lies graven in letters of fire upon the mind of each. It was uphill work, and often it was hopelessly incomplete, but those who were mourning their lost homes, and those who had at first resented so untimely an invasion overcame their grief and their grievances in the mutual effort for good.

I had known Jassy in other years – in the years of peace I had come to her sometimes, too seldom, though through no fault of my own, and always had she received me loyally, with manifestations of great joy. Now I had come to her a broken-hearted mother, a queen seeking refuge, like many other, an exile from my own hearth, and Jassy took me up in my hour of trouble and helped me, and little by little became my new home. I had always felt tenderly towards her, for in the days of my extreme youth, when first I came as a bride to this country, there had been rumors that we, the young ones, would settle down in the second capital of the land. Jassy desired it, and after my first visit to her picturesque solitude I would gladly have made my home within her walls. But the old sovereigns needed us. So long had they pined for children that they could not contemplate the thought of our living far from their side. Thus Jassy saw us seldom, but always with joy! I remember how the sun shone the first time I came to Jassy, I remember the welcoming faces that crowded the streets, the cheers, the flowers – the many flowers that were thrown into my carriage – I remember that I was but eighteen and full of hope...

How different was my last coming! I was in mourning, and there was no sunshine, no flowers, no glad cries of welcome, only anxiously inquiring faces, and no other sound but the far-off cannon tolling our fate. Unannounced, I stole into the town, a refugee, houseless, homeless, without my youngest child... Winter was approaching, and something like despair lay at the roots of my heart. Yet irresistibly hope rose anew, timidly at first, but each day stronger, little by little overcoming tears, sorrow and regret. Oh, Jassy! Shall we ever forget the past months spent within thy gates! Indescribable are the sufferings thy streets have witnessed; snow has lain mountain-high against thy house-sides, crowds of beggars have haunted thy pavements, and more than one, overcome by want, has lain down on thy stones to die! I have seen thee a picture of misery – shaken by dread, shivering with cold; into thy darkest and most dismal corners have I penetrated, searching for those who needed help – giving all I could, but it was always too little, for all my love and all my pity could ease but a particle of the distress I met at every step! Somber indeed was thy aspect during those winter months. Oh, Jassy! I felt how each house harbored hidden suffering, cruel secrets seemed hovering behind each wall. Food was scarce, wood still scarcer. Thy hospitals were overfull, so that those not yet completely recovered had to make place for others whose needs seemed more urgent; therefore did such pale faces haunt thy streets. Like ghosts, our underfed soldiers wandered from shelter to shelter, often finding nowhere to lay their fevered heads. We worked, we toiled, we tried to do marvels, but transports were insufficient, communication interrupted; everywhere the snow shut us away behind relentless barriers, cutting us off from what we would reach!... And there came a ghastly moment when the boards were insufficient for making coffins for the dead! Oh! The melancholy of those funerals stealing through thy streets! How many of them have I met... An old white horse, harnessed to a nameless something resembling a box the color of night. Bump, bump! Backwards and forwards it wandered over the uneven snow. Bump, bump! – The white horse each day more weary, more bony, more like a phantom horse! And many who met this uncanny vehicle turned away their faces, unable to bear the sight... Whilst overhead the crows darkened the heavens with their sinister flight...

I sometimes tried to get beyond the city, so as to relieve distress in other parts; but again and again did the snowdrifts baffle me, preventing my reaching the villages I had set out to seek. Sadly I had to turn back, but not before having contemplated great wastes become pathless, studded with bodies of fallen horses with stiffly outstretched legs, and on the horizon huts of misery buried in snow. And I knew that over there beyond, where I could not penetrate, there were misfortunes I hungered to relieve, but had to abandon to fate! And everywhere crows were feasting – they alone had enough to eat... Thus was the winter, the winter I spent in Jassy; yet, endless as it was, it came to an end!...

Doubly precious, because so ardently yearned for, spring at last dawned in glory over our distress – and then, oh, Jassy! How different was thy aspect; and, because of the sorrow shared with thee, we suddenly realized how close thou hadst grown to our hearts! All of a sudden didst thou become beautiful, oh, town of hunger, pestilence and tears! Thy gardens filled with flowers, and these were brought to me in great bunches by those who wished me not to pine too grievously for the gardens I had lost. Clusters of lilacs nodded to me over time-scarred walls, great beds of violet iris gladdened the humblest corner; once more, wherever I went, flowers were thrown into my carriage; even the trams had bouquets of blue scilla at-tached to their lanterns, and each passer-by carried a blossom in his hand… Like a dwindling nightmare, the dark hours rolled away; the most wretched, the most abandoned, crawling out to gaze at the sun, felt that somewhere there might still be hope! No more did our soldiers slink through the streets, vagrants who had nowhere to go; their step became lighter, less dragging, till once again they trod the earth like warriors be-lieving in victory, like heroes ready for battle and success...

Though my work was nonetheless arduous, it became sweeter; the hori-zons opened, the snow had melted – now I was free to wander far and wide. Then dear to me indeed became thy surroundings. Oh, Jassy! I dis-covered beauty in every place. Thy undulating hills were now a green glo-ry; fresh and marvelous, teeming with fresh life, was God's good earth; death seemed to have been defeated. Yet, in a quiet corner, I knew of a thousand and more crosses bearing evidence that the past horror had been no dream! Poor little forest of crosses, each marking the graves of ten men, a humble and insufficient memorial to those who had paid the price of war – bare mounds beneath the crosses, countless in number, which in vain I tried to cover with the sweet, bright flowers of spring… But there were too many crosses, too many graves – I could not even count them! Overcome, I stood before them with bowed head... And I knew that these were but a small number of those crosses, and that in all the four corners of our coun-try, and of so many other countries, there were silent places where these rough wooden effigies did not even bear the names of the dead. I know of many hidden cemeteries all around the town, where field had to be added to field, the space within the ancient boundaries having become too small. More than one pilgrimage have I made to these gardens of peace, and standing amongst the nameless mounds, with tears in my eyes, I have gazed towards the city, enwrapped in veils of mist – thinking of that other small grave I had to abandon over there with so much else! Ardent prayers have I breathed over those fallen sons of mothers who will never see them again... But the lilacs were in bloom, the birds were singing, and new life was springing – even out of the graves of the dead.

Everything had become easier since the snow no longer formed a barrier between us and the outer world; we were as prisoners released from bond-age; something like sacred joy filled our souls that had been so troubled, and much good work was done. Indeed, we were struggling against a widespread epidemic of typhus, part of our country was invaded, and oth-er terrors haunted our every step. But spring had overcome winter – was it not a sign that life must overcome death? Thus did each man go more light-ly to work and new confidence filled every heart. Verily it was resurrection, and all worked together so as to render it more complete, each man accord-ing to his means.

Every evening, when my work was over, I would have my horse saddled, and ride far out into the hills that surround Jassy, galloping for miles over unknown paths, coming to spots of green peace, wondrous in contrast with all the horrors I had seen. Each new beauty was as a balm to my sorrow-filled heart, yet awaking within me a fearful yearning for the home I had lost! Full of almost painful emotion were these evening hours in silent communion with nature's renewal; a great peace and at the same time an incommensurable sadness did I feel. God had made the world so beautiful, it was man who turned it into such a hell! There upon those billowing heights, far from noise, labor, and suffering, I once again recognized the earth as nature had made it, without the havoc man had wrought on its face. Oh! The glory of the sunsets over those quiet spots! Their inimitable perfection was an answer to many a question that weighted my soul, and dear to me beyond words became these regions revealed to me with the year's new awakening to hope.

Later, when the ground became too hard for riding, it was by motor that I prolonged my evening wanderings far and wide. Each day I discovered new places, each one full of its own charm; picturesque villages, deep forests full of shade, rivers like silver ribbons, winding through mist-softened plains, lonely churches and old convents hidden amidst trees. In each hamlet the children became my friends; my hands were never empty; wherever I went eager faces met me, and many a blessing has made sweeter my road… With the lengthening of the days, my drives also became longer, and ever more friendly these regions seemed to me. I began to love them dearly.

Day by day I saw the seed that had first resembled meadows of green grass grow taller and taller, ripening beneath the increasing heat of the sun, till the day came when cornfields in glorious abundance covered the low hills with their rippling oceans of gold. One thing never seen elsewhere filled me with rapture; enormous fields of sunflowers, acres and acres of these giants, a blazing sea of color, unlike aught else; I came upon them in many places, their resinous smell perfuming the air, whilst their large faces seemed eternally searching the great light which had given them their name; a glorious feast of color delighting the eye.

Another discovery did I make: Jassy was the town of lilies! There came a season when this city, lately but a world of darkness and sorrow, turned into one great garden in which this flower of flowers ruled supreme! Everywhere I found them in tall clusters of immaculate white – imparting a sacramental air to the poorest patch, giving strange dignity to the humblest cottage – their proud stems bending slightly beneath the wind's caress. Lilies having always been my favorite flower, this beautiful abundance was as a special revelation sent to endear the town to my heart; and all of a sudden my rooms that, in winter, had been so barren turned into a fragrant bower of the flower I loved best! Beauty has a strange power over man's heart; it helps him over many a grief, leading him through this "valley of tears" towards the secrets of God. When unexpectedly I come upon a bed of lilies sending up their proud glory out of a cracked and thirsting ground it is as though I must fall down and worship the Great Hand that creates such marvels; at those moments I suddenly seem to understand the mystery of hidden truths generally too deep for human hearts to conceive. At such hours no sadness seems to count, hope rises triumphant; the grave even loses its terror, and the infinite mercy of God lies like a benediction over the earth… But haltingly can I speak of such wonders, my words are too small, the soul's emotion cannot be contained within the speech of man! Yet, ofttimes, has a revelation of beauty lifted my heart above sorrow towards a deeper understanding lying beneath the dust that blinds our mortal eye. I cannot clearly explain why. But at such moments I have suddenly realized that suffering is the great master, and, as in a clear vision, I have understood that a people which has known how to suffer has also a right to live. No fire purifies as the fire of sacrifice, no flame mounts straighter to the Heart of God.

Therefore, oh, my country, never matter what thy tribulations have been, nor what they still may be! It is through the flame that the steel must pass before becoming a good strong sword. Let thy faith be unshaken and hold high thy hope; greater art thou because of thy troubles and because of the way thou hast borne them, more worthy art thou to win! The souls of our dead heroes have built your road to fame, earthly success has no meaning unless the honor of a country stand mountain-high. And if thou, Mircea, my little son, didst forsake me in an hour of darkness it was, perchance, so that those fallen heroes should find one of my children waiting to greet them in God's great sky above! Still, many an hour separates us from victory, but sacrifices so great and suffering so heavy cannot be all in vain. My country and people have passed through the fire, and because of their ever-growing heroism the day will come, little Mircea – of that I am certain – when, returning from exile, in an ecstasy of gratitude I shall fall down and kiss the stone of your grave. Dear God. Thus let it be…

Bran Castle

Before closing these pages, I would paint a last picture, a new picture, an after-war picture, but with something of the peacefulness in it of those pre-war visions so dear to my heart.

On the other side of our mountains, now no more barriers separating our people in two halves, stands a small castle on a steep jutting rock. It is but a rustic stronghold, in olden times a fortress, built perhaps by crusaders, but more probably a point of defence from the days of the Turkish invasions. Against a background of hills and mountains, of which the lower ones are thickly covered with forests of fir and beach; solid, stolid, and lonesome it stands, a watchman placed between plain and highland, guarding the entrance of a mountain-pass. Its walls, which are high and several yards in breadth, are built according to the level and shape of the rock, and are so welded together with their foundation as to have actually become one. Several irregular-shaped towers rise from these immense impregnable-looking walls, whilst a narrow stone stairway, composed of many, many steps, runs steeply up to a heavily barred door, sole entry to the fortress, a secretive, mysterious-looking little place. It has no special pretensions to beauty, no distinctive architecture; it is just a solid, primitive, pugnacious looking stronghold, and if it has a story, it has kept it locked away in its solitary stone heart.

In former days, many years ago, when it was still on alien ground, I had once driven past this queer little fortress; its extreme loneliness had attracted me; I wondered to whom it might belong and why it looked so forsaken and uncared for; it filled me with the desire to possess it and to awake it to life. It was but a fleeting vision, passed in a flash, effaced by the dust of my motor, just a dream-picture quickly left behind, but I never forgot it: strong, squat, uncommon of shape; standing out on its rock against a wooded background, guardian of the mountain road and of the several small villages lying at its feet.

When these regions became ours, one of my first visits was to this solitary fortress, which had made such a strong impression upon me, wondering if it still existed, fearing that it might have crumbled with so much else, since through this valley too the enemy had swept towards our plains. To my intense relief, there it stood untouched with its air of pugnacious strength, a stolid, lonesome, lifeless, almost eyeless thing. We decided to explore it; so, full of anticipation we climbed the precipitous road leading up to it, climbed its many steps of stone, and having secured its key, opened the secretive-looking door, sole entry to its mysteries... What a quaint, delicious little place! A small inner court entirely shut in by high, intensely thick walls, pierced here and there by small loopholes, rather shaky wooden galleries running round those walls somewhere near the top. Tiny disconnected stairs leading into the different towers, into several low-domed whitewashed rooms, others with heavily beamed ceilings, the whole squat, incredibly solid, in good repair, not at all a ruin, but as bare and empty as a forsaken heart. A silent, sad little place, but extraordinarily attractive, with a superb view from each wee window, and to me it seemed to have a sleeping soul longing to be awaked...

My children and I immediately began weaving dreams around Bran or Brana, the strange, solitary, fascinating little castle, which belonged to no one; whom nobody had ever cared for, which had never been loved nor inhabited as long as anyone could remember; Bran, Brana... That weird, picturesque, poetical, mysterious little place...

And one day… – for such are the opening words to events big and small – one day, a deputation from the town of Braşov, to which it seems Bran belonged, came to me, and with words resembling words used through all ages when offering gifts to royal people, Bran was offerd to me! Bran or Brana, the little castle, the solitary, rugged, pugnacious-looking little stronghold was offered to me!...

I could hardly believe my ears, but they had brought all sorts of papers with them, with seals and signatures and solemn-sounding formulas according to the law. I, too, had to sign my name; it was all done with much ceremony, many good wishes and blessings, and fine, kind words. Then the deputation departed, leaving me with that solemn, signed, sealed paper – and Bran was mine, was mine!...

Like the old gentleman who once, many years ago, had left me his forsaken villa in the melancholy weedgrown park, had the town of Brasov been pleased with the thought that their lonesome little castle should be given over into the hands of one who would care for it, and awake it to a life it had never known? I cannot say, but the glorious fact remained; whatever may have been their motive, they had come and had offered it to me. Henceforth, Brana, the beloved, belonged to me!

That was a glorious moment when I went to take possession of my own little fortress, and all the peasants from miles around rejoiced with me, for my coming was a blessed event in their careworn, colorless lives. Now the lonesome, soulless, masterless little stronghold would awake to life, would look down from its height, would suddenly become a point of gravitation, a protector watching over their weal and woe. They came in crowds to welcome me, all in their best Sunday costumes, to wish me good luck, good health, a long life; they came to express their satisfaction that the castle had become mine, they also came, of course, with their complaints and needs, and petitions, for one is not queen and mother of a people solely to receive congratulations and to hear expressions of content!

Oh! With what joy and interest I set about making my Bran liveable, putting in certain comforts, letting in more light, repairing the shaky galleries, creating new rooms in odd corners; making use of the huge timbered loft, using waste spaces, digging out secret little passages and stairs, turning queer little dungeons into living rooms, but withal taking greatest care to preserve the austere, primitive aspect of the place.

We have a dear old architect belonging to our household, inherited from King Carol's times. He, too, had always dreamed that one day it would be granted him to repair an old castle; now this quaint building has become his pet work. He has settled down there like an owl in an old wall and devotes all his love, all his skill, to make a real treasure out of my precious little place. But we are in no hurry to complete our work, we are like children with a beloved toy of which we never weary; each year we improve something, without allowing its original aspect to change. It is still the impregnable, pugnacious little fortress, but now it has been given a soul, its eyes are open, it is wide awake, joyfully alive...

Within, its walls are still severely whitewashed. Bran's rough, rustic appearance has been preserved, its several stairs are still steep and crooked, the rooms uneven of shape, built according to the rock beneath, nearly each one on a different level. You have to be careful not to stumble over the thresholds, not to hit your head against the low lintels of the doors; in fact, all the time you have to keep looking out because you are for ever turning unexpected corners and never know when you are going to encounter a step, a low ceiling, a projecting beam. Some of my own generation have shaken their heads, little approving of my taste for such an unpractical habitation; "at your age," they rather unkindly remarked! But I love it! And with that all is said! Something of the child has remained in my heart perhaps, a love of romance, discovery, adventures; besides, I invite few of my own generation to live there with me, they only come to see it, when I inhabit it; I take my children, their friends, or younger friends of my own, who see nothing but the virtues of my treasure!

Behind its incredibly thick walls I have collected a strange medley of old things of a more or less rustic kind: quaint carvings, ancient figures in wood, stone, or metal; figures which do not feel out of place in such austere medieval surroundings; strange old icons upon golden background, deliciously mellowed by time, old carpets and rugs, stone jars and mortars, bronze, copper, and brass vessels, peasant pottery from many lands; quaint old chests and cupboards, heavy old oaken tables, settles, and stools; but there are also huge soft easy-chairs, sofas, and couches, which, if the right colors and stuffs are chosen, harmonize agreeably with the rest, blending perfectly with their more austere companions. And everywhere, flowers, flowers, the brightest, the simplest, marigolds, calendulas, sunflowers, rubechias, representing a complete scale of oranges and yellows; then roses and asters, dahlias, lupins, larkspurs, and delphiniums, great flaming bunches of nasturtiums, huge proud nosegays of tiger-lilies and the beloved white cottage lily, each color finding its right background; taking a special value against the whitewashed walls, or on the time-blackened tables and chests, in the deep window embrasures, peeping from quaint little niches cut out in the tremendous thickness of the walls. I never saw any house love flowers as my little old castle does; its every corner wants them, accepts them, asks for them... All the galleries have boxes gorgeous with scarlet geraniums, and half of the inner court has been walled off separately and transformed into a little paved garden, one blaze of color. This wee garden is also the proud possessor of a well several hundred feet deep.

My old architect has a special talent for building the most delightful fireplaces; every kind of shape, generally walled into each room according to the size and style of the room ; they are mostly quite plain peasant-hearths, whitewashed, built of bricks with all sorts of odd corners and shelves jutting out from them, so that pots and jars and ancient icons can find the right little places to stand on, each object looking as though it had been there always, as though it had been made for that special place.

Below the castle lies an old orchard alongside of a damp emerald-green meadow, where forget-me-nots grow in masses. I am transforming the orchard into a sort of kitchen flower-garden, a veritable orgy of color, upon which the little fortress looks down with what formerly would have been a frown, but which today certainly more resembles a smile.

At certain dates, the poorest amongst the peasants climb the castle's steep stone steps and crowd into my fortress-enclosure, and there, feudal-wise, I distribute corn, maize, money and clothing. A more picturesque, tattered, end-of-the-world assembly can hardly be imagined; strange, long-haired old men with white shirts, broad leathern belts and earth-colored coats; tiny wizened-faced old women, like uncanny witches, come down from their far-off mountain-sides; larged-eyed pathetic war-orphans brought hither by careworn foster-mothers, already heavily burdened with innumerable children of their own; one and all, patient, respectful, all-enduring, full of quiet dignity in spite of their crushing poverty. They all crowd round me, kissing my hands, the sleeve or the hem of my dress, full of profuse thanks, which make my gifts seem much too meagre.

Then they all troop out again, old men and tottering old crones, careworn mothers and orphan-children, all calling down blessings on my head in the most picturesque language, wishing good luck, good health, long life, prosperity and a heart for their misery; begging me to come again, to come often, not to forget them, to "descend from my height" towards them and no end of other things, whilst I, feeling humbled, watch them climbing down my steep steps, limping off each with his small share, dispersing, going back to their poor little homes amongst the hills...

Occasionally, accompanied by one or the other of my children, or by some of my younger followers, clad in the bright costume of the country, astride a hardy mountain pony I ride up, up into the hills upon fearfully steep, uneven paths, in springtime but torrent-beds. Then it happens that quite unexpectedly we come upon some of those weird, wizened, limping old men and women, who assemble in my castle courtyard to receive alms. They greet us joyfully but with slowly dawning astonishment, wondering what ever could have moved the queen to wander into such far-off, never-visited corners, upon such ill-kept precipitous roads. I halt and hold converse with them, they shake their heads and sigh and smile, using quaint expressions, which nearly always end in some blessing or good wish, and the petition that we should be sure and come again...

Up, up, beyond beaten trails into shadow-filled fir-forests, dark, mysterious, sweet with the pungent perfume of sun-warmed resin, through dense thickets full of night, opening out on to moss-coated glades shut in by somber fir-trees, regular and magnificent, like an army of giants, the many-

shaded indigo mountains forming: a background, so magnificent, so perfect, so changeless in its strength and stability that gratitude rises suddenly
from my heart like a prayer. Beauty, beauty! Eternal, indestructible, beauty
of form, color, detail, ever again it is as a deep religion to me, making me
believe in things beyond this life, making me believe in hope, truth, goodness, the conquering of evil, of death... With dusk we return, picking our
way carefully over rolling stones, our shadows lengthening weirdly as
though we and even our ponies were walking on stilts.

I have also been at Bran, or Brana the Beloved as it sometimes amuses me
to call my castle, who through me has gained a soul, on an early winter's
night when the snow was on the ground, and a large moon was sending
her ghostly beams stealthily into my carefully locked courtyard, as though
trying to discover secrets we were anxious to conceal from the outer world.
The pugnacious small castle had that night a quite different aspect; it had
suddenly become ethereal, bodiless, a sort of dream, a vision of my own
fantasy. A waxen taper in hand, a thick, dark yellow taper made by the
nuns, smelling deliciously of honey, I began wandering all through my
stronghold, up and down its many steep stairs, in and out of ridiculously
low passages, carefully stepping over uneven thresholds, on to secretive-
looking galleries leading to squat towers with wee windows, whence I
could look down, down upon the peaceful valley beneath, with its river
winding through it like a shimmering path. There was no sound; only a
deep silence, the world lying fast asleep, all white under its first coating of
snow, silvered by the moon's intense light. A strange, incredible little place,
hardly to be imagined in our teeming, striving, bustling times, a lost little
corner of peace. I felt inconceivably far away from everyday life, almost a
stranger to myself, but oh, so much in sympathy with this old world, almost incongruous habitation, which I cared to share only with those who
understood its charm as I did. I kept my life here jealously apart from all
those who were too accustomed to a royal, conventional, over-comfortable
way of living.

Huh! But how cold it was! How ghostly, looking down, suspended over
such a giddy height, and how my honey-scented taper dripped in the sudden blasts of wind which caught me round each corner. I must hurry back
to the big flaming fire crackling on the huge hearth in the long low room,
which had once been a loft and where the others were assembled, chatting
and telling tales, occasionally listening to the wind whistling round the
ancient walls. Oh! How cozy it was round that giant fireplace, which made
quite a room in itself, walled within the other, with a big roof under which
one could creep close up to the flame.

But now to bed. We all scattered to our different apartments in the four
corners of the castle. I climbed down my own secret stairs, a tiny, steep,
stone flight hidden away in the thickness of the wall, with a niche at the top
and another at the bottom, and a wee antique oil-lamp flickering in each,

like those used centuries ago by Christians in the catacombs. There was something of the sensation of a catacomb about those dark little stairs leading down... down... as into a well. How the wind howled round my bedroom, an isolated chamber in one of the towers. Low-domed and white, it has quaint, perforated marble windows, remnants of some ancient Byzantine church which I brought back from Greece and which seem perfectly at home here. A fire was crackling in one of the little white hearths, characteristic of the house, the leaping flames filling the small room with ever-changing light and shade, gilding the white walls, making the old icons and the silver lamps hanging before them glow, throwing unexpected colors upon the soft, dark blue Chinese carpet. In a nook between the two windows, upon an old stone capital of a church pillar, stands a monk carved in wood. An austere figure with a wonderful ascetic face; he is the silent guardian of this room, the companion of my hours of solitude. A taper burns beside him, and a blue Persian jar, full of flowers that are always fresh, stands at his feet. His attitude is one of prayer; with bent head and closed eyes, he stands there, a perfect picture of patience and abnegation. Given to me once by my mother, he has been moved from house to house, but this low vaulted chamber, around which the four winds howl and whistle, chanting their dismallest dirges, is his right setting; here he has found his final home. He pays no attention to me whatsoever, but the ruddy glow from the flames gives him an uncanny look of real life. He watches over my sleep, and when I awake at dawn, there he is, praying still, his face pale and more austere than ever in the growing light...

Have I been able to describe some of the charm of Brana the Beloved? I fear not. The child who loves it best said: You will never be able to make anybody who has not seen it understand what it is really like! I am afraid this is true, but I have spoken about it as a lover singing of his love – it is the best I can do. You see, it is a love which has come to me in my riper years, on the other side of that chasm which cut my life in two – so it is something of a symbol to me, a sign that one can begin again – even after war and exile – a little differently, no doubt, but with that ever young energy and that undying renewal of faith and hope, of which, thank God, the human heart is eternally capable...

Band 1:

Silvia Irina Zimmermann

Unterschiedliche Wege, dasselbe Ideal

Das Königsbild im Werk Carmen Sylvas und in Fotografien des Fürstlich Wiedischen Archivs

348 Seiten. Paperback. **€ 39,90**
ISBN 978-3-8382-0655-4

Band 2:

Silvia Irina Zimmermann, Edda Binder-Iijima (Hg.)

"Ich werde noch vieles anbahnen"

Carmen Sylva, die Schriftstellerin und
erste Königin von Rumänien im Kontext ihrer Zeit

272 Seiten. Paperback. **€ 34,90**
ISBN 978-3-8382-0564-9

Band 3:

Silvia Irina Zimmermann, Edda Binder-Iijima (Hg.)

Das erste Königspaar von Rumänien
Carol I. und Elisabeta

Aspekte monarchischer Legitimation im Spiegel
kulturpolitischer Symbolhandlungen

192 Seiten. Paperback. **€ 29,90**
ISBN 978-3-8382-0755-1

Band 4:

Silvia Irina Zimmermann, Bernd Willscheid (Hg.)

Carmen Sylva: Heimweh ist Jugendweh

Kindheits- und Jugenderinnerungen
der Elisabeth zu Wied (1843-1916)

340 Seiten. Paperback. **€ 39,90**
ISBN 978-3-8382-0814-5

Bestellen Sie per Fax: 0511 26 222 01 | telefonisch: 0511 26 222 00
online: www.ibidem-verlag.de | in Ihrer Buchhandlung

Band 5:

Silvia Irina Zimmermann (Hg.)

Carmen Sylva & André Lecomte du Nouÿ

Monsieur Hampelmann / Domnul Pulcinel

Ein Märchen aus der Exilzeit der Königin Elisabeth von Rumänien (Carmen Sylva)

128 Seiten. Paperback. **€ 29,90**
ISBN 978-3-8382-1114-5

Band 6 & 7:

Silvia Irina Zimmermann (Hg.)

„In zärtlicher Liebe Deine Elisabeth" –
„Stets Dein treuer Carl"

Der Briefwechsel Elisabeths zu Wied (Carmen Sylva) mit ihrem Gemahl Carol I. von Rumänien aus dem Rumänischen Nationalarchiv in Bukarest

Teil 1: 1869-1890. 494 Seiten. Paperback. **€ 45,90**
ISBN 978-3-8382-0906-7

Teil 2: 1891-1913. 458 Seiten. Paperback. **€ 45,90**
ISBN 978-3-8382-1220-3

Set aus Teil 1 und Teil 2. 952 Seiten. Paperback. **€ 84,90**
ISBN 978-3-8382-1221-0

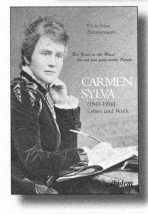

Band 8:

Silvia Irina Zimmermann

„Die Feder in der Hand bin ich eine ganz andre Person"

Carmen Sylva

(1843-1916). Leben und Werk

436 Seiten. Paperback. **€ 45,90**
ISBN 978-3-8382-0815-2

Bleiben Sie auf dem Laufenden und abonnieren Sie den Newsletter der Forschungsstelle Carmen Sylva unter:

www.carmensylva-fwa.de

Carmen Sylva

Aus Carmen Sylvas Königreich

Gesammelte Märchen und Geschichten für Kinder und Jugendliche

Herausgegeben und mit einem Vorwort von Silvia Irina Zimmermann, mit Abbildungen aus dem Fürstlich Wiedischen Archiv Neuwied, 2 Bände, im Set erhältlich für € 79,80 ISBN 978-3-8382-0495-6

Carmen Sylva

Gedanken einer Königin – Les pensées d'une reine

Gesammelte Aphorismen in deutscher und französischer Sprache und Epigramme der Königin Elisabeth von Rumänien, geborene Prinzessin zu Wied (1843-1916)

Herausgegeben von Silvia Irina Zimmermann

€ 49,90 ISBN 978-3-8382-0385-0

Silvia Irina Zimmermann

Der Zauber des fernen Königreichs

Carmen Sylvas "Pelesch-Märchen"

€ 24,90 ISBN 978-3-8382-0195-5

Silvia Irina Zimmermann

Die dichtende Königin

Elisabeth, Prinzessin zu Wied, Königin von Rumänien, Carmen Sylva (1843-1916)

Selbstmythisierung und prodynastische Öffentlichkeitsarbeit durch Literatur

€ 49,90 ISBN 978-3-8382-0185-6

Gabriel Badea-Păun

Carmen Sylva

Königin Elisabeth von Rumänien – eine rheinische Prinzessin auf Rumäniens Thron

Ins Deutsche übersetzt und mit einem Nachwort von Silvia Irina Zimmermann

€ 32,00 ISBN 978-3-8382-0245-7

Carmen Sylva
Gedanken einer Königin
Herausgegeben von Silvia Irina
Zimmermann
€ 24,90
ISBN 978-3-8382-0375-1

Carmen Sylva
Pelesch-Märchen
Herausgegeben von Silvia Irina
Zimmermann
€ 24,90
ISBN 978-3-8382-0465-9

Carmen Sylva
Prinz Waldvogel
Herausgegeben von Silvia Irina
Zimmermann
€ 24,90
ISBN 978-3-8382-0818-3